WHY MRS BLAKE CRIED

WHY MRS BLAKE CRIED

William Blake and the Sexual Basis of Spiritual Vision

Marsha Keith Schuchard

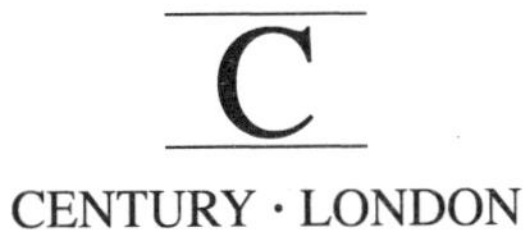

CENTURY · LONDON

Published by Century 2006

2 4 6 8 10 9 7 5 3 1

First published in Great Britain in 2006 by
Century
Random House, 20 Vauxhall Bridge Road,
London SW1V 2SA

Random House Australia (Pty) Limited
20 Alfred Street, Milsons Point, Sydney,
New South Wales 2061, Australia

Random House New Zealand Limited
18 Poland Road, Glenfield,
Auckland 10, New Zealand

Random House South Africa (Pty) Limited
Isle of Houghton, Corner of Boundary Road & Carse O'Gowrie,
Houghton 2198, South Africa

The Random House Group Limited Reg. No. 954009
www.randomhouse.co.uk

A CIP catalogue record for this book
is available from the British Library

ISBN 0712620168

Papers used by The Random House Group Limited are natural, recyclable products made from wood grown in sustainable forests; the manufacturing processes conform to the environmental regulations of the country of origin.

Typeset by Palimpsest Book Production Limited,
Polmont, Stirlingshire

Printed and bound in Great Britain by
William Clowes Ltd, Beccles, Suffolk

Contents

The great passions are the angels of God.
W. B. Yeats

Acknowledgements

This reconstruction of the lost religious history of the family of William Blake was made possible not only by my discovery of the Armitage-Blake family documents in the Moravian Archives in London, but by the work of many scholars who have brought to the surface much of the secret history of the mystical underground of the 'Enlightened' eighteenth century.

My greatest debts over the years have been to the late Ellic Howe, Mrs Cecil Roth and Gershom Scholem, who first urged me to dig in this difficult terrain. Susanna Åkerman, Craig Atwood, Allison Coudert, Keri Davies, John Patrick Deveney, Antoine Faivre, Deborah Forman, Clarke Garrett, Joscelyn Godwin, Matt Goldish, Olle Hjern, Don Karr, David Katz, Jeffrey Kripal, Stephen Lloyd, Jonathan Miller, Morton Paley, Michael Phillips, Richard Popkin, Sheila Spector, Elliot Wolfson and David Worrall all encouraged my research – even when it led to unexpected, uncomfortable and unattractive realms of belief and behaviour. Special thanks go to Arthur Versluis, whose generous support of heterodox scholars led to the publication of my exploratory article, 'Why Mrs Blake Cried', in his innovative, online journal, *Esoterica*.[1]

I am also grateful to the Trustees of the British Museum for permission to quote from the Charles Townley Papers; to Neil Chambers, Research Curator at the Natural History Museum, for permission to quote the Joseph Banks correspondence; to the Society of Antiquaries for permission to use the journals of the Society of Dilettanti; to Colin Smithson, archivist at Alnwick Castle, for permission to quote the Rainsford Papers.

Of further assistance were the staffs of the British Library, Royal Botanical Gardens at Kew, Wellcome Institute, Grand Lodge Library, and Swedenborg Society in London; the National Library of Scotland, Royal Order of Scotland and Grand Lodge Library, Edinburgh; the Royal Library and State Archives in Stockholm and the Diocesan Library in Linköping, Sweden. Members of the Interlibrary Loan Office at Emory University, Atlanta, Georgia, have located many rare volumes for me.

In 2001 the new cataloguing work and open-minded hospitality of Paul Blewitt, archivist at the Moravian Church Library in Muswell Hill, London, made possible my discovery of the Armitage-Blake family documents. In 2004 the succeeding archivist at Muswell Hill, Lorraine Parsons, generously shared her subsequent Armitage findings and expertly assisted my further investigations. I publish the Moravian documents with their permission.

Mark Booth and Hannah Black, my editors at Random House, helped me condense a very long and detailed academic study into a more streamlined and accessible book. Believing that my scholarly investigation of William Blake and the esoteric-erotic underground would appeal to a broader general audience, they determined to present this extremely complex and often abstruse material in a simplified and clarified narrative. For readers interested in pursuing further the research in this area, academic and historical publications are cited in the endnotes and bibliography.

My husband, Ronald Schuchard, spurred me on by reading passages from W. B. Yeats that continue the tradition of visionary eros maintained by Moravians, Swedenborgians, Kabbalists and Yogis – that motley crew of spiritual seekers who somehow found each other in the dark alleyways of eighteenth-century Fetter Lane.

List of Illustrations

Urethra'. Henry Gray, *Anatomy, Descriptive, and Surgical*, 20th rev. ed. (1858; Philadelphia: Leigh and Febiger. 1918), Fig. 1156.

Illus. 8a, p. 137 – MS. 'Das Christen ABC Buch' (1750), frontispiece. Ephrata Cloister, Pennsylvania Historical and Museum Commission.

Illus. 8b, p. 137 – 'MS. Das Christen ABC Buch' (1750), letter O. Ephrata Cloister, Pennsylvania Historical and Museum Commission.

Illus. 8c, p. 137 – William Blake, *Songs of Innocence* (1789). Copy B, title-page. Library of Congress, Washington, D.C.

Illus. 8d, p. 137 – William Blake, 'A Cradle Song', *Songs of Innocence* (1789). Copy B, plate 24. Library of Congress, Washington, D.C.

Illus. 9a, p. 139 – Herman Hugo, *Pia Desideria*, Editio 6. emendata. (1624; Antuerpia: apud Henricum Aertssens, 1634), plate 39. Engraving by Boëce van Bolsvert. Robert W. Woodruff Library, Emory University, Atlanta.

Illus. 9b and 9c, p. 139 – William Blake, *There is No Natural Religion* (1788), Copy L, plates 7 and 8. Pierpont Morgan Library, New York. William Blake Archive.

Illus. 10, p. 141 – William Blake, *For Children: The Gates of Paradise* (1793). Copy D, plate 9. Library of Congress, Washington, D.C.

Illus. 11, p. 164 – James Gillray, 'Love in a Coffin' (1784). Trustees of the British Museum, London.

Illus. 12, p. 166 – William Blake, 'The Ancient of Days', *Europe a Prophecy* (1794). Copy E, plate 1. Library of Congress, Washington, D.C.

Illus. 13, p. 175 – William Blake, 'The Dance of Albion, or Glad Day' (*c.*1803–1810). Lessing J. Rosenwald Collection, National Gallery of Art, Washington D.C.

Illus. 14, p. 176 – Catherine Blake, 'Portrait of the Young William Blake' (*c.*1827–1831). Fitzwilliam Museum, Cambridge.

Illus. 15, p. 185 – Anon., 'The Quacks' (1783). Trustees of the British Museum, London.

Illus. 16, p. 201 – Robineau, 'The Assault or Fencing Match which took place between Mademoiselle La Chevaliere D'Eon de Beaumont and Monsieur de Saint George (1787). Brotherton Library, University of Leeds.

Illus. 17, p. 207 – 'Eighteenth-century Cartoon Satirizing a Mesmeric Session'. Courtesy of Robert Darnton.

Illus. 18, p.211 – 'Le Doight Magique' (1780s). Courtesy of Robert Darnton.

Illus. 19, p. 225 – 'The Loss of the Prepuce, or Lord George Riot Suffering a Clipping to Become a Jew', *Rambler's Magazine* (September 1785), 342. The British Library Board, London.

Illus. 20, p. 230 – James Gillray, 'A Masonic Anecdote' (1786). Thomas Wright, *The Works of James Gillray* (London: H.G. Bohn, 1851), plate 37. Library of Congress, Washington, D.C.

Illus. 21, p. 242 – William Blake, *The Marriage of Heaven and Hell* (1790–1793), Copy D, plate 3. Library of Congress, Washington, D.C.

Illus. 22, p. 252 – William Blake, *Visions of the Daughters of Albion* (1793), Copy D, plate 3. Library of Congress, Washington, D.C.

Illus. 23a, p. 254 – William Blake, 'Portrait Sketch of Catherine Blake' (*c.*1805). Tate Gallery, London.

Illus. 23b, p. 254 – Frederick Tatham, 'Mrs Blake in Age' (*c.*1831). Trustees of the British Museum, London.

Illus. 24, p. 260 – William Blake, 'Adam and Eve' (1790–1792). *Manuscript Notebook*. Add. MS. 49460, f.52v. The British Library Board, London.

Illus. 25a and 25b, p. 265 – Lambert de Lintot, 'Chapter and Grand Lodge of England' and detail, 'Nothing Without the V Point' (1789). *Ars Quatuor Coronatorum*, 3 (1890), 37. Masonic Library, Atlanta.

Illus. 25c, p. 265 – Lambert de Lintot, 'Foundation of the Royal Order' (1789). Grand Lodge Library, London.

Illus. 26a, p. 274 – William Blake, 'The Book of Enoch. An Angel Teaching a Daughter of Men the Secrets of Sin' (1824–1827?). Lessing J. Rosenwald Collection, National Gallery of Art, Washington, D.C.

Illus. 26b, p. 274 – William Blake, 'The Book of Enoch. The Descent of the Angels to One of the Daughters of Men' (1824–1827?). Lessing J. Rosenwald Collection, National Gallery of Art, Washington, D.C.

Illus. 27a and 27b, p. 280 – William Blake, *Vala,* or *The Four Zoas* (*c.*1797–1807?), Add. MS. 39764. f.21c and 22v. Infrared negatives 35277 and 35278. The British Library Board, London.

Illus. 28, p. 286 – 'Ex-Voto of Wax presented in the Church at Isernia in 1780'. Richard Payne Knight, *A Discourse on the Worship of Priapus, and its Connection with the Mystic Theology of the Ancients,* rev. ed. (1786; London: privately printed, 1894), plate I. Pitts Theology Library, Emory University, Atlanta.

Illus. 29 p. 287 – William Blake, *Vala*, or *The Four Zoas.* (*c.*1797–1807?). Add. MS. 39764, f.13v. Infrared photograph. The British Library Board, London.

Illus. 30, p. 290 – Edward Moor, *Oriental Fragments* (London: Smith, Elder, 1834), plate IV. Library of Congress, Washington, D.C.

Illus. 31, p. 290 – William Blake, *Vala*, or *The Four Zoas* (*c.*1797–1807). Add. MS. 39764, f.13v. Infrared photograph. The British Library Board, London.

Illus. 32, p. 303 – William Blake, *Milton a Poem* (1804–1808?). Copy A, plate 29. Trustees of the British Museum.

Illus. 33, p. 306 – William Blake, *Milton a Poem* (1804–1808?). Copy C, plate 29. New York Public Library, New York.

Illus. 34, p. 307 – Moses Haughton, 'Narayana'. Edward Moor,

The Hindu Pantheon (London: Joseph Johnson, 1810), plate 20. Library of Congress, Washington, D.C.

Ilus. 35, p. 311 – William Blake, *Milton a Poem* (1804–1808?). Copy A, plate 38 (first state). Trustees of the British Museum.

Illus. 36, p. 313 – William Blake, 'When a Man has Married a Wife', *Manuscript Notebook*. Add. MS. 49460, f.2v. The British Library Board.

Illus. 37, p. 321 – William Blake, *Jerusalem the Emanation of the Giant Albion* (1804–1820). Copy E, plate 6. Paul Mellon Collection, Yale Center for British Art, New Haven.

Illus. 38, p. 323 – William Blake, 'Portrait of the Man who Taught Blake Painting in his Dreams' (*c.*1820). Tate Gallery, London.

Illus. 39, p. 330 – William Blake, *Jerusalem the Emanation of the Giant Albion* (1804–1820). Copy E, plate 14. Paul Mellon Collection, Yale Center for British Art, New Haven, Connecticut.

Illus. 40, p. 332 – William Blake, *Jerusalem the Emanation of the Giant Albion* (1804–1820), plate 28, suppressed version. PML 99486.16. The Pierpont Morgan Library, New York.

Illus. 41, p. 335 – William Blake, *Jerusalem the Emanation of the Giant Albion* (1804–1820), Copy E, plate 99. Paul Mellon Collection, Yale Center for British Art, New Haven.

INTRODUCTION

Why Mrs Blake Cried: The Sexual Basis of Spiritual Vision

When I first Married you, I gave you all my whole soul
I thought that you would love my loves & joy in my delights
Seeking for pleasures in my pleasures O Daughter of Babylon
Then thou wast lovely, mild & gentle, now thou art terrible
In jealousy & unlovely in my sight, because thou hast cruelly
Cut off my loves in fury till I have no love left for thee.
Thy love depends on him thou lovest & on his dear loves
Which thou has cut off by jealousy.

William Blake, *Milton* (1804–10)

IN DECEMBER 1825, in a genteel drawing room in London, an elderly man dressed in humble black boldly expressed his radical spiritual beliefs to a dumbfounded but fascinated barrister. Fortunately for posterity, the barrister, Henry Crabb Robinson, went home and jotted down in his diary what he could remember of the bizarre and shocking statements of William Blake, the sixty-eight-year-old engraver, artist and poet: 'Shall I call him Artist or Genius – or Mystic – or Madman? Probably he is all.'[1] Though he found Blake confusing, contradictory and sometimes distressing in his pronouncements about religion and sexuality, he tried to faithfully record what Blake told him.

Six months later, in June 1826, a dismayed but admiring Robinson noted that Blake was 'as wild as ever', with no great novelty:

> *except that he confessed to a* practical *notion which would do him more injury than any other I have heard from him. He says that from the Bible he has learned that* eine Gemeinschaft der Frauen statt finden solte *[there should be a community of women]. When I objected that* Ehestand *[marriage] seems to be a divine institution, he referred to the Bible – 'that from the beginning it was not so.'*[2]

The horrified diarist was so disturbed that he prudishly disguised Blake's words in German. For more than eighty years, until Arthur Symons's gleeful discovery of it, this revealing account of Blake's beliefs about sexuality and religious tradition remained unpublished.[3]

In 1828, a year after Blake's death, his long-time friend John Thomas Smith described 'the uninterrupted harmony' in which Blake and 'his beloved Kate' lived.[4] The artist's marriage had been 'a mutually happy one', with no hint of jealousy or sexual impropriety. However, in the 1850s, when another lawyer and art critic, Alexander Gilchrist, decided to gather biographical information on Blake, especially from Robinson and other surviving friends, he learned that he would have to correct Smith's picture of 'uninterrupted harmony'. Thus, in his *Life of William Blake, 'Pictor Ignotus'* (1863), Gilchrist wrote:

> *Such harmony there really was; but . . . it had not always been unruffled. There* had *been stormy times in years long past, when both were young; discord by no means trifling*

> *while it lasted. But with the cause (jealousy on her side, not wholly unprovoked), the strife ceased.*[5]

Though Gilchrist gave no examples of Blake's 'provokings', he did report a conversation in which Blake asked, 'Do you think if I came home and discovered my wife to be unfaithful, I should be so foolish as to take it ill?'[6] Gilchrist's informant assured him that Mrs Blake would have agreed and answered, 'Of course not!' But the informant assumed that Blake's pronouncement was only 'a philosophic boast'.

Gilchrist's reticence and euphemisms did not satisfy the poet Algernon Swinburne, who was preparing a critical study of Blake. In 1868 Swinburne commented:

> *Over the stormy or slippery passages in their earlier life Mr Gilchrist has perhaps passed too lightly. No doubt Blake's aberrations were mainly matters of speech or writing; it is however said, that once in a patriarchal mood he did propose to add a second wife to their small and shifting household, and was much perplexed at meeting on one hand with tears and on all hands with remonstrances.*[7]

In 1893, when Edwin John Ellis and William Butler Yeats brought out their ground-breaking edition of Blake's works, they repeated this report: 'It is said that Blake wished to add a concubine to his establishment in the Old Testament manner, but gave up the project when it made Mrs Blake cry.'[8]

Over the next decade Ellis became more convinced that Blake's descriptions of sexual and marital difficulties were not just symbolical but biographical. When he drafted *The Real Blake* in 1904, he included a melodramatic scene in which a passionate William and a prudish Catherine quarrel bitterly:

So Blake became half unfaithful to her in his anger. Half unfaithful only, however – the theoretic half. He fumed out at his wife a theory of matrimony as preposterously arrogant and patriarchal as was preposterously vestal. He claimed the right of Abraham to give to Hagar what Sarah refused.[9]

In the Old Testament story, Abraham's wife Sarah cannot bear children and urges her husband to sleep with Hagar, the serving girl. Despite Ellis's qualification that Blake was only theoretically unfaithful, he recognised that Blake was sincere in his antinomian sexual theosophy, which inverted the normative morality of his day. He boldly argued that Blake's illuminated prophecy, *Visions of the Daughters of Albion*, with its call for uninhibited sex in couples and groups, was 'composed as part of the education of Mrs Blake'.[10]

Just as early attempts were made to sanitise Blake's biography, so attempts were made shortly after his death to sanitise his art. All the nineteenth-century admirers of Blake lamented that Frederick Tatham, who was appointed executor by Catherine Blake, destroyed many of Blake's manuscripts and drawings – which included his most radical sexual, religious and political expressions. As William Michael Rossetti, a friend of Gilchrist and brother of the artist Dante Gabriel Rossetti, reported:

Notebooks, poems, designs, in lavish quantity, annihilated: a gag (as it were) thrust into the piteous mouth of Blake's corpse. The fact is – so I have been informed – that Swedenborgians, Irvingites, or other extreme sectaries, beset the then youthful custodian [Tatham] of these priceless relics, and persuaded him to make a holocaust of them, as being heretical, and dangerous to those poor dear 'unprotected females' Religion and Morals. The horrescent pietists allowed that the works were 'inspired'; but alas! The inspiration had come from the Devil.[11]

Tatham and the pious John Linnell, Blake's late-life friend, also erased many offending words and drawings, while some alarmed friend even drew underpants over the erect penis on Blake's nude self-portrait in *Milton*.[12] Fortunately, modern technological advances mean that much of the censored material can now be retrieved.

Though Ellis and Yeats were the first to publish the turbulent erotic verses of Blake's manuscript, *VALA or THE FOUR ZOAS, The Torments of Love & Jealousy in the Death and Judgement of the Ancient Man*, they did not discuss or reproduce the provocative illustrations of phallic and vulvic images. Ellis subsequently took the bold step of describing some of the erotic drawings, as well as the erasures made by Linnell. He revealed that Linnell 'used the india-rubber to one in particular, to make it less audaciously defiant of the proprieties':

The drawings were in pencil only. Their subjects included the distinguishing characteristic of the ancient god 'Priapus', an object fitted for sacred art before the degrading spirit of a later civilisation had vulgarised it, but not fitted for secular art, other than medical, at any period of the world's history. In one design to Vala, *the Priapic attribute is represented as nearly the height of a signpost: three figures are bowing down to it . . .*[13]

However, even Ellis was unwilling to discuss Blake's drawing of a nude woman with a Gothic chapel in her vagina. It was a missed opportunity, for these images of phallic and vulvic worship provided a key to the strange sexual-spiritual underworld that both nourished and troubled Blake's marriage.

Despite their efforts to recover biographical facts about

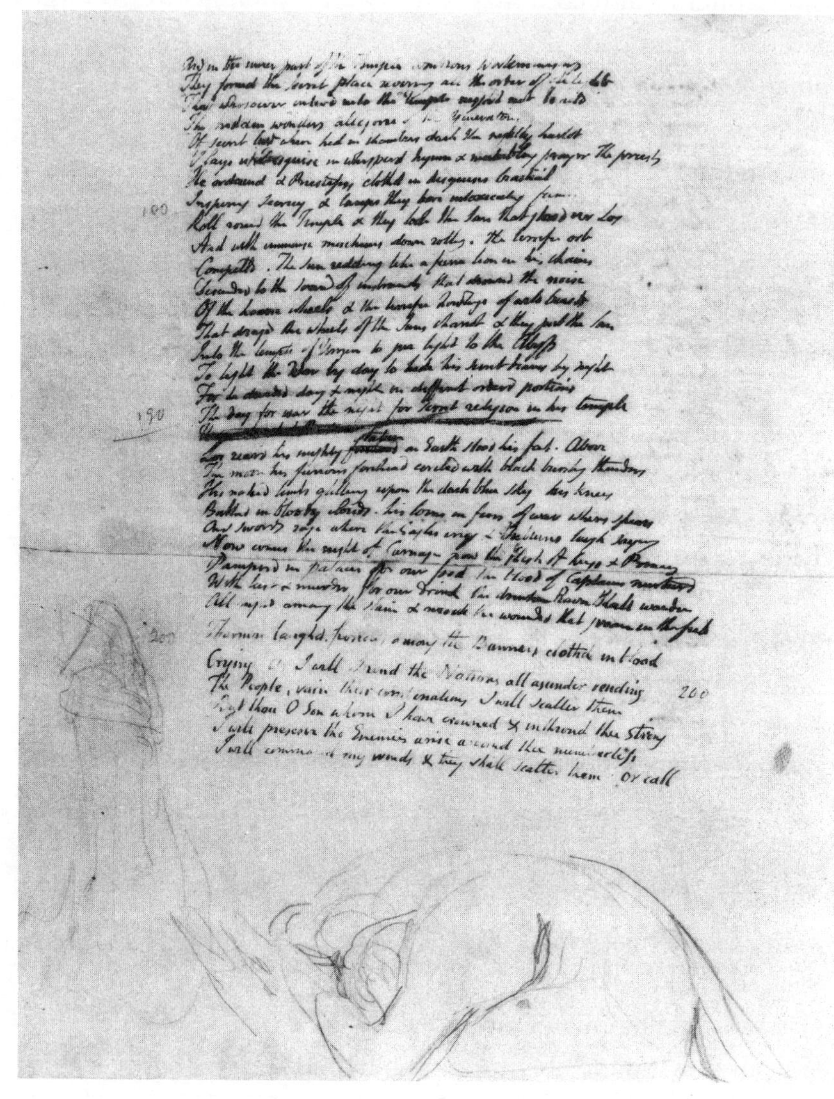
And in the inner part of the Temple wondrous workmanship
They formd the Secret place reversing all the order of delight
That whosoever enterd into the temple might not behold
The hidden wonders allegoric of the Generation
Of secret lust when hid in chambers dark the nightly harlot
Plays in Disguise in whisperd hymn & mumbling prayer The priests
He ordaind & Priestesses clothd in disguises beastial
Inspiring secrecy & lamps they bore intoxicating fumes
Roll round the Temple & they took the Sun that glowd oer Los
And with immense machines down rolling. the terrific orb
Compell'd. The Sun reddning like a fierce lion in his chains
Descended to the sound of instruments that drownd the noise
Of the hoarse wheels & the terrific howlings of wild beasts
That dragd the wheels of the Suns chariot & they put the Sun
Into the temple of Urizen to give light to the Abyss
To light the War by day to hide his secret beams by night
For he divided day & night in different orderd portions
The day for war the night for secret religion in his temple
Los reard his mighty stature on Earth stood his feet. Above
The moon his furious forehead circled with black bursting thunders
His naked limbs glittring upon the dark blue sky his knees
Bathed in bloody clouds. his loins in fires of war where spears
And swords rage where the Eagles cry & the Vultures laugh saying
Now comes the night of Carnage now the flesh of kings & Princes
Pamperd in palaces for our food the blood of Captains nurturd
With lust & murder for our drink the drunken Raven shall wander
All night among the slain & mock the wounded that groan in the field
Tharmas laughd furious among the Banners clothd in blood
Crying As I will I rend the Nations all asunder rending
The People, vain their combinations I will scatter them
But thou O Son whom I have crowned & inthroned thee Strong
I will preserve tho Enemies arise around thee numberless
I will command my winds & they shall scatter them or call

Blake, none of his nineteenth-century defenders attempted to research the actual historical context of his esoteric and erotic experiences – a context that could reveal the sources of his sexual-spiritual philosophy. From Gilchrist onwards, Blake's biographers agreed that he was influenced by the Swedenborgianism of his family, but they did not examine what Blake described to Robinson as the 'dangerous sexual religion' of the Swedish scientist-seer.[14] Nor did they inquire into the sexual beliefs of Blake's Swedenborgian friends, neighbours and associates. While Rossetti accepted the Swedenborgian claims, he also noted accurately the influence of Hermetic alchemists and Christian Kabbalists – such as Paracelsus, Agrippa and Boehme – on Blake's youthful development.[15] But even he did not relate the tenets of these writers to Blake's sexual pronouncements or, more importantly, to his erotic drawings and poetry.

As an initiate of the Rosicrucian Order of the Golden Dawn, Yeats was in a position to go further than Rossetti. Drawing on oral traditions and archival materials, he suggested that Blake was associated with a secret magical society, in which initiates learned the arcana of Jewish Kabbalism, Rosicrucian alchemy and Swedenborgian theosophy.[16] Yeats recognised that, like himself, Blake made a connection between the energy of sexual passion and the capacity for spiritual vision.

In an 1893 essay, 'William Blake and the Imagination', Yeats observed that Blake had learned from Jacob Boehme and from old alchemist writers that imagination was the first emanation of divinity, 'the body of God', 'the Divine members'.[17] Though 'it was a scandalous paradox in his time', Blake believed that the passions made the 'sensations of this foolish body . . . a part of the body of God' and that 'man shall enter eternity borne upon their wings'. Sworn to secrecy about his own Kabbalistic meditation and Rosicrucian rituals, Yeats did not explore the possible real-life effects of such a creed, in which

Mrs Blake became a sometimes unwilling sexual 'member' of the 'body of God'.

As modern photographic technology recovers Blake's erased drawings and expressions, it provides increasing evidence of the boldness and intensity of Blake's sexual and spiritual preoccupations. Thus, the need to unearth the submerged historical underworld that nourished his antinomian beliefs becomes more pressing. Ironically, a long-ignored claim made by William Muir (1845–1936), the great Blake facsimilist, holds the key to unlocking the sources of Blake's radical notions of sexualised spirituality (or spiritualised sexuality).

In the 1920s, Muir informed the biographer Thomas Wright that Blake's 'parents attended the Moravian Chapel in Fetter Lane' and that Moravian hymns influenced Blake's *Songs of Innocence and Experience*.[18] Blake's father subsequently 'adopted the doctrines of Swedenborg, whose followers, however, did not separate from other religious bodies until later'. Muir reiterated this claim to Margaret Lowery, who published it in 1940.[19] Unfortunately, in 1941, the destruction of the Fetter Lane Chapel during the German Blitz seemed to bury not only the evidence but scholarly interest in the alleged Moravian connection. Though two post-World War II critics mentioned a possible Moravian association, they provided no new documentation, and a confident critical consensus emerged that the Blakes were radical Dissenters, probably Baptist or Muggletonian, and opposed to the established Anglican Church.[20] Moreover, the long tradition of the family's early Swedenborgianism was dismissed as 'a Twentieth-Century Legend'.[21]

But Muir and Wright were definitely accurate in their Moravian claim and almost certainly in their Swedenborgian claim. Blake's mother Catherine, her first husband Thomas Armitage, and several Blakes were members of the Moravian congregation at Fetter Lane, at a time when Swedenborg also participated in its services. Thus they could have met the Swedish scientist-seer or learned about his writings from his Moravian publishers. As we shall see, the assertion that Blake learned Swedenborgianism 'at his father's knee' gains plausibility.

While planning to write a political and Masonic biography of Swedenborg, I learned of the important Kabbalistic and Rosicrucian influences on him – influences that also affected Count Nicolaus Ludwig von Zinzendorf, leader of the Moravians who met at Fetter Lane. Much to my surprise, I also discovered an esoteric tradition of psychoerotic mysticism, which revealed to Swedenborg and Zinzendorf the sexual techniques that achieve spiritual vision. These techniques – and the theosophy that lay behind them – seemed to illuminate the most occulted, inchoate and erotic of Blake's themes and symbols. However, these daring experiments in spiritual and sexual liberation had been suppressed and whitewashed by conservative church historians, because of attacks by hostile critics who published sensationalised accounts of the secret activities of the more radical Moravians and Swedenborgians.

As I took the scholarly plunge into this little-charted and always murky underworld, I discovered a colourful and bizarre cast of characters – mystical scientists, heterodox Jews, antinomian Yogis, Priapic antiquarians, revolutionary Freemasons, and even a transvestite spy – who exercised a significant, though little-known influence on the visionary artists in Blake's milieu. It is small wonder that sensible academic critics have cautiously refrained from taking the plunge, for this kind of historical detective work must reject much academic conventional wisdom about the eighteenth century. It must go beyond the surface of 'The Enlightenment' and dig deep into the esoteric underground of the mystical counter-culture. Despite decades of continuing repression by Church and State, this counter-culture maintained clandestine 'brotherhoods' that energised their enthusiasts and alarmed mainstream rationalists. It was an imaginatively rich and erotically charged milieu, in which sexuality was infused into spirituality and sexualised spirituality into revolutionary politics.

It was a milieu whose ideas provided a stimulating home and educational environment for the young William Blake. As we shall see, a key to his beliefs – and praxis – can be found in the once-suppressed but now recoverable history of the Moravians, Swedenborgians, Sabbatian Kabbalists and Illuminist Freemasons – secretive societies that inspired and disturbed his volatile imagination. The techniques developed by these societies to achieve sexual and visionary potency would sometimes provoke Mrs Blake to frightened and anguished tears but would also help Mr Blake survive the dangers of 'sexual religion' – and remain as a high-spirited sexagenarian, 'wild as ever'.

Part One

1

Religion of the Heart

What Pleasure doth a Heart perceive, that rests in the precious Hole, lives there, loves and sports . . .

Moravian hymn (1749)

On 10 May 1941, while London firemen battled the flames engulfing the Moravian Chapel in Fetter Lane, they little knew that Nazi bombers came perilously close to destroying the only evidence of the religious beliefs of William Blake's mother, Catherine, who was widely credited with nourishing his artistic imagination. Since her death in 1792 at the age of sixty-seven, researchers into Blake's life had been unable to learn anything about her, leading Alexander Gilchrist to lament, 'She is a shade to us, alas! In all senses: for of her character, or even her person, no tidings survive.'[1]

Not until 1992 did scholars finally discover that her maiden name was Wright and that she was a widow when she married James Blake, father of the artist; moreover, her first husband's name was Thomas Armitage, not the misspelled Hermitage.[2] These small discoveries made possible the major discovery in the Moravian Archives that in 1750–1 Catherine and Thomas Armitage were members of the Congregation of the Lamb that met in the Fetter Lane Chapel.[3] At the same time, several Blakes – including John Blake, arguably the brother of James Blake – also appeared in the Congregation diaries. At last, the shade of Catherine Blake can take on a flesh-and-blood reality, which will help us understand her influence on the artistic and spiritual development of her most unusual son, William.

The association of the Armitages and Blakes with the Moravians provided them with an unusual – even unique – access to an international network of ecumenical missionaries; an esoteric tradition of Christian Kabbalism, Hermetic alchemy and Oriental mysticism; a European 'high culture' of religious art, music and poetry; and a supportive political environment for opposition to current government policies. Significantly, their participation occurred during the 'Sifting Time' (*c.*1743–53), the most controversial, turbulent, creative and artistic period of Moravian history.[4] During these years the Congregation at Fetter Lane was exposed to a lurid but compelling theology of sex, wounds and blood, which inflamed the minds and hearts of the Brothers and Sisters of their *Unitas Fratrum* (their 'Unity of Brethren').

Though currently a nondescript street of impersonal office buildings, the Fetter Lane neighbourhood had an ancient history of unconventional, heretical and subversive inhabitants, who participated in a centuries-long struggle for the spiritual and political soul of Britain. In *London: The Biography*, Peter Ackroyd observes that the obscurity surrounding the derivation of the name Fetter Lane suggests that 'the city was trying to conceal its origins':

> *A more simple connection has been made with the workshops of the street which manufactured* fetters *or lance vests for the Knights Templar who also congregated in the vicinity . . . Throughout its history Fetter Lane acted as a boundary, or has been recorded as frontier territory; . . . it has attracted those who live upon 'the edge'.*[5]

The connection with the medieval Knights Templar, whose eighteenth-century Masonic revival would play a significant role in the Blakes' milieu, provides a provocative context for the long history of religious disaffection and government punishment on Fetter Lane, where both Papist and Protestant dissidents had periodically been hanged, drawn and quartered on the gallows that stood at each end of the street. Records show that not only Catholic recusants, Puritans and Anabaptists but also prostitutes, sodomites, pawnbrokers and 'the more dubious healers' found refuge in its dark alleys and enclaves: 'Their interest in Fetter Lane . . . lay in secrecy and seclusion.'[6] From 1738, when the Moravians took over a former Presbyterian chapel, until 1941, their presence infused an unusually mystical and artistic tone into the neighbourhood.

On 14 November 1750, Thomas Armitage and his wife Catherine penned highly emotional letters to the Elders of the Congregation of the Lamb. Addressing 'My Dear Brethren', Thomas wrote, 'My Dear Saviour has maid me Love you in Such a degree, as I never did Experience before to any Set of People; and I believe it is his will that I should come amongst you.'[7] Describing herself as 'a pore Crature and full of wants', Catherine pleaded, 'I do not Love our Dear Savour halfe enough but if it is his will to bring me among his hapy flock in closer conection I shall be very thankful.'[8] Sometime earlier, a certain John Blake – most likely the paternal uncle of William Blake – also made an impassioned appeal to join this highly selective, inner group: 'that I may come in a Closer connexont with them, that I may injoy those privilidged with our Dear Saviour as his Congregation have . . . O Lamb of God grant that I may be a membr of thy Congregation and may be quite happy.'[9]

What was it about this small, little-known, foreign-based Brotherhood that drew such ardent yearnings and promised such happiness? To understand the Armitages' and Blake's intensely emotional appeals, we must briefly explore the life and teachings of their charismatic leader, Count Zinzendorf, who brought to Fetter Lane the impassioned themes and rituals of his 'Religion of the Heart'.

The dramatic career of Nicolaus Ludwig von Zinzendorf (1700–60) continues to provoke controversy among historians, with most praising him as a creative theologian and pioneer of religious and racial toleration, and some condemning him as a Gnostic heretic and sexual pervert.[10] Born in Dresden, Saxony, to an aristocratic Lutheran family, he was early exposed to the Pietist movement, which sought to bring Christianity back to its simpler Gospel roots. He was raised by a remarkably spiritual and erudite grandmother, who corresponded with Leibniz in Latin, read the Bible in Hebrew and Greek, and studied Syrian and Chaldaean, while she exposed her young grandson to themes of Boehmenism and Christian Kabbalism.[11]

Like the young William Blake, Zinzendorf was considered a precocious child with 'a too vivid imagination and volatile temperament'.[12] At the age of nine he passed through a period of 'intense intellectual struggle concerning the reality of a transcendental God', which he resolved through his sense that he could converse directly and intimately with Jesus. He would often write notes to Jesus and toss them out of the window for him to pick up. So strong was his belief in a child's spiritual capacity that he would not have been surprised by the four-year-old Blake's claim that he *saw* God put his forehead to the window.[13]

From his grandmother's Pietist visitors, the eight-year-old Zinzendorf heard missionary reports from the East Indies and, as he told the Fetter Lane Congregation in 1753, 'there and then the first seed of missionary impulse arose in my soul'.[14] Two years later he was sent to the Pietist school at Halle, where his mentor August Hermann Francke informed him about the Collegium Philobiblicum, whose Hebrew scholars hoped to convert the Jews.[15] The relatively sympathetic attitude of the Pietist missionaries, who were willing to learn the languages and traditions of their targeted populations, encouraged Zinzendorf's own curiosity about foreign customs.

Fired with adolescent idealism, Zinzendorf and five other schoolboys organised a secret society, the 'Order of the Grain of Mustard Seed', a kind of spiritual knighthood, with the count serving as Grand Master. The first article of the Order affirmed that 'the members of our society will love the whole human family', and as crusaders for Christ they will seek conciliation with Jews.[16] This enterprise would bring Zinzendorf into unusual contact with heterodox Hebrew and Christian students of Kabbala, the esoteric tradition of Jewish mysticism, seen by many Pietists as a *via media* between the two religions.

However, his guardian determined to rid his ward of 'the taint of Pietism' and thus sent him at the age of sixteen to the University of Wittenberg, where his tutors were ordered to 'hold him with a tight rein' in order to break his proud and independent spirit. Their efforts failed, and when Zinzendorf undertook an extensive study tour in 1719, he deliberately sought contact not only with Jewish mystics but with Catholic intellectuals.[17] His curiosity about and tolerance towards different religions reinforced his distaste for sectarian divisions. Always deeply sensitive to art, he saw in the great European tradition of religious painting a means of transcending the antagonisms within Christianity. Thus, throughout his travels, he visited museums and galleries as part of his spiritual quest.

In a gallery in Düsseldorf he encountered a picture that deeply stirred him – and planted the seeds of his 'Religion of the Heart'. In his painting, '*Ecce Homo*, the Man of Sorrows', the baroque artist Domenico Feti portrayed Jesus suffering under the crown of thorns before his crucifixion. Under his wounded body scrolled a caption in Latin: 'All this I have done for you, but what have you done for me?'[18] As Zinzendorf later told his Congregation, 'My blood rushed because I was not able to give much of an answer, and I prayed to my Saviour to make me ride in the comradeship of his suffering with force.' The rushing blood, yearning for forced intimacy, comradeship in suffering – religious passions stimulated by a work or art – would intensify the young aristocrat's determination to serve Jesus and to identify with his fully humanised nature, which he came to believe included not only suffering but sexuality.

When Zinzendorf married an equally ardent and spiritual woman, Countess Erdmuth Dorothea Reuss, they both considered it a 'Militant Marriage' (*Streiter Ehe*), in which they were 'warriors for Christ'. He purchased his grandmother's estate at Berthelsdorf, where in 1722 he welcomed a band of Moravian refugees and then supported their settlement at nearby Herrnhut. Heirs to the radical reform movements of Jan Hus in the fifteenth century and Jan Amos Comenius in the seventeenth, the Moravian *Unitas Fratrum* struggled to preserve 'the Hidden Seed' of their ecumenical spiritual traditions.[19] In the eighteenth century, many of them studied the alchemystical writings of Jacob Boehme, Jane Leade and the Philadelphian Brotherhood, whose 'Sophia Mysticism' opened the door to new thinking about sexuality and divinity.[20] Through these works, the intensely passionate Zinzendorf learned that Christianised versions of Kabbala provided a spiritualising of sexuality that was emotionally and intellectually liberating.

According to Jewish Kabbalists, the unknowable hidden divinity – the *En Sof* – performed an act of love by manifesting 'his' essence in a series of male and female emanations, the *Sephiroth*, whose spiritual-erotic dynamics progressed from the original seminal point to the ultimate material cosmos.[21]

Using ritualised meditation, Kabbalists visualised this process in the image of the Sephirotic Tree and the microcosmic man, Adam Kadmon, who contains within his body all the spiritual and sexual potencies of the Godhead. The Fall from the primordial state of sexual equilibrium and bliss was caused by the unbalanced outgrowth of the female *Sephira* of strict judgement, which must be sweetened by the male *Sephira* of mercy. Through reverent meditation, the Kabbalist can achieve a visionary state in which he reintegrates the male-female emanations within his mind, and thus within Adam Kadmon and the Godhead.

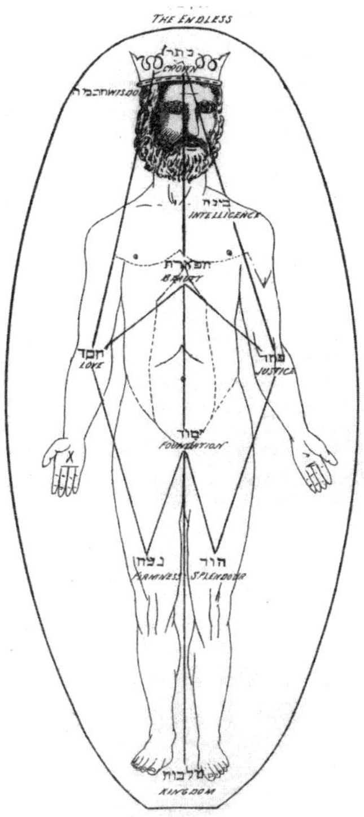

For many Christians, especially Protestants, this Jewish inclusion of sexuality within spirituality filled a void created by the elimination of the female from the orthodox Trinity. But, as B. J. Gibbons observes:

> *The divine feminine has, in fact, rarely remained behind the curtain in Western culture. If Diana and Isis were to leave the stage with the growth of Christianity, the Virgin Mary was also to make her entrance. The Protestant rejection of Mariology created a divine realm that was overwhelmingly masculine in tone, but this was compensated in some circles by the introduction of another manifestation of the divine feminine, Sophia . . .*[22]

By the 1730s Zinzendorf believed that an assimilation of these Kabbalistic notions into Christianity could save all the churches from their present state of arid theological disputes, desiccated spirituality and suppressed sexual energy. He had conversed with heterodox Jews, whose private sympathies for Sabbatai Zevi, the seventeenth-century 'False Messiah', led them to positions close to Christianity.[23] After Sabbatai's forced conversion to Islam in 1666, many of his followers developed an antinomian rationale for his apostasy.[24] Like Jesus, who was tortured and crucified, Sabbatai had to suffer debasement; like Jesus's salvific sacrifice, Sabbatai's self-chosen descent into the evil realm of false religion allowed him to ascend and proclaim the true religion of Kabbalistic Judaism. Thus, for Zinzendorf, a Judaised Jesus – a Christianised Adam Kadmon – should be passionately loved and intensely worshipped because of the *humanised* pain and suffering he voluntarily endured.

Zinzendorf began developing a new *Herzensreligion*, which drew on the Hebrew word for heart, *Lev*, the location of emotion and intellect. In the Old Testament, heart is the point of contact with God; *Lev* is 'more visceral and affective than the Greek word for the personality, *Psyche*'.[25] As Arthur Freeman explains:

> *Zinzendorf defined 'Heart' as the inner person which had five senses as did the outer person. The 'Heart', especially*

> *when it has been brought to life by the Holy Spirit, can perceive the Saviour objectively and directly. In modern terms we might speak of this as 'intuition' or 'extrasensory perception'. Zinzendorf's approach is very similar to Teresa of Avila's 'intellectual vision'.*[26]

Zinzendorf rejected the aridity and perplexity of abstract theological studies; instead, he advocated an intuitive, experiential, *felt* belief in the reality of Jesus's life on earth, in which the humanised God-Man enjoyed and suffered the full range of human experience. To honour the painful and degrading sacrifice he made on the Cross, one should meditate intensely on his human body, visualising and sharing his pain and desire. His sacrifice was so great that it atoned for the permanently sinful nature of man, who became a 'justified sinner' through his simple faith in Jesus. Thus, self-righteous and pious standards of behaviour, which led to joylessness and hypocrisy, were not the proper expressions of Christian worship, for one should utilise one's *Herz/Lev* to *sensate* Jesus's passionate love and to identify with his bleeding wounds, from the first wound of circumcision to the final wound in his side.

In order to utilise all the senses of *Herz/Lev* in their identification with Christ, the Moravians were urged to paint pictures of him, not only on canvas but in their minds and hearts. Whoever does not have 'a portrait of Jesus in his heart and before his eyes is an unconverted person'; thus, one must affirm the mental picture of Jesus's person, 'his holy humanity, as it forms itself'.[27] This visualisation focused especially on the bloody wounds of Christ, which the worshipper should 'taste, see, smell and touch', through the eucharist as well as intense prayer. This focus led critics to complain that Zinzendorf was becoming too carnal, a promoter of *Fleischliche Spiritualität* (fleshly spirituality).[28] It was a charge that would later be made against the drawings of Blake, who seemed to exemplify the Moravians' concept of *Herz/Lev*. As he explained to Crabb Robinson, 'I know what is true by internal conviction. A doctrine is stated – My heart tells me It *must* be true.'[29]

For Zinzendorf and his devotees, the 'Religion of the Heart' brought great imaginative joy and a full-bodied sense of religious ecstasy. In 1738, when a small group of his followers met in the Fetter Lane Chapel, they determined to bring this passionate new message to hungry listeners in London. Over the next years these would include Emanuel Swedenborg, Catherine and Thomas Armitage, John Blake and a host of other Blakes. And, though Zinzendorf's 'Love Feast' would eventually prove too rich and exotic for some early disciples, such as John and Charles Wesley, Blake's mother would bring a hearty (*herzlich*) appetite to his proffered meal.

2

The Mystical Marriage

The Man, whilst he conjugally embraces is a Vice-Christ, and His Wife ought to regard him as acting in the Name of the Creator.

Count Zinzendorf, *Sermon* (1747)

IN 1738 ZINZENDORF launched the *Judenmission* (mission to the Jews), in which he sent Hebrew- and Yiddish-speaking Moravians to live in the Jewish quarters of Amsterdam, London and other cities.[1] Though it was only one among his many missionary projects (which extended from the Americas to Africa to Asia), it was also closest to his heart. From his agents in the North American colonies, he heard of their collaboration with the native tribes, whom Zinzendorf believed were descendants of the Ten Lost Tribes of Israel. This belief was reinforced by his Hebrew and Kabbalistic studies and by his discussions with heterodox Jews in Germany and the West Indies.[2] By the time he made his first visit to London in April 1739, he was convinced that an infusion of Jewish mystical beliefs about marriage would enable the Moravians to enact the Kabbalists' cosmic marriage on earth.

Fundamental to Kabbalistic sexual theosophy was the ancient symbolism of the Cherubim, who guarded the Ark of the Covenant in the Holy of Holies in the Temple at Jerusalem. Portrayed in an ornate golden sculpture, the male and female Cherubim were entwined in the act of marital intercourse, thus forming an image of God's joyful marriage with his female emanation, the *Shekhinah*.[3]

When the Temple was sacked by the pagan Antiochus in 168 BC, the erotic statuary was paraded through the streets in order to ridicule the Jews. After the destruction of the Temple by the Roman emperor Titus in AD 70, Jewish mystics developed a meditative technique in which they visualised the rejoining of the Cherubim, and thus reintegrated the male and female potencies within the Godhead. This visionary cosmic drama was re-enacted within the androgynous body of Adam Kadmon, and the visualisation of the sexual dynamics between the male and female *Sephiroth* could also re-establish the original sexual equilibrium (a restorative process called *Tikkun*).

Most striking to Zinzendorf was the Kabbalists' further belief that the human couple could replicate the sacramental intercourse on earth, thus giving their humble bedroom a cosmic spiritual significance. When he arrived at Fetter Lane in 1739, he instructed the small group of Moravians to infuse his new 'Marriage Theology' into their teaching and practice.[4] By the time Catherine and Thomas Armitage joined the Congregation, this belief in the mystical marriage had become central to Moravian sermons, hymns and ceremonial. Moreover, they were attracted to the Brotherhood by some of the most passionate proponents of spiritualised sexuality – such as Peter Boehler and John Cennick.

In 1738 the Moravian missionary Peter Boehler returned from his work among the Negroes in the British colony of Georgia and organised a small group of sympathisers to meet in the Fetter Lane Chapel. A talented poet and musician, Boehler's eloquence soon gained him a reputation as 'the devout German, full of holy zeal'.[5] When John Wesley, leader of the Oxford 'Holy Club', met Boehler at the home of a Moravian merchant, he was greatly impressed by the German's opitimistic faith.[6] Like Zinzendorf, Boehler rejected the Pietists' emphasis on ascetic self-denial and morbid spiritual struggle – practices that had rendered Wesley miserable and guilt-ridden. Boehler preached the 'Religion of the Heart', proclaiming that Christ's bodily suffering was sufficient to save sinners, whose faith should then produce a joyful sense of relief and liberation. Echoing the seventeenth-century German mystic Jacob Boehme, who 'painted a picture of Adam's prelapsarian life as one of playfulness and freedom', Boehler went further to portray the fallen Adams – ordinary humans – as capable of spiritual frolic and emotional joy.[7]

Wesley introduced Boehler to the bookseller James Hutton, a member of a Non-Juring Anglican family, who hosted meetings of a private religious society in his home.[8] Encouraged by John and his brother Charles Wesley, who was teaching Boehler English, the group at Hutton's decided to organise a 'little society' on the 'Moravian model', as outlined by Boehler on 1 May 1738. John drafted eleven rules, but Boehler expanded them to thirty-three, which included a reference to the sex- and marriage-counselling that was becoming central to Moravian theology. Though never mentioned in official Methodist accounts of this historic meeting, Boehler's rule no. 21 hinted at this new sexual focus: 'That any who desire to be admitted into this Society be asked, What are your Reasons for desiring this? Will you be entirely open, using no Kind of Reserve, least of all, in the Case of Love or Courtship?'[9]

Twelve years later, when Catherine Armitage applied for membership in the Congregation, she knew that she was expected to answer personal and sexual questions, 'using no Kind of Reserve'. In her letter she indicated that 'if it is his will to bring me among his happy flock in closer conection I shall be very thankful', and 'I would tell you more of my self but itt is nothing thats good so now I will write of my Saviour that is all Love.'[10] Once accepted into the inner group, she would be intimately questioned about her religious, sexual and marital experiences. Boehler, who became her friend and protector, drew upon the practice at Herrnhut of organising congregations into 'bands' or fellowship groups, in which lay members examined each other's spiritual, psychological and sexual state. Colin Podmore observes that:

> *The bands were marked by total frankness on the part both of the member describing the state of his soul and of his fellow members in their criticism of him. Thus they had something of the function of the confessional and anticipated to some degree modern 'group therapy' . . . Such intimate discipleship groups were hitherto virtually unknown in the Church of England.*[11]

Meanwhile, in 1738, after John Wesley had a heart-to-heart conversation with Boehler, he 'accepted the Moravian understanding of salvation', which meant that he was saved 'from the *law* of sin and death'.[12] Defying the wishes of his parents, Wesley travelled to Germany to visit the Moravian centres; much to his disappointment, the Brethren considered him a *Homo perturbatus* and rejected his application for membership in the inner Congregation. Nevertheless, when he returned to London in September, he continued to visit Fetter Lane, where the members held Moravian-style 'Love Feasts', which combined food and drink with intense spiritual discussions.

These highly emotional sessions sometimes lasted all night, and they would later provoke much suspicion about the participants' behaviour. At one *Agape* in January 1739, Wesley recorded that at 3 a.m., 'The power of God came mightily upon us, in so much that many cried out for exceeding joy, and many fell to the ground' – a communal ecstatic state produced by 'the sudden effusion of the Holy Ghost'.[13] By October, when Zinzendorf's emissary Philipp Molther visited Fetter Lane, he reported that the 'sighing, groaning, whimpering and howling', which the participants saw as proof of the 'Spirit and Power of God', was 'enough to bring one out in a cold sweat'.[14] Adding to the excessive 'enthusiasm' were the bizarre actions of the French Prophets, who often burst into Fetter Lane meetings. In December, Charles Wesley was rooming with Isaac Hollis, a Prophet who was friendly with Boehler:

> *When we were undressing, he fell into violent agitations, and gobbled like a turkey-cock. I was frightened and began exorcising him . . . He soon recovered out of his fit of inspiration. I prayed, and went to bed, not half-liking my bedfellow. I did not sleep very sound with Satan so near me.*[15]

Under Molther's leadership, a temporary policy of 'Stillness' was implemented upon the unruly worshippers, while John Wesley – bitter at his rejection by the selective Congregation – nursed his resentment and planned his 'Methodist' breakaway from the Moravians.

During that year Zinzendorf and Samuel Lieberkuhn, his main missionary to the Jews, began to insert Hebrew and Kabbalistic terms (the *Sephiroth*, the *Shekhinah*) into Moravian hymns, and in October 1739 the Brethren and their Jewish converts began to celebrate Yom Kippur, the Jewish Day of Atonement.[16] A Dutch critic complained that the Moravians believe that 'One may be saved in the Profession of the *Pagan* and *Jewish* religion' and that 'Man is Part of the Divine Being'.[17] It was a belief that Blake would later affirm to Crabb Robinson: 'We are all co-existent with God – members of the Divine Body.'[18]

In 1741, inspired by what he was learning from his Kabbalistic studies, Zinzendorf set off for Pennsylvania, in search of the 'Jewish Indians'. With Boehler, who had taken over leadership of the Moravian settlement in Bethlehem, he visited a peculiar group of celibate Rosicrucians, who maintained a mystical community at Ephrata. The Pennsylvania Moravians had been impressed by the spiritual devotion of the Ephratans, who developed elaborate Hermetic and Kabbalistic rituals. While advocating celibacy in order to achieve marriage with Boehme's 'Divine Sophia', they incorporated the erotic symbolism of the *Zohar*, the thirteenth-century Kabbalistic masterwork, into powerful hymns, in which 'mystic exultation revels in rhythmic measure, and free use is made of the vocabulary of sensual love to symbolise religious ecstasy'.[19]

The count also visited the 'Zionitic Brotherhood', a radical branch of the Ephratan Rosicrucians, who developed Masonic-style initiation rituals. After participation in the sect's rites of illumination and rejuvenation, the local Moravian bishop began to wear an emblem of 'the Rosy Cross'. Zinzendorf's subsequent use of Masonic terminology in his sermons led his opponents to accuse him of running a quasi-Masonic secret society.[20]

Zinzendorf eventually quarrelled with Conrad Beissel, the autocratic leader at Ephrata, and he determined to counter Beissel's rejection of sexuality by 'embodying' the marriage of the Heavenly Bridegroom and Divine Sophia in the earthly life of the Moravians. Thus, he instructed Boehler to make Bethlehem a counter-movement to the celibacy rules of the Cloister at Ephrata. Like the Kabbalists, Zinzendorf advocated the sacred and mystical nature of conjugal intercourse, and he drew on Jewish ritual when he ordered the 'warriors' (ministers and missionaries) to perform their 'holy joining' on Saturday, the Jewish Sabbath.[21]

However, in order to avoid scandal and to ensure the sublimation of merely animal lust, he helped Boehler organise the community into bands or 'choirs' that were strictly segregated by sex, except for 'joining times'. Thus Bethlehem represented a paradoxical ideal of joyfully expressed sexuality in hymns and sermons combined with strong communal controls over sexual behaviour. For the next two years, Boehler tried to maintain the marriage theology in the face of bitter attacks by Beissel that the Moravians led 'disorderly lives' and had 'a carnal passion for making proselytes'.[22]

While Boehler struggled to implement the difficult sexual paradox (conjugal liberation and communal control) in Bethlehem, Zinzendorf carried it to England in early 1743, where he passionately preached his marriage theology. As Colin Podmore observes:

> *For him both the Church and the Individual Christian were brides of Christ and thus essentially female. Earthly marriage was an 'interim matter', preparing for and pointing to the heavenly marriage with Christ. In it the husband represented Christ as his 'procurator'; he was thus a 'vice-man' or 'vice-Christ'. Marriage and its consummation could therefore be described as* Gottesdienst *(the worship or service of God), as a sacramental act; it was the liturgy of . . . the marriage bed, where two people hold a daily* Gottesdienst . . .[23]

To overcome traditional Protestant prudery, Zinzendorf implemented a pioneering policy of 'sex education and marriage guidance'. Each choir was given only as much information as was considered necessary, and members were forbidden to talk about what they had heard to those in other groups: 'Between members of the married choir, however, such matters could be discussed openly and without shame.'[24] Zinzendorf had written detailed instructions for Boehler, explaining how members of the Married Choir were 'to teach sexual procedures and practices to newly wedded brothers and sisters':

> *The instructions emphasised the importance of consent by both parties in marriage, properly informing young men and women before and after marriage about sex, how and why their bodies and sexual organs were made holy by Jesus, the methods of sexual intercourse and how often it should be performed. Two methods of intercourse were suitable – sitting or lying – and couples should choose according to their own taste, using a chair or bench and towel with the first or a pillow with the second.*[25]

The teachers explained that the husband blesses the wife during ejaculation and suggested that they 'read aloud an appropriate verse while this is happening' (such as hymns describing 'the moment the stab occurred, / I leapt out, hallelujah!' or, more graphically, 'when my dear husband / lets his oil sizzle in me; / . . . this grace is a sacrament').[26] After they finished, couples prayed and discussed 'the liturgical importance of the event with others'. Thus the Congregation diarist at Fetter Lane could record in 1743 that 'Br and Sr Prusque wer much bless'd together last night in their Fellowship' (as intercourse was termed).[27]

Though the surviving Fetter Lane records of the sex- and marriage-counselling are generally euphemistic, the hymns and sermons written by Zinzendorf and his closest confidants after he returned to the Continent in summer 1743 express a much more explicit and even lurid fascination with the sexuality of Jesus, and a much more Kabbalistic sense of the psychosexual dynamics within the Holy Family and supernal world.[28] Now defining the Holy Spirit as female, the wife of God and mother of the God-Man, Zinzendorf composed erotically charged hymns, in which the Hebrew 'Mother *Ruach*' copulates with 'Christ's *Logos*', thus 'breeding the Creation'.[29] The hymns were sent to Moravian congregations in London, Yorkshire and other regions, where they appealed to growing numbers of listeners.

Given the emotional atmosphere created by sermon and song about the mystical marriage, it is tantalising that a Mr and Mrs Blake and a Mr Wright are listed as members of the Married Choir at Fetter Lane in 1743.[30] Were these the grandparents of William Blake? His mother's maiden name was Wright before she married Thomas Armitage, a haberdasher and hosier, on 14 December 1746. From their letters to the Moravian Elders in November 1750, it is clear that they had attended the public Moravian services for some time before they petitioned for membership in the inner Congregation. Moreover, the John Blake who also petitioned for membership was probably the brother and housemate of James Blake, haberdasher and hosier, who was the close neighbour of the Armitages in Golden Square.[31]

Thus Catherine probably knew the Blake brothers while she was married to Armitage and before she married James on 15 October 1752. If William Muir was accurate, then the new couple continued to attend services at Fetter Lane over the next decade. During the years of Armitage-Blake attendance, the Moravians participated in Zinzendorf's sexual and spiritual experiments, which produced the most creative and controversial period in the history of their church. During the 'Sifting Time', Zinzendorf and his more radical son, Christian Renatus, took the 'mystical marriage' far beyond its original definition, as they merged the psychoerotic techniques of Sabbatian and Hasidic Jews into the fervent 'wound mysticism' of Catholic and Jesuit visionaries. The result was a peculiar but passionate theology of 'sex, wounds and blood'.

3

Sex, Wounds and Blood

My dear Bretheren & Sisters, . . . at the love feast our Saviour was pleased to make me Suck his wounds . . . and I trust will more and more till my fraile nature can hould no more.

Catherine Armitage, application to the Congregation (1750)

IN 1746, ZINZENDORF ordered Peter Boehler to return to London and take over the Fetter Lane Congregation. Over the next years his eloquent preaching and passionate singing greatly appealed to John Blake, who wrote to 'Dear Brother Boehler', begging him to 'make me one of those who can Rejoyce in his wounds . . . May I become a happy Sinnor'.[1] The overwrought petitioner was responding to the main theme of the 'Sifting Time', in which Zinzendorf and Boehler urged the Brothers and Sisters to concentrate so intently on the fully humanised body of the crucified Jesus that they psychoerotically penetrated the bleeding wounds. The resultant sense of emotional and physical ecstasy would prove the most attractive and most dangerous state that the Moravians experienced. And it was one that Catherine Armitage cherished.

Zinzendorf took the German word *Siftung* from Luke 22: 31–2, where Jesus said to Simon Peter: 'Behold, Satan hath desired to have you, that he may *sift* you as wheat. But I have prayed for thee, that thy faith fail not: and when thou art converted, strengthen thy brethren.'[2] For the Moravians, the knowledge that Peter would thrice deny Jesus during his hour of peril was a challenge for them to remain faithful to the reality of his suffering and aware of their own weakness. The count's call for them to be 'warriors' for Christ, especially in their hazardous missionary activities, was in defiance of Satan's 'sifting' of their potential timidity or cowardice before hostile or dangerous adversaries.

Challenged by increasingly angry opponents, Zinzendorf intensified his focus on the physical body of Jesus and daringly merged Kabbalistic sexual theosophy with Christian wound mysticism. He revived the long-suppressed artistic tradition of *ostentatio vulnerum* (the showing forth of the wounds) and *ostentatio genitalium* (the showing forth of the genitalia), by which Renaissance painters and poets portrayed the full 'humanation' of Jesus.[3] Christian saints and artists stressed that the first cut on Jesus's penis prefigured the last spear-cut on the side of his chest; both served 'to destroy the error of them who would say he had taken on a phantasmal and not a true body'. As Leo Steinberg explains:

> *Linking beginning to end – the knife's cut to the gash of the lance – the wounds trace a passage on the body of Christ from man to God; the genital members broaching the mortal Passion, the breast yielding the gift of grace. Put into words, the anatomical consequence comes . . . as a shock – that Christ's redemptive Passion, which culminates in the blood of the sacred heart, begins in the blood of the penis.*[4]

In sixteenth-century England the newly Protestant Church dropped the word 'humanation', but the German version, *Menschwerdung*, survived in Lutheran 'wound mysticism'. Steinberg notes that, after the Renaissance, both Catholic and

Protestant churches suppressed the *ostentatio genitalium*, so that now, 'We are educated to shrink from such thinking. But it is Christian thinking.' Unusually for an eighteenth-century intellectual, Zinzendorf did not shrink from such thinking. Moreover, his Kabbalistic studies reinforced his determination to revive (at least verbally) this Christian artistic tradition, which was currently buried under layers of prudish over-painting that covered Jesus's genitals with aprons, veils and underpants. As we have already seen, William Blake would suffer similar artistic censorship.

With the assistance of a Jewish friend named Jakob, Zinzendorf composed the 'Litany of the Wounds of the Husband', which was sung in antiphonal choruses by the Congregation. He drew on the Kabbalistic concept of the circumcised penis as the visionary point of contact with God. The First Choir sang, 'May your holy first wound', and the Second Choir answered, 'Help us circumcise our heart'.[5] From his Jewish contacts, he gained access to the Kabbalists' elaboration of the meaning of *Lev* (heart), which identified *Lev* with the *Shekhinah*, who could vivify the heart, which was further identified with the phallus. According to Deuteronomy 10: 16, one must 'circumcise therefore the foreskin of your heart, and be no more stiff-necked'. Kabbalists interpreted this to mean, 'If one is sexually pure, then the male organ is the locus of beatific vision, but if one is impure, then this very location is transformed into a source of affliction and misery.'[6] Purity did not mean celibacy, which was always rejected in Judaism, but the proper religious exercise of conjugal and visionary sexuality.

By meditating intensely, with purity of intention, on the circumcised penis of Adam Kadmon, the Kabbalist could heal the phallic heart, for God's circumcised 'seal' upon the Jew corresponds to the 'breaking open of a path' – a path to an ecstatic visionary marriage with the *Shekhinah* and with God.

Clearly drawing on this Jewish tradition, Zinzendorf stressed that:

> *at the Moment when we obtain Grace, Absolution, and a Kiss of Peace from the Saviour's Mouth, He also tears in sunder, as it were, with his judicial Teeth as the Judge of all Flesh, the Fore-skin of our Heart: This is the Circumcision made without Hands. The pain attending it is call'd Compunction, or the Rending of the Heart* [Lev] *. . . When He kisses us the first time after forgiving us our Sins, then He does what the* Mohel, *or circumcising Priest among the* Jews *is wont to do with his Teeth or Nail. That Judge [Jesus], who was also himself circumcised, gives us a little bloody Mark, a Covenant-Scar or Notch, soon made but never to be worn out, a cutting Sense of his Sufferings, which takes place the same Minute with his reconciling Kiss.*[7]

The Kabbalistic sources shed a clarifying light on the Moravian hymns composed for adolescent boys:

> *Oh holy covenant slit, Oh holy wound, govern the true maleness of the sinful creature, whom you have sanctified as a marriage vessel with the circumcision of blood. The boys veil and hide themselves from secret prohibited [acts] because of this covenant. The young protect themselves before nature with seals which only the Creator can open.*[8]

Like the Kabbalists, for whom the semen was holy, the Moravians taught that wastage of male seed through masturbation or illicit sex was a heart- and phallus-breaking sin, a violation of the mystical marriage. Sexual realists as well as idealists, the Moravian youth counsellors spoke frankly about masturbatory impulses, nocturnal emissions and erotic dreams.

In one sermon Zinzendorf explained, 'Things that ought to be experienced physically at a certain Time, cannot be abolish'd. It would be a Chimaera, if the Children of God did not experience them; such as endeavour to put themselves above human Nature, become unhappy Boys and Girls.'[9] He told the Congregation that 'he had advanced nothing there, but what he knew very well, and had experienced himself in his Time, before the Society was in being'.

In order to sublimate, not suppress, the adolescent's normal sexual desire (a 'wild' but 'natural intoxication'), the sex counsellors urged the Single Brethren to focus on Jesus's 'holy covenant slit' and to envision the mystical marriage that awaits them. By transferring their own phallic energy to their visualisation of Jesus's penis and its purity, they could achieve a healthy release and catharsis. The spiritual and emotional intensity that this sexual meditation and sublimation created was evident in the Single Brethren's Love Feasts dedicated to the circumcision, one of which lasted nearly five hours. No wonder some young men described themselves as 'half-intoxicated from yesterday's lovefeast'.

Catherine Armitage, who had a young son (also named Thomas), probably learned about these meditation techniques, which were taught to parents as well as their male children.[10] In 1793, when her son William Blake wrote his paean to liberated sexuality, *Visions of the Daughters of Albion*, he seemed to refer to this Moravian effort to visualise the circumcised penis and to transmute, not repress, masturbatory impulses during 'the moment of desire!'

. . . the youth shut up from
The lustful joy, shall forget to generate & create an amorous image
In the shadow of his curtains and in the folds of his silent pillow.

Are not these the places of religion? The rewards of continence?
The self enjoyings of self denial? . . .[11]

Perhaps he heard from his mother about the early, uninhibited Moravian hymns and sermons that dealt with the adolescent 'blast of wild Fire' that raises 'Motions in the Flesh', natural urges that had a spiritual purpose.[12] He may have learned further that these writings were censored by the conservative Elders in the 1760s and subsequently disappeared from Moravian sex education.

Not only the penis but the vagina was honoured by Zinzendorf, who elevated the importance of the sexual female within Christian theology. In 1749, when Boehler celebrated the 'Day of our Saviour's Circumcision', he urged the couples to visualise intensely not only the penis but the womb:

We had in our View and also in our Heart all the Day Reflections suitable to both. *In the Married Q[uarter] of* hour Br Boehler *recommended to that Choir the reverent Thoughts of the human Frame, which our Saviours being a Male, and born of a Female, do demand.*[13]

Merging Jewish tradition into Moravian teaching, Zinzendorf went even further and stressed that:

the Womb of Woman is no more to be deem'd shameful, but the most awful of all the Members; it having become the happy Tabernacle, which the Holy Ghost both could and would overshadow, and wherein his Schechinah *did lodge, and quicken a divine Babe.*

The Babe himself receiv'd the Shape of a Boy, to the End that He might hereby turn the Male Shame also into Honour,

> *make it again a Member of the greatest Dignity, and worthy of the Creator . . . by that Rite [of circumcision] to be authentically declared a Boy; a Male that open'd the Womb.*[14]

Influenced by the Kabbalistic tradition of the *Shekhinah* who dwells between the male and female Cherubim in the Holy of Holies, Zinzendorf Christianised this image of divine copulation. Thus he identified the spear that pierced the side of Jesus with the penis and the resultant wound-hole with the vagina – a spear thrust that he 'compared to the ripping of the curtain of the Holy of Holies', a tearing open that would reveal the sacred intercourse.[15] It was no coincidence that in a previous hymn the Moravians sang, 'A great deal of power is uselessly spent/Condemning the Jews.'[16]

Influenced by his study of Renaissance paintings that portrayed 'the mystical Man of Sorrows' as a comprehensively sexual being with male genitalia and female side-wound, Zinzendorf urged the Moravians to keep 'all of Christ's body in their mind's eye'. Like the painter Andrea del Sarto, who portrayed a laughing baby Jesus who 'clutches his genitals while pointing to Mary's breast', Zinzendorf believed that 'the crucified God is one with frolicking infant', whose first phallic wound foreshadows the final vaginal wound that leads to man's salvation.[17] Thus he exhorted the Brothers and Sisters first to infantilise themselves and then to visualise so intensely the side 'Hole' that they felt absorbed into it, bathed in the warm blood, enwombed in its safety, aroused in spiritual-sexual euphoria.

In a beloved hymn that was probably known to Catherine Armitage, the Moravians sang 'heartily':

> *What Pleasure doth a Heart perceive, that rests in the precious Hole, lives there, loves and sports, works and*

> *praises the little Lamb, and tho' it storms and blusters without, feels nothing of it within this his Dwelling . . . My heart dwells in Jesus' Side, I kiss with the greatest Tenderness the Scars on his Hands and Feet. I kiss the Spear; how would I, O Soldier, run even to kiss thee for this Piercing . . . I lay myself in the Hole made by the Spear, sometimes Length-wise, sometimes Cross-wise . . . then the Loins I use for my little Bed, and the Hands and Feet serve me for a Pillow . . . God be praised! Soldier, for this Pricking with the Spear I give thee Thanks. I have licked all over that Rock Salt! O how well did it taste, on that Moment my little Soul is transported into the little Side-Hole.*[18]

In her application letter of 1750, Catherine Armitage revealed that she was so carried away at a Love Feast that she felt Jesus making her 'Suck his wounds', and she quoted a blood-and-wounds hymn, 'Here let me drink for ever drink.' Shocking as such words were to many of Zinzendorf's critics, they actually replicated those of late medieval and Renaissance poets and artists who described the side-wound as a nest, bedchamber, honeycomb, 'sweet luscious fruit' or 'the spout of a winepress, oozing the juice of the grape'.[19] Reviving centuries-old traditions of the magical, sexual and healing power of blood, the Moravians repeated the kind of 'writhing erotic symbolism' expressed in the visionary accounts of various Catholic saints, who immersed themselves in Jesus's blood 'in a laver of thirsting, slaking concupiscence', in which 'God is tasted mouth to mouth'.[20]

The gushing blood of the humanised Jesus redeemed all the organs of the human body, including the male and female genitalia. Noting that 'we believe in that Lamb of God, who put a happy End to the whole Career of natural Depravity', Zinzendorf affirmed that 'through the merit of his Wound of Circumcision, we trust to sanctify the Choirs or Conditions of Life' – that is, the stages of physical development.[21] He thus rejected the Christian term *Pudendum*, which made the vulva an object of shame that should be concealed, and called instead for a Kabbalistic respect for male and female sexual organs:

> *What in the Bible is mentioned an hundred, and more than an hundred Times, but on Account of the Fall, by Reason of Depravation, is call'd by the hideous Name* Pudendum; *this he (the Saviour) has changed into* Verendum, *in the proper and strictest sense of that Word: And what was chastised by Circumcision, in the Time of the Law, is restored again to its first Essence and flourishing State; 'tis made equal to the most noble and respectable Parts of the Body, yea 'tis on Account of its Dignity and Distinction, become superior to all the rest; especially as the Lamb would choose to endure in that Part his first Wound, his first Pain . . . I consider the Parts for distinguishing both Sexes in Christians, as the most honourable of the whole Body, my Lord and God having partly inhabited them and partly wore them himself.*[22]

To further honour the vagina-womb, he preached that it was deliberately formed as a chapel for worship by Moravian husbands and 'the whole Congregation of Souls'. In fact, the sexual organs were designed to make the mystical marriage possible:

> *All this we have, that we may become Saviours in this World, Saviours of the Member of that Body, which the Lamb has instructed us, of that little Model of a Chappel of God, of that Vice-Church, where also something represents itself of the Members of Christ, as in us Men, who are the Head.*[23]

Despite his oblique language, it is clear that Zinzendorf referred to the penis-like clitoris in the vulva – a reference that throws a new light on one of Blake's most provocative drawings. In the 1790s, during a period of intense psycho-erotic experimentation, Blake sketched 'a naked woman whose genitals have been transformed into an altar or chapel, with an erect penis forming a kind of holy statue at the centre'.[24]

For his enemies – and for many modern critics – Zinzendorf's obsession with the bloody wounds of Christ was the most repulsive theme in his theology. And certainly there were many shocking expressions in his sermons and hymns, which described the wounds as moist, gory, juicy and succulent. He even preached to the children that 'in the Holy Communion the communicants sacramentally eat the flesh and drink the blood of Christ on the "Cross-Delicatessen"'.[25] The spear's wound was called a 'Diet-Table, where my Mouth th' Side may dive, To revive'.[26] One diarist recorded that 'Our morning blessing was especially bloody and juicy.'[27] The Married People sang, and the youthful flock trembled 'with a blessed sensation of shaking from love's fever'. At Fetter Lane, when Boehler led the liturgy by singing 'Lick on Jesus Christ', he sometimes became so excited that he was 'transported' into a 'religious ecstasy'.[28]

Given the vaginal symbolism of the side-hole, these exhortations have proven fertile ground for modern psychoanalysts, who view Zinzendorf's obsession as pathological – that is, that the count 'found sexual release in fantasising about sucking and licking this ersatz vagina'.[29] However, Craig Atwood argues convincingly that 'the vivid phantasy life' expressed in the 'cult of the wounds' was *not* pathological; in fact, it was a key factor in the success of the Moravian communities:

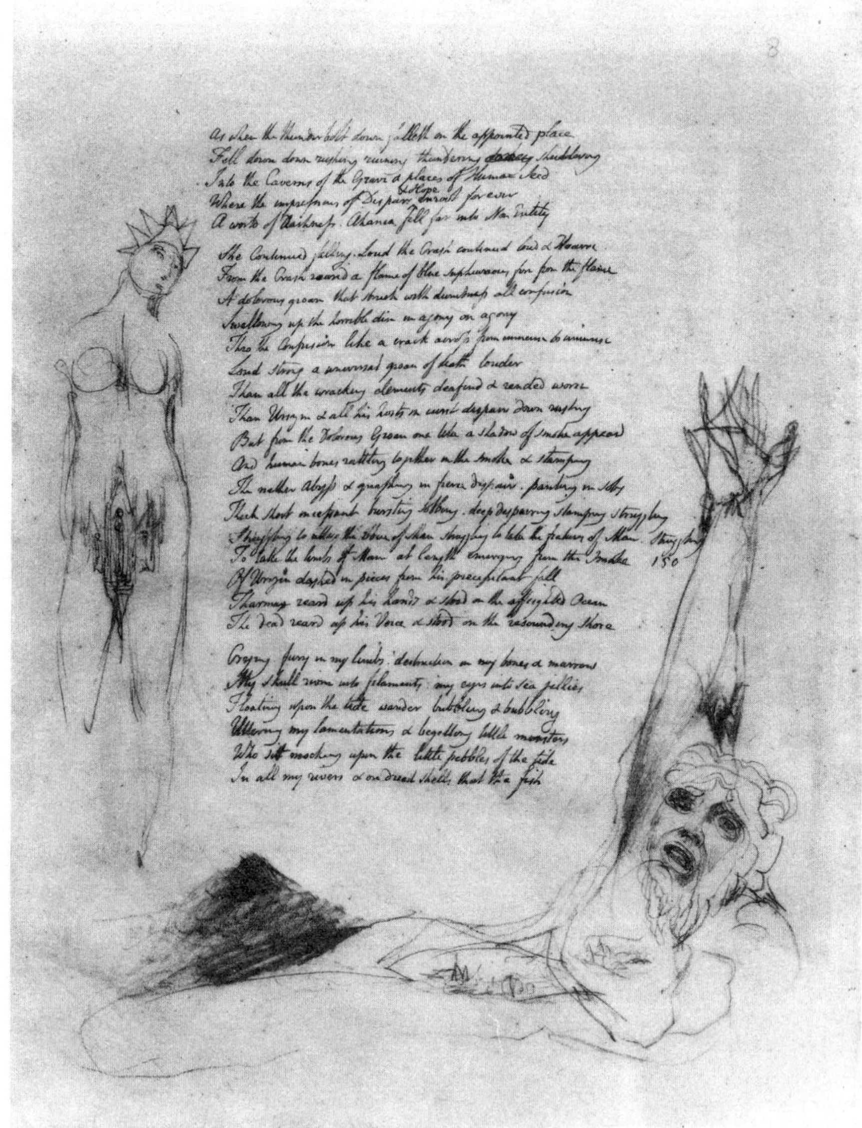
As when the thunderbolt down falleth on the appointed place
Fell down down rushing ruining thundering shuddering
Into the Caverns of the Grave & places of Human Seed
Where the impressions of Despair & Hope enroot forever
A world of Darkness. Ahania fell far into Non Entity

She Continued falling. Loud the Crash continued loud & Hoarse
From the Crash roared a flame of blue sulphureous fire from the flame
A dolorous groan that struck with dumbness all confusion
Swallowing up the horrible din in agony on agony
Thro the Confusion like a crack across from immense to immense
Loud strong a universal groan of death louder
Than all the wracking elements deafend & rended worse
Than Urizen & all his hosts in curst despair down rushing
But from the Dolorous Groan one like a shadow of smoke appeard
And human bones rattling together in the smoke & stamping
The nether Abyss & gnashing in fierce despair. panting in sobs
Thick short incessant bursting sobbing. deep despairing stamping struggling
Struggling to utter the voice of Man struggling to take the features of Man. Struggling
To take the limbs of Man at length emerging from the smoke
Of Urizen dashed in pieces from his precipitant fall
Tharmas reard up his hands & stood on the affrighted Ocean
The dead reard up his Voice & stood on the resounding shore

Crying. fury in my limbs. destruction in my bones & marrow
My skull riven into filaments. my eyes into sea jellies
Floating upon the tide wander bubbling & bubbling
Uttering my lamentations & begetting little monsters
Who sit mocking upon the little pebbles of the tide
In all my rivers & on dried shells that the fish

> *It provided a mythology and ritual that allowed the members of the society to sublimate a variety of personal drives and fears to the mystical realm for the good of the* Gemeine *[community] and its mission. The sense of ecstasy and joy experienced in the worship of the wounds, so often reported in the Bethlehem diary, was real. It was a religious experience, but inextricably connected with the religious experience was the deep psychological experience of catharsis and sexual release.*[30]

In Thomas Armitage's petition for membership, he admitted that he initially responded negatively to blood-and-wounds imagery: 'I could not bear the Doctrine of his Bloody Corps, till; very lately':

> *but my Dr Saviour could show me; perfectly, & he came over me so sweetly that I shall never forget, when I only went out of curiosity to hear Bro'r Cennick, which was to be the last Time I thought I wod care in hearing any of the Brethren; & my Jesus Show'd me that I had been seeking something else besides him, nor could I then bear the thought . . . of his Bleeding wounds, which I Experienced very Sweet & the only food for my Soul then.*[31]

For a mundane hosier – selling stockings and hats at his shop in Golden Square – such language may seem remarkable, but it reveals the intense emotional experience created by concentration on the blood and wounds. In a telling phrase, Thomas noted the moment when 'Jesus came over me so sweetly', which in Moravian parlance referred to the biblical account (I Kings VII: 21–2) when Elisha 'stretched himself upon the child three times', until 'the soul of the child came into him again, and he revived'. For Kabbalists, this moment of full-frontal, body-to-body embrace was fraught with mystical-erotic overtones.[32] It was an image that would later appear in Blake's works.

For the hosier's wife Catherine, the emotional effect of the blood and wounds was even more intense. At a previous Love Feast, Jesus 'was pleased to make me Suck his wounds and hug the Cross . . . more and more till my fraile nature can hould no more'. She concluded her letter with lines from the second stanza of a Moravian hymn, 'Here let me drink for ever drink / nor never once depart / for what I tast makes me to cry / fix at this Spring My heart.' In the first stanza she would have sung, 'Stream thro' the bottom of my soul, / Blood of the Son of God!'[33]

For John Blake, who apparently lived with another hosier, James Blake, the blood and wounds promised a kind of therapy for his state of depression and alienation. As he wrote to Peter Boehler:

> *I am a pore missarable unhappy Creature. But for such I know the Saviour Shed his Blood for. May that blood whith he Shed in ye Garden in the hall before Pilate and on the cross I say may that blood which me Clense and make me one of those that can Rejoyce in hiss wounds . . . O Lamb of God grant that I may be a memb'r of thy Congregation, and may be quite happy . . .*[34]

John also referred to the circumcision wound, the 'Smart and Pain', suffered by the infant Jesus, whose 'Tears' paid the price of the happy sinner's salvation.

In 1750–1, while the Armitages participated in the inner circle of the Congregation of the Lamb, the mythology, rituals and vivid phantasy life of 'the cult of the wounds' was so intensified by the more extreme Moravians that it triggered a barrage of scandals that would eventually force Zinzendorf to leave England and the Fetter Lane Elders to mount a campaign of censorship and secrecy about the 'Sifting Time'. However, in the extremists' artistic and poetic expressions one finds the possible sources of Blake's most radical psychoerotic and antinomian beliefs.

4

The Mirth of the Justified-Sinner Community

Christ can make Laws and abrogate them; he can make that to be moral which is against Nature; the greatest Virtue to be the most villainous Action, and the most virtuous Thoughts the most criminal.

Count Zinzendorf, *Sermon* (1747)

WHILE JOHN BLAKE yearned to become 'a happy Sinnor', Zinzendorf's stress on the total salvation given by the crucified Jesus led him to reckless statements about the uselessness of 'moral' behaviour. Thus he affirmed that 'a person regenerated enjoys a great Liberty', for he is responsible to what his heart senses is the Saviour's will'.[1] If that breaks the laws of conventional morality, so be it: 'It is only the sinner, such as Mary Magdalen, who is saved. The self-righteous saint must first be made a thief in order to be saved by the power of the wounds.'[2] Zinzendorf delighted in making deliberately shocking and paradoxical statements, which stimulated the imagination and opened the mind to new theological and psychological vistas.[3] He also used paradoxical language to conceal the secrets of sexualised spirituality; thus it is difficult to know how much he practised of what he preached. It is a question that also remains unanswered about Blake.

As more and more curious 'strangers' attended services at Fetter Lane, the count's daring sermons, which stirred powerful emotions in his ardent disciples, made him increasingly vulnerable to the attacks of his enemies. They also worried some of his earlier supporters. For example, he preached that Jesus 'is the rightful Husband of even the most miserable and pitiful creature, of even the most detestible prostitute'.[4] He further illustrated Christ's universal mercy by proclaiming that:

> *no human creature walks the street, there exists no human creature, be he whoring, drinking and living as he ever lives in all sins, who cannot, through the sovereign power of Jesus Christ, the Creator of the World, be delivered from his sins, be snatched out of his misery, be turned around, and be freed from the power of Satan. As soon as a yearning, a longing in wretchedness with themselves has begun in them, they will be grasped and carried home in the arms of the God and Creator of the universe.*[5]

His conclusion that the Saviour even prefers to deal with drunken whoremongers and prostitutes, rather than his loyal flock, was disturbing to the more cautious Brethren: 'The Saviour forgets, as it were, for a moment in His pasture the sheep of His hands, His bride, and occupies Himself with the miserable man, with that sinner there, with the harlot.' Believing that 'No one is more holy than a sinner who has grace', Zinzendorf even preached to the children that 'they must become sinners in order to be saved'. Reinforcing this message, Boehler 'spoke of the self-holy being made Sinners, and the real holy, the royal Priesthood, reclaiming their sinnership'.[6] Did Blake remember this Moravian paradox when he told Crabb Robinson that 'What are called vices in the natural world are the highest sublimities in the spiritual world'?[7]

In their application letters, the Armitages and John Blake seemed almost proud to declare their personal deficiencies and sins: Thomas referred to his 'base actions', Catherine called herself 'a pore crature and full of wants', noting that 'of my self . . . is nothing thats good'; John admitted to being 'a Sinnor' and 'poor missarable unhappy Creature'. All expected to be saved through their intense identification with the wounded body of Jesus. And, though there is no evidence that these simple shopkeepers practised the antinomianism that Zinzendorf and Boehler preached, the Moravians would soon be shaken by the 'immoral' sexual experiments undertaken by the count's charismatic young son, Christian Renatus.

At the German Moravian settlements in Marienborn and Herrnhaag, the eighteen-year-old 'Christel', as he was affectionately called, implemented the most extreme forms of Sifting Time sensuality and mysticism. While the count was in America, Christel organised the younger members into a secret group, 'The Order of Little Fools', which initially gained the approval of his indulgent 'Papa'. The close inner circle exulted in the glorification of the sexual organs, which produced 'a feeling of psychic liberation', expressed in elaborate ceremonies and works of art.[8] They took to heart sermons by Papa, which praised 'that precious Sign (*Membrum Virile*)' by which human husbands resemble Christ: 'Member full of Mystery, which holily gives and chastely receives the conjugal Ointments for Jesus's sake.'[9]

For the beautiful bachelor Christel, the confinement of such phallic reverence to marriage seemed too narrow, and he wrote hymns that compared the yearning for Christ to 'sexual arousal'.[10] In so doing, he seemed to draw on the meditation process practised by some Kabbalists among the Sabbatian and Hasidic Jews – techniques he could have learned about from Samuel Lieberkuhn, who lived for years among the Jews, and from converted Jewish Moravians, who often visited Herrnhaag.[11] Because sexual arousal is necessary for visionary copulation or 'converse with the *Shekhinah*', the mystical Hasidim:

> *deliberately give themselves erections during prayer according to the commandment of Rabbi Israel Baal Shem . . . who said to them that just as one who engages in intercourse with an impotent organ cannot give birth, so one should be potent at the time of prayer, it is necessary to unite with the Shekinah. It is therefore necessary to move back and forth as in the act of intercourse.*[12]

Zinzendorf attempted to solve the gender problem of male marriage with Jesus, the Heavenly Bridegroom, by declaring all souls female (*animas*); males would assume their true female nature (their inner woman) in the after-life. But Moravian hymns still pulsated with homoerotic language – a theme that opened the door for more radical interpretations.

Led by the androgynous Christel, the 'Little Fools' composed poetry and hymns that 'went so far in their contemplations about unification with Christ that they pictured themselves involved in a sexual act with Him'.[13] Christel urged them to implement his father's teaching about Elisha:

> *It is therefore an act when the Saviour spreads over a soul, like Elisha over the boy, so that happens to these two, to the Bridegroom and Bride, to the Lamb and the soul, what the Saviour says in Matthew 19 . . . they are glued together, they are attached to each other . . . so that something new comes out.*[14]

The impatient Christel could not wait for his soul to become female in the after-life, and he recommended that the Single Brothers enjoy 'the blissful passivity towards our Husband and His Sidehole, that one is to lay still and not move and one lets oneself be nuptially embraced by the Husband, to be cuddled, caressed and let him enjoy us'. This was risky advice to offer to young men living in a

Single Brothers' Choir and wrought to a high pitch of spiritual intensity.

Like the Moravians at Fetter Lane, the 'Little Fools' sang that they wanted to 'nuptially embrace' the side-hole, to 'go deep inside, deep inside'. It was a theme echoed by John Cennick, whose passionate sermons had attracted Thomas Armitage to the Congregation. A talented poet and composer, Cennick left his London preaching to visit Herrnhaag, where he was greatly moved by the young men's emotional singing: 'Draw us to thee, and we will come into the Wounds' deep places, Where hidden is the Honey-comb of thy sweet Love's Embraces.'[15] In 1746 Cennick wrote enthusiastically to the Fetter Lane Congregation about his participation in Christel's spiritual-erotic rituals: 'I am often too big and too great to get in yet . . . and pray the Lord to make me a dear little Bee that can go in and out and suck the honey from his Wounds which are like so many pretty Roses about his lovely Body.'[16]

Though Cennick expressed himself metaphorically, the reckless Christel would, two years later, declare 'how being inside the Sidehole is not to be taken spiritually but that one may and can realistically enter it'. Paul Peucker speculates that some kind of ritualised homosexuality was practised by the 'Little Fools', which was initially treated with relative tolerance. For the Elders, 'Sex between two men was not deemed any worse than other lustful sexual acts.'[17] Moreover, since the intercourse between two people was considered a sacramental act, 'the intention' with which husband and wife copulated was most important. The Kabbalists similarly taught that *kawwanah* – the right intention – was crucial to spiritualise erotic meditation and sexual performance. The count had warned the London Congregation that without proper devotion to Jesus as the 'Sanctifier' of their sexual organs, the Brother or Sister 'may be a mere Stallion (or else miserable Strumpet) under the Name of a human Creature'.[18]

John Cennick was inspired not only by Christel's erotic eloquence but by the vivid works of art that graced the walls of Herrnhaag and other centres in Germany. His open-mindedness to the powerful images of the Sifting Time was conditioned by his antinomian sense of being released from the repressive 'Law'. In London he had assured the Single Brethren, who 'were panting for Liberty', that 'The Spirit of the Law of Life / Has made us Children free / From Hell, and Sin, and Fear, and Strife / And giv'n us Liberty!'[19] When he returned from 'the poetic world of Herrnhaag', he continued to preach this message of erotic joy and liberation. It was perhaps no coincidence that William Blake would later be known as a 'Liberty Boy'.

Though the Congregation diaries at Herrnhaag for the years 1748–9 were destroyed, other evidence points to an intensification of Christel's radical experiments. A special 'cabinet' or room was provided where married couples, who lived in sexually segregated dormitories, could perform conjugal intercourse. After the act they would sometimes discuss its success or failure – spiritually and physically – with the Elders and members of the Married Choir. Aaron Fogleman notes that there is a reference in the Moravians' own records to couples having sex 'in the presence of everyone', but it is not clear 'if this meant that they entered and departed the *Schlafsaal* [bed chamber] with others watching or if others actually observed their sexual intercourse'.[20]

Sexual decorum was maintained most of the time, but Christel's innovations in late 1748 encouraged behaviour that would bring great scandal to the Moravians. Dissolving the gender divisions of Brothers and Sisters, he declared all souls female in the here and now; blending the whole Congregation into a single choir, he added a layer of heterosexual 'frolic' to his previous homoerotic titillations. After the Moravian men were declared to be women, they 'held Communion as maidens and the community of single brothers and single sisters became very large . . . Brothers were also called Sisters out of frivolity.'[21] The liberated young people caroused with joy, turning their religious ceremonies into near-orgies.

Andrew Frey, a friend of Cennick and an apostate Moravian, published a sensational account of the lavish ceremonies at Marienborn, which duplicated those at Herrnhaag. The 'whole Castle seemed on Fire' from the thousands of candles, and crowds flocked to see 'this famous spectacle, this Scene of Gluttony, Parade, Idolatrous Profuseness':

> *Here a spirit of Drunkenness and Debauchery seemed to be broke loose among the Community. The young Folks began to grow wanton, laughing, sporting, jesting, leaping, throwing one another on the Floor, and struggling till they were quite spent and out of Breath, besides many filthy and gross Indecencies . . . [They declared] that they would not give over till they had driven Piety out of the Community . . . and the* Life of Nature *or none, was what they would have.*[22]

To reinforce 'the gratification of the natural Life', the young people revelled in sensual music, including the strumming of guitars. One evening:

> *there was such an Uproar among them, as if a Mad-house had broke loose; . . . the Musicians never failed to heighten their Mirth with all Manner of wanton Tunes: and these* Orgia, *as they may be termed, lasted till One or Two in the Morning, with the most indecent Levity; and, what is worse, the Saviour's precious Wounds are made a Veil for these dissolute Practices.*[23]

When Frey and others complained to Zinzendorf, the count rebuffed them and praised 'the Mirth of the Justified-Sinner Community'. As Craig Atwood observes, the Moravian Church during the Sifting Time was 'primarily a youth movement', and its manifestation at Marienborn and Herrnhaag should be compared to the 'Summer of Love' in San Francisco in 1968, 'when a youth culture frightened the authorities'.[24] Like many 1960s parents, the indulgent 'Papa' maintained a state of denial about his beloved son's actions until the damage was already done.

Another 'renegade Moravian', Jean François Regnier, published a widely circulated account of the sexual shenanigans at Herrnhaag. A veteran of the Rosicrucian rituals at Ephrata, he had left Pennsylvania to join Zinzendorf in Germany. He now turned on his friend and accused the Moravians of being sexual perverts, who created a 'mysterious evil' that, like whoredom, denigrated men.[25] He provided a detailed description of the 'blue chamber' at Herrnhaag where couples arranged to have liturgical sex, calling it a 'bordello'.

As a spate of hostile pamphlets appeared in Germany, Papa got a wake-up call. After persistent complaints from the Elders and a particularly shocking letter (evidently about Christel), Zinzendorf issued a 'Reprimand to the Brotherhood'. Sent from London on 10 February 1749, it banned all unapproved 'private societies' and 'private liturgies'; all 'fleshly-sounding discourses', all 'lip-smacking' and 'indecent' kissing; and all unsupervised meetings between boys and girls.[26] In a world-weary statement, the count concluded:

> *We are a people (Volk) born from Jesus' side: this is our spiritual nature, but outwardly we consist of worldly people: Moravian farmers, rich and poor persons, adventurers, gross sinners, atheists, Socinians, Arians, Hussites, Waldensians, and we have had to leave all together and not selected.*

> *Since a person still remains a person, even if at the same time he becomes a man of grace, so it can not and will not be appropriate to let an untamed freedom of the flesh enter through the back door . . .*[27]

Was this an allusion to Christel's oblique hint that the anus was another side-hole, a new place to consummate the mystical marriage?

Zinzendorf now ordered Christel and his party to leave Herrnhaag and move to London, where they arrived in May 1749. Few in the Congregation at Fetter Lane were aware of the attacks in Germany, and they welcomed Christel with open arms. Soon he was idolised by Brothers and Sisters, 'who seemed to have been infatuated by him'.[28] One young Englishman who fell in love with him was Benjamin La Trobe, who almost certainly knew the Armitages and who would later play a significant role in William Blake's artistic milieu. Though no evidence survives in the London archives about 'irregular' activities by Christel, several passages in Swedenborg's diaries suggest that the unreformed son and his *Schätzeln*, his male and female 'Sweethearts', secretly carried on their erotic ceremonies. We do not know if the Armitages and Blakes were aware of such clandestine ceremonies, but the Congregation as a whole was enamoured of Christel.

While the Moravians in Europe struggled against hostile attacks and territorial expulsions, Zinzendorf was engaged in a campaign to gain recognition of the *Unitas Fratrum* as an ancient Episcopal church, historically connected to the Church of England. Utilising his considerable aristocratic charm, he garnered enough support to pass the Bill in Parliament in April 1749.[29] Thus, at the same time that a secretive infusion of Sifting Time extremism was brought from Herrnhaag to London, the Moravians also reached the high point of their reputation in England. For four halcyon years, until 1753, the scandals were held at bay, but they would eventually wreck Zinzendorf's dreams and drive him out of England.

During these years Thomas and Catherine Armitage experienced both joy and sadness, while they participated in the Congregation of the Lamb. Having first notified the Elders in August 1750 that they desired 'to come closer to ye Brn.', they formally applied for membership in November.[30] Unlike John Wesley and Emanuel Swedenborg, they made it through the difficult vetting process (administered by the Elders and settled by casting the Lot, which was supposed to reveal the will of Jesus). At the Love Feasts, which resonated to the passionate hymns of sex, wounds and blood, they gained their hearts' desire, and they must have attempted to implement the mystical marriage in their humble home.

However, their happiness was short-lived, for the Register of Burials reveals that on 'Fri. 1 March 1751. Thomas, the child of Br. & Sisr. Armitage was buried in the Ground near Bloomsbury.'[31] This crushing blow for Catherine was compounded by the deteriorating health of her husband, which evidently drained their finances. In September the Congregation diary recorded: 'Br. Armitage being sick, and having long desired it, had the H. Communion delivered to him privately.'[32] On the same day Catherine probably attended the Sabbath Love Feast held at Bloomsbury, where the Congregation would pray for her husband. On these occasions the flamboyant Christel often led the Congregation in joyous singing, theatrical displays and elaborate ceremonies.

On 19 November, Thomas went 'home to the Side-Hole', and four days later his biographical obituary was recorded, which revealed how difficult the last months had been for Catherine:

His sickness was a slow consumption, of which he died . . . Towards the latter end a little Fretfulness clouded his Love, which he always bore to his nearest Hearts; but the Night before he departed, he desired they would forgive this, & took a cordial Leave afterwards of his Wife.[33]

On 20 November, Peter Boehler had expressed some concern about Thomas's attitude and behaviour:

Br. Boehler took notice of Bro. Armitage not being in so good a condition in his heart the latter end of his life as the Brn. Could wish – He observed that such things did not please the Brn. & that they shd be very Cautious of what they did in Receiving Persons to Fellowship and especially to the Lord's Supper. Further said [word illegible] of what has happened with Bro. Armitage he wd not mention him in the Liturgy as being uncertain of his Estate etc.[34]

Though the exact nature of Thomas's offences is not known, other diary notes reveal that Boehler's main concern (since Christel's arrival) was the indiscreet revelation of the sexual teachings about marriage to those who were not deemed ready by the Elders.[35] Two months earlier, in September 1751, when Thomas desired Holy Communion as a demonstration of his intimacy with the Congregation, Boehler spoke to 'a few Marrieds':

The Holy Manner, separate from the usual Lust, wherein Marriage is carried on among us, can scarce be conceiv'd or credited by any, who had not been train'd up in the Congregation from his Childhood; and so avoided all the prepossessions of the corrupt ideas of the World . . . All the Transactions of the Married Pair from the very Beginning, til the last Act . . . can be and are highly holy and happy.[36]

He had obviously heard the charges circulating in Germany that sexual intercourse was performed in front of the Congregation:

> *It is not customary in our Congregation (as some maliciously reported) to perform the Marriage-bed Act in front of the Assembly; but it is certainly perform'd in the presence of our Saviour himself; and the gracious Tranquillity, Innocence and Nearness of his Heart bestow'd upon us, is the Seal that it has been done as it ought.*

Even more worrying to the Elders was the insufficiently reverent attitude of some carnally minded Brethren to the sexual arcana taught in the inner circle – secrets that were being leaked to outsiders. Boehler's colleague Brother Schlicht agreed and conferred with the Married Choir:

> *He took notice how dangerous it is to speak full and close upon the Subject to People, before one knows them well, because sometimes, seeing no way to shake off their Corruptions and become as is spoken, they grow desperate and worse than before . . . Our Saviour alone knows the Manner how he communicates to us the Quintessence of his own Body, but we feel it with a tender, and awful yet welcome shuddering of our whole Frame; and his Blood, the Sap of Life: Those who have once this Enjoyment cannot do without it . . .*[37]

The widowed Catherine Armitage was apparently in better graces with Boehler, who worried that her husband had left her in difficult straits. Thus, on 4 December, he asked some of the Brothers if they would 'undertake Sis. Armitage affairs', because Br. Armitage 'had made a very unrequitable will obliging his Widow to pay 80 pounds to his Bro. In case she

Marry's again.'[38] As we shall see, she would marry again and would infuse into her new family many of the themes of the Sifting Time.

But, over the next years, those themes would receive new elaboration by a Swedish visitor to Fetter Lane, who expanded the Moravians' mystical marriage on earth into Swedenborgian conjugial love in heaven.[39] As a mysterious intelligence agent, who operated on earth and in heaven, Swedenborg witnessed and recorded the secret erotic ceremonies of the radical Moravians, and his influence on the Blake family would eventually supersede that of Zinzendorf.

5

Swedenborg and Kabbalistic Science

If you will believe the Jews, the Holy Spirit hath purposely involved in the Words of Scripture, every Secret that belongs to any sort of Science, under such Cabalisms as these.

Charles Wilkins, *Mathematical and Philosophical Works* (1710)

On a July evening in London in 1744, a Moravian watchmaker, John Paul Brockmer, became alarmed at the strange behaviour of his Swedish lodger, Emanuel Swedenborg, who emerged from his room, ran after him and looked very frightful:

> *his hair stood straight up, and he foamed a little at his mouth. He wanted to talk with Mr Brockmer . . . he had something very particular to communicate: namely, that he was the Messiah; that he was come to be crucified for the Jews; and that as he had a great impediment in his speech, Mr Brockmer was chosen to be his mouth, to go with him the next day to the synagogue, and there to preach his words.*[1]

Brockmer knew that Swedenborg already had contacts with Jews, two of whom visited him in his room. When Swedenborg went into an *ecstasis* or trance, they allegedly tried to steal his watch, but he refused to prosecute 'these good Israelites'.[2]

He now assured Brockmer that an angel would appear at his bedside in the morning to confirm the messianic mission to the Jews.

When the angel did not show up, the Moravian urged the distraught Swedenborg to go to 'our dear Dr Smith, with whom you are intimate', who would provide beneficial medicine. However, Swedenborg went instead to the Swedish Embassy, where he was refused admittance. He then ran to the nearby Gully-hole, a huge drainage ditch, 'undressed himself, rolled in very deep mud, and threw the money out of his pockets among the crowd'. Brockmer reported that before this manic behaviour, 'the Baron behaved very decently in his house; he went every Sunday to the chapel of the Moravians in Fetter Lane'.

Surprisingly, no record has been found in Moravian archives for Swedenborg's participation in their affairs, and no Moravian historian has ever mentioned it. However, in his posthumously published *Journal of Dreams* and *Spiritual Diary*, Swedenborg revealed an otherwise unknown extension of Moravian experimentation in Kabbalistic and Yogic meditation rituals – techniques that provided a sexual basis for spiritual vision. He associated with the Brethren in London in 1744–5 and 1748–9; though he broke with them in the 1750s, he continued to use Moravian publishers and booksellers in London. Thus, by recovering the previously lost Swedenborgian-Moravian-Jewish-Yogic history, we can shed new light on William Blake's development into a visionary artist, antinomian theosopher and difficult husband.

Before his breakdown in London in 1744, the fifty-six-year-old Swedenborg had spent most of his life as a scientist, engineer and political intelligencer – the latter role accounting for the extraordinary secrecy that he maintained over many of his activities.[3] Born in Stockholm in 1688, Swedenborg was the third son of Jesper Swedberg, a royal military chaplain who became Theology Professor and Dean of Uppsala University.[4] The energetic and blunt-speaking Swedberg was raised in a copper-mining family, and believed in the robust and practical application of Lutheranism – that is, that faith must be demonstrated in good works. At the same time he sympathised with the Pietist movement, which attempted to restore Christianity to its primitive roots.

For Swedberg, those roots were essentially Jewish – a belief that would be important for Emanuel and his later associations with Jews and Moravians in London. Swedberg was especially influenced by the learned Hebraist Edward Edzard, with whom he lived for ten weeks in Hamburg in 1685.[5] Encouraged by the failure of Sabbatai Zevi's movement, Edzard launched a campaign to convert the Jews of Hamburg by emphasising their 'vain looking' for a Sabbatian messiah.[6] Drawing further on his knowledge of the Talmud and Kabbala, Edzard succeeded in baptising 148 Jews – a singular accomplishment that greatly impressed his Swedish house-guest. On his return to Sweden, Swedberg and his Orientalist colleagues attempted similar approaches to Sabbatian, Karaite and other heterodox Jews.[7] However, their efforts were frustrated by the conservative Lutheran clergy, who in 1685 pressured a reluctant King Carl XI to ban the practice of Judaism in Sweden.

In the meantime, Swedberg had deliberately 'Judaised' his own children. Citing Old Testament precedent, he deviated from Swedish custom and gave his sons Hebraic names rather than family names. He was following the example of Edzard, who had laid his hands upon the heads of his children and blessed them, 'just as the patriarch Jacob blessed his sons Ephraim and Manasseh, and just as Christ blessed the little children'.[8] Swedberg affirmed that 'the name of my son Emanuel signifies "God with us": that he may always remember God's presence, and that intimate, holy and mysterious conjunction with our good and gracious God'. Such stirring words would make Emanuel especially susceptible to the Moravian belief in intimate 'marriage' with the God-Man.

In Uppsala, Swedberg made his home a centre of Hebrew studies and intense prayer, which he believed led to communication with angels. He had confided to Edzard that when he conversed with angels they spoke Swedish, but they used Hebrew among themselves: thus, 'I shall know what they say, for I understand that tongue.'[9] He gave the seven-year-old Emanuel a Hebrew grammar and was pleased that the child spent hours meditating on Hebrew and biblical studies.[10] Whenever Emanuel uttered pious thoughts, his parents announced that an angel seemed to speak through him.[11] With such encouragement, the child soon reported that angels visited him in the garden.

His father's religious enthusiasm made an indelible impression on the sensitive child, and Swedberg's huge shadow would loom over Emanuel's turbulent dreams and psychic experiences. Like most Swedes of that time, Swedberg's attitude towards the world of spirits was essentially medieval and magical, and he believed that he could influence the spirits to work for him in pious causes.[12] He performed exorcisms and even claimed to raise a girl from the dead. But he was most proud of his healing powers, which he achieved through intense Bible readings and hypnotic personal persuasion. He claimed to possess second-sight or clairvoyance, a gift that Emanuel would later demonstrate.

At the same time, Emanuel's resident tutor, the medical student Johan Moraeus, stimulated in him a sense of wonder at the intricacies of the human body, which represented God's temple on earth. In a pattern that would later produce startling psychic effects, the boy learned to combine intense self-scrutiny of his own bodily processes with intense meditation on spiritual studies. While holding his breath for long periods of time during morning and evening prayers, he became aware of a relationship between his thinking and his breathing. He later recalled that 'when he tried to make the rhythm of his breathing correspond with the beating of his heart, his thought-life became almost dormant'.[13] This ability to achieve a state of semi-trance would later be enhanced by Kabbalistic meditation techniques.

After Swedberg was appointed Bishop of Skara in 1703, he left the fifteen-year-old Emanuel in Uppsala, where he moved into the home of his brother-in-law, Eric Benzelius, newly appointed university librarian. Over the next seven years, Benzelius guided his young protégé through his university studies, and his influence soon superseded that of Bishop Swedberg. Surprisingly, Benzelius's forty-year role as Emanuel's primary intellectual, spiritual and political mentor has been largely unexamined by Swedenborg's biographers.[14] But it was through his researches and contacts that Swedenborg first gained access to rare Kabbalistic and Sabbatian lore, material that would influence his later spiritual-sexual theosophy of 'conjugial love'.

Having mastered Hebrew by the age of nine, Benzelius became a sophisticated scholar of Jewish and other Oriental traditions. During a foreign study tour in 1697–1700, he visited the German philosopher Gottfried Wilhelm Leibniz and his collaborator, Frances Mercury Van Helmont, son of the famous Paracelsan physician, Jan Baptiste Van Helmont. Leibniz had long credited his study of the Kabbalistic *arte combinatoria*, the transposition of Hebrew letters and numbers, for his breakthrough in developing the differential calculus. With Benzelius in Hanover, he and Van Helmont discussed the Kabbalistic theories published in Knorr von Rosenroth's Latin translation of Jewish mystical texts, the *Kabbala Denudata* (1677–84), a work that would later influence Swedenborg.[15]

While studying in England for several months, Benzelius

also met members of the Philadelphian Brotherhood, a neo-Rosicrucian society that espoused the Christian Kabbalistic, Hermetic and Boehmenist themes of Jane Leade, John Pordage and Dr Francis Lee. From the last, he could have learned about a recent Sabbatian movement in Poland, which had attracted many Jews before fizzling out.[16] When Benzelius returned to Sweden, he learned that one of the participants in the movement, Rabbi Moses ben Aaron Kohen of Cracow, was so disillusioned with its failure that he changed his name to Johan Kemper, converted to Christianity, moved to Sweden and became Hebrew instructor at Uppsala.[17]

'Rabbi' Kemper and Benzelius became close friends and scholarly collaborators; for sixteen years they worked together on editions of Philo Judaeus and a new Kabbalistic interpretation of the Gospel of St Matthew. Benzelius, who had inspected editions of the *Zohar* in the Bodleian Library in Oxford, was delighted by Kemper's argument that the truths of Christianity could be established on the basis of Jewish sources. The *Zohar* especially revealed that 'the messianic faith of the Christians was in fact the truly ancient Kabbalah of Judaism'.[18] Still influenced by the Sabbatian notion of 'the holy sin', Kemper taught that the key to the Kabbala lay in the pattern of debasement and subsequent elevation of the Messiah, which had its parallel in Matthew's account of Jesus. As noted earlier, these parallels would also pique the interest of Zinzendorf and the Moravian missionaries to the Jews.

From 1702 to 1710, while Swedenborg lived with Benzelius, it seems certain that Kemper was his Hebrew teacher, thus providing the young student with early access to heterodox ideas of Sabbatian and Christian Kabbalism.[19] The rabbi's lectures at the university had been supported by the late King Carl XI and by Bishop Swedberg, and he predicted a glorious Christian-Jewish rapprochement under the reign of the tolerant new monarch, the young Carl XII. For Benzelius, the new overtures to the Jews were promising signs of the opening of Sweden to progressive ideas in religion, science and economics. Elliot Wolfson notes that Kemper's usage of 'the bold hermeneutic of the Sabbatian form of Kabbalism' fit in with the larger cultural patterns of his historical moment and setting, 'attested in the post-Reformation fraternities of neo-Rosicrucians and Freemasons, which loosened considerably the boundaries between Judaism and Christianity, in large measure due to the interest of these occult fraternities in Jewish esotericism'.[20]

After graduation in 1710, Swedenborg made his own study tour in England. Armed with introductions from Benzelius, he sought out mathematicians and scientists with Rosicrucian and Masonic interests. But, most importantly, he read widely in English publications that emphasised the importance of Kabbala and alchemy to innovative thinking in science and religion. In a review of Basnage's *History and Religion of the Jews* (1710), Swedenborg read a disdainful but clear exposition of the basic tenets of the *Zohar*:

> *The Jews esteem the Caballa as a noble and sublime science, which leades men by an easy path in the Knowledge of God and His Works, which are unaccessible to the Ignorant. They pretend that this Service which the Patriarchs handed down directly from the Angels, hath been communicated from hand to Hand down to their Doctors, by an uninterrupted Tradition . . . This Caballa is the Art of Symboles, Allegories and Mystical Explications. 'Tis the Opinion of the Caballists, that there is no Letter nor Number, nor Name of God in the Scripture, but profound Mysteries may be found in it, if we set ourselves to it.*[21]

Basnage further discussed 'the mysteries contained in the Letters of the Human Alphabet; of the Relation these Letters have to Angels' and 'the Mysterious Significations attributed to Words of the Holy Scripture'. When these Kabbalistic tenets emerged in Swedenborg's theosophical writings, he claimed to be the first and unique recipient of them – via spirit communication.

Remembering Leibniz's linkage of Kabbalistic study and mathematic innovation, Swedenborg found reinforcement in the late Charles Wilkins's *Mathematical and Philosophical Works* (1710), which he described to Benzelius as 'very ingenious'.[22] A founding member of the Royal Society of Sciences, a student of Rosicrucianism and a confidant of several Freemasons, Wilkins wrote in 1641 that:

> *If you will believe the Jews, the Holy Spirit hath purposely involved in the Words of Scripture, every Secret that belongs to any art or Science, under such Cabalisms as these. And if a Man were expert in unfolding them, it were easie for him to get as much Knowledge as Adam had in his Innocency, or Human Nature is capable of.*[23]

That the Kabbalistic 'sciences' had a real methodology and technique of learning was revealed to Swedenborg when he read John Smith's *Select Discourses* (1660). A Cambridge Platonist and friend of Henry More and F. M. Van Helmont, Smith responded eagerly to their Kabbalistic theories. He was especially interested in the ancient Jewish schools or colleges of 'Prophetic Education', which taught the techniques of achieving prophetic visions and communication with angels. The 'Hebrew Masters' tell us that the old prophets had 'some Apparition or Image of a Man or Angel presenting itself to their Imaginations'.[24] Smith also explained that 'the Cabalistical Jews' revealed in 'the book *Zohar*' that the Law delivered upon Mount Sinai was 'a Device God had to knit and unite the Jews and the Shechinah or Divine Presence together'.

Swedenborg also learned that this knitting together was fraught with sexual significance. In the works of John Norris, another friend of More, there was a rare exposition of Kabbalistic sexual arcana.[25] In *The Theory and Regulation of Love* (1688), Norris published his letter to More, in which he challenged the orthodox Christian belief that sexuality was sinful: 'I can see no reason why that sort of Corporeal Indulgence which is emphatically called *sensuality*, should be charged with any moral turpitude.'[26] In his reply, More directed Norris to 'my *Cabbala Philosophica*', which contains 'the choicest secrets of the *Jewish Theosophy* or methaphysicks'. He then answered Norris's question about the spiritual role of sexuality. Referring to 'the *sixt sense*' or '*Tactus Venerens*', More explained:

> *There must . . . be watchfulness over a mans waies, over the inclination of his mind . . . and devotional addressed to God for further* Illumination *and strength to carry on the work of real* Regeneration *. . . and when his* true self *is awakened in him . . . all the* Trees of Paradise, *which God planted, the* pleasures of all the six Senses, *he may taste of, so long as . . . he is not* lessened above, *by* being captivated *by anything* below. *The pleasure of the sixt sense is not forbid, nor is there anything forbid in the* Paradise of God, *but the irregularity of our own lust and will.*[27]

Norris heeded More's advice and explored thoroughly the Jewish mystical writings on sexuality. He concluded that 'even the grossest Pleasure of Sense, is one of the Remoter Participations of God: For it must be granted a natural good, and every particular good . . . is a Ray and Emanation of the universal good . . . nothing of God can be *simply* and *absolutely* evil.'[28] Foreshadowing Zinzendorf's valorisation of the sexual organs, Norris affirmed that 'in the Human frame God has prepared Organs and Instruments of Sensual Pleasure'; it is a Tree of God's own planting, and 'there can be nothing evil in the *Paradise* of God'.

Though Swedenborg read more about these concepts of divinised sexuality during this first visit to London, he would not practise the meditation techniques until he received training from Moravian and Jewish associates in the 1740s. Then he would apply the scientific discipline of precise analysis and objective experiment – the 'modern' methodology he learned from Royal Society scientists – to the psychological and physiological processes of the Kabbalistic erotic trance. In the intervening decades, before his manic illness and messianic mission to the Jews of Fetter Lane, he would endure political persecution, scientific suppression and spiritual frustration – experiences that made the Moravian hymns of mystical marriage become the siren songs of his spiritual seduction.

6

Erotic Dreams and Ecstatic Visions

In a vision . . . there was an inward and sensible gladness shed over the whole body . . . like the joy that a chaste man has at the very time when he is in actual love and in the very act with his mate.

Emanuel Swedenborg, *Journal of Dreams* (1744)

DURING THE 1720s, while the Swedenborg and Benzelius families suffered under the ruling oligarchy, their plans for religious, scientific and economic reform were constantly thwarted.[1] While working as a mining engineer and serving in the Swedish parliament, Swedenborg sought refuge from his frustrated ambitions in the radical Pietism and Hermeticism espoused by Johan Conrad Dippel, who visited Sweden in 1726–8, and then in Moravianism, which attracted many disaffected souls in Sweden.[2] Zinzendorf too had been attracted to Dippel's theosophy, which focused on the *Ur-Mensch* (the original man), his version of Adam Kadmon. But Zinzendorf withdrew from collaboration with Dippel, whose extreme anti-clericalism seemed to threaten the foundations of all churches. Swedenborg was stimulated by the alchemystical notions of both men, and he began to move beyond the natural to the supernatural sciences.

In the early 1730s, while travelling in eastern Europe, Swedenborg began to search in neo-Platonic, Hermetic and

Kabbalistic literature for the means of demonstrating scientifically the reality of the soul. He studied the works of Comenius, the spiritual father of the Moravians, who attempted to portray the soul in human form, using 'a hieroglyphical signification'.[3] In Prague, he visited the Jewish quarter, whose leader Rabbi Jonathan Eibeschuetz was a devoted Kabbalist and crypto-Sabbatian.[4] The local Moravians had established communications with some of these mystical Jews, and decades later followers of Eibeschuetz would establish relations with Benjamin La Trobe and the Brethren in Fetter Lane.[5]

Perhaps inspired by his contact with some (unnamed) Jews, Swedenborg undertook psychic experiments aimed at reaching heightened states of spiritual and scientific 'illumination'. He described certain 'operations' (a magical term) that produce 'a supremely subtle sympathy and communion of souls and angels, and their correspondence with our soul'.[6] Hoping to demonstrate 'the mechanism of the soul', he revealed that 'Acts of the imagination are clearer when existing alone, than when existing together with sensation'; moreover, the soul 'is seen in dreams; when we are alone, and when we are in ecstasy'.

While in Leipzig to oversee the printing of his scientific treatise, *Opera Philosophica et Mineralia* (1734), he added some of the fruits of his recent experiments. Eberhard Zwink argues that in the 'The Principia' section, Swedenborg drew on Zoharic notions of the seminal point, the nexus between the divine and natural worlds, which he interpreted in terms of mathematics and geometry.[7] From this point, emanations of the universal aether emerge, which form the descending chain of creation. For Kabbalists, the seminal point was also the seminal drop, which triggered the downward spiralling of the sephirotic emanations into the world of sexual generation.

In another treatise, Swedenborg tried to define 'The Mechanism and Intercourse between the Soul and Body', examining the role of angels who mediate between man and God.[8]

Evidently stimulated by Kabbalistic and Moravian notions of the sexual dynamics within the Grand Man, he read the works of Martin Schurig on sexual generation, including spermatology, gynaecology, genital physiology and copulatory sensation.[9] Schurig combined 'quasi-scientific and erotic material', while analysing the ancient belief that 'the whole soul is in the body'.[10] Especially appealing to Swedenborg was the ability of the learned physician to maintain a religious perspective on sexuality.

In 1736 Swedenborg returned to the Continent, where he combined political intelligence work with further explorations of Moravian and Jewish theosophy.[11] In Hamburg he met Arvid Gradin, a Swedish Moravian friend, who evidently informed him about Moravian overtures to the local Jews.[12] Swedenborg then visited the local synagogue and recorded the Hebrew inscription over the door: 'This is the entrance gate to Jehovah.'[13] After residences in Paris, where he allegedly participated in *Écossais* or Jacobite Masonic affairs, and in Rome, where he visited the Jewish ghetto, Swedenborg returned to Amsterdam in summer 1739, when he achieved a significant psychic breakthrough. While investigating the human body as a microcosmic image of the universal soul, he studied the texts and illustrations in anatomical books, concentrating on the physiology of the heart and lungs.

Resuming the breath-control experiments of his childhood, he induced the imaginative experience of depersonalisation and trance.[14] As he later remembered, 'hardly a day passed by for several months in which a flame was not seen by me as vividly as the flame of a household hearth; at the time, this was a sign of approbation, and this happened before spirits began to speak with me *viva voce*'.[15] He observed that 'while the mind is intensely pondering on the different relations of things, the brain in general with the lungs is comparatively quiescent; hence it avoids drawing breath through the nostrils'.[16] In volume I of *Oeconomia Regni Animalis* (*The Economy of the Animal Kingdom*), published in Amsterdam in 1740, he described this 'synchronism and concordance of the cerebral and pulmonary motions', which, when coupled with intense meditation, produces a sensation of great pleasure in the brain.

While 'intently exploring the secrets of the human body', Swedenborg described the mental euphoria achieved by intense meditators. After a long course of reasoning, they make a discovery of the truth, and 'straightaway there is a certain cheering light, and joyful confirmatory brightness, that plays around the sphere of their mind; and a kind of mysterious radiation . . . that darts through some temple in their brain':

> *the soul is called into a more inward communion, and has returned at that moment into the golden age of its intellectual perfections. The mind that has known this pleasure . . . is carried wholly in pursuit of it . . . and in the kindling flame of its love despises all in comparison . . . all merely corporeal pastimes.*[17]

Modern neurologists explain that the reduced breathing deprives the brain of oxygen and stimulates it to produce electrical discharges, which create a sensation of light-flashes, and to release endorphins, the morphine-like chemicals that produce a sense of cerebral pleasure (or 'high').

Swedenborg's meditative technique bore striking similarities to that of Jewish mystics, who concentrated intensely on the dynamic (sephirotic) relationships between different organs of the Grand Man's body, while regulating their breathing and heartbeat. He possibly received instruction from the Jews who participated in the Moravian *Geheimbund* (secret society), organised by Zinzendorf and Lieberkuhn in the Jewish quarter of Amsterdam.[18]

These heterodox students of Kabbalah were undoubtedly aware of the writings of Rabbi Moses Hayim Luzzatto, which shed revealing light on Swedenborg's developing technique for achieving psychoerotic visions. In 1735 Luzzatto had been forced to move from Padua, Italy, because of accusations that he was a secret Sabbatian.[19] In the more tolerant atmosphere of Amsterdam, he privately taught and wrote about his method of interpreting dreams and summoning angels and spirits. He maintained 'remarkable' friendships with Christians and was possibly initiated into Freemasonry, for Jews and Christians mixed freely in the Dutch lodges.[20] In terms that echoed Masonic terminology, Luzzatto wrote that the aspiring visionary must undergo 'a course of apprenticeship, just as in the case of other disciplines and crafts'.[21] Critics of the Moravians suspected that Zinzendorf also maintained a secret connection with Masonry in Holland.

In 1739, through his friend Arvid Gradin, Swedenborg established contact with the Moravians in Amsterdam, and possibly learned of Luzzatto's teaching from participants in the *Judenmission*. In 1740, when he made a secretive journey to London, he could glean more information from Leonard Dober, missionary to the Jews in the city's East End, who also maintained connections with Swedenborg's Moravian friends in Sweden.[22]

In volume II of *The Economy*, which Swedenborg began in London but finished in Amsterdam, he made a decided shift towards Jewish and Kabbalistic phraseology. Hinting at the theories of sexual potencies and male–female equilibrium that permeate Kabbalistic theosophy, he observed that 'the liberty of acting or the wife, is very easily divorced from the understanding, or husband. And this separation in the marriage-bed of the mind is often more complete in the intelligent than in the simple-minded.'[23] He added that marriages are literally made in heaven, and he yearned for 'a calculus about the nature of love' and 'other marvellous sympathies'.

As his language became more allusive to Jewish ritual and symbolism, he noted that rational truth may look 'into the holy of holies, though not enter it'; however, he was 'not forbidden to approach the divine sanctuary by means of comparison'. For Kabbalists, the Holy of Holies was the site of the sexually joined male and female Cherubim, who represented the 'marriage-bed' of God's mind and who could be visualised by linguistic, mathematic and sephirotic analogies. Swedenborg also drafted a manuscript in which he assigned numerical values to letters (a Kabbalistic technique), and he promised a treatise on correspondences.[24]

After Swedenborg's return to Sweden in 1740, his political party (the pro-French, pro-Jacobite 'Hats') aggressively pursued war against Russia, and he was caught up in political and military affairs, while he sought spiritual relief in esoteric and mystical readings. He was especially intrigued by the Kabbalistic sexual-spiritual theories revealed in the Rosicrucian novella *Le Comte de Gabalis, ou Entretiens sur les Sciences Secrétes* (1670). According to Gabalis, the ancient Hebrews could communicate with 'the Aerial People' and converse with 'all those Inhabitants of the Air'.[25] The Rosicrucians took their technique further, making possible a mystical copulation between initiated human 'Sages' and the celestial and elemental spirits. Through the 'philosophic procedures' of mystical breathing, the Sage could achieve 'philosophic love making'. Despite the light-hearted tone of the book, Swedenborg seemed to take it seriously and included it in his list of important authors to be quoted.[26]

As the Swedish war effort began to collapse, Swedenborg and other Hats tried to find a spiritual rationale for their failure. Worried by a flood of anti-Hat pamphlets that invoked dreams, visions and prophecies, the Prime Minister consulted Swedenborg (and his cousin, Carl Linnaeus) for interpretations of these mystic portents.[27] Attempting a scientific explanation,

Swedenborg revealed more about his own visionary states. In a remarkable foreshadowing of modern descriptions of the 'near-death experience', he observed that it is 'a state of body and soul separated, while life still continues':

> *Some persons are wont to fall into ecstasy before the death agony, and in respect to the soul to be elevated outside the world, as it were, but to again return into this humble abode or prison house . . . In northern regions [Lapland], certain persons skilled in the art of magic are credited with being able to fall spontaneously into a kind of ecstasy in which they are deprived of the external senses and of all motion, and with being engaged in the operations of the soul alone, in order that after resuscitation they may reveal thefts and declare desired secrets.*[28]

Continuing his scientific explanation, Swedenborg wrote that 'in persons subject to ecstasy the circulation of the blood seems to have stopped; for the pulse of the arteries is felt nowhere except in the cervical artery, where it is very feeble; the respiration is also gone'.[29] He concluded that 'therefore, for the leading of the ecstatic life, a peculiar disposition is required . . . Nor would it be entirely contrary to reason to add that there are also some who are able to throw themselves into ecstasy by natural means, whence comes the belief in magic.'

In August 1743 Swedenborg left for Amsterdam, determined to study 'the Hebrew language, as well as the correspondences, according to which the whole Bible is composed'.[30] He was thereby 'put in a position to receive instruction from the Lord who is the Word'. Over the next eleven months he ventured ever further into the esoteric psychic world of Kabbalistic Jews and Moravians. In the muli-layered entries in his *Journal of Dreams* (1743–5), he revealed his disturbed state of mind – torn between his hazardous political responsibilities and his dangerous visionary experiments. Though he often feared for his physical safety and mental health, he also experienced great joy, as he progressed through the stages of mystical initiation.

Despite the Moravians' attempt to maintain secrecy about their Jewish overtures, their enemies publicly accused them of 'Judaisation'. In 1743 an English critic charged that the Brethren in Amsterdam allowed salvation to unconverted Jews; even worse, they recruited youths and women by appealing 'to their affections and passions'.[31] An angry John Stinstra claimed that they used 'lucious Expressions' from the Canticles of Solomon to inflame the young: 'The *Fanaticks*, in general, take great care to keep the Imagination in a continual Heat and Agitation. For this purpose, they affect a lofty Stile, full of high-strained Expressions taken from the Oriental languages, bold Metapors, unnatural Figures and far-fetched Emblems.'[32] Recognising the Jewish influence on this language, Stinstra scoffed, 'The *Cabala* of the *Jews*, what is it else but a Production of disordered Brains, a Medley of Imaginations, and a Chaos of Dreams, on the different Orders of Spirits, and their Marvellous Operations.'

While Swedenborg recorded his turbulent dreams, he was probably aware that Zinzendorf spoke about visualisation of the God-man through dreams 'in Sleep' and other 'extatic Methods'.[33] The Moravian apostate from Herrnhaag, Andrew Frey, described the psychological manipulation practised by some Brethren, who utilised 'their Stygian Magic and Power of Illusion', often 'operating in Dreams or by Inspiration'.[34] He revealed that he was once 'deceived' by a seemingly benign Moravian 'who was possessed of this magical Talent', by which he could 'inject Dreams into me, and in those Dreams get from me what he would. It is in this respect that God complains of the Dreams of the Jew.'

Within this Moravian-Jewish context, the dreams and visions recorded in Swedenborg's diary seem rooted in real world conditions. He first approached this visionary *arcana* through dream analysis – and possibly through Luzzatto's teachings on the subject. In *Derech ha-Shem* (*The Way to God*), Luzzatto described how 'the bond between the body and the divine soul should be loosened while man sleeps'.[35] Then the 'freed portions of the soul can move about in the spiritual realm' and can 'interact and associate with spiritual beings as the angels who oversee natural phenomena'. Instructed by a master, the student of dreams learns that 'God manipulates man's power to dream, and uses it as a means to transmit a prophetic vision'. Explaining the nature of 'bestowed illumination', Luzzatto resorted to scientific images drawn from optics and his experiments with lens-grinding to hint at the 'allegories and metaphors' (what Swedenborg called correspondences and representations), that help to induce the trance state.

Like the Moravians, the Kabbalists emphasised the sacramental importance of marital intercourse, but Luzzatto taught that the adept must abstain from physical sex on days when he hopes to obtain 'erotic conjunction with God'.[36] This abstention was also stressed by Rosicrucians, as revealed in Swedenborg's copy of *Le Comte de Gabalis*: 'The Sages will never admit you to their Order', and you cannot achieve Wisdom, unless you 'renounce all sensual relationships (*la commerce charnel*) with women'.[37] The Rosicrucian doctrine was reaffirmed by Giacomo Casanova, the great libertine and practising Kabbalist, who had studied Jewish lore in Luzzatto's home town of Padua. Casanova was told by the local Rosicrucians that adepts must give up women: 'They held that such a renunciation was the chief condition which the elemental spirits enforced upon those who have a desire to have commerce with them.'[38]

Such a requirement would initially prove difficult for

Swedenborg, who recorded that 'the inclination to the other sex' had been 'my strongest passion'.[39] According to G. E. Klemming, who first published the *Journal of Dreams* in 1844, 'It is evident that Swedenborg until 1744, and during that year, had led an irregular life in respect to the other sex. This has not been known publicly until now, but the fact has been handed down, quietly, by tradition among the older and higher adepts in Sweden.'[40] Swedenborg reportedly kept mistresses in Sweden and Italy, and his many descriptions of sirens and whores suggest his familiarity with brothels.[41]

Certainly he valued his own experiences of sexual intercourse, which he described happily and analysed anatomically in 'The Generative Organs', a treatise he began drafting in Amsterdam:

> *While the sexual love is proceeding from the first effort to the final act, and when at length the state is hot, so sweet a tremble and so bland a soothing seizes upon the whole nervous system, that all the fibres whatever in the brain, and all whatever in the body, expand in every way with innermost delights . . . This highly pure tremble which is present, shows . . . that the expansion extends to the fibre that terminates in the testicles . . .*[42]

However, Swedenborg also noted that the ageing process (he was now fifty-six) made abstention from sex and 'the delicious affection' easier. As he continued his meditation experiments, he recorded how his 'inclination to the other sex so suddenly ceased'.[43] Nevertheless, given his still-powerful sex-drive, his struggle for sublimation was difficult, as reflected in the sexually disturbed scenes recorded in his diary.

By March 1744 Swedenborg had moved beyond mere dream analysis and was now able to deliberately induce waking trances. He noted his 'wakeful ecstasies' that occurred 'before and after sleep'.[44] Luzzatto had described this state as preliminary to superior illumination, when the adept makes contact with spirits and angels.[45] Critical to the meditative discipline was the capacity to maintain *kawwanah* or 'the right intention'. The adept must concentrate intensely and lovingly on the totality of God and not be distracted by impure thoughts or preoccupation with lesser spirits. As he focuses on each male and female *Sephira* or emanation of God, he climbs the mystical ladder. But he must hold in his mind all the *Sephiroth* at once.

Gradually mastering the difficult meditation technique, Swedenborg penetrated into a new level of consciousness, in which spirits began at first to speak to him and then appear to him. He struggled to maintain *kawwanah*, but was distracted by lower spirits: 'I was in waking trances nearly the whole time' and tried 'to keep clear thoughts about things', but then 'I set myself against the Holy Spirit'.[46] According to the Moravians, the Holy Spirit was a female potency, equivalent to the Kabbalists' *Shekhinah*, and when Swedenborg opposed her he saw 'hideous spectres', the *Lilith* demons of perverted sexuality. But he soon learned 'by actual proof the meaning of the injunction not to love the angels better than God' – that is, not to be distracted by lower *Sephiroth* from visualisation of the divine whole.

The intense struggle between opposing forces within Swedenborg's mind or psyche, while he struggled to master the visionary methodology, revealed the genuine danger to human sanity of the demanding process. He veered between ecstasy and misery, between spiritual consummation and psychological disintegration. At times he perspired and trembled from the mental strain: 'thoughts invaded me which I should never be able to control; yea, so hard that I was withheld from all other thought . . . so hard, that if God's grace had not been the stronger, I should surely have fallen therein, or gone mad'.[47] However, when 'the movement and power of the spirit' came to him, he felt that he 'would rather go mad'.

The reward for Swedenborg's increasing mastery of the process was psychic or spiritual ecstasy that made death or martyrdom seem easy or even desirable. The Kabbalists described this euphoric state as 'the Death of the Kiss', a state that Swedenborg joyfully described: 'I found in myself like beams of light that it was the greatest happiness to be a martyr in regard to indescribable grace connected with the love of God.'[48] He experienced 'in mind and body a kind of consciousness of an indescribable bliss, so that if it had been in a higher degree, the body would have as it were dissolved in mere bliss'.

The disciplined sublimation of erotic drives, the meditative balancing of male and female forces, the visionary yearning for consummation of the divine marriage – all contributed to the ecstatic joy of the adept. Thus Swedenborg lay awake, 'but as it were in a vision':

> *In the spirit there was an inward and sensible gladness shed over the whole body; it seemed as it were shown in a consummate manner how it all issued and ended. It flew up* (abouterade) *in a manner, and hid itself in an infinitude, as a centre. There was love itself* (amor ipse) *. . . This love in a mortal body, whereof I then was full, was like the joy that a chaste man has at the very time when he is in actual love and in the very act with his mate; such extreme pleasantness was suffused over the whole of my body, and this for a long time.*[49]

Despite his oblique language, Swedenborg seemed to draw upon the Moravian teaching that 'directly linked an erotic female image of the side wound of Jesus to human male orgasm during ritualised sex between married couples'.[50] But, through his greater mastery of the Jewish technique, he achieved the visionary state called 'the pleasure of the bridegroom and the bride', in which 'an actual experience of sexual contact is not essential for the ecstatic Kabbalist'.[51] His odd usage of the word *abouterade* suggests the sexual arousal necessary to achieve 'the Death of the Kiss'. The French verb *aboutir* means 'to lead to and end in', 'to come to a head and burst', 'to gather (as an abscess) and come to a head'. This ecstatic-orgasmic experience convinced him that 'the inward and actual joy came from this source' – from the visionary-phallic penetration of the divine vagina.

For Kabbalists the visionary identification of the female genitals with the 'Holy of Holies' – the inner sanctuary of the Temple – was an *arcanum* reserved for the highest adepts. In a peculiar dream description, Swedenborg referred to these highest sexual mysteries:

> *something holy was dictated to me, which ended with* 'sacrarium et sanctuarium'. *I found myself lying in bed with a woman, and said, 'Had you not used the word* sanctuarium, *we would have done it. I turned away from her. She with her hand touched my member, and it grew large, larger than it ever had been. I turned round and applied myself; it bent, yet it went in. She said it was long. I thought during the act a child must come of it; and it succeeded* en merveille.[52]

For Moravians and Kabbalists, the ejaculatory process was sacramental and the semen holy. For Swedenborg, his psycho-erotic penetration of the Holy of Holies was a life-changing experience:

> *This denotes the uttermost love for the holy; for all love has its origin therefrom; is a series; in the body it consists in its*

> *actuality in the projection of the seed* (projectione semenis)*, when the whole . . . [ejaculation] is there, and is pure, it then means the love for wisdom. The former woman stood for truth . . .*[53]

Swedenborg's description was strikingly similar to Luzzatto's: 'The gates of divine grace, open wide when the Temple stood, were shut when it was destroyed . . . From that year onwards events took place in accordance with the stages which require *tikkun* [reintegration, restoration] so that each day has its own illumination.'[54] Like Swedenborg, Luzzatto defined the *projectione semenis* as the holiest of acts, which stimulates the Zoharic marriage:

> *The secret of the Zohar is that it is all inwardness, unlike all plain meanings which belong to the external . . . The Zohar belongs in the category of the seminal drop which comes from* Yesod *[the phallic* Sephira*]. Now it is well known that all providence proceeds by means of copulation so that everything depends on the influence of the seminal drop. When it is merited that the seminal drop comes down into the lower world all is put right by means of a great* tikkun, *for by means of that drop are all things perfected in every way . . .*[55]

Affirming that 'this is the mystery', Luzzatto warned that every *tikkun* – every act of psychosexual reintegration – 'depends for its effectiveness on the degree of preparation undergone by the recipients'. Swedenborg similarly warned that the sexual-visionary technique should be kept secret: 'we ought to be silent (*tacendum*) about this matter, and let no one hear of it; because for the worldly understanding it is impure, in itself, pure'.[56]

Despite his fear that he might go mad, Swedenborg treasured his visionary experience of marital *tikkun*. He visualised a woman who owned a beautiful estate and whom he was to marry. She signified piety and wisdom: 'Even when I was with her and loved her in my accustomed fashion, I seemed to obtain wisdom (*quod*) in place of the intercourse itself.'[57] Similar visions were recorded by contemporary Kabbalists among the Hasidic Jews, for whom 'it is recommendable to imagine a naked woman while praying, in order to reach the known degree'.[58] The adept should look 'at her body and blinding beauty' until he is 'overcome by great holiness' and makes himself stop. He should only contemplate, not carnally desire, the visionary woman. By controlling himself, he 'will pass the test and rise to a high degree. And enough said for him who understands.'

In May 1744, an inspired and disturbed Swedenborg set out for London, accompanied by a Moravian friend who would direct him to the Fetter Lane Chapel. His subsequent attempt to 'pass the test and rise to a high degree', while participating in Moravian and Jewish affairs, would stretch his sanity to the breaking point and make clear what William Blake meant when he told Crabb Robinson that Swedenborg's 'sexual religion is dangerous'.

7

Sacramental Sexuality

These generative organs are organs of more perfect nature, for they are the campus of the exercise of Loves, and are the native land, or Cyprus of Venus, and thus the Olympus of all delights.

Emanuel Swedenborg, *The Animal Kingdom* (1744)

IN MAY 1744, Swedenborg arrived in an England that was preparing for a Franco-Jacobite invasion, which was secretly supported by the Swedish government. Though preoccupied with his spiritual explorations, Swedenborg was charged with an intelligence mission by his friends in the Hat party, which placed him in a dangerous political position.[1] When he landed, his Moravian travelling companion, Johann Seniff, was arrested and interrogated, and Swedenborg feared that his own papers were actionable.[2] In the symbolic language of his dream journal, he intermingled his political fears with his psycho-erotic explorations; it was an ingenious method of encoding that could protect him from English spies.

For example, he referred to his compatriot, Johan Archenholtz, who opposed the Hats' support of the planned invasion:

I lay with one that was no by means pretty, but still I liked her. She was made like others: I touched her there, but found that at the entrance it was set with teeth. It seemed that it was Archenholtz in the guise of a woman. What it means I do not know; either that I am to have no commerce with women; or that in politics lies that which bites.[3]

Swedenborg recorded dreams in which he was attacked and arrested; thus, 'I had to provide myself against a godly shoemaker [Seniff] who was with me on the road and with whom I lodged at that time.'[4] Given his secret mission, it would be risky for him to live with a man already under government suspicion, so Seniff sent him to another Moravian Brother, Johann Brockmer, who lived near the Fetter Lane Chapel.[5]

At this time, John Blake (William's paternal uncle?) participated in Moravian affairs and knew both Seniff and Brockmer; thus he may well have met Swedenborg. Certainly both men shared in the soul-searching that characterised the Sifting Time and in the political vulnerability of the Congregation at Fetter Lane, which was accused of Jacobite sympathy and repeatedly attacked by anti-Papist mobs. During Swedenborg's association with the Brethren in London in 1744–5 and again in 1748–9, he was attracted to the same Moravian beliefs that inspired John Blake and Thomas and Catherine Armitage. Though he broke with the Brotherhood after 1749, they had given him rare access to not only Kabbalistic but Rosicrucian techniques of meditation – techniques that transformed him from a scientific explorer of the natural world into a visionary traveller in the supernatural world.

In April, just before leaving for England, Swedenborg experienced an overwhelming vision:

there came over me a strong shuddering from head to foot, with a thundering noise as if many winds beat together; which shook me and prostrated me on my face . . . I held together my hands and prayed, and there came forth a hand, which squeezed my hands hard . . . At that same moment, I sat in his bosom, and saw him face to face; it was a face of holy mien . . . Thought, what can this be? Is it Christ, God's son, I have seen? But it is sin to doubt thereof. But . . . it is commanded that we try the spirits . . . Wakened, with shudderings.[6]

After praying and struggling, he concluded that it was Jesus himself, but he later identified the spirit as his internal man externalised:

The remarkable fact was that now I represented the internal man and was as it were another than myself, so that I saluted my own thoughts, frightened them, the things of my own memory, that I accused another one. Thus now there has been a change so that I represent the internal man.[7]

The changed identification from Jesus to internal man reflected his increasing mastery over the form of meditation practised by Luzzatto's disciples. In *The Way of God*, Luzzatto described the moment of divine influx in terms strikingly similar to Swedenborg's: 'When God reveals Himself and bestows His influence, a prophet is greatly overwhelmed. His body and all his limbs immediately tremble, and he feels as if he is being turned inside out.'[8]

However, neither Jewish nor Christian visionaries were always sure about the identity of the *maggid*, defined as the externalisation of one's soul into an angelic or spiritual mentor. In a revealing letter, Luzzatto described his first vision of a *maggid*:

while keeping in mind a cabbalistic formula, I fell asleep, and when awaking heard a voice saying in Aramaic: 'I came down to reveal hidden secrets of the Holy King.' I stood trembling . . . he told me was a Maggid sent from Heaven . . . I heard his voice speaking out of my mouth . . . Also there are holy souls who come . . . and they tell me things I write down . . . All these things I am doing while falling on my face, and while seeing the holy souls as if through a dream in human forms.[9]

For the Kabbalist, the achievement of such spiritual communication creates a physical sensation of being coated with oil, an obvious reference to the sexual fluids exuded during intercourse: 'I was still speaking to God' and the oil 'anointed me from head to foot and very great joy seized me which for its spirituality and the sweetness of its rapture I cannot describe'.[10] When Swedenborg experienced the holiness of the *projectione semenis*, he recorded, 'it seemed to me that a quantity of oil with some mustard mingled with it was floating about; which perhaps may be my life to come'.[11]

In the multi-layered symbolism of his dream language, he seemed to refer to his desire to join Zinzendorf's Order of the Mustard Seed, whch included members important to the Hat-Jacobite political agenda. Influenced by his initiatory experiences at Ephrata, the count had recently transformed the Order into an international, hierarchical secret society, in which 'members were often kept unknown to each other, and their connection with the Order carefully concealed from all'.[12] To ensure secrecy, the 'candidate never knew the *frater* who received him'. According to C. G. von Murr, the new Order of the Mustard Seed was a 'pale imitation of the Society of Rosicrucians' and a form of 'spiritual Freemasonry'.[13] While critics charged that Zinzendorf 'bestows orders of knighthood', his initiates wore a 'Templar style cross'.[14] Thus Swedenborg's reference to the oil and mustard suggests his desire to join the intensely secretive Order of the Mustard Seed, whose Rosicrucian rituals would give him new life.

Zinzendorf had long been interested in alchemy, both in its practical and symbolical forms.[15] Some Brethren actually experimented with chemicals and crucibles, while others explored spiritualised alchemy. He observed that the Moravians' 'Notion of Divinity is apt to appear almost like Alchemy, or the Art of Making the Philosopher's Stone'.[16] He further described a Rosicrucian-style transformation of the human body: 'As the outward Tabernacle, the Corpse of Jesus which it has partaken of, will by a more than Chymical Process, refine it: so that before Any one imagines, the concentrated heavenly Body, which is to last for ever, will be ready.' Swedenborg too described the alchemical transformation of the body, including the all-important sexual organs and fluids:

> *Animal nature is almost universally occupied in her peculiar chemistry or alchemy: that is to say, in preparing a series of menstrua, more and more universal, to prolong the life of the body; and indeed, to perpetuate it . . . All the glands are so many workshops . . . All the viscera . . . the genital members – aye, and the very brain itself, are chemical organs.*[17]

He also recorded his association with some gold-makers and his desire to spiritualise their alchemical process.[18]

During Swedenborg's first weeks in London, he was accompanied by a Swedish friend, Niklas von Oelreich, a Hat activist and alchemist. While recently in Paris, Oelreich had collaborated in Hermetic experiments with the fabulously wealthy and eccentric Marquise d'Urfé, whose farcical attempt to achieve Rosicrucian intercourse with the elemental spirits (*à la* Gabalis) would receive comic immortality in the *Memoirs* of Giacomo Casanova.[19] Employing a low-life cast of criminals and prostitutes costumed as spirits, Casanova convinced her that his 'Genius' could impregnate a virgin with a male child, who would reveal the ultimate Kabbalistic *Word* to the *grande dame*, by kissing her and simultaneously killing-off her previous female embodiment. Casanova would later claim that *Madame* died of an 'overdose of the Panacea'.

Oelreich was aware of d'Urfé's mystico-copulatory ambitions, while they worked together in her alchemical laboratory. And in Swedenborg's diary, his descriptions of his own and Oelreich's sexual escapades suggests their participation in psychoerotic rituals. On 20 May, Swedenborg recorded, 'Still I could not at all keep myself under, or hinder myself from seeking after the sex; though I was far from any intention of committing acts . . . I was in company with Prof. Oelreich in certain places.'[20] In another entry, he noted: 'It seemed to me that I was with Oelreich and two women; he laid down and afterwards it seemed he had been with a woman. He admitted it. It occurred to me, as I also stated, that I also had lain with one.'[21] Swedenborg then linked their sexual experiences with his spiritual quest: 'It seemed that a rocket burst over me spreading a number of sparkles of lovely fire. Love for what is high perhaps.'

After Oelreich returned to Sweden, where Rosicrucian rituals were soon infused into the Masonic high degrees, Swedenborg gained access to a mysterious Jewish alchemist, whom many believed to be a Rosicrucian.[22] It was through a Moravian friend that Swedenborg apparently met Dr Samuel Jacob Falk, who gained notoriety as 'the Baal Shem of London' (master of the Kabbalistic names of God).[23] Over the next decades, Falk's mystical and Masonic career would be mysteriously intertwined with Swedenborg's and, according to W. B. Yeats, the 'brothers Falk' would provide William Blake with Kabbalistic and Rosicrucian knowledge.

In summer 1744, when Swedenborg suffered a severe illness and mental breakdown, his Moravian landlord Brockmer sent him to 'our dear Dr Smith, with whom you are intimate'.[24] Brockmer referred to Dr William Smith, who had earlier helped to found the Jacobite Masonic 'Order of Heredom' and who currently participated in Moravian affairs.[25] It was probably Smith who introduced Swedenborg to the two Jews who visited him at Brockmer's and witnessed his ecstatic trance. Smith

was a friend and student of Dr Falk, who with his factotum Hirsch Kalisch were possibly Swedenborg's Jewish visitors, whom he called these 'good Israelites'.[26]

Smith found lodgings for Swedenborg near his home in Cold Bath Fields and visited him daily, until his medical treatment eventually produced a cure. The physician's mystical theories of physiology and neurology were similar to Swedenborg's, for he believed in a universal cosmic aether, which holds the body and soul together. When the cosmic aether gets out of balance with the animal aether, nervous diseases emerge. Thus, by studying the analogies and correspondences between spiritual and material essences, the doctor can diagnose disease and prescribe for its cure. More importantly, through achieving true equilibrium and spiritual illumination, the patient – or any man – can raise himself to 'the pure state of man in Paradise' and achieve 'ETERNAL BLISS!'[27]

That such BLISS! included an exaltation of the senses – especially touch and sexuality – explains why Dr Smith was so interested in the Moravians and Kabbalists. He believed that the Methodists, who broke away from the Moravians, suffered from sexual repression, which they projected into morbid religious enthusiasm:

> *As for the religious elect or methodist saints, if any female among them fancies that she has got a cobler in her belly, I should neither deny the enthusiastic vision, nor the reality of the fact; for I sincerely believe there are many methodists, more for the sake of those visions, new births, and holy over-shadowings, than for a desire of serving and worshipping God acceptably. Many of them, I am sure, have a greater inclination to get, than to be begotten; to generate than to be regenerated.*[28]

According to a later friend of Swedenborg, he eventually moved into the house of Dr Smith, 'who was a man of a strange turn of mind'.[29] Some of that strangeness was his fascination with Jewish lore and his Kabbalistic collaboration with Dr Falk. After his arrival from Germany around 1739, Falk attempted to support himself by providing clients with Kabbalistic knowledge, alchemical transmutations and magical healing. Smith often visited the Baal Shem at his residence near Wellclose Square, which was directly behind the Swedish Church where Swedenborg attended services.[30] The physician was especially interested in Falk's

Kabbalistic healing techniques, which he used in cases of epilepsy, mental illness and fevers. In a later medical work, Smith revealed that his theory of mental illness and recuperation was rooted in his studies of Jewish works, especially the Talmud, the *Zohar* and a host of Kabbalistic treatises.[31]

Given Smith's interest in the negative health effects of sexual repression, it was relevant that Falk concocted potions to cure impotence and create lustfulness in males. He also possessed a repertoire of folk remedies and hypnotic skills, which enabled him to produce some surprising psychosomatic cures. According to the diary of Kalisch, these 'medical' treatments often verged on the grotesque and comical: 'To know if a sick man will live – take milk and put it into his urine; if it sinks he will not live, but if it floats up he will live.'[32] For pregnancy, 'smear the woman's womb with bear's fat', and for a woman who hates her husband, 'take a calf's eye, burn to ashes and spread on his foreskin during intercourse'.

The Baal Shem was a great admirer of Luzzatto's work and carried his books with him at all times. Thus he could have been another source for Swedenborg's Luzzattoan-style dream interpretation and meditation techniques. Though Falk maintained a public reputation for piety, his own dream diary suggests that he taught his clients some kind of erotic meditation ritual (similar to that of contemporary Hasidim). In Falk's dream, he saw his pupil Cosman Lehman 'standing before and looking at me':

> *I saw his penis which was so hard that it stood by itself, and he was using his body and his mouth to make it erect. When he needed to hold his penis in his hand, he did it very quickly. He drew on his penis and then cast his sperm (his dirt) to the south and to the north four times without stopping and then the penis lost its erection.*[33]

According to Luzzatto and the Kabbalists, such 'vitiation of the penis' would spoil the magical process and prevent the achievement of vision.

Like Luzzatto, Falk was accused of Sabbatianism, and his orthodox enemies sought to blacken his reputation. They claimed that he married 'a woman whose conduct gave much cause for complaint', with Rabbi Jacob Emden calling her 'the infamous whore'.[34] However, given the much-publicised adultery and debauchery among upper-class Christians (graphically satirised by William Hogarth's 'Marriage à la Mode'), it is not surprising that some Jews imitated their so-called superiors. In 1746 the wealthy Ashkenazi physician Meyer Schomburg published a shocking account of the antinomian and promiscuous conduct of London's Portuguese Jews:

> *They live with women, daughters of the gentiles, as if they were fulfilling a commandment, without shame . . . Some of them are so addicted to lewdness and adultery that they even associate with their friends' wives . . . In spite of this they think they do not transgress the Holy Commandment, 'Thou shalt not commit adultery.'*[35]

As we shall see, similar charges would subsequently be brought against the radical Moravians in Zinzendorf's inner circle. Moreover, in his *Spiritual Diary*, Swedenborg later recorded his London experiences in an antinomian and promiscuous society that included Jewish magicians and Moravian mystics.

During his first months in London, Swedenborg intensified his meditation on the Hebrew letters, which can be visualised in the form of male and female bodies. While the adept transposes and manipulates the linguistic forms, their sexual positionings and couplings reveal the celestial dynamics of the *Sephiroth*, which strive towards unification within the God-Man. They also stimulate the desired sexual arousal. On 4 July,

Swedenborg recorded an erotic dream vision: 'Seemed to take leave of her with particular tenderness, kissing. When another appeared a short way off; the effect while I was waking was as if I was in continual amorous desire.'[36] Four days later, he seemed to visualise the divine vagina, which he described in his usual oblique dream language:

> *Saw how an oblong globe condensed itself to its highest part from the bottom of the globe; taking the form of a tongue; which then afterwards spread and spread out. Signifies, I believe, that the innermost is a sanctuary, and served as a center of the lower globe; and that this thing in great part shall be thought out, as the tongue manifested. Believed that I am destined to this . . . all the objects of the sciences presented themselves to me in the form of women.*[37]

At this time Swedenborg was writing his anatomical treatise 'The Generative Organs', and he felt no inhibitions about visualising the physiology of the female genitals, especially the clitoris as a tongue:

> *the female parts are adept in enlarging and constricting, and by their very nature open, then seize, embrace, and fit closely to and with. This is the end of the fissure at the orifice, of the nymphae, carunculae, the folds of the vagina uteri; and also of the penis-like clitoris itself . . . Moreover, there is the cavernous texture of the inner surface of the vagina, which renders its expansion easy. The clitoris too cooperates . . . the accelerator muscles also correspond to the acclerators in the male organs . . . The innermost or intimate excitements are those which have their seat in the soul and mind . . .*[38]

In these strange passages Swedenborg applied a scientific explanation to the Moravian practice of visualising Christ's side-wound as a vagina or womb. Zinzendorf often exhorted the Brothers and Sisters to achieve a 'clear image' of the wound, which was opened by the phallic spear-thrust and thus birthed new souls.[39] He hinted at the resemblance between penis and clitoris, referring to the vagina as 'that little Model of a Chappel of God', where 'something represents itself of the Members of Christ, as in us Men'.[40]

To aid their visualisation, the Moravians produced small cards, painted with striking watercolours, which depicted the side-wound in the form of the female genitalia, which in turn contained a picture of an ordinary domestic activity taking place within the 'womb-like wound' . [41] In some of the emblematic vulvas, the bed and chair utilised for marital intercourse in the *Schlafsaal* were depicted. As 'a form of devotional art', these cards were used in the sexual instructions given to married couples; thus the Moravians directly linked the erotic image of the vagina-wound 'to human male orgasm during ritualised sex between married couples'.

The Moravians also visualised Jesus's penis, and the wives – 'Ye holy Matrons' – were urged to 'honour that precious Sign (*Membrum Virile*)' by which their husbands resemble Christ.[42] In passionate sermons, Zinzendorf praised the 'Member full of Mystery, which holily gives and chastely receives the conjugal Ointments for Jesus's sake'. Swedenborg could have learned from Dr Falk or his Jewish visitors that some Kabbalists stress that the male member must be erect, 'vital with joy and pleasure', during prayer in order to give birth to the divine vision.[43] This meditative practice may explain one of Swedenborg's most cryptic statements: 'Afterwards in a vision . . . I now arose a whole God up. God be thanked and praised . . . [Thou] wilt not take away from me Thy Holy Spirit which strengthens and upholds me.'[44]

In his manuscript on 'The Generative Organs', Swedenborg revealed his study of the anatomy and function of the cremaster muscle in the scrotum, which 'draws up, sustains, compresses

Gloria dem
Seitenhöhlgen

Wie warm sichs liegt im Seitelein
Ehre dem Seitenschrein

Da halt ich Mahlzeit früh u. spat.

and expresses the tunica vaginalis and the testicle'.[45] The English translator notes that 'expresses' is used 'in the sense of squeezes out the juices from'. Swedenborg's scientific understanding of the role of the cremaster in raising the testicles and allowing or preventing ejaculation would eventually provide him with a new key to achieving sexual and visionary bliss. In the meantime, he became so fascinated by this investigation that he proclaimed, 'if the structure of the testicle be properly examined, it will be evident, that it is so wonderfully constructed on geometrical principles, that anything more perfect cannot be'. Reflecting his and the Moravians' current interest in alchemy, he referred to 'the alchemical preparation of the seed in the testicles'.

While Swedenborg worked on his sexual-anatomical treatise, he probably discussed his theories with Dr Smith, especially the physiological reinforcement for the Kabbalistic notion of male and female reunification within the God-Man:

> *The parts of the woman answer to those of the male, as though they had first been naturally united, and afterwards naturally separated; and when united they resembled only a single body . . . The female parts so correspond to the male, that during the time of carnal copulation they resemble one and not two bodies, and so far coalesce that in the moment of orgasm . . . in the height of ecstasy . . . the soul tries to go forth out of its body.*[46]

For some reason Swedenborg did not publish 'The Generative Organs', but he did assimilate its physiological processes into an unusual and charming work, *De Cultu et Amore Dei* (*On the Worship and Love of God*), which he issued in London. The book would certainly have appealed to Moravian and Rosicrucian readers, for it describes in poetic prose the betrothal in Eden that takes place within the 'marriage-chamber of the mind' and the 'marriage chamber of Heaven itself'.[47] When the young maiden first sees her destined bridegroom, a flame 'beautifully tinged her, like a rose', while he was sexually aroused by her celestial beauty: 'This ardour increased even to this day, in which it was appointed by Divine Providence, that his wound, which then lurked in his inmost veins, should be healed by enjoyment.'

The healing of the sexual wound 'by enjoyment' reflected Moravian teaching, which at this time Swedenborg fully accepted. Though he had not gained admittance to the inner Congregation of the Lamb, he continued to attend the public services at Fetter Lane. Four years later, when he returned to London, he would be shocked to learn that a secretive group of young Moravians – probably led by the charismatic Christel – were taking the more reckless and antinomian exhortations of 'Papa' Zinzendorf to scandalous extremes.

But Swedenborg also gained access to new Yogic meditation techniques, brought back by the Moravians' Asiatic converts, that went beyond the Kabbalistic methods of Dr Falk and his 'brotherhood'. These radical innovations took place while John Blake and the Armitages participated in the Congregation of the Lamb; thus it should not be surprising that many of these themes would later emerge in William Blake's most audacious works.

8

Judaised Yoga

'Tis pretended, that the Cabala has taken a great part of its Follies from the Philosophy of Phoe, the Indian philosopher. And in this confus'd Heap of Rabbinism and Magick, something is discover'd, that comes near to the Doctrine of the Learned Chinese.

. . . La Créquiniére, *The Agreement of the Customs of the East-Indians with Those of the Jews* (1705)

AFTER SWEDENBORG RETURNED home in August 1745, his Hat colleagues launched a bold project to recruit wealthy Jews to Sweden.[1] In a new journal, known as his *Spiritual Diary*, he recorded many spirit-conversations with Jews, which were evidently based on the real-world negotiations undertaken with Jewish agents who arrived in Stockholm. While he worked on Hebrew conjugations and Kabbalistic interpretations of Scripture, he wrote that 'These words are written in the presence of many Jews who are around me.'[2] He further stressed, 'That it is no phantasy can be clearly known by those in Sweden, etc., with whom I have conversed. It can also be evident from an historical account of my life, if opportunity be afforded for describing this.'

At first he seemed hopeful that the Moravian dream of a universalist society of Jews, Christians and Gentiles could be realised. 'The end of the entire new creation is that, at the end of the ages, the spiritual man, or the great society which is to be formed from the spiritual man will grow together into one body by means of the Messiah.'[3] This kingdom will consist of Jews and Gentiles, but 'because the Messiah should be born of Jewish stock', the Gentiles should be 'grafted on the same stock, namely the Jewish, as branches on the tree of life'. Over the next months the Jewish negotiations became bogged down in a partisan struggle over control of the Swedish East India Company, and Swedenborg expressed frustration that the Jews would not accept his Christian messianic message.

However, he continued his Hebrew studies and occasionally praised the better Jews for assisting him or alerting him when some arcana must not be revealed.[4] Perhaps with their help, he used his meditation on Hebrew letters as 'a ladder' to descend and ascend to 'Jehovah, the only begotten Son of God'. He visualised the heavenly spirits 'consociated together to form one body', which was 'the very effigy of the kingdom of God'.[5] The 'resulting sweetness and happiness' were so great that 'they penetrated deep into the fibres and inmost marrows and affected them'. The Messiah then allowed him 'to sensate this effigy several times, and to sensate the heavenly sweetnesses and felicities'. The ecstatic state was achieved by envisioning the copulating Cherubim in the Holy of Holies, for 'in the tabernacle and temple, it is God Messiah who is represented, because there, as in a center, are angels, who make a small effigy of his kingdom.'[6]

By May 1747, the Swedish immigration project had fizzled out and the Jewish negotiators left Sweden. Disappointed and confused by his failure to convert them, Swedenborg sensed that he was called for a mission and must return to Amsterdam.[7] His subsequent contacts in Holland and England suggest that he considered himself part of the Moravian *Judenmission*, as well as a Hat agent of *Rose-Croix* Freemasonry.[8] While residing in Holland until September 1748, Swedenborg made an intensive study of Hebrew. Unfortunately, his cautious heirs deliberately removed (and even cut out with scissors) the annotations on his Hebrew Bible.[9]

At this time the Amsterdam Moravian Congregation included a converted Jew named Pauli, who assured the Brethren that there were many more ready to join their society.[10] Though Swedenborg wrote many stereotypically anti-Semitic comments in his journal, he also referred to one Jew 'who was with me for some time and who still perceived more interior things, and he was greatly instructed'.[11] Others were 'so deeply moved by the truth, that confessing their iniquities, they devoutly supplicated the mercy of God Messiah.'

Swedenborg now learned new meditation techniques, by which the adept is taken in a chariot (*Merkabah*) to see the holy palaces (*Heikhalot*).[12] In Jewish Gnostic traditions of *Merkabah*, the novice is taught how to ride the chariot of vision until, if he is worthy, he achieves a vision of 'the body of God' (*Shiur Komah*), complete with all its members and organs.[13] The Kabbalists further developed the technique to achieve a vision of Adam Kadmon. As Luzzatto explained, 'The realm of the *Sephiroth* is called "World of Emanation", or *Adam Kadmon*, the God-man, because the figure of a man is used in symbolic representations of the ten Ideas or Attributes.'[14] Moreover, 'all reality is but the image of one man, of whom all creations form the parts of the body', and the roots of God's rulership 'are to be found, hinted and revealed in the human body'.

In January 1748 Swedenborg achieved the vision of the Grand Man that would become central to his developing theosophy:

> *It is a great mystery that the entire angelic heaven is so formed that in every respect it corresponds to man in the universal and singular, and to all his members; and that Grand Man* (Maximus Homo) *has become altogether perverse by lapses, so that things inferior dominate those that are superior.*[15]

After more intensive study and meditation, Swedenborg penetrated into the great mystery of the Kabbala – that human sexual intercourse, when performed with the right intention (*kawwanah*), stimulates a similar joy within the Godhead: 'It is a great arcanum, that conjugial love may so enter into heaven . . . as to reach the inmost with a perception of felicity.'[16] As the Kabbalistic couple experience sexual joy, 'it enters from them into heaven'. Raphael Patai explains that God flowed into the act while the act flowed into God, thus 'aiding the Divinity himself in achieving a state of male–female togetherness which God is just as much in need of as man'.[17]

After this stunning revelation, Swedenborg left for London in September 1748, thus re-entering the Moravian milieu during the same period when John Blake and the Armitages sought spiritual inspiration from the passionate preaching and hymns of the Brethren. He now expanded his studies in Jewish theosophy to new explorations of Asian mysticism, a subject that had long fascinated Zinzendorf.[18] Though the count's early plan to travel to Asia did not materialise, in the 1740s he sent his 'Disapora' missionaries to Malabar, Ceylon, China, Tibet and Tartary.[19] Zinzendorf was familiar with Marco Polo's thirteenth-century account of the combined Yogic-alchemical traditions of Malabar, and with François Bernier's popular *Travels in the Mogul Empire* (1670), which presented Yogic mysticism as a form of Kabbalism.[20] The French traveller described his encounters with naked Indian Yogis, who became absorbed in 'profound meditation' and went into 'vaunted ecstasies'.[21] He explained that the trance, and the means of enjoying it, forms 'the grand Mystery of the Kabbala of the Yogis as well as the Sufis'. The Yogis were not only Kabbalists but alchemists, whose medicines cure diseases and produce rejuvenation.

Bernier further claimed that this Yogic-Kabbalistic-Hermetic philosophy was the same as that of Robert Fludd, the seventeenth-century English adept, and thus part of the Rosicrucian tradition.[22] This perceived linkage was reinforced by Samuel Richter ('Sincerus Renatus'), who reported in 1710 that 'all Rosicrucians have left Europe and gone to India'.[23] According to Christopher McIntosh, Yogic traditions of 'sexual alchemy' were almost certainly known to eighteenth-century Rosicrucians in Britain and Europe.[24]

Reports of such mystical exotica arrived at the Moravian centres, and the letters of their missionaries and converts were read to the Congregations. In Madras and other Indian cities, not only Hindus but Jews attended Moravian services, where the ecumenical 'Religion of the Heart' and 'mystical marriage' aroused much curiosity.[25] Though Zinzendorf aimed at Christian conversion, he recognised the validity of Jewish and Asian beliefs. At Fetter Lane he asked, 'who can tell, but if thou hadst been born a Jew, thou wouldst have believed what the Rabbi taught thee'; if a pagan, what the yogic 'Lama' taught.[26]

By 1743 there were many Moravian converts in Ceylon, and when Christian Dober returned to Holland in 1744, he brought with him a Malabaran Hindu, who was baptised into the Congregation in 1746.[27] The Moravians' praise of the human genitalia would seem familiar to the Malabaran, for the artists of his homeland lovingly depicted the *Lingam* (phallus) and *Yoni* (vagina) in sculpture, emblems and jewellery, which were often used for yogic meditation.[28] A Moravian artist, in turn, portrayed Zinzendorf preaching to Asian converts whose costume (nude except for a white loincloth) suggests that they were Yogis.[29]

Christian's cousin Leonard Dober, leader of the *Judenmission*, must have noticed the similarities between Jewish and Hindu mysticism. As Gershom Scholem explains, many of the meditation techniques of Kabbala are 'a kind of Judaised Yoga'.[30] Swedenborg, who had read about the mutual influence between the Jews and Hindus of Malabar, perhaps discussed their

sexual and mystical rituals with his Moravian friends in London.[31] He owned Arvid Gradin's book, *A Short History of the Bohemian-Moravian Protestant Church of the United Brethren* (London, 1743), in which his friend described the Moravian missionaries to Ceylon in the East Indies.[32] On their return, they gave accounts of the conversion of the 'Heathens', whose confessional testimonies were read by the Congregations in England, Holland and Germany.

Swedenborg also acquired a rare book that explicitly linked the Yogic and Kabbalistic mystical traditions, La Créquiniére's *Conformité de la Coutoumes des Indiens Orientaux avec celles des Juifs* (1704), which was translated into English by the radical pantheist John Toland and provoked much interest among Masonic students of the esoteric sciences.[33] The French author argued that there were shared phallic and magical practices among Asians and Jews: 'We find among the Indians,

Temples dedicated to Priapus, tho' under several different names', and it is certain that 'this abominable Idol did formerly meet with Worshippers among the Jews'.[34] The Priapic rites remained in India until Solomon's time and then, 'in the sixty-fifth year of Jesus Christ, they were carried into China'. Scornful of the Jews, he noted that it is 'pretended that the Cabala has taken a great part of its Follies from the Philosophy of Phoe', an Indian philosopher, and 'in this confus'd Heap of Rabbinism and Magick, something is discover'd that comes near the doctrine of the learned Chinese'.

Moving beyond his Hebrew studies, Swedenborg experienced a *Drang nach Osten*, an impulsion towards the East. In the visionary scenes of his *Spiritual Diary*, he described Zinzendorf's conversations with 'some of the gentiles in western India', who believed the count because 'they held the idea of God as a Man'.[35] He referred to 'a certain spirit from India of those who adored graven images in their lifetime', and he knew from La Créquiniére that these were erotic images.[36] He would later refer to a secret society in which 'spirits from Asia' teach initiates how to meditate on emblems of conjugial love, carved in stone or cast in silver.[37]

During their visits to Herrnhaag, Samuel Lieberkuhn, Christian Dober and their respective converts could have shared their knowledge of Yogic and Kabbalistic beliefs with Christel's 'Order of Little Fools'.[38] Thus it is suggestive that a mutual influence possibly developed between Moravian missionaries and the heterodox Indian sect of Kartabhajas. Like the Moravians, these Tantric mystics believed in an incarnated God called 'The Man of the Heart', advocated an egalitarian and universalist 'Religion of Man' and held weekly 'Gatherings of Love', which almost duplicated Christel's Love Feasts:

> *Held in the strictest secrecy, these involve the communal singing of Kartabhaja songs, and the sharing of food . . . In*

> *their most intense forms, as the singing and dancing reached the height of power, these gatherings were designed to culminate in a state of spiritual intoxication and devotional ecstasy, with the spontaneous display of the symptoms of divine madness – tears and laughter, writhing on the ground, trembling with joy, etc.*[39]

In 1748 at Herrnhaag, Christel's youthful disciples enacted similar scenes. At the Festival of the Single Brethren, he led them in choral singing, elaborate ceremonials and erotic prayers to the 'Side-hole', until many of them burst out in wails and moans.[40] While prostated *en masse*, they pictured the Side-hole lying on top of them, just like Elisha: 'they all embraced one another on the floor and "everyone was gone"'. After Christel declared all souls feminine and blended the male and female choirs together, the ceremonies became almost orgiastic.

A horrified Andrew Frey described scenes that were sometimes grotesquely comical: 'Revellings on Birth-days . . . throwing one another on the Floor, and struggling, with many filthy and gross indecencies – one brother breaking Wind over another's Tea-Cup, etc.'[41] Like the 'horripilations of joy, laughter, trembling, gnashing of teeth' at the Indians' 'Gatherings of Love', Christel and the Little Fools created their own riotous 'Summer of Love'.[42]

Echoing charges made against Zinzendorf's Order of the Mustard Seed, critics compared the Kartabhajas to the Freemasons, because of their secretive rites of initiation and magical practices.[43] Curiously, the burning of spark-emitting mustard seeds was a 'standard feature' of the Tantrists' sorcery.[44] The Moravian missionaries and the Indian mystics were persecuted by the British East India Company, and extremists in both fraternities found refuge in increasingly erotic and antinomian forms of mysticism.

The Kartabhajas practised a form of Tantric Yoga that

emphasised seminal retention and sexual intercourse as vehicles of vision.[45] The individual male utilised intense meditation and regulated breathing in order to control the 'pingala vein', in which the arrested semen was transferred to the brain and alchemically transmuted into the divine nectar. The male–female couple exercised phallic and vaginal muscles to prolong sexual arousal, achieve erotic euphoria and spiritual vision.

For Zinzendorf and Swedenborg, one Tantric belief was especially relevant. Though most Kartabhajas practised individual meditation, they believed that 'the practice of conjugal love is also a path. But it is a very hidden one. It is not to be discussed openly . . . Conjugal love is also a path to discovering the Man of the Heart.'[46] The more radical Tantrists also indulged in adultery, communal sex and bizarre sexual positions. Like the Moravians, they elevated the sexual fluids and blood to a spiritual level and stressed the sucking and revelling in these elements of the God-Man's physiology.

Given this Moravian-Indian context, Swedenborg's spirit descriptions become surprisingly relevant. He remembered a naked sorceress and magicians, who were skilled in 'abominable arts, from the influx of those who were from Eastern India'.[47] Referring to the spirits of souls 'from the Indies', he described initiation rites in which they 'worshipped the Greatest God' and established communication between 'their Magnate' and Swedenborg by 'a kind of respiration'.[48] The Indian spirits 'then magnified themselves in a certain manner' before prostrating themselves 'as little worms'. Swedenborg had earlier read descriptions of human sperm as 'little worms'; did he refer to a technique of semen (worm) control, which first enlarged and then shrunk the penis?[49]

Echoing Moravian missionary reports, Swedenborg described Chinese spirits 'from Asiatic regions', who were won over by visiting Christians; the latter revealed that charitable 'gentiles' would be welcomed into the universalist heaven.[50]

Later he remembered a peculiar vision, in which he discussed a Hebrew text with a 'spirit from Asia', who 'supposed therefrom' that he himself was Jewish.[51] The Judaised Asian thus perceived 'the interior effect of his adoration to be more holy than ever occurs with any Christian, and, indeed, to be more interior'. Most revealing, however, was Swedenborg's dream-memory of meditating Yogis, who sit in the lotus position in a state of *nirvana:* 'I was in bed, and slept sweetly and most deliciously . . . when I awoke, there were above me, at a distance, Chinese, sitting there, as the Indians are wont to do, with the feet crossed . . . they were in the tranquillity of peace.'[52]

Several Swedenborgian scholars suggest that Swedenborg practised Yogic-style meditation, but they insist that he invented the process by himself.[53] Wilson Van Dusen notes that Swedenborg's dream of a ship-deck, where the people were arranged like the cardinal points of a compass, was a *mandala*, a geometric emblem upon which Yogis meditate.[54] He points out similarities between Swedenborg's vision of 'the inward man separated from the outward', when 'the shudders all started from below in the body and went up to head', and the trance process in 'the Hindu *Kundalini*', when the *chakras* of energy rise from the genitals up to the brain.

Sigrid Toksvig observes that Swedenborg's technique of listening to heart sounds while he regulates his breathing 'is one way of reaching that condition of ecstasy which the Hindu yogins call samadhi'.[55] She goes further to vaguely suggest a combined Yogic-Kabbalistic influence on his 'marriage mysticism':

> *Except for certain forms of Hinduism or Tantric Buddhism, it is doubtful if in any advanced form of religion so much stress has been laid on the symbolic significance of sex . . . Certain Kabbalists used sexual imagery to describe the union*

of God and his 'Shekhinah' – the feminine element in God – and saw this union as the central fact in the whole chain of divine manifestations in the hidden world.[56]

Similar parallels have been noticed by historians of the Moravians. Jacob Sessler argues that the Moravians' 'extensive use of theological symbols for sexual themes', which 'dominated the whole community', is common and traditional in the Orient: 'Hindu symbolism analogous to Zinzendorf's can be found in extreme forms of Bhakti and in the Tantric literature.'[57]

As we shall see, this combined Kabbalistic-Yogic technique of meditation will help to explicate some of Swedenborg's most bizarre descriptions in his *Spiritual Diary*, while the orgiastic context of Christel's secret ceremonies will place them in a real-world context. Was it the real-world context of William Blake's mother – the erotic and exotic Love Feast that later nourished his own bizarre and orgiastic visions?

9

Phallic Feet and Tantric Toes

Pain was also felt in the great toe of the left foot . . . the great toe communicates with the genitals; for the genitals correspond to the Word . . .

Emanuel Swedenborg, *The Spiritual Diary* (1752)

IN SEPTEMBER 1748, Swedenborg arrived in London, where he undertook a year-long mission for Louis XV and the pro-French Hat party. His announced purpose was the writing and publication of *Arcana Caelestia*, an allegorical explication of Genesis, which would Christianise his Kabbalistic theories of the 'celestial arcana' enclosed in each Hebrew letter and word, as well as the correspondences between the human body and the Grand Body. When Louis XV gave Swedenborg a secret subsidy for the book, he possibly intended it as a cover for his intelligence activities.[1] According to the rules of the French king's clandestine diplomatic network (later known as the *Secret du Roi*), he must publish anonymously, leave no paper trail and maintain a low profile.

Perhaps this virtual incognito explains the lack of references to Swedenborg in Moravian archives, for his diary suggests that he immediately sought out 'the Moravian church, among whom an image of the primitive church is preserved'.[2] His later spiritual *memorabilia* reveal that he gained access to the 'abominable secret tenets' reserved for the radical inner circle, when two friendly Brethren 'led me down to a place, where I was brought in'.[3] At this location he 'frequented their sacred assembly' and thus discovered 'their arcana'. After accounts of such secret meetings became public in 1753, Zinzendorf complained that in some congregational buildings there were too many dark corners where people could retreat 'for doing bad things'.[4]

Swedenborg then claimed that other Brethren threatened him and 'declared me guilty of death', because he had witnessed their clandestine ceremonies.[5] The apostate Moravian Andrew Frey reported similar threats from the radicals at Herrnhaag, claiming that he was persecuted by 'Invectives and magical Cruelties, which threw me into extreme Anguish, Terrors and Tremblings'.[6] According to the hostile Henry Rimius, Zinzendorf believed that his condemnations and excommunications had the power to kill his victims.[7]

Swedenborg further recorded that the Moravian extremists were 'almost Socinians', who 'utterly deny the Lord's Divine' and claim that 'He was not conceived of Jehovah God, but was a bastard'.[8] He thus echoed charges made against 'Rabbi' Lieberkuhn, leader of the *Judenmission*, who refused to stress the divinity of Jesus in his dialogues with Jews.[9] By 1748 Lieberkuhn had recruited enough London Jews to convince Zinzendorf that the Fetter Lane Elders should buy a house in the Jewish quarter, to provide a meeting place for a Christian-Jewish *Kehille* (Yiddish for congregation).[10] As in Amsterdam, this mixed congregation should operate clandestinely in order to avoid opposition from rabbinic authorities.

Though few records survive about this London *Kehille*, it may have received sympathetic support from Zinzendorf's son Christel, who met Lieberkuhn and some of his Jewish recruits when they visited Herrnhaag. In fact, it was one of those recruits, Abraham Herz, who would later accuse Christel of anal sodomy and his followers of general debauchery.[11] As noted earlier, when Christel arrived in London in May 1749, few in the Congregation knew about the scandals in Germany, and he soon won them over with his charismatic personality. The Congregation diaries reveal his leading role in bringing many of the poetic, artistic and theatrical rituals from Herrnhaag to Fetter Lane, where the 'infatuated' Congregation enjoyed them.

From several weird passages in Swedenborg's *Spiritual Diary*, the question arises of whether Christel also brought the homoerotic and promiscuous practices to an inner circle of his devotees.[12] Even more intriguing, did they join with Sabbatian radicals in the *Kehille* to experiment with new forms of spiritual eroticism? Led by two friendly Brothers, Swedenborg entered a murky underworld in which sexual magic merged with spiritual ecstasy. It initially attracted but eventually repelled him.

Swedenborg described a preceptor, or preacher, who proclaimed that the Lord took away all evil and pollution, 'so that with man there is nothing of it left'.[13] With him were spirits 'who favour promiscuous marriage, from the persuasion that very good should be held in common'. The preacher justified his sexual beliefs by extracting 'foul representations and shameful nakednesses' from the Sacred Word, 'which it is not permitted to relate'. Eventually the preacher confessed that he was 'leagued with the adulterers', and disclosed the manner in which 'those abominable, promiscuous marriages were conducted, both in darkness and light':

> *They court obscurity, but when those they fear withdraw, they bring a light and kindle it, when their rites are detected, which from their abominableness are not to be described; and as they say the intercourse is to be common, so they act promiscuously, that a wife may not know by whom she is pregnant, and thus the progeny will be common to all.*[14]

While the orgiasts acted independently, they confessed that because 'this preacher of the king' sometimes participated, 'they had done it with less shame'. The usage of 'king' seems to reflect Christel's language, in which the erotically aroused *Schätzeln* (sweethearts) 'sleep in the arms of the King', both symbolically and literally.[15]

Alfred Acton, the New Church editor, makes the odd comment that 'the scenes here portrayed were really transacted in the natural world, but under the instigation of spirits such as those whom Swedenborg describes.'[16] Though Swedenborg may have exaggerated and distorted the real-world behaviour when he transferred it to the spirit world, other critics of the Moravians described similar scenes.

Andrew Frey portrayed a youthful minority among the German Moravians, whose indulgence in communal sex revived 'the Spirit of the Evites', followers of the Boehmenist prophetess Eva Buttlar, whose promiscuous actitivies caused much scandal earlier in the century.[17] Repeating Frey's charges, Rimius reported that George II's Consistory in Bremen and Verden banned the Moravians in 1749, predicting that they 'will fall into those abominations, which in former times were detected in Buttlar's gang'.[18] In a helpful note for his English readers, Rimius explained that the Evites acted out their heterosexual Trinity and proclaimed that 'no true love could arise between them, unless they carnally mixed together, which they called a matrimonial mystery'.

After several months in London, Swedenborg changed lodgings and moved to Wellclose Square, where he became a close neighbour of Dr Falk, whose fellow Sabbatians were accused of similar orgiastic behaviour. One orthodox opponent accused the 'heretics' of engaging in a study of Kabbala with their hearts full of lust and therefore materialising much of its spiritual meaning: 'in consequence of the fact that they saw reference to copulation, kissing, embracing, and so forth, they yielded to lascivious passions, may God preserve us, and committed great evil'.[19] It is certainly possible that Dr Falk, who taught Kabbala to Christians, was associated with the Moravians' mixed Jewish-Christian *Kehille*.

However, Swedenborg's further 'spirit' descriptions suggest another layer of influence on the orgiasts' behaviour – that of Tantric Yoga. He had earlier read that in Malabar the Brahminical Yogis got to sleep with other men's wives, even the king's, and that the women had so many sexual partners that they did not know which ones were the fathers of their children.[20] His subsequent references to Moravian contacts with Asians, and his own visions of Hindu magicians and Chinese Yogis, have already been discussed. It is clear that he learned something about Asian sexual rituals and techniques of erotic meditation. In fact, a merged Kabbalistic-Tantric context provides a possible explication for Swedenborg's most bizarre description of the secret practices of the preacher's disciples:

> *It was shown to me of what sort the filthy loves of these people, truly in the way they support* (confirmant) *such loves with filthy calculations* (spurcis ratiociniis), *by means of sensations induced on the region of the genital members, first into the little glands of the groin* (glandulas inguinales), *then through a certain sensible approach [touch, massage] from the area of the belly toward that area [genital region]; then through the induction of sensation into the genital member itself, successively in the direction of the glans penis* (bulbum), *and then with a fiery burning of such a kind in the glans* (bulbo)*; it [glans] came to be fiery. By these things it was signified in what manner they will have progressively encouraged* (confirmant) *and incited themselves with filthy calculations, indeed in those most gross of natural things which are made known through the burning of the nail of the big toe of the left foot.*[21]

William Blake would later seem to draw on this passage, when he portrayed himself with a fire-charred, erect penis, while the flaming star of spiritual illumination plunges towards the tarsus (sole) of his foot.[22] Thus it will be useful to examine Swedenborg's account in some detail.

Swedenborg accused the preacher of screening himself behind the more innocent participants and attempting to justify his conduct: 'He then scraped together whatever he could from the Word – some things respecting Adam, and others respecting the Prae-Adamites – which I had not heard before.'[23] Swedenborg later claimed that the Moravian radicals justified their antinomian sexual practices by perverting the commandments forbidding such things by 'sinister interpretations' – a charge also made against contemporary Sabbatians. Despite the weirdness of Swedenborg's language, his reference to 'filthy calculations' provides a clue to his meaning, for Jewish techniques of interpretation of Hebrew scriptures by *Gematria* (letter-number manipulations) were often defined as 'calculations'.[24]

Combining *Gematria* with the physiology of the Divine Body, the Kabbalists interpreted the feet as 'a euphemism for the genitals' or 'a phallic symbol for the masculine aspect of God'.[25] The ten toes represent the ten demonic powers who struggle with the ten fingers or 'ten holy emanations' (*Sephiroth*). The unification of male and female feet constitutes the *hieros gamos:* 'When the divine feet are united [in intercourse] the Jews will be released from entrapment in the feet of the demonic power. This is the esoteric knowledge attained by one who calculates by means of the measuring line.'[26]

Were the 'filthy calculations' of Swedenborg's orgiasts a reference to such sexual-mystical mathematics? In his diary he described the magical power of numbers, which allowed an erotic female spirit to attract him 'more strongly'.[27] He further described the evil spirits who 'took possession of the soles of the foot', and the pain felt 'in the great toe of the left foot', which shows that 'the great toe communicates with the genitals; for the genitals correspond to the Word'.[28] Moreover, 'It has been often granted me to sensibly perceive that communication.'

Since La Créquiniére claimed that Jewish Kabbalists received their phallic rites from the East Indians, Swedenborg's reference to the sorceress, skilled in the abominable arts from Eastern India, who was cast into hell 'under the sole of the right foot', suggests a Yogic extension of Kabbalistic foot symbolism and a merger of meditation techniques. As Jeffrey Kripal explains, in Indian culture 'feet are the sacred meeting point of the human and the divine', and 'for the sake of liberation, the yogi ponders in his heart the lotus feet of Kali', the vulvic goddess.[29] In the antinomian symbolism of Tantric Yoga, Kali stands with her feet on the chest of the phallic god Siva, in an emblem of 'reversed sexual intercourse', which nevertheless produces an erection in Siva (as portrayed in numerous Indian temple carvings and medallions).

Provocatively, Swedenborg seemed to draw on this notion of reversal, especially in relation to the seminal flow. As he affirmed in 1744, controlled projection of the semen (*projectione semenis*) is crucial to the erotic trance. By delaying or preventing ejaculation, the seminal energy can be transported up the spine to the brain, where it produces visionary ecstasy. At that time Swedenborg had difficulty in arresting the seminal flow, but four years later he understood better – and evidently practised – Yogic disciplines of seminal control.

Perhaps he learned from the Moravians' Asian converts about the 'hydraulic' or 'fountain-pen' technique of urethral suction that draws the semen back from ejaculation.[30] Or he may have drawn on Chinese manuscripts and oral lore, brought to Sweden by his friends in the East India Company, about the techniques of 'The Manual of Immortals', in which the adept uses certain breathing and touching techniques to make the semen 'come back from the Stalk of Jade and mount upwards to the brain'.[31] Though his spirit-description suggests that the Moravian initiates abused such rituals, it also hints at his own experimentation.

Swedenborg described an approach by touch or massage that moved from the belly to the groin, glans penis, great toe and sole of the left foot. According to Tantrist Yogis, ritualised touching of the area below the umbilicus awakens the serpent of wisdom (*kundalini*), which engenders a fiery sensation as it moves through the body. While arousal progresses, the Yogin changes the breath flow by massaging the great toe, where a nerve terminates that regulates all cyclic changes and rhythms in the entire body. At the same time, he meditates on the connection between great toe and genitals. With an ascending breath along the *sumna*, the central breath channel, the Yogin can remove gradually all sensory qualities:

> *He visualises a fire arising from his right big toe that burns all the impurities of the elements located in the body. The imagined fire, following the path of reabsorption upward from the toe, purifies his gross body just as the visualised reabsorption of* tattwas *[five essential elements] into their source-substances purified the subtle body.*[32]

Some adepts then achieve an extraordinary mastery over their genital muscles, which cannot normally be controlled, which allows them to arrest the semen and in-breathe it back: 'This is no more remarkable than the fully-trained adept's ability to suspend breath or heart-beat or to control nerves and circulation.'[33] Given Swedenborg's detailed scientific study of the genital muscles, he was unusually capable of understanding this Tantric process. His odd use of the words *bulbum/bulbo* suggests his familiarity with the *bulbo spongiosum* muscles at the base of the penis; when sexual arousal commences, these powerful muscles constrict and keep the penis erect.[34] He also studied

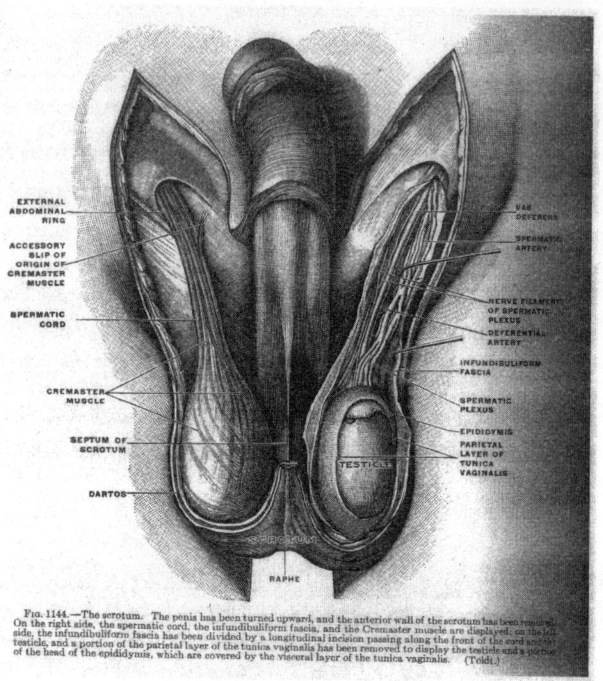

FIG. 1144.—The scrotum. The penis has been turned upward, and the anterior wall of the scrotum has been removed. On the right side, the spermatic cord, the infundibuliform fascia, and the Cremaster muscle are displayed; on the left side, the infundibuliform fascia has been divided by a longitudinal incision passing along the front of the cord and the testicle, and a portion of the parietal layer of the tunica vaginalis has been removed to display the testicle and a portion of the head of the epididymis, which are covered by the visceral layer of the tunica vaginalis. (Toldt.)

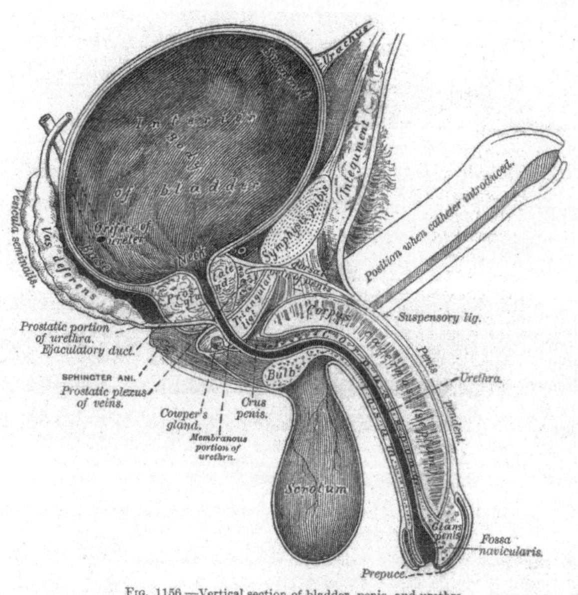

FIG. 1156.—Vertical section of bladder, penis, and urethra.

in detail the cremaster muscle in both promoting and preventing ejaculation.

Discussing 'the link between the cremaster and Tantric sex', André Van Lisebeth explains:

When one is close to the point of no return – to ejaculation – the scrotum as a whole shrinks, and the cremaster brings the testicles to both sides of the lingam's base, thus in a way 'cocking' the penis, setting it ready to fire, ready to ejaculate. This happens automatically, and we don't even notice it. On the razor's edge, if the Tantrist relaxes the cremaster, it 'de-cocks' the penis . . . and the testicles leave their ejaculatory position, making it easier to control oneself.[35]

In order to gain control over the cremaster, the Tantrist 'breathes slowly, deep down in the abdomen', while he concentrates on the scrotum and tries to 'contract whatever one feels inside it'. Swedenborg seemed to refer to this technique when the 'spirits' showed him 'abdominal respirations pertaining to the region of the genital members and loins'.[36] By regularly contracting and relaxing the cremaster, the adept becomes capable of lifting or lowering the scrotum at will.

Swedenborg also understood the Tantric role of the urethra, as the carrier of both semen and urine. As he described the orgiasts, he traced the burning sensation from great toe to 'the urethra', which 'pertains to the filthy bladder':

Thus have their fetid loves proceeded, for they prize their partners the lowest and regard their spouses as urinary vessels, into which each one is permitted to pour his urine, to such an extent do they hate and abominate their partners, and conjugal love, indeed the whole female sex.[37]

Scholars of Tantra explain that the same passage that conveys the semen – the urethra – also conveys urine from the bladder. Thus the penis is provided not only with neutralising agents to protect the sperm from the destructive effects of urine but with sets of special muscles for ejecting urine or semen, and to constrict the urethra or raise the penis in erection: 'it is by developing extraordinary control over some of these muscles that yogis may practise the retention of semen'.

The aspiring adept should begin with attempts at urinary control: 'One who, after a deep inspiration, restrains the flow of his urine – releasing it little by little and again holding it back – and practices this every day as per direction of the guru, achieves mastery over his seminal fluid also.'[38] When engaged in Yogic meditation, whether alone or with a female partner, and the moment of ejaculation is reached, the Tantrist applies pressure on the urethra in the perineal area, thus diverting the secretion into the bladder.[39] This diversion (the most important technique in antinomian, 'left-hand' Tantra) is extremely difficult and requires disciplined 'pumping and expulsion of fluids from the urethra' while the semen is arrested.[40]

From the Moravian missionaries or Swedish scholars who visited Tibet and Tartary, Swedenborg could have heard the well-known story of the Fifth Dalai Lama (d. 1680), a famous mystic and notorious womaniser, who defied his critics by boasting of his Tantric prowess. Admitting that he had many women, he stressed that copulation for him is not the same thing as it is for them:

> *He then walked to the edge of a terrace and urinated over it. With the force of gravity the stream of urine flowed down from terrace to terrace, finally reaching the base of the palace. Then, miraculously, it re-ascended the terraces, approached the Dalai Lama, and re-entered the bladder from whence it had come. Triumphantly he turned to those who had been*

abusing him: 'Unless you can do the same, you must realise that my sexual relations are different from yours.'[41]

However, even among Tantrist masters, success in this urethral technique is rare. No wonder the neophyte Moravian-Kabbalists ended up using their wives as 'urinary vessels'! It is possible that Swedenborg himself failed in a Tantric attempt in 1744, for he recorded a dream-vision of himself urinating before a woman in his bed, who then showed him 'her secret parts and her obscenity', which led him to decline 'any dealings with her'.[42]

Despite the high failure rate, these Tantric rituals were said to produce rejuvenation and longevity. Modern scholars of Tantra note that the repeated sexual arousal 'stimulates the gonads to secrete more rejuvenation hormones', while preserving the energising semen; thus, 'male Tantrists, instead of becoming sexually and physiologically weaker with age, remain very active and surprisingly youthful when they are old'.[43] Traditional Tantrists claim that by saving their own *bindu* (semen), the Yogis conquer death. Swedenborg had earlier recorded his own rejuvenation (his improving eyesight and angelised appearance) and intiation into the society of immortals. In 1748, his repeated use of *confirmant* hinted at a process of sexual healing and rejuvenation, though he was sarcastic about the results of the promiscuous group sex.

In the 1790s, when some of Blake's Swedenborgian friends transcribed and studied the manuscript of the *Spiritual Diary*, they perceived Swedenborg as a precursor of the Orientalist and Tantric scholars who brought esoteric lore from Asia to England. As we shall see, Blake would infuse mixed Kabbalistic-Yogic themes into his most puzzling and provocative 'illuminated prophecies'. It was a multi-cultural transfusion that began in the shadowy sub-cultures of Fetter Lane and Wellclose Square – and which possibly reached into Golden Square.

Part Two

10

Moravian Deaths and Blake Beginnings

We allow the greatest possible freedom with the hearts of our children.

Count Zinzendorf, *Sermon* (1740)

THE EXOTIC AND erotic experiences of Swedenborg and the Moravians of Fetter Lane may seem distant from and alien to the modest household of Catherine and Thomas Armitage in Golden Square. The question of the Armitages' awareness of the radicals' activities remains unanswered, and Swedenborg's claim that two-thirds of the Moravians participated in the orgies was an exaggeration.[1] Despite rumours about scandalous behaviour at Herrnhaag, the Congregation was devoted to the gifted and eloquent Christel,[2] who brought to London his 'high culture' of poetry, music and art. Catherine Armitage definitely participated in this sophisticated artistic and compelling emotional milieu, and she would eventually transmit the imaginative vision of Zinzendorf and Swedenborg to her fourth son, William Blake. But that transmission was initiated by sad events at Fetter Lane.

Though Catherine must have been overjoyed when she was accepted into the Congregation, her happiness was soon blighted by the deaths of her son and husband in March and November 1751. The Moravians were then plunged into near-hysterical grief by the sudden death of Christel, at the age of twenty-four, in May 1752. Boehler had loved the young man, but he now had to defend the Congregation from scandalous accusations, provoked by rumours about the Order of Little Fools.[3] In the midst of these troubles, Boehler also worried that the late Thomas Armitage had not been properly counselled. In December, he asked Brothers Masons and Syms to 'undertake Sis. Armitage's affairs', because 'Br. Armitage had made a very unrequitable will obliging his Wid[ow] to pay 80 pounds to his Bro. In case she Marry again & it is tho[ught] she has little more if any left her & Bro. Boehler wish'd the [illegible] would be advised by the Brn. When they made their will.'[4]

At this time, Zinzendorf's extravagances had brought the *Unitas Fratrum* near to bankruptcy, and the Brethren had to solicit financial donations and inheritances from its members. Though they tried to take good care of the Widows, inviting them into a special band or choir, the women lost their elite membership if they married outside the Congregation. Thus the following entry in the 'Church Book of the Brethren' is suggestive: 'Catherine Armitage – m [arried] s[iste]r. Born Walkingham, Nottinghamshire, Nov. 21 1725. Received 26 November 1750. Became a Widow and left the Congregation.'[5]

Did she leave only the Congregation of the Lamb, which made time-consuming demands on its members, and continue to attend public services at Fetter Lane? Was she accompanied by James Blake, her neighbour in Golden Square, whom she married on 25 October 1752? An odd record for 20 March 1753 suggests that she was still associated with the Moravians, for Brother West – who had presented Thomas Armitage's petition for membership – was instructed to speak to 'Sis. Arm.' about some financial matter.[6] Perhaps the use of her Armitage surname was a mere slip of the tongue or pen by her old friends.

The possibility that her new husband was sympathetic to the Moravians, though not a member of the inner Congregation, is suggested by the many references to Blakes in the records.[7] James Blake, who had earlier lived with John Blake, moved into Thomas Armitage's residence-cum-shop at 28 Broad Street, Golden Square. The new couple may have benefited from Boehler's sexual instruction, for their first child, James, was born 'almost exactly nine months after their marriage'.[8] Catherine went on to bear four more children, with her most unusual son, William, arriving on 28 November 1757.

The parents christened William in the Anglican Church at St James, Piccadilly, which belies the conventional wisdom that the Blakes were dissenters.[9] According to Catherine's previous Moravian beliefs, one should remain within one's national church, even while participating in the Brethren's affairs.[10] She had probably heard Zinzendorf affirm that 'he perceives that the Church of England retains that Charity and Largeness of Mind, which in smaller Sects is scarcely to be met with'.[11] In the years since 1749, when the Moravian Church was recognised by Parliament as an episcopal ally of the Anglican Church, the Brethren had suffered from a barrage of published attacks, which drove Zinzendorf out of England in 1755. After his death in 1760, the Fetter Lane Elders began a conservative retrenchment, in which they censored the hymnbooks and sermons and officially distanced themselves from the themes of the Sifting Time.

However, many Moravians still cherished those themes and maintained them in the privacy of their homes and small gatherings. While Catherine and her new husband allegedly attended services at Fetter Lane, she courageously implemented many of Zinzendorf's teachings about art, music and spirituality in the education of her young child. As discussed earlier, the Moravians stressed the visualisation of the God-Man's body, and many participants reported seeing visions of him, the maternal Holy Spirit, angels and spirits. Catherine was aware that Zinzendorf believed that infants and young children were capable of spiritual and visionary experiences.

Crabb Robinson recorded that Blake claimed to possess the faculty of vision 'from early infancy'; at the age of four, he saw God put his forehead to the window, which set him 'a' screaming'.[12] At the age of eight or ten, William had another vision on Peckham Rye, where he saw a tree filled with angels, 'bright angelic wings bespangling every bough like stars'.[13] Having returned home, he related the incident and, 'through his mother's intervention', escaped a thrashing from his honest father for telling a lie. On another morning he saw haymakers at work, and 'amid them angelic figures walking'. His older brother James 'had his spiritual and visionary side too' and talked of 'seeing Abraham and Moses'.

It has been assumed that Blake's visionary and volatile temperament motivated his parents' decision to keep him out of school, but the home-schooling his mother undertook for her children was consistent with Zinzendorf's notions about education. The count long remembered the unhappiness of his early school days, when he yearned to be with his family rather than at school, under the instruction of puritanical pedants. From his own intense religious experiences, he knew that children were capable of a rich spiritual and emotional life. He admired the 'pansophic' educational theories of the reformer Comenius, who stressed the innocence of childhood, the importance of parental affection, the healthy effects of outdoor free play and the use of pictorial images to inculcate religious sentiments.[14] He implemented these dicta in his voluminous sermons, songs and lessons for children.

What was surprisingly modern in Zinzendorf's ideas was his belief that even embryos and infants were receptive and that 'the process of religious education and socialisation began *in utero*'.[15] Within the 'embryo choir', the pregnant mother was pampered and counselled; after birth, she and her infant became part of the 'suckling choir', and joyous Love Feasts were held for them. As the child grew, Zinzendorf advocated family-based education. In 1751 he told the Fetter Lane parents, 'I hope that the time may soon come that all parents may train their own children.'[16] In 1753 he exhorted them to build a home 'for a Christian family life which will make possible the ideal church in the home with proper religious training for children'. Moreover, 'parental training is the natural method as compared with institutional training which is artificial'.

Unusually for the time, he emphasised the importance of the mother and minimised that of the father: 'We do not presume to require of a son that he should follow the same maxims as his father', for 'we allow the greatest freedom with the hearts of our children'.[17] As Blake's early biographer Allan Cunningham stressed, the boy 'was privately encouraged by his mother'.[18] Most significant for Catherine Blake and her imaginative son was Zinzendorf's emphasis on the role of art, music and poetry in the development of religious feelings and beliefs.

According to the scornful Rimius, Zinzendorf proclaimed, 'I would choose *Fancy* rather than *Philosophy*. Feeling is ascertained by Experience; Reasoning is hurtful, or makes us lose ourselves.'[19] Theological abstraction desiccated the imagination and led to hypocrisy and cruelty. Other mystics described God as 'Darkness, Nothing, Source, Unendlessness, hidden Majesty' – like Blake's later negative portrayal of 'Nobodaddy', who was silent, invisible and hidden in clouds.[20] Zinzendorf argued instead that God's essence can only be apprehended in the human figure of Christ, the 'body of the deity' or the 'concentrated God'.

At Fetter Lane, he rejoiced that 'we have been freed by the blessedly happy thought that our Creator has become a human and that the divine essence has finally, after a long wait, assembled an image'.[21] In order to sensate that image of the God-Man in one's heart (*Herz/Lev*), mother and child must 'view, picture and meditate about the Saviour from head to foot'.[22] These injunctions were sung by the mother in the home and by the children in catechistical hymns. In a method that shocked many contemporaries, Zinzendorf believed that children should be exposed to the full sex, wounds and blood theology, which they would absorb according to their innocent capacity.

He was apparently familiar with sixteenth-century paintings that portrayed the infant Christ with an erect penis, who gives a flirtatious 'chin-chuck' to his adoring mother.[23] When Blake later wrote his provocative 'Cradle Song', he seemed to draw on the Moravians' infant and maternal sexual psychology. In Blake's song, the mother strokes the soft limbs, the babe's face and heart respond with smiles and a peaceful beat, and she recognises the erotic pleasure stimulated in the infant:

> *Sweet Babe in thy face*
> *Soft desires I can trace*
> *Secret joys & secret smiles*
> *[Such as burning youth beguiles –* deleted*]*[24]

Though Blake deleted the last line, he went even further in his paean to free love, *Visions of the Daughters of Albion*, where he proclaimed:

> *. . . Take thy bliss O Man!*
> *And sweet shall be thy taste & and sweet thy infant joys renew!*

Infancy! fearless, lustful, happy! nestling for delight
In laps of pleasure . . .[25]

Zinzendorf preached that the school of the female Holy Spirit was 'a family school, that is a school on the lap, in the arms of the eternal Mother', which was replicated by the earthly mother and infant and celebrated in hymns for the embryo and suckling choirs.[26] When he sang 'That your child lay naked and bare on your lap', he drew further on the double meaning of the German word *Schoss* as lap and womb.

Following Comenius's teaching, the Moravians advocated maternal breastfeeding, rather than farming children out to wet-nurses. Catherine Armitage must have heard Boehler's talks to the Married Sisters, when he stressed that 'suckling', like sexual intercourse, was a liturgical act: it must be done with 'gracious ideas as a Divine Worship'.[27] Decades later William Blake would lament that so many selfish parents reject this beneficial practice: 'The child springs from the womb . . . The young bosom is cold for lack of mother's nourishment, & milk / Is cut off from the weeping mouth.'[28]

Determined to make the sensating of Jesus a joyous experience, Zinzendorf advocated that parents and children – of every class and background – should participate in a rich Renaissance-Baroque 'high culture' of painting, architecture, poetry and music. In this stress on the value of the visual arts, the Moravians differed dramatically from British Dissenting and Calvinist Reformed denominations. As he explained to the Fetter Lane Congregation, the Old Testament prohibition against graven images (Exodus 20: 4) no longer applies: 'In the New Testament this commandment is at an end: we have *seen*. Therefore the Lutherans are right in leaving this commandment out of their catechism, for it no longer has a relation on earth to us.'[29] Moravians believe that a person not only 'may' but 'should make an image'.

From 1749 until 1755, while Zinzendorf was resident in England, he made Lindsey House (an aristocratic mansion in Chelsea) the centre for his artistic mission. Ever since the overwhelming religious experience provoked by Feti's painting of Christ as the 'Man of Sorrows', he encouraged the production of religious art that would enhance the worshipper's ability to achieve precise and definitive visions. As a highly educated lawyer, he admitted his own struggle to move beyond intellectual abstraction to imaginative visualisation. He granted that the capacity for vision – 'that extraordinary state' when one is 'in the spirit' – was not equally shared by every member. The spiritual vision may occur with more or less sense experience, distinctness and visibility, 'as the different human temperaments and natural conditions can allow':

> *One person attains more incontestably and powerfully, the other more gently and mildly; but in one moment both attain to this, that in reality and truth one has the Creator of all things . . . standing in the form of one atoning for the whole human race . . . this individual object stands before the vision of one's heart, before the eyes of one's spirit, before one's inward man.*[30]

Blake would later echo this belief, telling Crabb Robinson that all men possess the faculty of vision, 'to a greater or less degree', but it has to be cultivated.[31] During the period of Moravian participation by Blake's mother, that faculty was cultivated by Zinzendorf's pedagogical employment of religious art. He exhorted the Congregation at Fetter Lane that each man, woman and child should be able to say, 'I see him clearly as if he were here: I could paint him right now', for then 'He remains engraved in one's heart. One has a copy of this deeply impressed there; one lives in it, is changed into the same image.'[32]

To increase their capacity to 'see' and 'engrave', Zinzendorf commissioned Moravian artists to embellish the walls and altars at Fetter Lane and Lindsey House with vivid, colourful and passionate depictions of Christ and his disciples, often merged with dramatic incidents from Moravian spiritual and missionary experiences. Unfortunately, because of the sale of Lindsey House in 1774 and the bombing of the Fetter Lane Chapel in 1941, most of these paintings were dispersed or destroyed. However, from contemporary accounts and surviving works in other Moravian churches, it becomes clear that Blake's family had access to an unusual treasure trove of religious and historical painting.

Among the Moravian artists who practised in London, the most interesting and relevant to Blake was the Danzig-born Johan Valentin Haidt (1700–80), who moved to England in 1724, married a Huguenot woman and opened an academy in his home, where he and his students studied live nudes.[33] Vernon Nelson points out that Haidt's comment about the importance of the nude model may be 'the earliest such reference for English art'.[34] With his friend, the Swiss-born artist George Michael Moser (1704–83), he started 'a predecessor to the Royal Academy of Arts' in his house, which influenced Moser's later role in co-founding the Royal Academy. In 1779, when William Blake applied to study there, it would be Moser, 'the venerable Keeper', who evaluated his work and oversaw his subsequent lessons.[35]

However, it was Haidt's role as a Moravian artist – known as 'the Painting Preacher' – that is most suggestive when exploring the Blake family's attitudes towards art. Always deeply religious, Haidt was attracted by the dramatic preaching and passionate singing he heard at Fetter Lane. In 1740 he sold his house and business and travelled to Herrnhaag, where he achieved a mystical experience that he remembered all his life. At Herrnhut, Zinzendorf commissioned him to paint a series of large symbolic works with life-size figures, who included the Jewish, Asiatic, native American and other 'exotic' converts to the Brotherhood.

Returning to London in 1749, Haidt brought with him the ardent devotion to the arts that he had observed in Germany. Deeply versed in the blood-and-wounds theology, he sensed that the Londoners were veering away from it (as indicated in Thomas Armitage's initially negative response).[36] He vowed that if they 'will not preach the martyrdom of God anymore, I will paint it all the more vigorously'. He soon filled the walls at Fetter Lane and Lindsey House with richly coloured, intensely spiritual paintings, before moving to Pennsylvania in 1754.

Despite the destruction of his Fetter Lane paintings, Haidt's surviving work makes clear that his emphasis on the role of art in children's education inspired much of the creative and imaginative teaching in Moravian families. That Blake, as a young child, could have seen Haidt's and other Moravian paintings is suggested by the report of his friend, Benjamin Heath Malkin: 'Mr William Blake, very early in life, had the ordinary opportunities of seeing pictures in the houses of noblemen and gentlemen, and the king's palaces.'[37] However, those opportunities were not really 'ordinary', and in the 1760s were quite limited for lower-class students. He certainly could have seen the collections at Lindsey House and possibly at the residences of Zinzendorf's aristocratic friends. Since these visits took place before his tenth birthday in 1767, he must have been taken by a parent, probably his mother, who would have been aware of the vivid paintings at Lindsey House and Fetter Lane.

For Zinzendorf, it was through art, poetry and music that the full impact of the 'mystical marriage' could be experienced. At Lindsey House the brilliant paintings inspired intense study and meditation, which were further enhanced by coloured transparencies, theatrical scenes and symbolic architecture. In a deliberate attempt to appeal to the children, Christel introduced some peculiar rituals at Fetter Lane. In the wall of the chapel he built a niche, covered with red cloth, into which children were placed to symbolise their dying in Christ's 'Side-hole'. For the adults, he built another 'Side-Wound' through which the Congregation marched.[38]

Given the vaginal symbolism of the 'niche' and 'hole', some psychoanalytic critics have viewed this return to the womb by children and adults as perversely erotic. Even worse, of course, were Christel's displays and ceremonies at Herrnhaag, which expressed both vaginal and anal symbolism. However, the richly coloured artwork and the elaborate ritual processions, which had a 'dance-like quality in their complexity', produced thrilling experiences for the artisans, shopkeepers and housewives who joined their aristocratic 'Brothers' in the services.[39] From the Fetter Lane records in 1750–1, it seems likely that Blake's mother observed and participated in these ceremonies.[40]

There is also clear evidence of another Moravian influence on William's early work in 'illuminated printing'. While visiting the Rosicrucians at Ephrata, Zinzendorf and Boehler observed the German artistic technique of *Frakturschriften*, the ornamental breaking or fracturing of letters, which represented the breaking of the artist's self-will and opening to marriage with Christ.[41] Each scribe had 'the birthing process in himself', and from the breaking open and rebirth, 'a florid paradise sprouted in many Ephrata calligraphy pieces'.[42] The 'illuminations' were usually drawn with pen and ink, and then embellished with vigorous colours. The ability to create *Fraktur* was regarded 'as a spiritual grace', while the actual practice, with its intense concentration and visualisation, could produce mystical states.[43]

Though Zinzendorf rejected the ascetic-celibate symbolism

of Ephrata, he incorporated the technique of *Fraktur* into the interior decorations and musical compositions of the Brethren. Hanging on the white walls of chapel and mansion were Moravian verses with decoratively painted letters, often in elaborate German Gothic script, while the hymns were surrounded by swirling ornamentation that gave them a florid quality.[44] Within this context, Bentley's comment about Catherine Blake's artistic influence on her son William takes on a new resonance. 'Catherine was a tender and sympathetic mother', who privately encouraged her strange son to make designs and, in the solitude of his room, 'he used to make drawings, and illustrate them with verses, to be hung up together in his mother's chamber'.[45] Perhaps it is not coincidental that an art historian sees striking similarities between the illuminated *Ephrata ABC Book* and the illuminated songs of Blake.[46]

Blake's mother could also have introduced him to the mystical emblem tradition, which he later used in tiny illustrated tracts.[47] Zinzendorf agreed with Comenius's advocacy of emblem books, which can 'explain the whole of pansophy' and which function like the 'signatures of Paracelsus and Boehme'.[48] Closer to home, Catherine had further access to the esoteric 'science of emblematics'. Thomas Armitage had been inspired by the preaching of John Cennick, a talented poet and composer, who won him over to the blood-and-wounds theology. With the Congregation, Cennick often discussed Hermann Hugo's *Pia Desideria,* a seventeenth-century Jesuit emblem book.[49] From descriptions in the Congregation diaries of 'our little childlike Hieroglyphicks', 'many childlike emblematical Doings, with Candles, Leaf-work' and 'emblematical Pictures, suddenly shifting & successively presenting themselves to the Eye', it is clear that Cennick encouraged the implementation of Hugo's theories.[50]

As the Italian scholar Mario Praz explains, Jesuit emblematics aimed at 'making ethical and religious truths accessible

A CRADLE SONG
Sweet dreams form a shade,
O'er my lovely infants head.
Sweet dreams of pleasant streams,
By happy silent moony beams
Sweet sleep with soft down,
Weave thy brows an infant crown.
Sweet sleep Angel mild,
Hover o'er my happy child.
Sweet smiles in the night,
Hover over my delight.
Sweet smiles Mothers smiles,
All the livelong night beguiles.
Sweet moans, dovelike sighs,
Chase not slumber from thy eyes.
Sweet moans, sweeter smiles,
All the dovelike moans beguiles.
Sleep sleep happy child.
All creation slept and smil'd.
Sleep sleep, happy sleep.
While o'er thee thy mother weep
Sweet babe in thy face,
Holy image I can trace.
Sweet babe once like thee,
Thy maker lay and wept for me

to all, even to the illiterate and to children, through the lure of pictures'.[51] At the same time, emblematics incorporated hieroglyphic techniques, which created an esoteric language that only a few could understand. Cennick, who greatly admired the Moravian paintings and engravings that he observed in Germany and England, recognised the relevance of the Jesuits' emblematic technique to Zinzendorf's artistic-pedagogic goals:

> *They made the supernatural accessible to all by materialising it. Rather than mortifying the senses . . . the Jesuits wanted every sense to be keyed up to the pitch of its capacity . . . The picture eventually became animated with an intense, hallucinatory life, independent of the page. The eyes were not alone perceiving it; the depicted objects were invested with body, scent and sound . . .*[52]

Hugo's great popularity arose from his use of the Song of Solomon, whose metaphors suggested 'emblems with the Oriental lusciousness of their appeals to the senses'.[53] Zinzendorf similarly compared the visualisation of Christ to the bride's in the Song of Songs. Quoting the line 'This is my beloved', he stressed that her lover is actually Christ, and 'there he is painted piece by piece'.[54] In *Pia Desideria* the emblematic characters emit tears, sighs, voluptuous swoonings and subtle pains: 'Love darts from his mouth a quivering tongue of flame, and, caressed by that heat', the bared breast of Anima burns, until the nocturnal garden is 'all a-bubble' with fertilising springs. At Fetter Lane, when Zinzendorf's birthday was celebrated with 'illuminated Pictures' showing 'Fountains springing' and the count 'solacing himself in a Garden where the Fountains spouted Blood', Jesuit icono-mysticism received a full-blooded Moravian expression.[55]

Hugo's most famous illustration, 'Anima trying to soar on

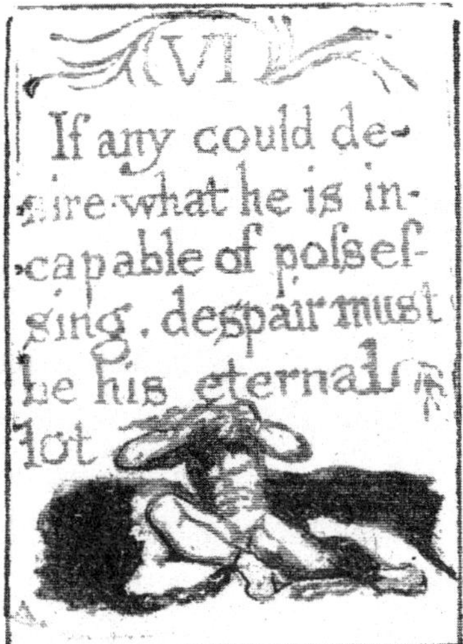
VI
If any could de-
-sire what he is in-
-capable of possess-
-sing, despair must
be his eternal
lot

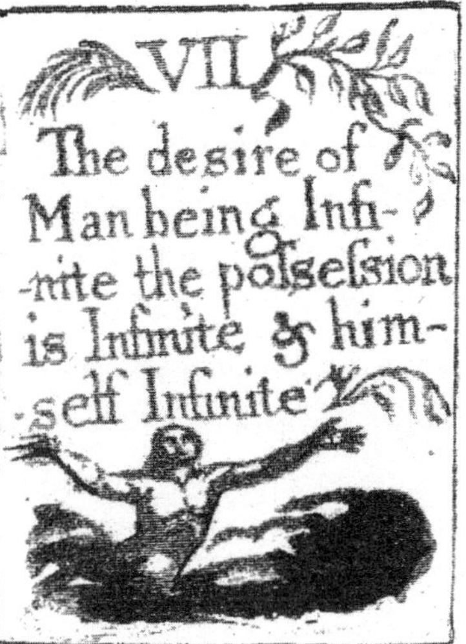
VII
The desire of
Man being Infi-
-nite the possession
is Infinite & him-
-self Infinite

wings, but held back by a weight tied to her foot', would later be echoed in Blake's tiny emblem book, *There is No Natural Religion.*[56] On plate V, Blake drew a figure soaring with hands raised, while the inscription reads, 'More! More! Is the cry of a mistaken soul, less than All cannot satisfy Man.'[57] On plate VI, he drew a naked man chained and fettered by his ankles, with the text, 'If any could desire what he is incapable of possessing, despair must be his eternal lot.' Like Cennick and Zinzendorf, Blake admired the theosophical works of the French mystic Madame Guyon, which were discussed at Fetter Lane gatherings. In her popular edition of Hugo's emblems, she stressed that worshippers must become child-like before they can realise their passionate desire for union with Jesus, '*le Désiré*'. Dedicating her edition to 'the interior Christian', she wrote, 'Lord, all my desire is exposed to your eyes.'[58]

Perhaps Blake drew on childhood memories when he engraved *For Children: The Gates of Paradise*, which included an emblem of a young man preparing to climb a ladder to the rising moon, while an embracing couple urge him on. The caption reads, 'I want! I want!'[59] Echoing Hugo and Guyon, Blake affirmed that 'The desire of Man being Infinite, the possession is Infinite, & himself Infinite.' While Catherine Armitage Blake home-schooled her children, did she introduce them to Hugo's little books of emblems, which offer to the eyes 'charming *Zinnepoppen,* or dolls for the spirit . . . the toys of a bewitched kindergarten'?[60]

Within the humdrum routine of shopkeeping, Catherine created a Moravian-style 'school on the lap' for her children, one of whom – William – would learn to fully express Zinzendorf's conception of the sensating and visionary heart (*Herz/Lev*). As the Fetter Lane preacher James Hutton explained, the Brethren believed that children should receive ingenuous and affectionate treatment, without force or violence: 'O! My Lord, could you but see the heartiness of

9
I want! I want!

our children, you would be touched.'[61] For Moravians, and probably for the Blake family, 'heartiness' was a multi-levelled quality; *Herzlichkeit* meant passionate, enthusiastic and imaginative visualisation of and engagement with the body of the God-Man. By the age of ten, William Blake was determined to become a truly 'hearty' artist.

11

School of Art and Eros

The spiritual Preceptor, an experiment Picture . . . This subject is taken from the Visions of Emanuel Swedenborg . . . The works of this visionary are well worthy the attention of Painters and Poets.

William Blake, *A Descriptive Catalogue* (1809)

THOUGH BLAKE'S MOTHER is credited as the primary inspiration for his artistic and spiritual life, his father eventually supported his son's artistic bent. The love of designing and sketching grew upon the child, and 'he expressed his anxious desire to be an artist'.[1] Though James Blake had intended his son for the hosier's shop, he and Catherine may have remembered Haidt's insistence on the importance of an independent spirit in the young artist, for talent 'is a gift of God, and whosever is sure of that and convinced of it, he can paint'.[2] Moreover, 'Each one knows best what his inclinations are, and he should follow them.'

While William wrote and illustrated poems and songs for his mother, recognition of his talent expanded beyond her chamber. His father 'began to be pleased with the notice his son obtained'.[3] Thus in 1767 he paid the fees to enrol the ten-year-old William in Henry Pars's Drawing School in the Strand, where he would find teachers and comrades sympathetic to his parents' religious interests. Pars's school had been founded in 1755 by William Shipley, an aspiring painter, to 'train Youths of genius' and introduce them to 'masters of several

Arts and Manufactures', in which 'Correctness of Drawing' is required.[4] It was a branch of the 'Society for the Encouragement of Arts, Manufactures and Commerce', organised two years earlier by Shipley and Dr Husband Messiter, with whom Shipley resided in Great Pulteney Street, Golden Square.[5] As close neighbours of the Blake family, they may have recommended the school to James Blake.

The Swedish-born Messiter shared with Shipley an admiration for Comenius's educational and scientific theories. In 1753 they determined to implement the reformist plans of seventeenth-century Rosicrucians and Freemasons for a non-partisan, non-sectarian society to develop a 'national scheme of social regeneration'.[6] Messiter was also a Freemason, and he may have met Blake's father at meetings of the Ancient Lodge, no. 38, for a James Blake was listed as a member from 1757 to 1761.[7] Some of the Armitage men also joined the Ancient system, which opposed the autocratic policies of the pro-government Modern lodges.

The Ancients also drew on the Kabbalistic themes of earlier 'Celtic' and *Écossais* Masonry, which included a solemn dedication to Solomonic art and architecture. Their chief spokesman, Lawrence Dermott, an Irish painter and crypto-Jacobite, proclaimed that 'the Masons at Jerusalem and Tyre were the greatest Cabalists then in the World'.[8] He urged each brother 'to be a lover of the Arts and Sciences' and 'to take all Opportunities to improve himself therein'. As an erudite student of Hebrew, Oriental and Hermetic lore, Messiter also believed the visual arts were the highest expression of such Solomonic aspirations.

In 1754, Messiter was one of the judges who awarded Shipley's apprentice, the thirteen-year-old Richard Cosway, the Society's prize for the best drawing.[9] At this time Cosway lodged with Shipley and Messiter in the latter's Golden Square residence.[10] It was probably through Messiter that Cosway met various Moravians, such as James Hutton and Benjamin La Trobe, for the physician had known Zinzendorf and mixed in Moravian company. Intellectually and spiritually curious, Cosway soon acquired Zinzendorf's *Nine Public Discourses . . . Preached in the Fetter Lane Chapel* (1748) and developed lasting friendships with various Brethren.[11]

Messiter and Cosway also became early readers of Swedenborg, who visited London in 1758, 1764 and 1766.[12] It was apparently during the last visit that Swedenborg met Messiter, who became his personal physician and confidential friend. He may also have met Messiter's protégé Cosway, who soon became William Blake's art teacher. This context lends some plausibility to the nineteenth-century tradition that Blake's father was an early reader of Swedenborg and acquired the *Arcana Caelestia* (1749–56), issued anonymously by John Lewis, the Moravian publisher.[13] Young William allegedly imbibed Swedenborgianism 'at his father's knee', while his older brother James 'would at times talk Swedenborg'.[14]

At the Society for Arts, Messiter and his committee often awarded premiums for drawing to their own pupils, and Blake's parents probably learned that Cosway's prize opened the door for lucrative commissions (by the age of seventeen). Thus they must have been pleased that the upwardly mobile Cosway was an instructor at Pars's School. The ten-year-old William was soon exposed to a liberal, even libertarian, world of free-spirited artists, who must have encouraged his precocious production of paeans to joyful sexuality.[15]

The pioneering use of nude models by Haidt was not followed at Pars's School and plaster casts of classical sculpture had to suffice. Evidently there were not enough for close study, and James Blake eventually purchased casts for his son to copy at home. He also supplied him with money to buy engraved prints of Raphael, Michelangelo, Romano, Dürer and others. Though William's choices were condemned by his youthful companions, 'who were accustomed to laugh at what they called his mechanical taste', his parents perhaps followed the advice of Haidt, who stressed that students should study engravings of these artists' works, as well as casts of classical sculpture.[16]

Influenced by Moravian and Swedenborgian reverence for sacramental sexuality, Blake's teacher Cosway combined an interest in erotica and esoterica. Three years before Blake became his pupil, Cosway allegedly met the Italian adventurer Giacomo Casanova, who visited London in summer 1764. An expert in Kabbalistic sexual and predictive techniques, Casanova commissioned Cosway to paint an obscene miniature on a portrait ring. Curiously, he assumed that Cosway was Jewish, which leads one art historian to observe that Cosway 'obviously had a great deal more to do with Judaism than we know about'.[17] By 1767 similar commissions for pornographic miniatures on rings and snuffboxes, from English ladies as well as foreigners, had brought him unusual prosperity, which must have impressed his students and their fee-paying parents.

Given Cosway's 'highly sexed nature' and mystical interests, his continuing friendships with Moravians and readings in Swedenborg would provide a spiritual sanction for his uninhibited sexual expression and behaviour.[18] If Blake had heard about Swedenborg's ideas from his father, he would not have been shocked by Cosway's flamboyance. Moreover, when Swedenborg returned to London in 1769, he brought with him copies of *Amore Conjugiale* (1768), a work in Latin, whose full title provoked both curiosity and scorn: 'The Delights of Wisdom Concerning Conjugial Love, After Which Follows the Pleasures of Insanity Concerning Scortatory Love'. No longer subject to Louis XV's rules of secrecy and anonymity, he placed his name on the title-page and assumed a more public persona in London. Despite his criticism of the Moravians in his unpublished diary, he employed Mary Lewis (Moravian widow of John Lewis) to sell the new work, which suggests an overlapping readership of Moravians and Swedenborgians.[19]

Among those readers was Cosway, who had long been curious about the notions of 'mystical marriage'. Like Swedenborg, who drew heavily upon it, Cosway owned and studied Nicholas Venette's *Mysteries of Conjugal Love, or, the Pleasures of the Marriage Bed Considered* (1754).[20] Reporting that 'the ancients ranked the *Viril Member* among the number of their gods', Venette affirmed that 'the pleasures of the wedlock are something divine'.[21] The medical historian Roy Porter argues that the French physician developed a magical-scientific philosophy of marital sexuality: 'Eros, in Venette's view, is Nature's occult *Wisdom*.'[22]

While 'the libido' provides initial attraction, 'it is the translation of sexual desire into the public estate of matrimony that transforms the passions into order'.[23] Thanks to the cunning of nature, the 'most exquisite sexual pleasures' are those experienced within 'settled conjugal alliance'. For Venette, the return to Nature is a 'mystery' – a two-sided notion, a secret; yet, 'a mystery is also a craft, a knack'. Harking back to the Renaissance corpus of esoteric and Hermetic wisdom, Venette portrayed love as a rite, as magic: 'Venette's reference point is an occult art, a bag of magical tricks.' No wonder Swedenborg and Cosway found his book fascinating.

Swedenborg and Cosway also acquired *Onania: or, the Heinous Sin of Self Pollution*, in a 1754 edition.[24] While railing against the practice of masturbation, the anonymous author noted that the Bible forbids the wastage of seed, while neither 'the Jewish rabbins, nor the most extravagant Cabalists' fantasised about onanism, despite their 'monstrous conjectures on other things'.[25] Praising the Jews' high regard for marriage, he stressed that self-pollution is the opposite of conjugal love. In passages that would have appealed to Jacobites (and their

Swedish supporters), he lamented the widespread practice of masturbation among English youth, while he praised the native Irish and Scottish Highlanders for rejecting the practice and therefore maintaining much greater fertility.[26]

For Swedenborg, who was repelled by the radical Moravians' moral antinomianism and sexual promiscuity, a reformist theology of conjugal love could have positive spiritual and political ramifications. In his voluminous manuscript, 'Apocalypsis Explicata', which he began in London in 1759, he drew on his increasing knowledge of Kabbalistic theosophy to extend the positive effects of conjugial intercourse into the heavens, where spirits revealed to him their own sexual experiences:

> *They declare they are in continual potency, that after the acts there is never any weariness, still less any sadness, but eagerness of life and cheerfulness of mind, that the married pair pass the night in each other's bosoms as if they were created into one, that effects are never so closed as to be lacking when they have desire . . . They declare that the delights of the effects cannot be described in the expression of any language of the world.*[27]

In Swedenborg's terminology of correspondences, 'effects' were the organs and sensations of the body that materialise the spiritual form of the Grand Man. In the sexual organs, spiritual form found its most sublime expression.

Because of the Hats' decades-long military alliance with Turkey (which provided a northern and southern flank against Russia), Swedenborg was interested in and relatively tolerant towards Muslim ideas of the after-life. He read that Muslims believe they will become 'ever young and sprightful' in their 'sense-ravishing' paradise.[28] He copied passages revealing the belief that 'the soul and body are conjoined even to the end of the world' and that 'the pleasure of paradise consists in embracing and kissing most beautiful women'. John Wesley, who met and initially admired Swedenborg, would later call him that 'filthy dreamer', who turned the Bible into 'the Christian Koran', which 'exceeds even the Mahometan'.[29]

As Swedenborg added new sections to 'Apocalypsis Explicata', he wrote a running commentary on the Ten Commandments, probably in response to Zinzendorf's antinomian 'perversions' of the Law. His greatest concern was the violation of the commandment against adultery, which had generated much negative publicity against the Moravians. During his tenure at Fetter Lane, Zinzendorf had recklessly announced that the Old Testament commandment against adultery 'could oblige us no more in the New Testament, because it was at a Time, when one Man had five or six wives'.[30]

His enemies claimed that Zinzendorf had an improper relationship with Anna Nitschman, whom he made an Eldress at the age of fourteen, for he travelled with Anna and 'was frequently alone with her'.[31] Even worse, Zinzendorf's erotic descriptions of Mary Magdalene, whom he hinted had a romantic relationship with Jesus, were 'intended to justify the Count's strolling about with Anna'.[32] His relations with his wife, who bore him twelve children (few survived), became strained and they lived mostly apart. After her death, he arranged a morganatic marriage with Anna in 1757, which made him even more vulnerable to charges of sexual impropriety.[33]

During Swedenborg's 1766 visit to London, he again took lodgings in the King's Arms Tavern in Wellclose Square, where the Swedish landlord Johan Bergström hosted meetings of Ancient and *Écossais* Masonic lodges. Directly across the small square was an imposing mansion, in which Dr Falk now performed his magical ceremonies and instructed curious Masons in Kabbala.[34] As Swedenborg began writing *Amore Conjugiale*, his most explicit explanation of visionary sexuality, he referred several times to a special parchment with Hebrew writing, which contained the arcana of earthly and heavenly spirituality.[35]

He directed his spiritual-sexual revelations to 'the company of the wise', who make up an 'order of knighthood' and who gather in assemblies in temples decorated with mystical columns and pyramids – an apparent reference to his Masonic brethren.[36] In the higher Rosicrucian degrees of *Écossais* Masonry, the adepts were often called 'angels', and Swedenborg had earlier described himself as becoming angelised. In *Conjugial Love*, he described an angel-guide who leads the 'initiates' into the temple, where the higher adepts explain the Solomonic symbolism, lead the novitiates in prayer and instruct them in meditation techniques: 'Take great care that, within yourselves, you think of nothing and, with your companions, speak of nothing but what is holy, pious and religious.'

After those cautionary words about maintaining the right intention (*kawwanah*), Swedenborg revealed to the initiates that sexual desire remains in the after-life, especially among 'those who become spiritual on earth'.[37] Moving beyond the Moravians' mystical marriage in this world, Swedenborg argued that sexual abstinence is an affront to God, even in the world beyond, where 'the sphere of perpetual celibacy infests the sphere of conjugial love, which is the sphere of heaven'. Human sexual activities, when performed with proper reverence and techniques, can stimulate sexual delight in the celestial world – that is, in the Grand Man who is God. Thus the delights of true conjugial love 'ascend and enter into heaven':

> *I have heard those angels, that when these delights ascend from chaste partners on earth, they perceive them to be exalted from themselves and infilled. Because some of the bystanders were unchaste, to the question of whether this applied also to the ultimate delights, they nodded assent and*

> *said tacitly, 'How can it be otherwise? Are not those delights the other delights in their fullness?'*[38]

Swedenborg elevated the sense of touch into the highest spiritual gift, noting that it is dedicated to conjugial love, as proved by 'its every sport and from the exaltation of its refinements to the supremely exalted'.[39] This notion was currently propagated by Sabbatian Jews, who may have informed the Moravians about it, especially during the last years of Zinzendorf's life, when he sent emissaries to establish relations with the Sabbatian followers of Jonathan Eibeschuetz and Jacob Frank in Europe.[40] But Swedenborg may also have learned this Sabbatian theme from Dr Falk in Wellclose Square. As explained by Eibeschuetz's son:

> *The patriarchs came into the world to restore the senses, and this they did to four of them. Then came Sabbatai Zevi and he restored the fifth, which according to Aristotle and Maimonides is a source of shame to us, but which has now been raised by him to a place of honour and glory.*[41]

Three decades later, William Blake would portray the sexual sense of touch in the mythic figure of 'Tharmas', whose degradation and exaltation form a theme of *Vala, or The Four Zoas.*

However, Swedenborg also made clear that physical sexuality is only an instrument of the mind, which receives influx from the spirit world. For those who are united in conjugial love, the 'forms of their minds terminate in these organs' of generation.[42] He then revealed the mental or psychic disciplines that produce the married couple's visionary sexual experience. By meditating together on the arcana of love – that is, the sexual polarities and commminglings of Hebrew letters and Kabbalistic *Sephiroth* – the man and wife can achieve a conjunction of minds and not at the same time of bodies.[43] When their minds are 'conjoined conjugially', their thoughts 'kiss each other spiritually, and these thoughts breathe their virtue or potency into the body'.

This supreme state of 'interior spiritual friendship' was strikingly similar to that described by contemporary Hasidic Kabbalists, who taught that a 'telepathic' sexual relation, without physical or visual contact, was possible between male and female 'fantasisers'.[44] It is not surprising that later enemies of the Hasidim compared their visionary writings to those of Swedenborg.[45] These meditative techniques were also similar to those of Tantric Yogis.[46] For Swedenborg, Kabbalists and Tantrists, this shared psychoerotic state could only be achieved if the male mastered the meditation process that creates 'continual potency' – a prolonged erection with arrested or delayed ejaculation. The husbands must 'keep the ideas of their thoughts on high and hold them in the air, as it were, so that they do not descend and press on that which makes that love'.[47]

The natural basis of earthly potency – good health – is elevated by meditative technique from the primitive sphere to the ideal sphere: 'a man who is continuously sound and enjoys stable health, is not lacking in vigour. His fibres, nerves, muscles and cremasters do not become torpid, relaxed or feeble, but continue in the strength of their powers.'[48] Swedenborg had earlier written about the cremaster muscles in 'The Generative Organs', and he evidently learned the Tantric role of the cremasters in 'cocking and decocking' the *Lingam* (first erecting the penis, then preventing ejaculation). Thus his anatomical and Yogic studies gave him a unique understanding of the physiology of the erotic trance.

He argued that control and prolongation of the male erection is crucial to the visionary state, for the presence of 'the virile powers' elevates the mind and 'their absence depresses, this absence causing the mind to droop, collapse and languish'.[49]

The modern Tantric scholar Lisebeth explains that to reach 'the razor's edge', without proceeding to ejaculation, is the key to ecstatic vision: 'The supreme art, for a Tantric male, is to remain indefinitely on the verge, and by doing so, he has access to the "sexual heaven" in the brain, paving the way to the true male orgasm.'[50]

Swedenborg also warned that this Tantric technique is difficult, for the cremaster control is not always successful:

> *It should be known, however, that neither with men or angels is conjugial love wholly chaste or pure . . . With those who are in conjugial love, the chaste is above and the non-chaste below, and between the two is interposed, by the Lord, a hinged door, as it were, which is opened by determination, care being taken that it does not stand open, lest the one should pass over into the other and commingle.*[51]

The 'hinged door' was the seminal duct, which the adept controlled in order to arrest or in-breathe the semen, which then nourished the brain – thus producing visionary states and communication with spirits.[52]

According to eighteenth-century Hathayogic texts (describing practices in India, Tibet and China), the hinged door is initially opened and then closed by a combination of postures, 'together with a number of respiratory and "hydraulic" techniques, for the immobilisation of the breaths and the diaphragmatic retention that trigger the rise of the *kundalini* and all that follows'.[53] The 'hermetic seals' or 'locks' in the abdomen, thorax and head work hydraulically to 'effect internal changes in pressure, such that breath and seed become immobilised or begin to be drawn upward'.

Eighteenth-century Kabbalists also referred to a hinged door, which regulates the seminal flow as the adept progresses towards the trance state. Luzzatto described 'the phallic force of *Yesod* that opens the closed door' and allows visionary union with the *Shekhinah*.[54] For the mystical Masons who studied Kabbala with Dr Falk and who read Swedenborg's *Conjugial Love*, Luzzatto's linkage of this sexualised meditation to the psychic rebuilding of the Temple would have been provocative: 'the construction of the destroyed Temple in the messianic age ensues from the phallic gradation of *Yesod*, stimulated by the exposition of Kabbalistic secrets'.

This was heady stuff indeed for the liberated artists and spiritual seekers in London, who soon infused Swedenborgian sexual theosophy into secretive rituals in *Écossais* lodges. In 1767, a French physician, Dr Benedict Chastanier, established in London a lodge of *Illuminés Théosophes*, which assimilated Hermetic and Swedenborgian themes.[55] Another French Mason, Lambert de Lintot, infused Swedenborgian symbolism into the Kabbalistic 'Rite of Heredom', which included Dr Falk among its members. As we shall see, its erotic emblems would later seem to influence William Blake.

When Blake completed his studies at Pars's Drawing School in 1772, he left a small but sympathetic world of aesthetically and spiritually inclined artists and patrons. At the age of fifteen he would move into another artistic and Masonic milieu, in which he received further encouragement for his esoteric and erotic explorations.

12

Apprentice in Art and Romance

Sing now the lusty song of fruits and flowers.
The narrow bud opens her beauties to
The sun, and love runs in her thrilling veins.
William Blake, 'To Autumn' (*c.*1770s)

AFTER SWEDENBORG LEFT London in summer 1769, his friends and admirers eagerly read *Amore Conjugiale*, a work that would inspire and disturb them over the next decades. For Blake's teacher Cosway, the book reinforced his interest in non-English sexual customs. He had recently aquired *Hymen – An Accurate Description of the Ceremonies Used in Marriage by Every Nation in the Known World* (1760), authored by 'Uxorious', or 'one who is dotingly or irrationally fond of his wife'. The author expressed a relatively tolerant attitude to sexual practices in foreign cultures, describing the Jewish reverence for marital sexuality, the Venetian and Spanish permission for adolescent erotic experimentation, the French tolerance for adultery, and a Chinese fraternity's condoning of full sexual freedom for wives.[1] In *Amore Conjugiale*, Cosway found a further rationale for his powerful libido.

Though Swedenborg's ideal was love between husband and wife, he recognised that many young men could not marry because of financial deficits or official duties and that the delay meant their natural sexual drives must find another outlet. A young man's roving instinct was normal and healthy, because 'with men is love of the sex in general and with women love of one of the sex; this is because those who have love of the sex have freedom to look around and also to decide'.[2] Claiming that he had 'new information from heaven', Swedenborg revealed that pre-marital sex with prostitutes or a mistress is not sinful, as long as the man maintains a belief in true conjugial love.

In passages that would shock many readers, he argued that for some men 'love of the sex cannot without harmful results be totally restrained from going forth into fornication'.[3] For those men 'who from superabundance labour with burning heat', excessive repression can produce harmful results. It is otherwise with those whose sexual energy is 'so scanty that they are able to resist the urgings of lust'. As Blake would later write, 'Those who restrain desire, do so because theirs is weak enough to be restrained.'[4] Because the preservation of sexual potency is crucial for spiritual vision, Swedenborg argued, 'therefore in populous cities brothels are tolerated', and bachelors should seek 'refuge' and 'asylum' by taking a mistress.

For a high-spirited and passionate young man like Cosway, this mild permission must have seemed almost a *carte blanche* for well-intentioned 'pellicacy', which Swedenborg defined as 'a more ordered and sane fornication', from which the young man 'can learn and see the distinctions'.[5] It was an attitide shared by several of Cosway's artistic colleagues, such as Charles Townley, a wealthy collector and antiquarian. Scion of a Catholic family whose support of the Stuarts led to executions, persecution and exile, Townley joined other frustrated Jacobites in a nostalgic sexualisation of politics, in which the courts of Charles II and James II were remembered as havens of sexual, artistic and intellectual freedom.[6] Townley, Cosway and their friends believed that these havens were destroyed by the 'usurpation' of William of Orange, a Calvinist, whom the Jacobites accused of sodomy.

This sexualisation of politics also infused their artistic imaginations during Blake's student days. Like the Scottish Jacobites who organised 'The Beggers' Benison', a defiantly irreverent and phallic mock-Masonic fraternity, Townley was inspired by the Priapic art excavated at Herculaneum and Pompeii, which provided an ancient religious context for liberated sexuality.[7] During art collecting tours in Italy, Townley worked with the eccentric scholar Baron d'Hancarville (*ci-devant* Pierre François Hugues), a specialist in pornographic art, and with the engraver-dealer Giovanni Casanova, brother of the libertine adventurer Giacomo. Both men influenced his developing belief that Priapic art expressed universal religious truths.

The French-educated Townley, who was 'much given to gambling and whoring', passed on his erotic and artistic interests to Cosway, who in 1772 sent an astoundingly uninhibited letter to him in Italy:

> *I must not omit telling you how much you are regretted by everybody here . . . there can be no life here without you. Wynne is envellop'd in* Cunt *– but, Alas, tis his Wife's. I believe you don't envy him . . . with respect to* shagging, *it is much the same as when you left us (your part omitted) – but as to myself, I stick as close to Radicati's arse as Bum Bailiff to Lord D——'s [illegible]. Italy for ever I say – if the Italian women fuck as well in Italy as they do here, you must be happy indeed – I am such a zealot for them, that I'll be damned if I ever fuck an* English *woman again (if I can help it) . . .*
>
> *. . . Addio – nothing on Earth (fucking Radicati always excepted) can make me so happy as hearing from you, when you have an Hours relaxation from Virtu and fucking . . .*[8]

One wonders if Giacomo Casanova had introduced Cosway to his Italian courtesans when he was in London in 1764.

Cosway further reported to Townley that there were no fewer than eight divorce cases under consideration at Doctors Commons and, even more amusing, 'a clergyman has just publish'd *openly* a treatise on *fucking* under the title of the Joys of Hymen – so that on the whole you see that things go on as they shou'd do'. Cosway referred to *The Joys of Hymen, or, the Conjugal Directory: A Poem in Three Books* (1768), published anonymously by a supposedly pious churchman, who claimed that he did not intend 'to excite lewd desires, or to provoke lawless love'.[9] The author stressed that his poem was unlike 'those more serious books, which under the notion of *science* have really corrupted our youth'. Instead, 'I sing the raptures of the Marriage Bed':

> *Whilst innocence among mankind remain'd*
> *And Nature's laws implicit were retain'd,*
> *With mutual rapture, both the sexes strove*
> *To gain the height of ecstasy in love.*[10]

Despite his bawdy tone, Cosway responded positively to this theme of ecstatic conjugal love.

In 1771, while Cosway was teaching Blake, he began work on a large painting of Townley and his 'carousing' antiquarian friends. Stephen Lloyd points out that the initial idea for the group portrait was explicitly lewd, as revealed in the preparatory drawing: 'the six connoisseurs are seen sexually arousing themselves while watching a third man fondle one of the marble Venuses. In the finished painting this sexual element is toned down, although the voyeurism remains clear.'[11] Cosway probably took his students to see the important classical collection of Townley, who would later befriend Blake and employ him as an engraver.[12]

When the fifteen-year-old Blake completed his studies at Pars's Drawing School, he decided to apprentice himself as an engraver rather than continuing his studio art classes. His parents may have remembered the elevated status that Zinzendorf gave to engraving, which he considered a 'high art', closely connected with visualisation of the God-Man. Preaching at Fetter Lane, the count urged the Congregation 'to take the spirit's stylus and etch – yea engrave – the image of Jesus in the fleshly tablets of the heart'.[13] Blake's mother probably knew the lines from the 1749 hymnbook, 'let me paint that melting Look', but 'paint thyself with thy own Hand; Deep in my Heart engrave Thee, O Lamb'.[14]

In August 1772, Blake was apprenticed to James Basire, who had recently been commissioned by John Nourse (who printed and stocked Swedenborg's works) to engrave the frontispiece for James Harris's odd work of sexualised linguistics, *Hermes, or a Philosophical Inquiry Concerning Universal Grammar* (1771). Drawing on Linnaeus's sexual classification of plants, Harris applied similar analyses to language, which he related to the hieroglyphics and correspondences of Hermes Trismegistis: 'The whole Visible World exhibits nothing more, than so many passing Pictures of these immutable Archetypes.'[15] In a passage that would have appealed to Blake, Harris praised the role of 'Imagination or Fancy', which preserves the Archetypes even as the world of memory and the senses fades away. Perhaps Blake and his father interpreted such a commission as a sign of similar spiritual interests in Basire.

Young Blake now moved into the engraver's studio at 31 Great Queen Street, where for the next seven years he was situated in the heart of London's Masonic world. Directly across the street was the Freemasons' Hall and Tavern, where many of his artistic and theosophical friends would gather. With the launching of an ambitious project to construct on the site a magnificent Masonic Temple, a temporary truce was implemented between the Ancient and Modern Masons, and Great Queen Street received visitors from all the branches of Masonry from Britain and abroad. While Blake was still at Pars's School, he probably witnessed the public Masonic procession on 21 May 1772, when Ancients and Moderns paraded to the Crown and Anchor Tavern on the Strand, close by the drawing school, and held a grand gala in honour of Freemasonry. Cosway apparently attended the event, for he acquired the special edition of William Preston's *Illustrations of Masonry* (1772), which described the ceremonies and was distributed to initiated friends.[16]

While Blake lived with Basire, he engraved designs for the Society of Antiquaries, which had a large Masonic membership, including many admirers of the Gothic cathedrals (considered the high point of architectural history by Ancient Masons, but the low point by classical art critics). He was sent to study the sculptured monuments in Westminster Abbey and other Gothic churches, which stimulated his admiration for the master masons who designed and built them. On his engraving of 'Joseph of Arimathea among the Rocks of Albion' (1773), Blake wrote, 'This is one of the Gothic Artists who Built the Cathedrals in what are called the Dark Ages Wandering about in sheep skins & goat skins of whom the World was not worthy; such were the Christians in all Ages.'[17]

Like the early Scottish stonemasons, who practised the mnemonic art of visualisation, Blake's concentration on the architectural design and stone carving sometimes provoked him to visionary states, in which he saw the aisles and galleries 'suddenly filled with a great procession of monks and priests . . . and his entranced ear heard the chant of plain-song and chorale, while the vaulted roof trembled with the sound of organ music'.[18] Thus the young apprentice fulfilled Zinzendorf's teaching that artistic visualisation and powerful music could evoke a state of euphoric trance.

In 1773, Basire added a second apprentice, James Parker, who became the friend and eventual business partner of Blake. Though little is known about Parker's background, he may have come from a Moravian family, for several Parkers are listed as members of the Congregation from 1745 to 1752.[19] The surprising compatibility between the careful, methodical Parker and the impulsive, visionary Blake perhaps arose from a common religious background. If so, both apprentices would have been aware of the developing interest among Moravians in the works of Paracelsus, Boehme and Swedenborg. Mary Lewis sold not only Swedenborg's works, but *A Compendious View of the Ground of the Teutonick Philosophy* (1770), which drew on the Kabbalistic, Paracelsan and Boehmenist views of John Pordage and the neo-Rosicrucians. Swedenborg's Moravian friend, Francis Okely, would also publish Boehme's works.

Given this sympathetic milieu on Great Queen Street, it is not surprising that Blake read works by Paracelsus and Boehme during his teen years (before 1776), and that he would write poems of 'sexual daring'. Gerald Bentley observes that 'their sexual suggestiveness is astonishing at a time when feminine limbs and passions were invisible and unmentionable'.[20] However, for an adolescent exposed to Moravian sermons, hymns and art, as well as the erotic alchemical imagery of Paracelsus and Boehme, such suggestiveness should not be surprising.

In 'To Spring', Blake expressed his theosophy of desire: 'all our longing eyes are turned / Up to thy bright pavilions'.[21] In passionate lines he appealed, 'O thou with dewy locks . . . Come o'er the eastern hills . . . scatter thy pearls / Upon our love-sick land.' According to Nelson Hilton, these lines suggest 'a correspondence between dew and other genital juices, semen especially'.[22] Portraying England as a yearning woman, Blake urged the seminal Spring to 'pour / Thy soft kisses on her bosom; and put / Thy golden crown upon her languish'd head'. Was he already aware of the Kabbalistic meaning of the Hebrew word for crown, *Atarah*, which signifies sexual consummation?

If, as Hilton suggests, Blake's luscious descriptions of vallies in another poem, 'To Summer', evoke the popular etymology, '*Vulva*, as it were *vallis*, a valley', then their call to ruddy, virile Summer completes the theme of *Atarah*: 'Throw thy / Silk draperies off, and rush into the stream: / Our vallies love the Summer in his pride.' In 'To Autumn', Blake proclaimed, 'Sing now the lusty song of fruits and flowers. / The narrow bud opens her beauties to / The sun, and love runs in her thrilling veins.'

Perhaps echoing Swedenborg, Blake hinted at the celestial significance of earthly love. In 'To the Evening Star', he called upon the 'fair hair'd angel of the evening' to 'Smile upon our evening bed! / Smile on our loves.' In the visionary song 'To Morning', the dreamer meets his maiden, whose angelic limbs are 'beaming with heavn'ly light' and who speaks with 'the voice of heaven'. To the two lovers, 'nothing impure comes near'. Like the young Cosway, who took Swedenborg's approval of pre-marital 'pellicacy' as a rationale for happy promiscuity, Blake rejoiced in his roving freedom, but he also recognised that 'the prince of love' could shut him in the 'golden cage' of matrimony and mock his 'loss of liberty'.

Though these poems certainly reeked of 'sexual suggestiveness', Blake was probably aware of the even greater liberty taken by Cosway in his obscene miniatures or, more intriguingly, by another artist with a Moravian background, James Gillray, who became England's most famous caricaturist. Through their parents' Moravian association, Blake and Gillray could have met early in life, and Blake later followed his career carefully.[23] Gillray was born in 1756 near Lindsey House in Chelsea, where his father served as sexton of the

Moravian burial plot. His parents participated in the Congregation during the same period as Catherine and Thomas Armitage and John Blake.[24] The Gillrays remained active in Congregation affairs for the next forty-five years, and they hoped to raise their children according to Zinzendorf's notions of education.

In 1762–4 their son James was sent to the Moravian boarding school at Bedford and probably next to one at Fulneck, where he received a high-level, 'European' education. In a surprisingly inaccurate account, Richard Godfrey, curator of the great Gillray exhibition at London's Tate Britain (2001), described Moravianism thusly: 'The Moravians were an austere and unattractive religious sect. They deplored all joy and pleasure. They continually contemplated death . . . Their children were forbidden all games.'[25] Noting that Gillray was surely 'marked by the grim nature of his upbringing', Godfrey admits that we cannot be certain of his education, 'but it was sufficient to produce a very literate and intelligent man'. Though he was, from childhood, set on a career as an artist, 'the nature of his background precluded entry into the profession in any elevated manner'.

Given such a distorted perception of Moravianism, it is small wonder that Gillray scholars seem puzzled by the precocity of his artistic commitment and the sexually explicit nature of his early drawings. After a rebellious adolescence, Gillray returned to his parents' home, lived there until 1793 and supported Moravian activities.[26] Thus he must not have sensed any contradiction between their reverence for the erotically wounded God-Man and his graphically sensual portrayals of the human body. In early unsigned etchings, he uninhibitedly displayed 'perverse scenes in and around brothels', such as a whore examining her private parts in a mirror held by her bawd, while the bedposts are constructed of stacked penises. In voyeuristic plates that were later suppressed, he used much excremental and phallic imagery.[27]

However, Gillray also used his obscene pictures to hint at his Moravian concern about the current degradation of Jesus's sacrificial wounds. In a disturbing print, 'Love in a Coffin', he portrayed Death holding a broken (phallic) spear, while he clutches and laughs at the wound in his side, in 'an unmistakeable reference' to Christ's final side-wound.[28] While an adulterous couple make love in a coffin, an inscription reads, 'Here lies Stella after coition, in hope of bodily resurrection.' For the disenchanted Gillray, there was evidently no room in the salvific side-hole for such corrupt worldly lovers.

From Moravian artists, especially Haidt, Gillray gained an ardent admiration for 'high Baroque excesses of movement and form', while 'the constraints of reproductive engraving may be seen as a barrier against which his creative energy pushed and shoved until it burst into a torrent of innovation and vitality'.[29] Godfrey observes that the only artist in Britain who could match Gillray's inventive powers was Blake, but he cannot imagine 'any meeting between the two as being anything but uncongenial'. Another Gillray scholar comments that Gillray and Blake were 'strange bedfellows in a category by themselves'.[30] However, one clue to their similarities is found in their mutual Moravian backgrounds, while another clue to their differences is revealed in Gillray's permanent bachelorhood and Blake's movement on to Swedenborgian 'conjugial love'.

In the last years of Blake's apprenticeship, he was a witness to the revolutionary developments within Ancient Freemasonry, which became dramatically visible on Great Queen Street. On 23 May 1776, the magnificent new Freemasons' Hall was dedicated with spectacular public parades and ceremonies. In an eloquent oration, Dr William Dodd stressed the roots of the fraternity in the ancient Jewish building guilds: 'We are told by the Jewish historian [Josephus] that "the foundation of Solomon's Temple was prodigiously deep".'[31] But, 'remote as this system is, we date not from thence the commencement of our art. For though it might owe to the wise and glorious King of Israel some of its mystic forms and hieroglyphic ceremonies, yet certainly the art itself is coeval with man.'

Dodd coyly hinted at the Kabbalistic mysteries reserved for high-degree initiates and noted that in Gothic times the Masonic builders 'took their ideas of symmetry from the human form divine'. In a performance of *Solomon's Temple, an Oratorio*, Uriel – the Angel of the Sun – sang: 'The Lord Supreme, Grand Master of the Skies! / Who bid creation from chaos rise, / Truths of Architecture engrav'd / On Adam's Heart.' This image of Uriel would later be echoed (and reinterpreted) in Blake's mythic figure of 'Urizen', his ambiguously portrayed Divine Architect.

Many foreign Masons attended the dedication of Freemasons' Hall, where in the prevailing atmosphere of fraternal unity the

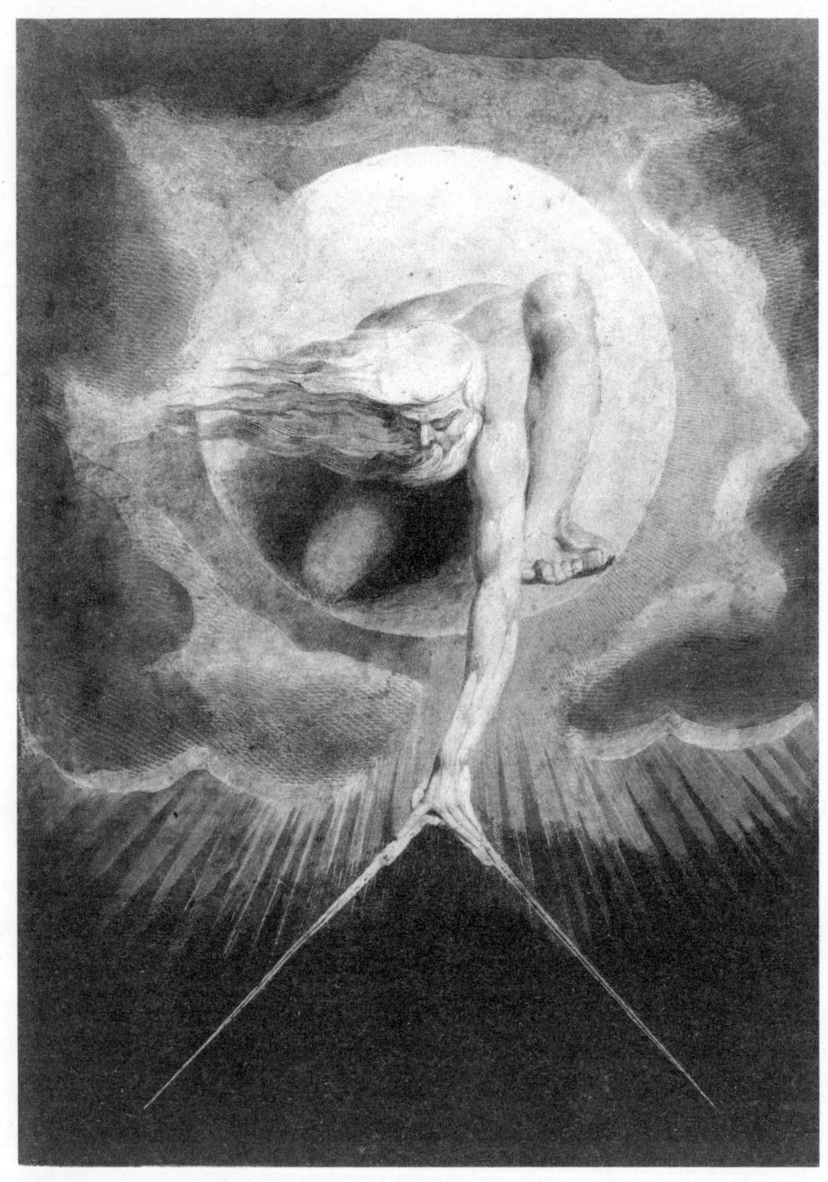

rivalries between Ancient and Modern systems were glossed over. Inspired by this apparent *bonhomie*, Dr Benedict Chastanier, founder of the *Illuminés Théosophes*, launched a secret Masonic organisation, 'The London Universal Society for the Promotion of the New Jerusalem Church', which had the public purpose of the 'Preservation of Baron Swedenborg's Posthumous Works'.

Chastanier vowed to do all he could 'to make these works as publicly known as possible', for he plainly saw that 'they brought the *very key of Salvation*, to a *Benighted World*'.[32] From his current work as a male-midwife, Chastanier came to see Swedenborg's spiritualised treatment of sexuality as the key to restoring the degraded body to its paradisal dignity. The politically liberal and religiously heterodox Freemasons (the *Illuminés*) who joined the Universal Society would play a significant role in the Swedenborg Society that William Blake and his wife Catherine joined in the 1780s.[33]

While living in Great Queen Street, the centre of London's Masonic world, the adolescent Blake shared the Universalists' millenarial views of the American Revolution. With the Declaration of Independence on 4 July, the political tensions within Masonry were reignited, for the Ancients tended to support the rebels and the Moderns the government. Like the *Illuminés*, Blake viewed the rebellion in terms of Paracelsan and Boehmenist theosophy. As he later recalled of this tumultuous period:

Paracelsus & Behmen appeared to me. Terrors appeard in the Heavens above
And in Hell beneath & mighty & awful change threatend the Earth
The American War began All its dark horrors passed before my face
Across the Atlantic to France.

Like Townley, Cosway and the frustrated Jacobites, he found spiritual refuge in the sexualisation of politics, a psychoerotic process that would soon move beyond the secretive Temple of Illuminist Masonry to the sensationally public Temple of Hymen, showplace for the 'Celestial Bed'.

13

The Celestial Bed

Such are the pleasures of performing the act of venery under the powerful influences of electric fire! – At the critical effort nature is like to spring up to the heavenly regions!
Dr James Graham, *The Art of Propagating* (1783)

WHEN BLAKE FINISHED his apprenticeship in 1779, he was accepted as an engraving student at the Royal Academy, where George Michael Moser (old friend of the Moravian artist Haidt) evaluated his work for admission. Blake soon found colleagues who shared his radical and enthusiastic views. James Gillray had recently returned to his Moravian home, after his brief 'bohemian' rebellion, and now studied engraving at the Academy. Besides Cosway, a Royal Academician since 1771, Blake met new friends who were interested in theosophical and Illuminist ideas, such as the sculptor John Flaxman, engraver William Sharp and painter Thomas Stothard, and he was probably aware of their liberal political sentiments and Masonic associations.[1]

More intriguing was Blake's probable meeting with Philippe Jacques de Loutherbourg, a French artist who had earlier studied under Francesco Casanova, brother of Giacomo, in Paris.[2] Though no evidence has yet turned up to prove that Blake knew Loutherbourg, their overlapping activities and interests make it seem certain. While working as a theatrical scene designer for David Garrick, Loutherbourg had the rare distinction of meeting both Swedenborg and Dr Falk. He painted Swedenborg's portrait from life, shortly before his death in London in 1772.[3] According to Stephen Lloyd, he also painted the great mystical portrait of Falk, which features Kabbalistic and Masonic symbols.[4] An early member of Chastanier's Universal Society, Loutherbourg now joined his friend Cosway in exploring the esoteric and erotic potential of conjugial love. They both collected works of occult sexology, while indulging in non-marital affairs, carrying out Swedenborgian-style 'pellicacy'. Blake and other Royal Academy students may have shared their esoteric-erotic interests. In 1779 Blake subscribed to Jacob Duché's *Discourses on Various Subjects* (1779), for which his friend William Sharp engraved a frontispiece that 'caused much remark at the time'.[5] The design showed male and female angels and thus 'correlates with a Swedenborgian doctrine – the existence of sex in heaven', which provoked both curiosity and embarrassment among readers. Sharp was not just an employee, for he arranged and paid for the printing, which suggests a close relationship with the author.

Duché was an Anglican minister and loyalist refugee from Pennsylvania, who had been attracted to Moravianism during a visit to London in 1762. On his return to America, he explored the Kabbalistic and Rosicrucian theories of the Ephrata community. An eclectic spiritual quester, he presented himself as 'a Mystic Divine, a Moravian, or any Thing to please various company'.[6] By the time of his move to London, he was a student of Boehme and his English interpreter William Law. He now added Swedenborgianism to his studies, probably under the influence of Sharp or other artists associated with his son, Thomas Spence Duché, a student of Benjamin West. Sharp and members of the Universal Society often gathered at Duché's Hampstead home to discuss Swedenborg and other mystical writers. If Blake joined them, then Duché's gatherings were perhaps the object of the long walks to Hampstead that Blake remembered taking in his youth.[7]

Though Duché had served as Chaplain of the Continental Congress, he feared that the Americans' rebellion would be crushed. When he indiscreetly warned against military action, he had to resign his position and leave the country. Nevertheless, he shared the apocalyptic sense of politics of his more radical friends in London. Blake similarly viewed the revolution as dangerous but believed it was worth the risk. In addition to his youthful poems of millenarian sexual desire, he referred to the political storms that rolled from America to England. In 'Gwin, King of Norway', he described a land desolated by a war-making Giant: 'He shook the hills, and in the clouds / The troubl'd banners wave. / Beneath them roll'd, like tempest black, /The num'rous sons of blood.'[8]

In an odd fragment, 'Then She Bore Pale Desire', Blake linked the oppressive sins of pride, greed and militarism to 'Self Love', the chief Swedenborgian sin because it prevents true conjugial love: 'Go See more strong the ties of marriage love. Thou Scarce Shall find but Self love Stands Between.'[9] For Blake, egotistic repression of sexuality leads to military suppression of liberty. He would later declare that 'The Roman pride is a sword of steel / Glory & Victory a phallic Whip.'[10]

The most radical public display of this linkage between sexual and political liberation was made by Dr James Graham, a Scottish physician and Ancient Mason, who advocated a new religion of 'pacifist sexology'.[11] In 1779, Graham moved into David Garrick's former residence in the Adelphi, which he transformed into the 'Templum Aesculapio Sacrum', initially known as the Temple of Health and then as the Temple of Hymen. Having studied electromagnetic therapy in Philadelphia and Paris, Graham assimilated it with Swedenborgian-style theories of conjugial love. In fact, he may have gleaned some of his ideas from Swedenborg's writings, for he later called himself a member of the 'New Jerusalem True Church'.[12] A staunch supporter of the American revolutionaries, Graham called for an end to government financing of wars, arguing that taxes should be spent to encourage early marriage, sexual potency and reproductive fertility.

Graham shared Swedenborg's belief that 'love for the holy' is expressed in the 'projection of the semen'. As Roy Porter explains, Graham believed in 'the sublime order of the spermatic economy', in which the 'exquisitely penetrating seminal liquor' was the elixir, the principle of vitality, almost the world soul.[13] During his lectures in the Temple of Hymen, the flamboyant doctor railed against masturbation, which was lethal because it wasted semen: 'Without a full tide of this rich, vivifying, luminous principle, continually circulating in every part of the system, it is absolutely impossible that either man or woman can enjoy health, strength, spirits or happiness.'

Echoing the basic Hermetic-Kabbalistic cosmology of the theosophers, Graham portrayed the world as a creature of an ambiguous nature, partaking of both sexes: 'The *higher* part of our system, namely, the Celestial, being active and *masculine*, the *lower*, or more gross *elementary* part, of the passive and *feminine* nature.'[14] When heaven and earth copulate, the cosmos is serenely in equilibrium. Sharing the visionary cosmology of Swedenborg, especially concerning the cosmic aether and auras, he argued that the male seed embodied the principle of vitality, in which 'the animating and vivifying powers of Nature all found expression in vital fluids, such as celestial fire, electricity, magnetism, and of course semen'.

As we shall see, the emerging Mesmerist movement, which based Animal Magnetism on similar fluidic theories, would soon claim Swedenborg as a precursor. Though Graham did not go as far as Swedenborg, who used Kabbalistic-Yogic techniques to transmute physical orgasm into visionary *nirvana*, he did affirm that proper regulation of the projection of the semen was the basis of 'celestial tranquillity of mind'.

Like the author of *Onania*, Graham admired the physical

vigour of the native Irish and Highlanders, but even more the American rebels – who supposedly did not indulge in masturbation, like the spoiled and effete English oppressors. Each of these young men was a hero, a Hercules, an angel, almost a God, 'in point of health, beauty, brilliancy, of body and mind; when compared to those poor creeping, tremulous, pale, spindle-shanked wretched creatures who crawl upon the earth, spiriting, dribbling, and drawing off alone'.[15] By infusing electromagnetic energy into his copulating couples, he hoped to propagate 'beings rational, and far stronger and more beautiful than the present, puny, feeble, nonsensical race of probationary mortals, which crawl, fret and politely play at cutting one another's throats for nothing at all, on all parts of the terraqueous globe'.[16]

In order to carry out his plan of pacifist sexology, Graham plastered London with advertisements inviting 'the Adepts! The Cognosenti! Et les Amateurs des delices ecquises de Venus' to his lectures on Health and Hymen. Within the grandiose, elaborately decorated Temple, he placed in the Holy of Holies a spectacular 'Celestial Bed', twelve feet by nine feet, which was infused with electromagnetic currents, perfumed with Oriental incense, rhythmically rocked to ethereal music, and decorated with paintings and sculptures of Cupid, Psyche and Hymen. For a mere £50 a night, a couple could prolong their sexual pleasure, turning the 'critical moment' into the 'critical hour' and could 'partake of the heavenly joys it affords by causing immediate conception'.[17] Stimulated by electric fire, 'all the organs of sensation are so exquisitely delighted, till at last they think they are no longer inhabitants of this earth, but of heaven'.[18]

Graham's dream was that his sexual therapy would usher in a new breed of men, who would turn from the arts of war to the arts of peace. He prayed that the children of those presently trained for war would be taught 'to ordain the sciences, embellish the arts, or to illuminate the human mind – instead of hewing down like savage monsters, their fellow creatures – or of eating up, like drones, the bread of children and industry'.[19] Blake would later express strikingly similar sentiments in his bitterly radical *Songs of Experience*.

Graham was not a mere quack, though certainly a showman, and he attracted 'the radical chic fringe of the *bon ton*', including imaginative artists, idealistic theosophers, anti-war activists and liberal politicians, such as Charles James Fox, who had the political support of the Blake family.[20] To the applause of many disaffected Londoners, an even greater political hero emerged from the 'adepts' of the Temple of Health, for the revolutionary Scottish pacifist Lord George Gordon was reportedly infused with the electrical energy of the Celestial Bed.[21] To his admirer William Blake, Gordon would soon represent Albion rising – the 'Glad Day' of political, spiritual and sexual liberation.

In June 1780, while Blake was living at home in Golden Square and attending classes at the Royal Academy, Gordon launched his peculiar but potent campaign against the Catholic Relief Bill, which he believed was aimed at the recruitment of Catholic Highlanders and Irish to fight against the American rebels.[22] After his election as President of the Protestant Association, Gordon led massive demonstrations against the Bill, which cloaked its militaristic aim under a pretence of religious toleration. When the protesters were joined by *agents provocateurs* and drunken looters, the peaceful demonstrations turned into violent riots, which threatened to engulf London and overthrow the government.

While many of the troops sympathised with Gordon and refused to fire on the rioters, Blake was swept into the crowd that marched on Newgate Prison, set it in flames and liberated 300 prisoners. As Blake's biographer Thomas Wright noted, 'these terrific scenes – the flaming houses and chapels and the occurrences at the

WB inv 1780

jail – affected him extraordinarily, and gave him ideas for many a startling print in *Europe*, *America* and other prophetic books'.[23] After Gordon's arrest and imprisonment in the Tower, which his supporters feared would end in his execution, Blake drew 'Glad Day' (1780), which he later engraved and inscribed, 'Albion rose from where he laboured at the Mill with Slaves / giving himself for the Nations he danc'd the dance of Eternal Death.'

David Erdman argues that in this drawing Blake referred to Gordon and his followers, who united into 'Albion the ancient Man' and rebelled against the despotic government; the image also had Swedenborgian overtones.[24] On a mountain top, arms in a gesture of tremendous energy and confidence, stands the 'naked multitude' portrayed as a single giant, in keeping with Blake's theory that 'Multitudes of Men in Harmony' appear 'as One Man'. Albion's facial expression 'must be read as that of one offering himself a living sacrifice', while his hair is twisted into 'flame-like points'. Provocatively, the portrait of Albion-Gordon could almost be a self-portrait of Blake, whose swirling locks of golden hair 'stood up like a curling flame, and looked at a distance like radiations'.[25]

During Gordon's eight months in the Tower, before his unexpected and startling acquittal by a London jury, his critics spread stories about his intense sensuality, prompting the quip that 'the Whore of Babylon is the only whore his Lordship dislikes'.[26] They charged that his 'over heated imagination' led to his religious fanaticism and cavorting with prostitutes.[27] Reports circulated about his electrification in the Celestial Bed, which was deemed indicative of his political role – electrified sex equalled electrified rebels. After many of the rioters were executed, Mrs Montague, 'Queen of the Blues', sardonically portrayed him as a lightning rod, who prevented infinitely more mischief than he had done: 'I look upon him as a political conductor, he has brought down the electrical matter that threatened our whole state, and buried under the Gallows what would have levelled our palaces and Senate Houses.'[28]

The 'flame-like points' of Albion's glowing hair perhaps referred to such electrification, which, when coupled with his proudly exposed genitals, suggests that Blake was aware of the Gordon-Graham connection. For the plugged-in adepts of the Celestial Bed, sexual energy was 'the litmus of bodily well-being', for 'the genitals are the true pulse and infallible barometer of health'.[29] Certainly, Blake's young Albion was not a 'pale, spindle-shanked' self-polluter, but a virile and vigorous embodiment of physical beauty and sexual health – what Graham envisioned as the revolutionary new Body Politic. As Blake would later proclaim, 'The head Sublime, the heart Pathos, the genitals Beauty.'[30]

Unfortunately, some visitors to the Royal Academy did not see the beauty of the genitals. In spring 1781, the 'venerable Keeper' George Michael Moser acquiesced to complaints about the explicit nakedness of the male statues. Blake's friend George Cumberland reported that 'an amputation of a most singular nature' was performed, and on each cast a 'plaister of fig-leaf was applied as a token, I suppose, of remorse'.[31] He expected soon to find the statues clad 'each in a pair of buckram trousers' – a form of sartorial censorship that would later be imposed on one of Blake's most sexually startling engravings.[32] Despite the 'ridiculous fig-leaves', Moser perhaps remembered his and Haidt's early advocacy for study of the naked body, when he 'apparently forgot to obscure a priapus'.

It is no wonder that Blake finished his student days at the Academy with a very low opinion of its policies: 'The Enquiry in England is not whether a Man has Talents & Genius, But whether he is Passive & Polite & a Virtuous Ass.'[33] Perhaps he had heard of Zinzendorf's frequent complaint – that those prudes who tried to suppress the erotic artistic expressions of the Moravians were determined to 'spiritually castrate them'.[34]

As electrified sex and politics fired Blake's imagination, he experienced at first hand the power of government to suppress the liberated artist. While enjoying a sketching and boating trip on the River Medway, Blake, Stothard and Parker were arrested and charged with being spies for the French, with whom England was at war.[35] They appealed to members of the Royal Academy to vouch for their loyalty, and – ironically – it was probably the castrating Keeper, Moser, who secured their release. Despite this help, Blake was relieved to finish his studies at the Academy and turn his attention to more serious matters – the search for an ideal wife. It was time to send the electrical charge from his own conjugal bed to the celestial bed above.

14

The Temple of Hymen

Hail Matrimony made of Love . . .
The Universal Poultice this
To cure whatever is amiss
In Damsel or in Widow gay
It makes them smile it makes them skip
Like birds just cured of the pip.

William Blake, *An Island in the Moon* (c.1786)

THOUGH LOUTHERBOURG, COSWAY and Blake enjoyed their pre-marital roaming and expressed their joy in youthful sensuality, all three looked for the ideal bride of Swedenborg's conjugial love. Loutherbourg was the first to commit, in May 1774, when he married Lucy Paget, known as 'the most beautiful woman in the kingdom'.[1] He now reformed the promiscuous ways of his first French marriage and left behind his adulterous escapades in the Parisian studio of Francesco Casanova. However, he did not abandon the esoteric-erotic studies that had attracted him to the Kabbalistic teachings of Swedenborg and, allegedly, Falk.

Like the more mystical Masons, especially those in the Rite of Heredom, Loutherbourg combined symbolic dramas of initiation with magical and visionary scenes.[2] His technical and talismanic skills were put to full use in December 1781, when the enormously wealthy connoisseur and pederast William Beckford invited the Loutherbourgs to stage a three-day ritualistic and magical celebration of his twenty-first birthday at Fonthill, his fantastic country estate. The couple produced a sensual orgy of theatrical and artistic effects that astonished the host and his intoxicated guests, a motley crew of closet homosexuals and lascivious nymphs.

An aged Beckford later remembered 'the delight into which our young and fervid bosoms were cast by such a combination of seductive influences'.[3] Chilled by age, he still felt 'warmed and irradiated by the recollections of the strange, necromantic light which Loutherbourg had thrown over what absolutely appeared a realm of Fairy, or rather, perhaps a Demon Temple deep beneath the earth set apart for tremendous mysteries.' Beckford immediately began writing his Gothic romance, *Vathek*, 'thoroughly embued with all that passed at Fonthill during this voluptuous festival'. It was probably Loutherbourg who stimulated Beckford's interest in Swedenborg's works, for the eccentric youth soon acquired several English and foreign editions.[4]

Both Beckford and Loutherbourg were friendly with 'Dicky Cosway', who was the next to abandon his roving ways and take the conjugal plunge. In January 1781, he married the much younger Maria Hadfield, daughter of a Catholic-Jacobite refugee from Manchester, who had moved to Italy. It was apparently Charles Townley who introduced Miss Hadfield, a talented artist and musician, to Cosway, for he had befriended the family in Florence and gave her away at the wedding.[5] This connection with Townley's antiquarian circle, who maintained 'a dual passion for Venuses living and dead', meant that the couple's conjugal happiness would be severely tested.[6]

After keeping Maria isolated in order to train her in the expected social graces, Dicky launched his wife into the world of the *bon ton*, and they soon became London's most celebrated artistic couple. And, according to rumour, they became adepts of Dr Graham's new Temple of Hymen. Cosway had attended Graham's Temple of Health in the Adelphi, and in 1780 he painted an erotic miniature of Emma Hart, the nubile sixteen-year-old whom Graham featured as 'Hebe Vestina, the Rosy Goddess of Health'.[7] A former prostitute (by the age of thirteen), the beautiful Emma proved so attractive that Graham moved into larger quarters in Schomberg House in Pall Mall in 1781. Two years later, when Graham was driven out of London, the Cosways moved into his former premises in Pall Mall, where they reportedly kept the Celestial Bed.[8]

The most successful, but least predictable, nuptial tie was instigated by Blake in summer 1781 when, on the rebound from rejection, he impulsively proposed to a pretty but illiterate servant girl, the nineteen-year-old Catherine Sophia Boucher.[9] Blake had been so heart-broken over the rejection of his romantic overtures to the flirtatious Polly Wood that he became ill and moved to the home of William Boucher, a market-gardener in Kew, 'for a change of air and renovation of health and spirits'.[10] Perhaps he was advised to do so by Cosway, who had studied Jacques Ferrand's *Erotomania, or a Treatise on Love-Sickness* (1640), which warned that sexual frustration and melancholy could lead to states of fury, hysteria and mania.[11]

In an 1832 manuscript, Frederick Tatham recorded a sentimental version of Blake's cure at the Boucher residence:

> *He was relating to the daughter, a girl named Catherine, the lamentable story of Polly Wood, his implacable Lass, upon which Catherine expressed her deep sympathy, it is supposed, in such a tender & affectionate manner, that it quite won him, he immediately said with the suddenness peculiar to him 'Do you pity me?' 'Yes indeed I do' answered she. 'Then I love you' said he again. Such was their courtship.*[12]

Tatham gave not only a romantic but a mystic tone to their meeting, claiming that when Blake first came into the room,

Catherine 'instantly recognised (like Britomart in Merlin's wondrous glass) her future partner & was so near to fainting that she left his presence until she had recovered'. Having 'recruited his health & spirits', Blake returned to Golden Square and did not see Catherine for a year, while he earned the money to make their union possible.

At that time, Catherine was a slender, dark-eyed, 'blooming' beauty, and he must have been impressed that she shared not only the forename of his mother and sister, but the middle name (Sophia) of Boehme's figure of theosophical wisdom. Dr Graham was also enamoured of the divine Sophia, who was present when God created the world and to whom the great lover Solomon dedicated 'his sublime description of Wisdom'.[13] Perhaps Blake saw the earthly Catherine Sophia through 'Merlin's wondrous glass'.

Finally, on 18 August 1782, the young couple married in the parish church of Battersea. As Tatham rapturously summed up, 'Nimble with joy & warm with the glow of youth, this bride was presented to her noble bridegroom. The morning of their married life was bright as the noon of their devoted love, The noon as clear as the serene Evening of their mutual equanimity.' Though Blake's father was greatly disappointed at his son's choice of an illiterate servant girl, he eventually accepted the match. The new couple took up residence at 23 Green Street, Leicester Square, and their simple home was soon filled with ambitious dreams of conjugial love and visionary art.

Over the next decade, the marriages of Loutherbourg, Cosway and Blake would be imbued with Swedenborgian, Kabbalistic and Grahamian spiritual-sexual ideals, and the attempt to put them into practice would produce exhilarating, turbulent and sometimes dangerous experiences. For all three artists, Dr Graham's pronouncements in the Temple of Hymen gave public utterance to a terrestrial version of Swedenborg's celestial sex. Like his Swedish predecessor, who believed that finding the right soulmate was the most important task on earth (or, if necessary, in heaven), Graham argued that the wisdom of the species made sex ecstatic, but only when enjoyed under healthful circumstances, within matrimony.

As Roy Porter observes, Graham wanted easy and early marriage, saw household activities as 'a kind of perpetual fore-play', and gave intimate advice to 'exalt and prolong the pleasure of the marriage bed'.[14] Surely Zinzendorf would have approved of such teachings, for his Moravians drew pictures of household chores taking place within the emblematic vulva. Like Graham, Swedenborg lamented the conditions that prevented early marriage, but he allowed the bachelor to use a prostitute or keep a mistress, so long as the ultimate goal was conjugial love. The more practical Scot called for changes in the tax laws and a ban on prostitution to avoid such semen-wasting practices.

The location of Graham's new Temple of Hymen in Pall Mall – a mansion divided into artists' homes and studios – placed him at the centre of London's artistic milieu, and it seems certain that Blake was aware of his popular lectures. While the guardians of artistic morality at the Royal Society covered the genitals of classical sculpture, Graham extolled the benefits of sexually explicit art. Couples should have 'their passions aroused and excited by the sight of rich, warm, or what are called lascivious prints, statues and paintings'.[15]

Determined to expand his audience to more affluent and respectable females, Graham enhanced the role of Emma Hart, who had posed nude for the life classes at the Royal Academy.[16] Now appearing merely half-naked, draped in pearls and undulating to the magnetic rhythms of the Temple orchestra, the Rosy Goddess delivered lectures 'whose precepts are so rational, whose language so chaste, and whose delivery so admirable' that ladies of the 'nicest delicacy' flock to hear 'the *warm effusions of a female soul*'.[17] Blake's close friend George Romney became so infatuated with Emma that he regularly attended her performances and began the obsessive painting of her portraits that he continued for decades.[18]

Graham soon faced a formidable rival, Dr Gustavus Katterfelto, another electromagnetising Freemason, who claimed to have demonstrated his therapeutic arcana before Grand Lodges all over Europe and the British Isles.[19] Katterfelto used electrified cats and giant microscopes during his 'scientific' shows, which led the racy tabloid *Rambler's Magazine* to comically compare him to Graham. 'The Hymeneal Doctor' had acquired a tabby cat, 'famous for her electrical powers, as well as the enormous size of her *tail*, as far superior to the *Katterfeltonian black cat*, as the *celestial bed* is to the solar microscope'.[20] Palmer Brown argues that Blake was familiar with Katterfelto's exhibitions, which influenced his portrayal of the eccentric scientists in *An Island in the Moon*.[21]

In Emma Hart, Graham still possessed the most popular attraction. To compete with the Rosy Goddess, Katterfelto dressed his daughter in a huge steel helmet, with leather straps under her armpits, and raised her to the ceiling by 'the attractive power of a single magnet'. The cartoonists had a field day with satirical prints on the electromagnetic battle between Graham and Katterfelto. One wicked print, published anonymously by Gillray's employer William Humphrey, showed both showmen astride giant phallic rods, marked 'Largest in the World' and 'Positively Charged'.[22] The barrage of ridicule took its toll, and Graham was forced to close his Temple at Pall Mall in summer 1783. Taking some of his equipment (but not the Celestial Bed) to Edinburgh, he was imprisoned in August for publishing 'lascivious and indecent advertisements' and delivering 'wanton lectures'.

For readers of Swedenborg, the attacks on Graham were instructive, for they paralleled those of John Wesley on their author, whom Wesley had earlier admired but now scorned.

In a pattern similar to his initial respect for and then vilification of Zinzendorf, Wesley used his *Arminian Magazine* in 1783–4 to portray Swedenborg as a lunatic, who 'ran stark naked, rolled in the mire, and proclaimed himself the Messiah'.[23] Even worse, 'that filthy dreamer' perverted the commandment against adultery and portrayed a sensual Islamicised heaven. Calling Swedenborg 'this highly *illuminated* author', Wesley lumped him with the irrational enthusiasts who spouted Boehme's turgid Teutonic themes and the reckless libertines who flocked to Graham's lectures.

Charles Frederick Nordenskjöld, a visiting Swedish *Illuminé*, had heard from his English correspondents in the Universal Society about Graham's Temple of Hymen. However, when he arrived in London in December 1783, he learned about the negative campaigns against the doctor, which belied English claims to be the land of liberty. Nordenskjöld was curious about the alleged similarities between Boehme, Swedenborg and Graham, so he immediately called on 'the hymeneal doctor', who had just returned to London from his imprisonment in

Edinburgh. In January 1784, Nordenskjöld sent a report to his fellow *Illuminé*, Charles Bernard Wadström, in Stockholm:

> *Dr Graham, who lives in Pall Mall, shows the 'celestial bed', and has an excellent electrical apparatus . . . I paid a visit to this king of charlatans . . . in the beginning he made much noise and gained many followers and much money. At that time he kept the finest equipage in the whole city, and all thought that Doctor Graham was so great a physiognomist that he saw into the heart of every Englishman.*[24]

Though Nordenskjöld suspected Graham of 'chicanery', he was also struck by the doctor's theory of correspondences, which was strikingly similar to Swedenborg's. In one pamphlet given to his Swedish visitor, Graham stressed the 'analogy which universally and certainly subsists between *natural* and *supernatural* things'.[25] In the natural, moral and intellectual worlds, there is a 'most harmonious analogy, relation, connection in and between each and every being and thing in the Universe from GOD HIMSELF!!!' After chastising the corruption and brutality of repressive Church and State, Graham promised his reader that, after death, the soul will progress through celestial worlds 'from pleasure to delights, from delights to raptures!, from raptures to extacies!!'

Nordenskjöld also became acquainted with Richard Cosway, who moved into Graham's former quarters in Pall Mall in early 1784 and reportedly purchased the Celestial Bed. As one journalist slyly asked, 'Why does Mr Cosway still retain over his house the insignia of Dr Graham?'[26] Nordenskjöld met the artist at secret meetings of the Universal Society and described him as 'Mr Cosway, Painter in History'.[27] Over the past two years, Chastanier had expanded the society's membership by appealing to 'the Elite among Alchemists, Kabbalists and Freemasons, and all students of the occult sciences'.[28] On

1 April 1783, Chastanier placed an advertisement in the *Courier de l'Europe: Gazette Ango-Française*, which appealed to new readers and which clearly linked the London society with Masonic lodges at Stockholm, Paris, Avignon and Berlin.

According to Chastanier's published *Plan*, the Swedenborgian *Illuminés* would lead initiates through hierarchical grades of esoteric learning, which replicate 'the human form'. He especially appealed to artists to join, for they would study the symbolic arts in their highest expression.[29] A Swedish journal reported that many artists responded, who evidently included Philippe Jacques de Loutherbourg, William Sharp, Thomas Spence Duché and possibly William Blake, whose name may be lost in the 'etc., etc. etc.' on Nordenskjöld's list of readers of Swedenborg.

Nordenskjöld brought to the Universalists many of Swedenborg's unpublished manuscripts, including sexually explicit excerpts from the *Spiritual Diary* and *Apocalypsis Explicata*. As the son of Finnish Moravian parents and nephew of a Rosicrucian alchemist, Charles Frederick and his brother Augustus Nordenskjöld fully accepted the most esoteric and erotic of Swedenborg's visionary teachings.[30] As we shall see, their advocacy of concubinage and eternal virile potency would later set off a firestorm in the Swedenborg Society that William and Catherine Blake attended – and would provide some answers to 'why Mrs Blake cried'.

Though the Universal Society functioned secretly, the printer Robert Hindmarsh decided to form a more public organisation, the 'Theosophical Society', which would publish Swedenborg's works and target a larger reading audience. When Chastanier wrote about this development to his Illuminist colleagues in France, the Marquis de Thomé decided to visit London in early 1784 in order to observe both societies.[31] Since founding a Swedenborgian Masonic rite in Paris in 1773, Thomé had studied Kabbala with Dr Falk in 1776 and hosted Chastanier during a Parisian visit in 1783. He was currently investigating the popular rage for Animal Magnetism and aerostatic ballooning.

To his enthusiastic audience in London, the marquis held forth on his plans to launch a Swedenborgian balloon expedition to Africa. Inspired by Swedenborg's tributes to the spiritually and sexually potent Africans, he envisioned Illuminist colonies that would become 'Paradise Restored'. According to the passionate anti-slaver Nordenskjöld, who would later try to implement this African project, Thomé believed 'it will be the second Noah's Ark, which shall save the faithful from the frightful desolation soon to overcome Europe'.[32] He criticised Hindmarsh's Anglocentric plans for the Theosophical Society but supported the Universalist agenda. Though the Frenchman's haughty ways and unembarrassed enjoyment of his mistress annoyed some of the English Swedenborgians, the *Illuminés* recognised that their Master gave permission for such 'well-ordered fornication'.

Another visitor to the Universal Society was James Glen, a Scottish-born planter from Demerara, who was so inspired by his experience that he took their publications to Philadelphia and Boston, where he lectured in June–July 1784 on the Swedenborgian science of hieroglyphics and its preservation in 'the Modern Freemasonry'.[33] Glen's practice of walking naked through the Guyanan jungles during his Swedenborgian missionary efforts will throw an interesting perspective on the Blakes' nudist interludes in their own Edenic garden.

Unlike the lodges of Modern English Masonry, the Universalists allowed women to participate in their meetings. If the Blakes joined them, the mystically eclectic and multinational make-up of this Swedenborgian sub-culture provides a new background for the theosophical and millenarian themes expressed in William's poetry and designs. From his publication of *Poetical Sketches* (1783) to his drafting of *An Island in the*

Moon (*c*.1786), Blake and his wife Catherine seemed to respond to the electrifying currents surging from the Continent to England.[34] Like Dr Graham's electrical sex therapy in the Temple of Hymen, Blake would portray 'Matrimony made of Love' as the 'Universal Poultice', which will 'cure whatever is amiss / In Damsel or in Widow Gay'.[35]

15

Merry Making and Edifying Discourses

In the Moon, is a certain Island near by a mighty Continent, which small island seems to have some affinity to England & what is more extraordinary . . . you would think you was among your friends.

William Blake, *An Island in the Moon* (*c.*1786)

SOON AFTER THEIR marriage, the Blakes were invited by John Flaxman to attend the social gatherings held by the Anglican minister Anthony Stephen Mathew and his wife Harriet, where the guests recited poetry, sang their musical compositions and discussed art and philosophy. At Flaxman's urging, the Mathews sponsored the printing of William's youthful poetry, *Poetical Sketches* (1783), which first introduced him to the literary world. Though the rather insipid nature of the Mathews' gatherings has led to doubts about their importance to Blake, some evidence suggests that they were interested in Moravianism and Swedenborgianism.[1] Thus, besides hosting their own *conversaziones*, they may have attended similar meetings in other homes, where a variety of mystics, philosophers, artists and musicians were discussed.

It has long been believed that the Blakes attended such gatherings at Jacob Duché's residence at the Lambeth Asylum for Female Orphans, where the Duché family moved in July 1782. Given Thomas Spence Duché's artistic, electromagnetic and Hermetic interests, these gatherings almost certainly included artists and occultists beyond those of the Mathews' coterie.[2] Such a context could explain the poems expressing Swedenborgian themes that Blake added to his adolescent poems of joyful sensuality in *Poetical Sketches*.

For example, in 'Samson', the narrator refers to Swedenborgian-style spirit-dictation, when he prays to the white-robed Angel to 'guide my timorous hand to write'.[3] In 'The Couch of Death', a dying youth overcomes his fears when 'a visionary hand wiped away his tears, and a ray of light beamed around his head', while angels gather round to take his joyful soul into eternity.

The bachelor Blake had feared that matrimony would lead to 'loss of liberty', but he recognised that 'Self love' (a central Swedenborgian term) too often stands between 'the ties of marriage love'. However, the husband Blake affirmed that 'Love and Harmony combine, / Around our souls intwine, / While thy branches mix with mine, / And our roots join together.' Was this a gloss on the Kabbalists' sephirotic tree and Swedenborg's conjugial love?

Blake acquired the second edition of Swedenborg's *Treatise Concerning Heaven and Hell*, published in 1784 with a subsidy from the Theosophical Society. Though critics have assumed that his annotations were not made until later, he could well have read the book in 1784,[4] Several of Blake's drawings of 1784–5 suggest his interest in Swedenborgian themes – such as 'The New Jerusalem Descending', 'Angels Gathered Around a Book' and 'A Number of Angels Instructing Children in the Spiritual World'.[5]

Probably in early 1786, Blake drafted *An Island in the Moon*, a light-hearted burlesque on the high-minded gathering of his friends, 'this improving company', who combined 'merry making' with 'edifying discourses'.[6] He targeted a motley crew of artists and readers, whose shared theosophical and artistic interests brought them together in often fractious and comical combinations. Michael Phillips argues that Blake drew on Swedenborg's *Earths in the Universe* for his lunar locale, and it is relevant that Cosway owned the 1758 Latin edition.[7] Blake used as his mouthpiece the character 'Quid, the Cynic', who sings irreverently about conjugial love:

Hail Matrimony made of Love
To thy wide gates how great a drove
On purpose to be yok'd do come
Widows & maids & Youths also
That lightly trip on beautys toe
Or sit on beautys bum.

Hail fingerfooted lovely Creatures
The females of our human Natures
Formed to suckle all Mankind . . .[8]

At this time Chastanier had informed the Swedenborgians about the publication of an abbreviated French translation, *Traité curieux des charmes de l'Amour Conjugal dans ce monde, et dans l'autre* (1784), by Guyton de Morveau, an *Illuminé* known as 'Brumore'. The Universalists were anxious to publish a more correct English translation, and at their various domestic gatherings there were heated discussions about the French version and Swedenborg's controversial sexual theories.

Blake's opening lines suggest these links with and reverberations from France: 'In the moon, is a certain Island near by a mighty continent, which small island seems to have some affinity to England.'[9] When Quid sings his jaunty tribute to the 'Universal Poultice', which makes females 'skip / Like birds just cured of the pip', he offends a character called 'Little Scopprell', who responds indignantly, 'Go & be hanged . . . how can you have face to make game of Matrimony.' Scopprell, who displays his skills in musical composition, conducting and playing ('Your out of key . . . Rap Rap Rap / Fiddle, Fiddle, Fiddle'), was possibly based on the French composer and violinist Francis Barthelemon, an early Swedenborgian *Illuminé* who especially valued *Conjugial Love*.[10] Barthelemon is also a candidate for one of the 'musical professors' who wrote down musical notations for Blake's songs.

In Quid's ribald lyrics, which urge maidens and swains to 'be eased of all your pains / In Matrimony's golden cage', Blake was possibly influenced by the popular satiric comedy on Graham's Temple of Hymen, *The Genius of Nonsense: A Speaking Pantomime*, by George Colman. Blake's friend Isaac Reed, who received a copy of *Poetical Sketches*, had attended Graham's lectures, and he enjoyed Colman's satire so much that he saw it repeatedly.[11] Reed's description of the comedy could almost be applied to Blake's bantering style in *An Island*. Describing *The Genius of Nonsense* as 'this original, whimsical, operatical, pantomimical, farcical, electrical, local extravaganza', Reed noted that the dialogue, which mimicked 'the Emperor of the Quacks (the noted Dr Graham)', may be said 'to comprise the whole extent of an ancient gossip's conversation, viz., a string of questions, with an insipid remark at the end of them', punctuated by giddy 'catches sung by Dame Turton, Goody Burton and Gammer Durton'.

A combined Swedenborgian–Grahamian background is further suggested by Blake's allusions to the *soirées* now held by the Cosways in Graham's former residence in Pall Mall, which still featured the advertisements for the Temple of Hymen. At this time Cosway was receiving lavish commissions from the rakish Prince of Wales, which made him the target of envious attacks by less fortunate artists and journalists.[12] Scandalised critics charged that the prince had a passageway made for Cosway from Pall Mall to the royal residence at Carlton House, so that the artist could act as a 'Pandarus'. Satirists such as John Wolcot ('Peter Pindar') claimed that Cosway went 'whoring after praise' and sexually exploited his wife's charms: 'he has got her engraved in a wanton attitude for the amusement of every ragged rascal in the metropolis'.[13]

John Williams ('Anthony Pasquin') further hinted that Cosway, 'Tiny Cosmetic', was complaisant to a liaison between Maria and the prince. Noting that the 'macaroni painter' had gone into 'a partnership with his master', Williams portrayed Cosway boasting to his friends that 'the Prince, you must know, adores Maria', who 'is a damned fine woman'.[14] The heir apparent was drawing in the same room with 'my dear angelic Maria', who was painting a design of the Gordon Riots: 'but the Prince not giving Maria entire satisfaction by his performance, what does Maria do, but lay hold of the Prince's *hair pencil*'.[15] He then 'catches my wife's *brush!* ha! ha! Ha! – though it was covered with hog's hair, as stiff as the beard of a Jew Rabbi, and as black as my hat'.

Always alert to the latest gossip, Williams apparently learned that the Prince of Wales had recently been elected to 'The Beggars' Benison', whose members solemnly intoned the blessing, 'May Prick nor Purse never fail you.'[16] Certainly, the Scottish sex club's emphasis on maintaining a rigid 'hair pencil' would make the prince and Maria even greater satirical targets. Despite their mockery, both Wolcot and Williams recognised Cosway's many good points and praised his generous efforts to help other artists. In Blake's comical allusions to the Cosways, he similarly combined satire with praise, for Richard was indeed a generous friend and included the young couple in his glittering parties. In *An Island in the Moon*, the character 'Miss Gittipin' becomes fed up with the men's philosophising and complains that she 'might as well be in a nunnery', except when she goes to the home of 'Mr Jacko', the name given to Cosway by the satirists because of his resemblance to the circus monkey Jacko:

> *I hardly know what a coach is, except when I go to Mr Jacko's, he knows what riding is & his wife is the most agreeable woman . . . and I do believe he'll go in partnership with his master . . . he says he has Six & twenty rooms in his house, and I believe it & he is not such a liar as Quid thinks he is* [but he is always Envying]. *Poo poo hold your tongue hold your tongue, said the Lawgiver.*[17]

The 'Lawgiver', modelled on the pious Swedenborgian John Flaxman, was friendly with the Cosways and discounted the slanderous gossip about them. From Blake's sly allusions to the sexual-monetary 'partnership' and 'riding', it is clear that he was familiar with the satirical accounts. Though he and Catherine were jealous of the golden guineas showering on Cosway, he admitted that his mouthpiece Quid 'was always envying'. At this time the Blakes naively hoped to make hundreds of thousands of pounds from his new method of 'illuminated printing', so they welcomed the chance to meet wealthy patrons at the Cosways' ebullient parties.

Another of Blake's Islanders, 'Etruscan Column the Antiquarian', was modelled on a regular attendee at Graham's Temple of Hymen – the love-besotten George Romney.[18] The artist became interested in Etruscan antiquities when living in Italy in the 1770s, but his infatuation with Emma Hart transformed that interest into a jealous obsession. Blake had probably met Emma when she posed at the Royal Academy, for the character 'Mrs Gimblet' seems a wickedly amusing portrayal of her self-centred relationship with Romney.

After leaving Dr Graham's employment and being cast off by her next 'protector', Sir Harry Fetherstonhaugh, the pregnant Emma gained more access to artistic circles in 1782, when she became the mistress of the antiquarian collector Charles Greville. The insensitive Greville cavalierly commissioned her portrait by the miserable Romney, who in 1784 drew the two in company with Blake's friend William Hayley.[19] In 1785 Greville made a stir in the art world when he published Francesco Bartolozzi's fine engraving of the Etruscan 'Barberini' vase, recently brought to England by his uncle, Sir William Hamilton. Greville believed that the mysterious scenes in bas relief portrayed fertility rituals, such as the death and resurrection of Adonis.[20] He and Emma must have been amused at Hamilton's other prizes – sets of phallic 'toes' (wax votives) and erotic Greek drawings.

For the morbidly sensitive and painfully shy Romney, to have Emma in the company of these 'Etruscan' hedonists seemed intolerable, especially since Greville was making arrangements with Hamilton to take Emma off his hands. It was a mercenary trade that deeply offended Romney and depressed the no-longer rosy Goddess. In real life, Emma took for granted Romney's devotion, while in *An Island* the diffident 'Etruscan Column' seems unaware of the female vanity that keeps 'Mrs Gimblet' from even noticing his artistic ambitions. 'Well she seated & seemd to listen with great attention while the Antiquarian seemd to be talking of virtuous cats' (that is, the virtuoso casts studied by artists), but 'it was not so, she was thinking of the shape of her eyes & mouth and he was thinking of his eternal fame'.[21]

Like the bartered-for Emma, Blake's Islander takes to the bottle: 'Mrs Gimblet came in [tipsy – *deleted*]. The corners of her mouth seem'd . . . as if she hoped you had not an ill opinion of her.' But Quid's song only reinforces her discomfort:

Little Phebus came strutting in
With his fat belly & his round chin
What is it you would please to have

Ho Ho
I wont let it go at only so & so
Mrs Gimblet lookd as if they meant her.[22]

By March 1786, Emma Hart was on her way to Italy with her purchaser Hamilton, leaving a bereft Romney behind. She would eventually enjoy revenge on her mockers, when she became the famous Lady Hamilton and mistress of Lord Nelson. We will return to Greville, Hamilton and their circle of randy antiquarians when their influence emerges in Blake's works of the 1790s.

In the character of 'Inflammable Gass the Windfinder', Blake seemed to portray another observer of Graham's Temple of Hymen, the flamboyant French artist Loutherbourg, who was running a rival show at his residence on Lisle Street, Leicester Square. The Blakes had been close neighbours in 1782–4, when they lived at 23 Green Street, just off Leicester Square, and they must have been aware of Loutherbourg's popular exhibit – the 'Eidophusikon; or, Various Imitations of Natural Phenomena, represented by Moving Pictures'.[23] To construct and operate this six-by-eight-foot model theatre, Loutherbourg combined his innovations in illusionistic scene design with his Hermetic experiments – sulphureous clouds, phosphorescent rays, painted transparencies, magic lanterns, glass harmonicas, etc. – to produce spectacular light and sound effects.[24] The whole London art world flocked to the Eidophusikon, and Loutherbourg's commercial success became the envy of other artists.

In early 1786, Loutherbourg hired a manager for the Eidophusikon and moved to Hammersmith, where he and his wife Lucy plunged into alchemical, electrical and magnetic experiments.[25] The couple saw themselves as reincarnations of the medieval alchemists Nicolas and Pernella Flamel, whose conjugal relationship engendered Hermetic illumination.

Though Blake's character 'Inflammable Gass' may be a *portmanteau* figure, who combines various occult scientists, many telling details suggest Loutherbourg as the primary inspiration. Inflammable Gass is a Francophile, who speaks with a foreign accent and who admires the inquiries into nature made by Voltaire and the *Philosophes*. Arguing that Voltaire 'found out a number of Queries in Philosophy', he rejects the criticism of 'Obtuse Angle' that 'Voltaire understood nothing of the mathematics'.[26] As a former protégé of Denis Diderot, Loutherbourg would have agreed with Inflammable that Voltaire was 'the glory of France'.

Changing the subject to the new sciences, Inflammable Gass declares, 'I have got a bottole of air that would spread a plague' and discourses for half an hour, before announcing that 'I have got a camera obscura at home.' Despite Quid's cynicism about the flamboyant showman-scientist, the Islanders happily flock to his house, where he shows off the full range of his experiments. After greeting the guests, his wife 'Gibble Gabble' says to her husband, 'Come Flammable . . . & lets enjoy ourselves bring the Puppets.'[27] Answering with a foreign accent (a kind of Germanic French suitable to Loutherbourg's origins in Strasbourg), Inflammable replies: 'Hay Hay, said he, you sho, why ya ya, how you be so foolish – Ha Ha Ha she calls the experiments puppets.' Then 'he went up stairs & loaded the maid, with glasses & brass tubes, & magic pictures.' Blake was evidently aware that the Eidophusikon was popularly viewed as a variety of puppet show, but as George Speight explains, 'No plays were performed and no puppets were used; the attraction of the exhibit was strictly pictorial.'[28]

The Swedenborgian musician Francis Barthelemon collaborated with Loutherbourg on theatrical productions and was familiar with his mania for experiments. Blake's character 'Little Scopprell' helps the Islanders, while they play with a microscope, slides and bottle of 'bog house' (privy) water. However, their boisterousness leads to disaster, and despite Gibble Gabble's help, they smear the slides with water and damage the air pump. An infuriated Inflammable breaks the glasses, pictures and 'bottles of wind & let out the pestilence'. Running from the room, he shouts, 'we are putrified, we are corrupted. Our lungs are destroyed with Flogiston.'[29] The other terrified Islanders tumble after him down the stairs 'in a heap'.

A similar story about the Loutherbourgs, with more alchemical detail and sexual innuendo, was later published by John Williams ('Pasquin'). In Loutherbourg's lab, 'he pondered, he floundered', until the good sense of a relative (his wife) saved him from local perdition. She burst upon his nocturnal studies when he was keenly watching a transmutation, 'in company with a *charlatan*, from the Lower Rhine':

> *The reddening fair caught them in the raging of the enchantment; when they were calcining* Venus *with the butter of the daughter of* Luna, *and fixing* Luna *herself into* Sol – *she broke his crucible to shivers, enfranchised the simmering metal, extinguished his fires, and seizing the forcepts, took his adult associate by the nose, and led him into the street, where the enraged lady broke his head with a urinal.*[30]

Blake could have drawn on Williams's portrayal of Loutherbourg in *The Royal Academicians: a Farce*, published in early 1786. In annotations to the text written 1 May 1786, Williams located the farce at 'Porridge Island' and identified 'Monsieur Lethimhumbug' as Loutherbourg, who speaks with a Franco-Germanic accent: 'me ver glad to see you – sur mon honneur . . . cot damn'.[31] Though Blake mocked the pseudo-scientific pretensions of Inflammable Gass, he also mocked his own envying nature. There was much to admire in

Loutherbourg, despite his commercial opportunism and financial success. Described as amiable, unpretentious and tolerant in private life, he would soon demonstrate his political courage by his support of persecuted radicals.

One final Islander to be discussed – 'Mr Femality' – provides a clue to the controversial question of dating Blake's manuscript, for the character was almost certainly based on the Chevalier d'Eon, the famous French transvestite, who became Blake's close neighbour when he/she arrived from Paris on 18 November 1785. The *bon ton* were immediately informed by *Rambler's* yellow pages that 'Mlle D'Eon, who is just arrived in England, is to be naturalised: after which she means to represent *Middlesex*' (a pun on the chevalier's ambiguous sex and Blake's voting district).[32] Blake and his wife would not have far to go to visit D'Eon, who resided at 38 Brewer Street, Golden Square, just a few blocks from the Blakes' current home at 28 Poland Street, Golden Square.[33]

After an exciting career as an espionage agent serving Louis XV's *Secret du Roi*, D'Eon was persecuted by political rivals who spread rumours about his sexuality (he had disguised himself as a woman in Russia).[34] When the new king Louis XVI forced him into handing over his secret diplomatic papers, he ordered the chevalier to wear female dress. As one of Europe's greatest swordsmen, with broad shoulders and muscular arms, D'Eon made a grotesque figure in his powdered wig, painted face, revealing bodice and voluminous petticoat. Mocked by the cartoonists, he found solace in Kabbalistic, Hermetic and Swedenborgian studies, which portrayed the Divine Human as androgynous, and in Freemasonry, which welcomed all varieties of men to universal brotherhood. However, he was disappointed to learn that Modern British Masons rejected him as a brother; unlike the *Écossais* and Illuminist Masons, they would not accept a sister, much less a brother/sister.[35]

The Assaut, or Fencing Match; which took place at Carlton House, on the 9th of April, 1787, between
Mademoiselle La Chevaliere D'EON DE BEAUMONT. and Monsieur DE SAINT GEORGE.
In the presence of His Royal Highness the Prince of Wales, Several of the Nobility & many eminent Fencing Masters of London.

On the last page of the *Island* manuscript, Blake referred to the visit of Quid and 'Mrs Nannicantipot' (Catherine Blake) to the salon of 'Mr Femality'. He also hinted at his efforts to educate and train his wife in literacy, drawing and engraving – based on his determination to have a truly conjugial union of minds as well as bodies. However, Catherine's lowly origins could not be completely disguised. At a previous gathering of Islanders, the self-righteous and pretentious 'Mrs Sigtagatist' (Mrs Mathew?) condescendingly insulted Quid's wife as an 'ignorant jade', which leads some critics to speculate that 'Blake's break with the Mathew clan resulted from his wife's unsophistication'.[36]

Optimistic and ambitious, Blake had great plans for his pliant wife, and he was sure that their new method of 'Illuminating the Manuscript' would make them wealthy.

However, when Quid boasts about their mutually high abilities, their acquaintances become 'eat up with envy'. Quid consoles his wife, Mrs Nannicantipot: 'My dear, they hate people who are of higher abilities than their nasty, filthy [souls – *deleted*] selves. But do you outface them & and then Strangers will see you have an opinion.' More importantly, at their next society party they should make their presence known to the guests (and potential customers). Quid then plots their strategy: 'I think we should do as much good as we can when we are at Mr Femality's do you snap & take me up – and I will fall into such a passion Ill hollow and stamp & frighten all the People & show them what truth is.'[37]

For the ambitious Quid and his wife, Mr Femality provided a stimulating and welcoming salon, where among the 'oysters and champagne, in the French style', the Cynic's vehement opinions and outrageous behaviour would appear *piquant* rather than truculent.[38] For the Blakes, invitations to D'Eon's glittering salon provided an entrée into a free-spirited, cosmopolitian, radical and often risqué company. Moreover, in D'Eon's great library – which contained rare editions of the *Zohar*, manuscripts on Hebrew rites and Kabbalistic magic, treatises on alchemy and Hermetic healing, and a unique collection on the rights of women – Blake gained access to many of the arcane symbols and antinomian themes that would emerge in his designs and poetry.[39]

In the 1790s, when D'Eon once again became Blake's neighbour in Lambeth, his mixed sexual nature seemed to provoke Blake's troubled preoccupation with hermaphroditism: 'Male form'd the demon mild, athletic force his shoulders spread / And his bright feet firm as a brazen altar', but also 'Female her bright form bright as the summer but parts of Love Male'.[40] Blake would long struggle with the cosmic and personal ramifications of the fragmentation of the God-Man into male and female emanations. Thus 'Mr Femality' posed an intriguing and perplexing theosophical problem: 'the two-fold form Hermaphroditic and the Double-sex'd / The Female-male and the Male-female.'[41] After D'Eon's death in 1810, the autopsy revealed that the 'male organs were perfectly formed', but the body had many feminine characteristics such as 'breast remarkably full' and 'unusual roundness in the formation of the limbs'.[42]

Though Blake seemed to welcome the freshening winds from France, his mockery of the pseudo-science of Inflammable Gass the Windfinder could not stop the powerful currents of electromagnetic forces flowing from the 'mighty continent'. Soon he and the Islanders would find the visionary science of Swedenborg merged with the experimental science of Animal Magnetism. It was a development that would positively charge and negatively shock his wife Catherine.

16

Animal Magnetism and the Furor Uterinus

The greater number of women who are magnetised are not really ill . . . their senses are not impaired . . . the visage fires by degrees, and the eyes light up with desire . . .

Report of the French Commission on Animal Magnetism (1784)

IN THE MONTHS before the Blakes attended D'Eon's soirées, they had undergone some trying times. After the death of Blake's father in 1784, his mother and brother James took over the Armitage-Blake family business and encouraged William and Catherine to move next door at 27 Broad Street.[1] With a small inheritance from his father, the young couple established a print shop in partnership with his fellow apprentice James Parker, who moved in with them. The shop proved a financial disappointment and was closed in autumn 1785, when the Blakes moved to 28 Poland Street. Nevertheless, Blake was happy in the daily companionship of his younger brother Robert, to whom he taught the art of engraving and printing. However, Robert's presence caused some friction in the marriage, predictive of future contests of the will between William and Catherine.

One day, when Catherine got into a heated disputation with Robert, William ordered her to 'Kneel down and get Robert's pardon directly, or you will never see my face again!' According to Gilchrist, 'Being a duteous, devoted wife, though nowise tame or dull of spirit, she *did* kneel down.'[2] Robert smoothed over the quarrel, but it would not be the last confrontation; as William would later write, the female, 'Once born for the sport & amusement of Man', is 'now born to drink up all his Powers'.[3]

From the surviving drawings of William and Robert, it is clear that they shared an interest in Druidic, Gothic and fairy lore.[4] They also seemed to play at spiritualistic communications and millenarial concerns. At this time William's drawings of supernatural figures were still staid, measured and classical – illustrating lines on 'the insubstantiality of vision'.[5] Then, in February 1787, Blake was deeply shaken by the illness of his brother, and he nursed him night and day until Robert's death. Gilchrist reported that Blake's 'visionary eyes beheld the released spirit ascend heavenward through the matter-of-fact ceiling, clapping its hands for joy'.[6] Until this traumatic event, Blake's personal vision had been unfocused, his execution hesitant. However, he soon benefited from the 'substantialised spiritualism' of Animal Magnetism to not only focus his vision but communicate with the spirit of Robert.

As Blake later told Crabb Robinson, all men partake of the 'faculty of Vision', but 'it is lost by not being cultivated'.[7] In the wake of Robert's death, Blake cultivated his own faculty until he visualised his dead brother and received instruction from his spirit on 'accomplishing the publication of his illustrated songs, without their being subjected to the expense of letter-press'.[8] This technological breakthrough by means of spirit-communication encouraged his further experiments in deliberate vision inducement. Soon 'Joseph, the sacred carpenter, appeared in a vision and revealed the secret of mixing and binding his colors. Apelles, the ancient Greek painter, revealed his system of coloring and praised Blake's mastery of it.' For the Swedenborgians, these technical visions would not be surprising, for certainly their master made similar claims about chemical and physiological discoveries.

But how did Blake 'cultivate' his visionary faculty, and how did he train his wife also to see visions? In 1907 Edwin Ellis wrote that 'we are forced into seeing that Blake, in his inspired moods, had the power of hypnotising himself – unless indeed other powers of spiritual nature, as he himself suspected, hypnotised him'.[9] Ellis was on the right track, but he was unaware of the actual historical context of developments in hypnotism – or Animal Magnetism, as it was called – in the 1780s. This exciting new 'science' was imported from France to England, where it was eagerly taken up by radical artists, Swedenborgians and Freemasons.

One reason why Dr Graham had to give up his Celestial Bed for the less dignified 'Earth Bath' (burial up to the neck in mud) was the growing competition from other electro-magnetising doctors. He was especially challenged by those who had travelled to Paris to learn the new techniques developed by the Viennese physician Franz Anton Mesmer, whose *séances* in Animal Magnetism were causing a sensation.[10] Though this psychosomatic therapy seems comical today, it played a cultural role similar in importance to Freudian and Jungian psychology in the twentieth century.

Drawing on Hermetic, Paracelsan and astrological theories of microcosmic man and the universal magnetic fluid, Mesmer modernised them by adding recent experimental discoveries in electricity and magnetism. With encouragement from the Mozart family, who shared his magnetic and Masonic interests, Mesmer made his psychotherapeutic sessions into a mystical initiation process that resulted in blissful, even orgasmic 'equilibrium'. When he moved on to Paris in 1778, he took advantage of the participation of aristocrats, intellectuals and amateur scientists in Masonic assemblies, including the ladies' 'androgynous' lodges.

Claiming to address the questions that Newton failed to answer, Mesmer presented Animal Magnetism as a new science that made room for religious impulses and placed man's body and spirit in a celestial world of gasses, currents and fluids. An enthusiastic J. H. Meister described this halcyon period in Paris: 'In all our gatherings, at all our suppers, at the toilettes of our lovely women, as in our academic lyceums, we talk of nothing but experiments, atmospheric air, inflammable gas, flying chariots, journeys in the air.'[11] It is not surprising that 'Inflammable Gass' Loutherbourg became an early student of the fashionable pseudo-science.

When would-be adepts gathered in Mesmeric temples, they formed a human chain around a large magnetic tub, which dispensed the fluid through movable iron rods and ropes, and waited with ardent expectation for the feel of the 'flow'. According to Mesmer, sickness resulted from an obstacle to the flow of the fluid through the body, which was analogous to the magnet: 'Individuals could control the fluid's action by "mesmerising" or massaging the body's "Poles" and thereby overcoming the obstacle, inducing a "crisis", often in the form of convulsions, and restoring health or "harmony" of man with nature.'[12]

Having studied the techniques of the Swabian exorcist Johann Gassner, Mesmer added psychological manipulation to his materialistic gadgetry. He and his followers learned to throw their patients into epileptic-like fits or ecstatic trances, which resembled those produced by Kabbalistic or Swedenborgian meditation techniques. His notion of the magnetic 'marriage' – in which the operator achieves *rapport* with the patient – struck a responsive chord among readers of Swedenborg. Rather than focusing on Hebrew letters and male and female emanations, the patient focused on the magnetiser's eyes, which produced hypnotic effects through the power of the 'magnetic gaze'.

As Barbara Stafford explains, the mass appeal of 'touching vision', its ability to 'exteriorise hidden desires and to compel enthusiasm', represented the zenith of the ancient tradition of 'fascination'.[13] Like Swedenborg's, 'this magical and talismanic medicine was grounded in a nature spun from immaterial correspondences invisibly shaping the material world'. Thus, an 'Inmost Spirit' situated in the fourth ventricle of the brain and also existing in the *anima mundi* emitted a plastic virtue. The term 'touching vision' was based on the combination of hypnotic gaze and strategic stroking, a practice made famous by the seventeenth-century Irish healer Greatrakes the Stroker.

As one witness observed, the Mesmerists sat with the patient's knees enclosed between their own and ran their fingers all over the patient's body, seeking the poles of the small magnets that composed the great magnet of the body as a whole: 'Most Mesmerists concentrated on the body's equator at the hypochondria, on the sides of the upper abdomen, where Mesmer located the upper sensorium.'[14] Not surprisingly, 'the practice stimulated gossip about sexual magnetism'. Mesmer took the term hypochondria from Paracelsus and J. B. Van Helmont, who called it the *Archaeus* and described it as 'a sort of demon presiding over the stomach', producing all the 'organic changes which take place within the corporeal frame'.[15] Lisebeth points out the striking similarities between Helmont's *Archaeus* and the Tantrists' 'organic overmind', which connects bodily organs with 'the appropriate mental imagery'.[16] Like the Tantrists, Helmont further claimed that by virtue of the *Archaeus*, man could be approximated to the realm of spirits.

Thus, in the trance state, the 'exalted sensibility' of the epigastric region transferred perception from the brain to the abdomen (including the erotically susceptible 'loins'). The magnetiser manipulated the transfer of sensibility from one organ to another, in order to clear the flow of lucidity (health) from obstruction (disease). As we shall see, when Blake learned these techniques, he similarly described – with vivid mythic overtones – 'the Four States of Humanity in its Repose':

The First State is in the Head, the Second is in the Heart:
The Third in the Loins & Seminal Vessels & the Fourth
In the Stomach & Intestines terrible, deadly, unutterable
And he whose Gates are opend in those Regions of the Body
Can from those Gates view all these wondrous Imaginations.[17]

For Blake, the principal regions of vision were Bowlahoola, 'the Stomach in every individual man', and Allamanda, 'the Loins & Seminal Vessels'. His strange physiology was entirely consistent with that of Animal Magnetism, especially in the Helmontian-Swedenborgian form later developed in London.

In the meantime in Paris, while increasing numbers of excited women flocked to Mesmer's sessions, the government and medical establishment became not only annoyed but alarmed. In 1784 an official commission, which included Benjamin Franklin, proclaimed the so-called science a fraud, based on the power of imagination and gullibility. In a secret appendix sent to Louis XVI, the investigators revealed their real concern. Claiming that most women who are magnetised are not really ill, they described the erotic titillation involved in the therapy.

The magnetiser has his patient's knees between his own, his hand is applied to the hypochondriac region, and 'sometimes over the ovaries'. Touch is exercised over the most sensitive parts of the body, causing the 'reciprocal action of the sexes' to act with all its force:

> *When this state of crisis approaches, the visage fires by degrees, and the eyes light up with desire . . . the eyelids become moist; the breathing hurried and irregular; the bosom heaves violently and rapidly, and convulsions and sudden twitchings take place in particular limbs, and sometimes over the body. In lively and sensitive women, the most agreeable termination of their emotions is often a convulsion.*[18]

When Blake later complained about his wife's resistance to his magnetic overtures, he remarked that 'The look of love alarms / Because tis filld with fire.'[19]

In the wake of the French government's crackdown, political radicals took up Mesmer's cause, claiming that he was persecuted by jealous and reactionary authorities, who wanted to keep this liberating new science out of the hands of 'the people'. Mesmer became so depressed by the barrage of attacks that he left Paris and travelled to England in August 1785, hoping to establish a Mesmeric Masonic lodge.[20] However, in September a rival magnetiser – Dr John Bonniot de Mainaduc – arrived from Paris and soon dominated the London scene.

LE DOIGT MAGIQUE

A frustrated Mesmer gave up and left for the Continent.

Mainaduc soon played an important role in Blake's artistic and Swedenborgian circles, and it seems likely that Blake knew him.[21] While Blake was a student at the Royal Academy, he studied anatomy under Drs John and William Hunter (he satirised John as 'Dr Tearguts' in an *Island in the Moon*). During the same period, Mainaduc studied medicine under the Hunters, before leaving for Paris to study Animal Magnetism. Though he was eventually rebuffed by Mesmer, he had learned enough to develop his own, more spiritualistic system. When Mainaduc launched his London campaign, he had the advantage of a ready-made clientele from his large midwifery practice and – more importantly – from his Masonic and Swedenborgian associates, who soon included several of Blake's friends and possibly Blake himself.

Probably informed by the Marquis de Thomé, who also attended Mesmer's sessions and who was currently in London, Mainaduc knew about the Swedenborgians' great interest in Animal Magnetism. Thomé brought with him a copy of his 'public letter' on Swedenborgianism and Mesmerism, which was published in the *Journal Encyclopédique* (September 1785). Chastanier, with whom he was staying, then reissued the full text in London. Thomé argued that Mesmer plagiarised Swedenborg and distorted his theories in ways that were 'vicious in point of morals, but also very dangerous in a physical respect'.[22]

This Swedenborgian attack on Mesmer must have impressed Mainaduc, for on 12 December 1785 he initiated Benedict Chastanier into 'this Modern Magical Science'.[23] The two knew each other from their mutual midwifery practice, but Mainaduc now profited from Chastanier's ability to link Swedenborg's 'divine influx' with the magnetic trance. Over the next ten months, Chastanier acted as Mainaduc's chief assistant at his lavish clinic in Bloomsbury Square, and he eventually opened his own clinic at 62 Tottenham Court Road.

Among the 270 paying customers listed by Mainaduc were more than a dozen Swedenborgians, who would play leading roles in the Swedenborg Society that the Blakes joined in 1789.[24] Also taking instruction were his artistic colleagues Maria and Richard Cosway, P. J. de Loutherbourg and William Sharp. They shared what they learned with Thomas Spence Duché as well as Blake's friends and fellow engravers Thomas Trotter and Thomas Holloway. Though Blake could not afford Mainaduc's high-priced course, he may have benefited from Chastanier's inexpensive lessons or from private tutelage by his friends.

An enthusiastic Cosway painted Mainaduc's portrait, which was later engraved for the posthumous publication of the doctor's lectures in 1798. From the revelations in those lectures, it is clear that he and Chastanier developed a form of Swedenborgian magnetism that exercised a powerful influence – for better or worse – on William and Catherine Blake. Through the clouds of magnetic miasma, we will begin to penetrate a turbulent atmosphere of sexual and visionary experimentation and start to learn 'why Mrs Blake cried'.

According to Mainaduc, the emanating atmosphere of the human body may, by the magnetiser's effort, 'be attracted from, or distended to, any unlimited distance'; it can then 'penetrate any form of nature'.[25] The magnetic healing occurs when, through the infuence of Volition (or Spirit), the emanations are forced out of their natural course or attracted into the pores of the Operator. The therapist is effective according to the Intention or Energy of his or her 'spiritual Volition'. Mainaduc instructed the Examiner to focus on some part of the patient's external or internal Form: 'then, turning the backs of his hands, with fingers a little bent, he must vigorously and steadily command the Emanations and Atmospheres, which derive from that part, to strike his hands, and most closely attend to whatever Impressions' are produced. Blake's subsequent descriptions of male and female emanations, which move in and out of swirling vortexes, suggest that he transferred his personal 'Volition' to his mythic cosmos.

As the magnetic fad spread, Mainaduc and Chastanier soon had stiff competition, for new rivals entered the field. In France the Puysegur brothers promoted 'induced hypnosis' and 'magnetic sleep', in which the entranced patient speaks with spirits and displays clairvoyance. Calling their technique 'Somnambulism', they brought forms, figures, motions, colours, and places 'to sight' by 'a physicalisation and exteriorisation of unseen energies'.[26] It was a form of 'substantialised spiritualism' that Blake would practise in invoking the spirit of his dead brother.

The Somnambulists also extended the Kabbalists' and Swedenborgians' exteriorisation of the internal man to medical diagnosis, in which they saw the internal organs of their patients in externalised visions. An indignant Mainaduc complained that this 'new food' of Somnambulism 'is grasped at with avidity by impostors', and many 'entertain their acquaintances with the wonder of their last comatose dream'.[27] Even worse, 'a most scientific lass, wishing me to believe she saw my brain', said it 'resembled an oyster'.

Despite his caveats, many of his students added Somnambulism to their repertoire, citing Swedenborg's descriptions of his internal man as their rationale. Cosway and Sharp magnetised Henry Tresham (a friend of Blake) and told him he had a hole in his liver, 'the form of which Cosway drew'.[28] Blake probably referred to this magnetic effect when he proclaimed, 'Their ears nostrils & tongues roll outward they behold / What is within now seen without.'[29]

As noted earlier, Blake's weird descriptions of Bowlahoola and Allamanda seemed to draw on the magnetiser's concept of the *Archaeus*, the ganglion of sympathetic nerves in the abdominal region. Where Mainaduc and his disciples got into trouble was in their technique of stroking the *Archaeus*, a technique that recalls Swedenborg's bizarre description of Tantric stroking by the Moravian orgiasts. The magnetiser was taught that the fluids are to be conducted upwards, slowly, softly and gently, in order to carry them from stomach to brain: 'the operation is to commence at the pit of the stomach, and the first intention must be to separate the plexus, or heap of nerves, situated in that part'.[30] The nerves must then be pursued, 'through the diaphragm up the pleura, and into the skull to the Brain'. Perhaps Chastanier showed Mainaduc the Tantric passage in Swedenborg's *Spiritual Diary*, for Chastanier spent years transcribing the manuscript.

The predictable effects of such eroticised psychotherapy delighted the cartoonists, and charges of sexual manipulation reverberated in the conservative press. Maria Cosway became a special target, for she possessed great 'spiritual Volition' and was easily 'entranced'. As she informed a sceptical Thomas Jefferson, who became her lover in Paris, 'I am susceptible and everything that surrounds me has great power to magnetise me.'[31] Satirists ridiculed her and the high-born women who flocked to Mainaduc as princesses of the 'House of Libidinowski'.[32]

With snide innuendo, a journalist reported that Mrs Cosway has become so proficient in 'the magnetic mysteries of Dr de Mainaduc' that by certain 'bewitching communications, and tantalising touches, she can throw her patients, whether male or female, into a temporary delirium, from which she can relieve them at pleasure'.[33] For the anti-magnetisers, that delirium was a dangerously orgasmic experience, which led one critic to claim that he saw 'a woman thrown by the magnetic process into a *Furor Uterinus*'.[34]

Richard Cosway must have been amused by these exaggerated accusations, as he read the prurient case histories of erotically aroused women in his copy of D. T. De Bienville's *Nypmphomania, or, a Dissertation concerning the Furor Uterinus* (1775).[35] Under an obfuscatory cloud of medical jargon (complete with graphic descriptions of the vagina, clitoris and uterus), the French doctor portrayed young women on the road to perdition (that is, the 'uterine fury') because of inflamed imaginations. For Cosway, Blake and anyone exposed to Moravian hymns and sermons and to Swedenborgian descriptions of conjugial love, De Bienville's diatribes would work as incitements rather than warnings.

In a chapter headed 'Observations on the Imagination, as connected with Nymphomania', he argued that 'It is the imagination which is almost constantly the principle, or the mother of the greater part of the passions, and of their excesses.'[36] The natural vehemence of females is stimulated by reading 'luxurious novels' which cause the heart 'to glow with lascivious flames' and is further fuelled 'by learning the most amorous songs'. In the first stage of nymphomania, often stimulated by consuming too much chocolate, reason and virtue struggle against erotic 'glowing in the imagination'. But then the female's mind and heart take a different turn: 'she enjoys without disquiet' and asks herself, 'what can be so delightful as to give a loose to amorous desires?'

Though their husbands might laugh at such puritanical hysteria, many women were terrified by De Bienville's warnings, which were widely bruited by both the popular press and puritanical sermon. For poor Maria Cosway, mocked mercilessly as a princess of Libidinowski, the doctor's prediction would certainly be distressing. Such erotic imaginings, whether stimulated by the magnetiser's powerful eye and stroking fingers or by lewd novels and erotic music, could lead to a uterine '*Mania or Furor*' and actual brain damage. While Swedenborgian *Illuminés* stressed visualisation of male and female potencies within the Grand Body, De Bienville argued that such obscene thoughts lead females into 'such lively, and deep meditations, that the salacious ideas' fatigue the brain fibres, producing oscillations and tension, 'until the fibres begin to change their tone'. Then a potentially fatal '*Delirium* and *Fever* seize on the miserable sufferer'.[37]

However, the Swedenborgians would surely applaud one of De Bienville's conclusions: 'Marriage alone cures the *Metromania*, particularly if it arises from a violent passion for one whom the patient is, at last, permitted to possess.'[38] Unfortunately, even wives can become victims of *Nymphomania*, if they overindulge their imagination and appetite for chocolate; then purgings, bleedings, fastings and isolation from stimulative literature, art and music are the only hope. Though these injunctions went directly opposite to the teaching of Zinzendorf, Swedenborg and Graham, their widespread dissemination by journalists and churchmen meant that many women were genuinely too terrified to exercise their romantic or erotic imaginations.

For Catherine Blake, the increasing charges of female vulnerability to sexual depravity created an uncomfortable context, for her husband and his friends were jauntily exploring new territories of sexual, spiritual and psychological liberation. That context would become even more distressing when several erotically charged 'Men of Desire' brought their techniques of sexual magic and spiritual vision from 'the mighty continent' to the radical artists and Swedenborgians in the Blakes' London milieu.

17

The Men of Desire

The desire of Man being Infinite the possession is Infinite & himself Infinite.

William Blake, *There is No Natural Religion* (1788)

WHILE THE COSWAYS, Loutherbourgs, Sharps and other friends of Blake exercised the magnetic gaze and strove for magnetic rapport, the fashionable world of Animal Magnetism was disturbed by the arrival from France of two new practitioners – Count Thaddeus Grabianka and Count Alessandro Cagliostro – who infused an exciting and dangerous element of sexual magic into Mainaduc's spiritualistic science. As European emissaries of the theosophy of desire, these flamboyant *Magi* hoped to recruit fellow *Hommes de Désir* from the circles of radical artists, Masons and Swedenborgians in London.[1] Over the next decade, their influence would stimulate some of Blake's most startling visions and contribute to growing problems in his marriage.

For some years, the Swedenborgians had been corresponding with fellow Illuminists in Poland, Germany, Sweden and France, and they were eager to learn more about the mystical and millenarian prophecies emanating from their lodges. However, they got more than they bargained for when the charismatic Polish Kabbalist, Count Grabianka, swept into London on 7 December 1785. He moved into Dr Graham's old quarters in the Adelphi, where he was immediately welcomed by Chastanier and the Swedenborgians. As he revealed his fusion of Kabbalistic and magnetic techniques, he brought a strain of Sabbatian antinomianism into the rituals of Swedenborgian Masonry and into the controversies within the New Jerusalem Church.

Like the late Dr Falk (d.1782), Grabianka was a native of Podolia, where Sabbatian influences were strong among local Jews, and he imbibed many of their notions.[2] The count informed the awestruck Londoners that in his youth he had been told by a fortune teller that he would gain the throne of Poland and then transfer his capital to Jerusalem, where he would serve as 'King of the New Israel'. He was further initiated into the occult sciences by the nephew of 'a rich Cabbalon Philosopher', who bequeathed his magical manuscripts to his young heir.[3] The nephew then revealed to Grabianka and seven 'jocular companions' the secrets of the mystical book. It showed them how 'to get acquainted with your guardian angel, how to come to the enjoyment of a pretty girl you love, etc.'

When the companions examined the book, they learned that it was 'a compendium of the science called CABBALA', which teaches in its purity 'how to make questions, and to receive answers from the written word of God'. To operate the 'oracle' or *Sainte Parole*, the adept manipulated Hebrew letters and numbers and then interpreted the cryptic revelations and prophecies that emerged.[4] It was a technique known to Falk, Casanova and Swedenborg, but Grabianka gave it a more radical and millenarian cast. When his friends formed a 'Society', they were informed about 'great Revolutions, great Alterations in States, and Kingdoms' that would soon occur. One night, when they posed 'an essential question' to the oracle, they received 'a very singular answer: "Have not I declared these things to my servant, Emanuel Swedenborg? Follow ye him."'

Gathering together a multinational party of Swedenborgians,

Grabianka took them to southern France, where they established a Masonic lodge called the *Illuminés d'Avignon.*[5] Acting as their agent, Grabianka sought recruits among the London Swedenborgians. First, he revealed that the techniques of the 'old Cabbalon philosopher' were similar to those of Animal Magnetism.[6] Thus it may have been Grabianka, as well as his Masonic *frére* Thomé, who persuaded Chastanier to become Mainaduc's chief assistant on 12 December. Over the next eleven months Grabianka both charmed and alarmed the Swedenborgians, while he revealed to selected Brothers the secret teachings of Avignon.

In themes that strikingly resembled those of the radical Sabbatians (such as Jacob Frank, the Polish 'militant messiah'), Grabianka merged the Jewish *Shekhinah* with the Catholic Mary, who functioned as the female partner within the divine family. Rather than the all-male Trinity, he described a heterosexual *Quaternité*. For Blake, Cosway and Duché, who were familiar with similar Moravian concepts, this would not be shocking. Like the youthful radicals among the Moravians, who feminised and eroticised the Holy Spirit, the Avignonese developed a cult of the Virgin Mary, which assumed strange forms: 'They exorcised evil spirits in her name, and combined in Her person the attributes of Diana, Hecate and the Sybil of the Syrians.'[7]

Merging the hypnotic techniques of Animal Magnetism with the visionary techniques of the Kabbalists and Swedenborg, Grabianka taught his initiates to see visions and speak with spirits. He also attempted to cure diseases, by placing on the patient a talismanic 'Pantecula', whose source (according to Chastanier) was 'in the first Volume of Cornelius Agrippa's Works, page 657'.[8] Perhaps it was at this time that Blake studied Agrippa, for he would soon draw on the Kabbalistic chart of angelic names found in that work.[9]

In their elaborate rituals, the Avignonese utilised hallucinogenic chemicals and fumigations, which enhanced their erotic meditation on the Kabbalistic *Sephiroth* and emanations. To begin the process of 'illumination', the candidate had to strip naked, inhale and imbibe various potent chemicals, and undergo gruelling psychological manipulation (interrogation, sleep deprivation, solitary meditation, etc.).[10] Once accepted into the lodge, males and females participated in orgiastic ceremonies in darkened rooms, filled with incense and pulsating to exotic music. Soon, 'it was rumoured that less spiritual homage was paid in this atmosphere to less immaculate persons'.[11] Critics charged that females joined 'not to participate in the cult but to freely satisfy their passions'.

Grabianka revealed these rituals to selected Swedenborgians in London, and rumours began to circulate about their 'frivolous erotic practices'.[12] Though conservative New Churchmen later tried to cover up the impact of Grabianka on the London group, most were initially entranced by him, and a minority remained loyal to him over the next decade. Despite or because of Grabianka's uninhibited behaviour, the Cosways probably welcomed him, for they entertained many of his Polish friends, expecially the Lubomirskis, whose kinsman Marius married a Frankist and converted to Judaism.[13] When the critic of the magnetising Maria Cosway referred to the 'Princesses of Libidinowski', he included a pun on her exotic Polish visitors.

It is hard to imagine Catherine Blake feeling comfortable in Grabianka's flamboyant company. Nevertheless, we shall see that some of the most fantastic and obscene images in Blake's later work seem to reflect Grabianka's teachings, especially in 1796 and 1799–1800, when the fiery Kabbalist reportedly returned to London.

Grabianka was not the only Kabbalistic guru who arrived from France, seeking recruits among the London Swedenborgians. In June 1786, the embattled Count Cagliostro arrived in the city, a refugee from the dungeons of the Bastille and the persecution of the French court.[14] During earlier visits to London, when he sought work as an engraver and artist, Cagliostro met Dr Falk, with whom he developed new Kabbalistic rituals for their 'Egyptian Rite' of Masonry.[15] In the early 1780s, Cagliostro acted as the emissary of the 'Grand Cophta' (Falk), while he blazed a magical trail across Europe, winning respectable bankers, heterodox physicians and aristocratic ladies to the Egyptian Rite. He especially targeted those Masons who were already readers of Swedenborg and who wanted to learn more about Falk.[16]

In the process, Cagliostro became bolder and more risqué in his message of conjugial love. In Latvia, he boasted to his awed initiates that he was 'a half-god, a product of earthly copulation between humans and divinities long past' – a point obviously taken from *Le Comte de Gabalis.*[17] Cagliostro could also 'devise potions to make a woman lust for a man against her will'. In Russia, an indignant Catherine the Great described his mission to the gullible Masons. She reported that the *magus* came at just the right moment for himself, 'when several lodges of Freemasons, who were infatuated with Swedenborg's principles, were anxious at all costs to see spirits; they therefore ran to Cagliostro, who declared he had all the secrets of Dr Falk'.[18] After the empress drove Cagliostro out of Russia, she wrote blistering theatrical satires on him and his mentor Falk, giving her character the portmanteau name of 'Kalifalkerston'. Curiously, the London Swedenborgians interpreted these comedies as attacks upon themselves.[19]

Cagliostro then settled in Strasbourg, where Loutherbourg reportedly met him at the lodge of *Amis Réunis*. To his new brothers, Cagliostro praised Swedenborg, who had been unfairly persecuted by Swedish clerics and politicians. Adding that 'in vain the Swedes now want to almost resuscitate his ashes', he warned that 'they will discover nothing'.[20] He boasted that 'the greatest man in Europe is the celebrated Falk in London' and claimed that 'there are in that capitol some five or six Masons who possess the secret knowledge, but they still lack the key'. To his Masonic confidants, Cagliostro seemed 'to incline towards Judaism'.

After Falk's death in 1782, Cagliostro took on his title of 'Grand Cophta' and began recruiting high-ranking churchmen and aristocrats to the Egyptian Rite. His greatest catch was the wealthy Duke of Orleans, Grand Master of the Grand Orient, who had studied under Falk in London and who still wore his Kabbalistic talisman on his chest. However, Cagliostro's scheming with the Cardinal de Rohan to gain the favour of Queen Marie-Antoinette entangled him in the snares of the 'Diamond Necklace Case', which threw unprecedented mud upon the French king and queen. Cagliostro and his beautiful wife Seraphina were imprisoned in the Bastille, slandered in a lengthy trial and then – amazingly – acquitted by a rebellious Parisian *Parlement*.

Following the trial from Germany, Johann Wolfgang Goethe, himself an Illuminist Mason, prophetically observed, 'The affair is as horrifying to me as a sight of the Medusa's head. The intrigue is utterly destructive to royal dignity. The Necklace Case is the prelude to revolution.'[21] A furious Louis XVI banished Cagliostro from France, and he fled 'from slavery to freedom' in London, where he was initially lionised as a popular hero. The disaffected Prince of Wales and his brothers, who despised their autocratic father George III, welcomed Cagliostro and his supporter, the Duke of Orleans. Already an attendee at Mainaduc's clinic, where he was put into a deep trance, the rakish prince was always eager for the newest psychoerotic sensation.[22] Among radical artists and politicians, the count's *outré* appearance (Oriental turban, bejewelled robes, beribboned pigtails) was interpreted as the latest Parisian style.

The Cophta made an immediate and lasting impression on Blake's artistic colleagues and, as will be argued, on Blake himself. Cosway, who had frequently hosted Orleans and who travelled to Paris to paint his family, was eager to meet Cagliostro, whom he called 'The Wandering Jew' (his current epithet in press reports). According to Cosway's friend William Beckford, the artist arranged a secret meeting and subsequently boasted that he had seen 'wonders beyond all conception – but I am forbidden to communicate them'.[23] Cosway's former housemate, the engraver Francesco Bartolozzi, painted Cagliostro's portrait from life and then distributed prints of 'The Friend of Humanity' to shopkeepers, who boldly featured it in display windows.[24] The Loutherbourgs collaborated with the Cophta in alchemical experiments, and Philippe Jacques made a series of watercolour illustrations of ceremonies in the Egyptian Rite.[25] The usually sceptical George Cumberland, now a close friend of Blake, was intrigued by Cagliostro, collected four books about him and later visited him in his Inquisition prison cell in Rome.[26]

However, Cagliostro's most important – and dangerous – champion was Lord George Gordon, who had secretly converted to Judaism, allegedly through the influence of Dr Falk.[27] In September 1785, *Rambler's Magazine* had broken the conversion story in a wicked article entitled 'The Loss of the Prepuce, or Lord George Riot Suffering a Clipping in Order to Become a Jew'.[28] In the accompanying illustration, a cartoonish Gordon discusses international Jewish affairs with Mordecai, a Frenchified Jew, whose daughter Susanna uses a pair of scissors to clip his lordship's prepuce. From this date on, Gordon was satirised as 'Lord Crop', especially by James Gillray, who would soon make him a satirical target. In the *Rambler's* print, a bearded Jew dressed in slouch hat and black robes reads a Hebrew book; Gordon later adopted the similar garb of a Hasidic rabbi, a costume that would make a startling appearance on the frontispiece of Blake's illuminated prophecy, *Jerusalem*.[29]

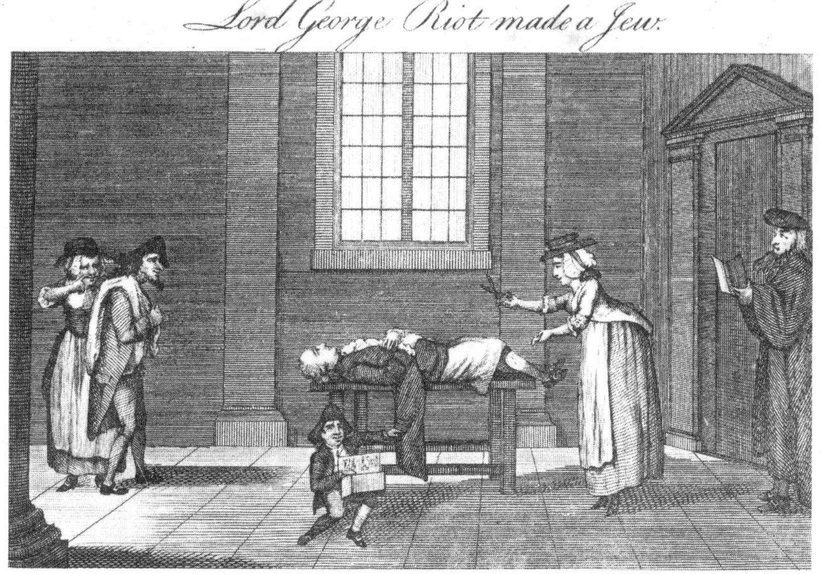

Gordon's rantings against the government eventually intimidated the Prince of Wales, who backed off from his support, taking with him many of the radical chic and *bon ton*. Seeking new backers, Cagliostro placed an ad in the liberal *Morning Herald* (1 November 1786), in which he appealed to 'all true Masons' to join with the Swedenborgians in a common effort at 'regeneration'. They should come to Freemasons' Tavern in Great Queen Street to 'plan for laying the first stone of the foundation' of the New Temple or New Jerusalem. He signed the ad 'a Mason and a Member of the New Church'. Though New Church historians would later try to cover this up, contemporary chroniclers (including Goethe) reported that the magician was welcomed by the Swedenborgians in London and attended meetings of their Theosophical Society.

A series of Blake drawings from this period suggests that

he was among the Swedenborgians who observed Cagliostro's Egyptian rituals. To serve as mediums, the Cophta often used children (*pupilles*), who kneeled around a specially lit crystal bowl of water and gazed into it until they went into a visionary trance. The children then reported the communications of the Seven Celestial Angels, who could be seen ascending and descending behind a screen.[30] In one drawing, Blake showed three naked children 'crouched round a bowl-like source of light'.[31] In three others he sketched 'An Incantation', in which a *magus*-figure raises his arms before an altar; a woman wearing 'an Egyptian head dress'; and 'haloed figures standing around a Hebrew-inscribed book from which 'rays of light emanate'.[32]

Cagliostro was so successful in creating these visionary and euphoric experiences for his initiates that some Swedenborgians sensed that they could emulate Swedenborg's angelic communication and spiritual intercourse. According to Cagliostro's inveterate critic, the pornographic journalist and spy Theveneau de Morande, the naive Swedenborgians tried to imitate the Cophta's theurgic rituals when he was temporarily away from the lodge. Using the hypnotic techniques of Animal Magnetism and the Hebrew incantations of Kabbalistic magic, they tried to raise the Seven Celestial Angels: 'Suddenly, in place of the seraphim in azure robes and silver that they were hoping for, there appeared a fearful horde of wild orang-outangs whose grimaces, insults and unworthy promiscuity the chaste idealists had to endure all evening.'[33]

In 1791, this story (minus the Swedenborgians) was repeated in the Inquisition biography of Cagliostro, which received wide publicity in London. Invited to assist 'at the principal lodge', the *magus* made use of 'four *pupils*, of distinguished birth'. However, a singular accident occurred, which he could not explain: 'Some ladies and gentlemen having petitioned for authority to make use of the *crystal vase*, etc., in the same manner as himself, he granted his authority accordingly; but their labours proved so unfortunate, that they beheld the apparition of monkeys and devils, instead of angels, as they expected.'[34] Cagliostro, who was undergoing torture, did not reveal to the Roman Inquisitors that the London theurgists were Swedenborgians, because he tried to convince them that he had rejected the Illuminist Masonry of Swedenborg and Falk.[35]

The Inquisitors also linked Loutherbourg to Cagliostro's evocation of the Seven Celestial Angels, and it seems likely that the artist used his theatrical skill at illusionistic effects to represent a scene from *Conjugial Love*, in which Swedenborg described the fate in the spirit world of unregenerated libertines who love to deflower virgins: 'Among themselves they do appear as men, but as seen by others who are allowed to look in there, they appear like apes, with a fierce face instead of mild, and a horrible countenance instead of pleasing.'[36] Loutherbourg was an expert in the use of magic-lantern techniques in which painted lenses projected eerily changing images, which could transform a human figure into a spirit, angel or ape.[37] He was also privy to the practice in some high-degree Masonic rites in which human actors portrayed good and evil spirits. Cagliostro employed a transparent screen to partially obscure his assistants, who may have impersonated apes and angels. Through proper meditation on conjugial love, the visualised ape could be regenerated into an angel.

Blake's later reference to the Swedenborgians' failed invocation suggests that he heard about or even participated in Cagliostro's ceremonies.[38] In 1791, when Blake had become angry at the conservative prudes among the Swedenborgians, he conjured up a painful memory of this bungled *séance*, when the 'chaste idealism' of certain Swedenborgians made them see brutally promiscuous baboons, whereas the sexually liberated Illuminists would see happily copulating angels. In *The Marriage of Heaven and Hell*, he parodied some of Swedenborg's spiritual *Memorabilia.* Gathering up the seer's publications, Blake drags one of the prudish 'Angels' through seven symbolic houses:

> *one we enter'd; in it were a number of monkeys, baboons, & all that species, chain'd by the middle, grinning and snatching at one another, but withheld by the shortness of their chains; however, I saw that they sometimes grew numerous, and then the weak were caught by the strong, and with a grinning aspect, first coupled with, & then devour'd . . . til the body was left a helpless trunk; this after grinning & kissing it with seeming fondness . . .*[39]

The conservative Angel responded that 'thy phantasy has imposed upon me, & thou oughtest to be ashamed'. But Blake answered, 'we impose on one another, & it is but lost time to converse with you whose works are only Analytic. Opposition is true Friendship.'[40] He then added, 'This Angel, who is now become a Devil, is my particular friend; we often read the Bible together in its infernal or diabolical sense.' E. P. Thompson suggests that the Angel was Benedict Chastanier, who struggled against the puritans and reactionaries in the Society.[41] Another candidate is the liberal Swedenborgian John Augustus Tulk, Blake's later neighbour in Lambeth.

Meanwhile, in autumn 1786, as attacks intensified on Cagliostro and the Swedenborgians, Gordon persuaded him to seek more support from the Ancient Masons. On 1 November, the Cophta, his lordship and a party of French disciples visited the Lodge of Antiquity, no. 2. Cagliostro explained the basic themes and broad humanitarian aims of his Masonic rituals, and observers reported that the brothers were 'very satisfied' with the Egyptian Rite.[42] This progress alarmed Morande, who was being paid by the French court to destroy Cagliostro's reputation. He thus turned to the most effective weapon of British libel – the biting caricature of James Gillray.

Taking advantage of his own Masonic affiliation, Gillray used his insider's knowledge of the Antiquity meeting to engrave a print entitled 'A Masonic Anecdote designed by a Brother Mason, a Witness of the Scene', which was published on 21 November.[43] Standing before the lodge, Cagliostro asks, 'Are you shot through the Heart? Take a drop of my Balsamo', a double allusion to Morande's charge that the so-called count was really the lowly Sicilian painter Joseph Balsamo, and to the Coptha's use of potent aphrodisiacs (a 'paste of Paradise' and 'Wine of Egypt') in his rituals. The English members, deep in their cups, shout 'Huzzas' and insult the visiting French *fréres*, who mutter, '*Quelle insolence!*' Beneath the print, a doggerel abstract of the Arabian count's 'memoirs' appears:

> *Born, God knows where, supported, God knows how,*
> *From whom descended . . . difficult to know.*
> LORD CROP *adopts him as a bosom friend,*
> *And madly dares his character defend.*
> *This self-dubb'd Count, some few years since became*
> *A Brother Mason in a borrowed name.*

In his hint at Gordon's circumcision, Gillray followed the exposé in *Rambler's Magazine*. Leaving behind the liberal sentiments of his Moravian youth, the sardonic caricaturist would later turn Tory and accept a secret government pension.

In January 1787, Gordon was charged with libel and sedition, but he continued to assail the corrupt government. Worried that Cagliostro would also be arrested, the Loutherbourgs persuaded him to take refuge in their Hammersmith home. As the artist later recalled, 'We proposed to make a living together, I by making him a partner of what I earned from my painting,

he by communicating to me everything that he knew and sharing the profits from his medicines.'[44]

By May, when Gordon made his first fiery appearance in court, the Loutherbourgs feared that Cagliostro would be implicated and they slipped out of England, on their way to Switzerland. In June, Gordon escaped to Holland, from where he planned to join Cagliostro in the Alps, but he was eventually arrested and shipped back to England under armed guard. Again he disappeared, only to be rearrested in the Birmingham ghetto in December, when he appeared with a long beard and Hasidic garb and announced his enthusiastic conversion to Judaism.

After Grabianka and Cagliostro left London, the Swedenborgians struggled to comprehend the positive visionary experiences they achieved, as well as the negative sexual gossip and political persecution they endured. In 1788, as Blake trained his wife not only to share his visions but to collaborate in his painting and engraving, he began to merge Illuminist notions of sexualised spirituality into his artistic credo. Transforming Swedenborg's divine influx into 'the Poetic Genius', he proclaimed in *All Religions are One* (1788) that 'the Poetic Genius is the True Man, and the body or outward form of Man is derived from the Poetic Genius'.[45]

This oblique hint at the Kabbalistic connection of the visionary imagination with its manifestation in the sexual body was elaborated in his annotations to Johann Caspar Lavater's *Aphorisms on Man* (1788), which drew on the Swiss physiognomist's studies of Zinzendorf, Swedenborg, Cagliostro and the revelations of 'Gablidone the Cabalistic Jew'.[46] Blake especially liked Lavater's aphorism no. 366: 'the purest religion is the most refined Epicurism. He, who in the smallest given time can enjoy most of what he will never repent . . . is the most religious and most voluptuous of men.' Blake enthusiastically responded, 'True Christian Philosophy'.[47]

Remarking that he did not believe in a literal hell, Blake explained that 'hell is the being shut up in the possession of corporeal desires which shortly weary the man for *all life is holy*'.[48] However, Blake did not agree with all of Lavater's propositions, which were limited by his Lutheran moralism and Christian conversionist agenda, which denigrated Jewish traditions: 'this mistake of Lavater & his cotemporaries is, They suppose that Woman's love is Sin; in consequence all the Loves & Graces with them are Sin.' For Blake, the liberating influence of the Men of Desire would open up a new chapter in his spiritual and conjugal life. He determined to become 'the most religious and most voluptuous of men'. In the process he would send his wife into floods of tears.

18

Perpetual Virile Potency

Love of the Sex, and the constant exercise thereof, which is the Virile Potency, is the very basis to the accession of all other kinds of Permanent Powers.

Augustus Nordenskjöld, *Plan for a Free Community upon the Coast of Africa* (1790)

BY 1788, WILLIAM and Catherine Blake were serious students of Swedenborg. They attended meetings of 'the society', where readers discussed and disputed passages in the writings. In his annotations to *The Wisdom of Angels Concerning Heaven and Hell* (1788), Blake revealed his intense interest in spiritual and visionary 'elevation'.[1] In one passage, Swedenborg foreshadowed the Somnambulists: 'Man, in whom the spiritual Degree is open, comes into that Wisdom . . . by laying asleep the Sensations of the Body, and from Influx from above at the Same time into the Spirituals of his Mind.' Blake commented that 'This is while in the Body. This is to be understood as unusual in our time, but common in ancient.'

However, the more conservative Swedenborgians wanted to distance themselves from Animal Magnetism, which provoked arguments with supporters of the 'new science'. To Swedenborg's statement that 'the natural Man can elevate his Understanding to superior Light as far as he desires it', Blake responded, 'Who shall dare say after this that all elevation is of self & is Enthusiasm and Madness.' He rejected as false the notion that 'love receives influx thro' the understanding, as was asserted in the society'. While one party pushed to organise the New Church as a dissenting sect, separated from the Church of England, Blake criticised the kind of man who 'is a Sectary therefore not great'.[2] Instead, he agreed with the Universalist position that 'the whole of the New Church is in the Active Life & not in ceremonies at all'.[3]

These disputes over spiritualism, magnetism and sectarian separation became so serious by autumn 1788 that a bipartisan group sent out invitations to 500 known readers to attend a conference at Great Eastcheap the following April.[4] The Universalist cause was helped by the arrival of two Swedish *Illuminés*, Augustus Nordenskjöld (brother of Charles Frederick) and Charles Bernhard Wadström, who worked with Chastanier, John Augustus Tulk and other moderates to patch together a compromise manifesto of Swedenborgian principles. When William and Catherine Blake signed the document, they must have sensed that the factions were reconciled.[5]

However, in May the apparent unity was shattered by Nordenskjöld's determination to include in the New Church credo Swedenborg's actual theories about conjugial love and concubinism. Like the Nordenskjöld brothers, Wadström came from a Moravian background, so Swedenborg's spiritual eroticism did not disturb them.[6] As clearly stated in *Conjugial Love* and the *Spiritual Diary* manuscript, which Wadström brought to London, the maintenance of prolonged 'virile potency' was crucial to the visionary process that achieved the ecstatic 'marriage within the mind'. For those men whose wives did not stimulate such erectile energies, Swedenborg's 'permission' for the husband to take a concubine should be honoured. However, the man must not continue sexual relations with his wife after he established concubinism.

In *Conjugial Love*, Swedenborg argued that sexual compatibility is so crucial to spiritual vision that a diminishment of mutual attraction is a cause for serious concern. Among just causes for the husband's separation from the marital bed are blemishes and diseases of the body, which produce from the whole organism exudings of 'hurtful effluvia and noxious vapours'; from the skin eruptions of 'malignant pox, warts, pustules, virulent itch'; from the stomach 'eructations constantly foul, rank and fetid'; from the lungs 'filthy and putrid exhalations'.[7] Blemishes of the mind also provide just cause, such as mania, memory loss, foolishness and idiocy, addiction to magical arts and sorcery. Finally, to keep her man, the wife must calibrate her sexuality to suit her husband, avoiding 'a shameless demand for the conjugial debt whereby the man becomes a cold stone', as well as 'the feebleness of advanced age, and hence a non-tolerance and refusal of actual love, while ardour still continues with the man'.

Conservative Eastcheapers claimed that Nordenskjöld's advocacy of concubinage 'opened the floodgates of immorality', and they would soon persecute and slander his unmarried brother Charles Frederick for acting out Swedenborg's permission for pre-marital fornication and roaming pellicacy. However, for Blake this permission was liberating, and he would eventually propose to his exhausted and unhappy wife that he add a concubine to their 'poor and shifting establishment'.[8]

The Swedes further shocked the prudes and appealed to Blake when they proposed a radical colonisation project. Swedenborg claimed that Africans possess the highest degree of virile and visionary potency; thus Nordenskjöld planned to travel to 'the dark continent' – hopefully by balloon – in order to establish a colony based on this singular premise.[9] Working with Wadström, who had recently visited West Africa, he published a *Plan for a Free Community upon the Coast of Africa, under the Protection of Great Britain; but Entirely Independent of All European Laws and Government* (1789).

Proclaiming that 'Man is born to liberty', he lamented the

sorry state of civil and conjugal affairs, for 'where Liberty is restrained', all true access to 'everything agreeable in life is shut up. Everyone feels a sort of Political and Oeconomical Slavery.'[10] Two things 'constitute the Political Hell of a Community; viz. The *Lust of Dominion*, originating in the love of self; and the *Lust of Possession*, originating in the love of the world'. In order to move past this corrupt and stagnant state, he advocated 'the Conjugial Life' as 'the basis of morality in all Communities'. So far so good, thought many of his liberal readers, who included Mrs Mathew and other pious ladies.

However, Nordenskjöld further argued that the basis of this African colony would consist of perpetual virile potency. Though 'the great secret of all *True Policy*' is at present entirely unknown, Swedenborg revealed that the ultimate foundation of all kinds of powers in individuals and communities consists in '*Virility* or *Conjugal Power*'.[11] If men deprive themselves of 'Love of the Sex', they will never become rich and great. 'In every Male there is an inexhaustible source of the *Virile Power*, capable of being exercised and cultivated to a perpetual Increase.' Therefore sexual love 'and the constant exercise thereof, which is the *Virile Potency*, is the very basis to the accession of all other kinds of *Permanent Powers*.'

Nordenskjöld won over the Universalists and Illuminists, but the angry sectarians expelled them from the Eastcheap Congregation and tore out the minutes that recorded the vehement arguments. Despite this setback, he continued with the second stage of his revolutionary agenda – the establishment of a secret interior order to practise alchemy, develop Hermetic medicines and achieve orgasmic visionary states: what he called the 'Tabernacling in the Body of a continual State of Bliss'.[12]

In a broadside distributed to 'the True Members of the New Jerusalem Church', he explained that his alchemical project was part of his radical political programme, for he hoped to abolish gold and establish egalitarian access to the wealth of the world. Blake almost certainly received Nordenskjöld's invitation, and the subsequent infusion of alchemical themes into his own radical poetry and designs suggests his sympathetic response to such Hermetic politics. The Swedes' emphasis on eroticised spirituality also struck a responsive chord, for their themes echoed Zinzendorf as much as Swedenborg. It is obvious that they retained much of the teaching of their parents and even tried to introduce Moravian-style foot-washing into services at Eastcheap.

Unlike the Illuminists, who believed that Swedenborg's *Conjugial Love* was the basic text for their religion, the conservatives argued that it was too provocative to be published in English. Instead, vetted members of the New Church should only gradually gain access to its teachings, and then through a rationalist understanding of its themes. Blake rejected this, noting that sexual love receives spiritual influx directly, not through the filter of reason. Over the next three years, he would struggle against the forces of repression, both in his wife and in society, which blocked the sexual path to spiritual vision.

Like the Swedes, Blake had long linked sexual liberation to political liberation. In 1788, he viewed the Regency Crisis, in which the Prince of Wales tried to replace the mentally ill George III, as a family psychodrama rooted in Kabbalistic sexual dynamics.[13] While the Illuminists supported the prince, the conservatives called for loyalty to the autocratic monarch. In *Tiriel*, Blake's unfinished satire on this crisis, he utilised Hebrew etymologies and Kabbalistic symbols to hint at the Royal Brothers' earlier association with Cagliostro's Egyptian Rite. Perhaps as a clue to his embedded code, he sketched on the back of the manuscript Hebrew letters in the form of human bodies. For the Swedenborgians, the king's insanity and subsequent political crisis were caused by his refusal to have sexual relations with his queen, while he pursued with frenzied erotomania a terrified lady-in-waiting. They argued that the king and Body Politic could only be cured by a resumption of conjugial love.[14]

However, the concubine and potency quarrels at Eastcheap led many Swedenborgians to back off from their earlier endorsement of visionary sexuality. Among the wives especially, the warnings of more prudish preachers began to take a toll. In Blake's subsequent writings, he hinted at such resistance in his own wife. In the illustrated poem or 'illuminated prophecy' entitled *Thel* (1789), Blake chided those females who do not recognise the importance of earthly intercourse, for God's sexuality can only be manifested through 'use'. Hinting at the visionary importance of removal of the hymen and prepuce, he asked, 'Why a tender curb upon the youthful burning boy! / Why a little curtain of flesh on the bed of our desire?'[15]

He drew upon Kabbalistic angelology in which *Theliel* is 'the angelic prince of love', invoked in ceremonial magic to procure the woman desired by the invocant.[16] But he knew that most readers would associate the name *Thel* (Greek for female) with a controversial book, *Thelypthora* (1780–1), by Reverend Martin Madan. Adding the Greek *pthora* (corruption) to the name, Madan addressed the growing problems of prostitution and venereal disease among English women. His work caused great scandal by its advocacy of polygamy, based on Jewish precedent, as the solution. Arguing that 'the Jews are more righteous and merciful' than 'we Christians are', Madan praised the former's sense of sacramental sexuality versus the latter's hypocritical debauchery.[17] Polygamy and concubinage are 'both dispensations from God, both modes of lawful and honourable marriage', which is made absolutely clear in the Hebrew Scriptures.

One of Madan's arguments would be worrisome to Catherine

Blake, for he stressed that the Jews maintained that a wife's barrenness justified her husband taking a concubine. After seven years of marriage Catherine was still childless, though it is unclear why. With a Christian minister expressing a positive attitude towards polygamy and concubinism (and Grabianka's *Illuminés* experimenting with group sex), Blake must have felt encouraged in his own daring advocacy of extramarital experiences. For his poor wife – rapidly losing her looks, burdened with overwork and subservient to her demanding husband – these radical pronouncements would certainly be disturbing.

Unlike the children of Moravians, Catherine had not been raised to accept sexualised spirituality as a legitimate part of religion, and the diatribes of puritanical preachers – at Eastcheap and in Dissenting and Anglican churches – evidently intimidated and frightened her. In William's annotations to Swedenborg's *Divine Wisdom of Angels Concerning Divine Providence* (1790), he revealed his increasing resentment at the repressive actions of the conservative New Churchmen, who pressured members 'to agree with Priests' interests'.[18] The uninhibited nudist missionary James Glen similarly complained that Robert Hindmarsh, a former Methodist, was 'becoming the Bishop of Babylon' and other Eastcheapers 'pronounced ecclesiastics'.[19] Glen would agree with Blake's judgement that they were turning Swedenborg's visions into 'Lies & Priestcraft'.

Fortunately, in autumn 1790, when the Blakes moved south of the River Thames to Lambeth, they became close neighbours of several Swedenborgians who would be sympathetic to his increasingly radical views. At the nearby Lambeth Asylum, the Duché family continued to gather readers of Swedenborg and other mystics. Grabianka had spent much time with them at Lambeth, and in 1788 Thomas Spence Duché travelled to Avignon, in the hope of a Kabbalistic cure for his consumption.[20] Francis Barthelemon and John Augustus Tulk also lived in the neighbourhood and continued to support the efforts of Chastanier and the Swedes to bring full knowledge of Swedenborg's regenerative sexual theosophy to the unregenerated world.[21]

The Nordenskjölds, who often stayed with Tulk, allowed him to read the more explicit manuscripts, such as 'De Conjugio', an unpublished draft for *Conjugial Love*. Thus Tulk learned that Swedenborg intended to write extensively about the 'increase of potency according to the opening of the interiors of the mind' and 'the correspondence of seminal potency with reception of spiritual truths through the Word'.[22] Swedenborg warned that there is no love truly conjugial unless consorts are in the spiritual marriage: 'where there is not this, neither can the love be given that descends to the loins. Where conjugial love is perpetual, there is perpetual potency.' Then, 'Enjoyment is the life of love.'

Drawing on Kabbalistic teachings, Swedenborg revealed that conjugial intercourse on earth stimulates pleasure in heaven, for the 'organs of generation have correspondence with the third heaven; especially the womb'.[23] As the Lord's influx descends on the genitals, 'conjugial love increases in potency and effect to eternity'. When the interiors of the mind are opened, both human and angelic 'conjunctions are delicious'. The manuscript material reinforced Tulk's determination that *Amore Conjugiale* should be published in English. Thus he provided funds to the Universalists to print *The New Jerusalem Magazine*, which issued monthly instalments of the work. When protests arose, one sympathetic reader wrote, 'What most are offended with, is the greatest beauty of the doctrine, the *everlastingness* of conjugial love.'[24] And, of course, that *lastingness* resulted from perpetual virile potency.

Of great interest to Blake was Swedenborg's revelation that

such conjunction made spirit-communication and celestial visions possible. However, of greater concern to his wife would be the emphasis on her responsibility in enabling her husband to achieve the prolonged erection necessary to the visionary process. In a long discussion of passages 23–4, the Universalists stressed that 'Light cannot exist without fire or flame. The wife is love or fire; the husband must first be kindled by that fire, before the light that is in him from the Lord can be fixed and received by the wife.' Moreover, 'the heat does not pass into conjunction, unless the husband is kindled by it'. It was crucial that both partners give up their will, because 'in spiritual persons the will-principle is totally lost'. However, for Swedenborg as well as Blake, it was really the female will that must be abolished, for she must submit to her role as the 'kindler' of fiery desire.

While Blake drafted his blistering satire on the New Church prudes, aptly titled *The Marriage of Heaven and Hell* (1790–3), he seemed to expect a friendly audience of Illuminists who shared his ambivalent reaction to Swedenborg's theology and his oppositionist stance to the narrow-minded sectarians. He further hinted at his access to the radically antinomian sexual beliefs of Jacob Frank and his crypto-Sabbatian disciples – access provided by those Swedenborgians who were collecting information on the strange Jewish-Christian sect.[25] Many of the more puzzling pronouncements in Blake's *Marriage* echoed Frankist prophecies and proverbs.

For example, on plate 5 Blake featured a nude female with welcoming arms spread wide open and flames emerging from her genitals; at the bottom, a female gives birth while an embracing couple flies into the flamy clouds. The illuminated text reads:

> *As a new heaven is begun, and it is now thirty-three years since its advent: the Eternal Hell revives. And lo! Swedenborg*

As a new heaven is begun, and it is now thirty-three years since its advent: the Eternal Hell revives. And lo! Swedenborg is the Angel sitting at the tomb; his writings are the linen clothes folded up. Now is the dominion of Edom, & the return of Adam into Paradise; see Isaiah XXXIV & XXXV Chap:

Without Contraries is no progreſsion. Attraction and Repulsion, Reason and Energy, Love and Hate, are neceſsary to Human existence.

From these contraries spring what the religious call Good & Evil. Good is the paſsive that obeys Reason Evil is the active springing from Energy.

Good is Heaven. Evil is Hell.

is the Angel sitting at the tomb; his writings are the linen clothes folded up. Now is the dominion of Edom, & the return of Adam into Paradise; see Isaiah XXXIV and XXXV Chap:

Without Contraries is no progression. Attraction and Repulsion, Reason and Energy, Love and Hate, are necessary to Human existence.

From these contraries spring what the religious call Good & Evil. Good is the passive that obeys Reason. Evil is the active springing from Energy.

Good is Heaven. Evil is Hell.[26]

Referring to 1757, the year of his own birth and of Swedenborg's 'Last Judgement in the Spirit World', Blake pointed the reader to chapters in Isaiah that prophesy the downfall of princes and the return of the Jews to Zion. At this time, such a dream was shared by Grabianka and Frank, who planned actual military marches to the Middle East.[27] After Frank's death in December 1791, his followers circulated his treatise, which focused on the same verses. In this sensational work, entitled 'The Prophecies of the Prophet Isaiah, Member of the Holy Sanhedrion, as Revealed by the Great Shaddai, Lord of White Magic', Frank transformed the biblical prophecies into 'an entire mystical theory of revolution'.[28]

Like Grabianka, Blake was now moving beyond Swedenborg, 'the linen clothes folded up', into a revolutionary vision of liberated sexuality. Like the Frankists, who preached 'the holy religion of Edom', Blake declared, 'Now is the dominion of Edom.' Though Edom was traditionally interpreted by Kabbalists to mean Christianity, Frank transformed it into the domain of 'holy sin', in which all rules – especially sexual norms – would be reversed: 'Edom symbolised the unbridled flow of life which liberates man because its force and power are not subject to any law.'[29] After Frank's death, his disciples appealed to a number of synagogues to band together in 'a sect called *Edom*', which accepts Jews and Christians alike.[30] Blake associated the 'dominion of Edom' with the transformation of hell into heaven and the return of Adam into paradise – an antinomian reversal similar to Frank's theology of reversal.

Blake described this cosmic transformation, when 'the whole creation will be consumed and appear infinite and holy, whereas now it appears finite & corrupt', and then affirmed, 'This will come to pass by an improvement of sensual enjoyment.'[31] To illustrate these lines, he drew two tiny worm-like squiggles among the nude spirit-figures; one is clearly a sperm whose triangular head encloses a Hebrew letter, the phallic *yod*.[32] The other apparently represents the vulvic *he*, for in the *Zohar*, when *yod* has intercourse with *he*, the secret world of angels and spirits is produced. The Frankists often exploited these linguistic-celestial couplings to justify their orgiastic and illicit behaviour.

Inverting the traditional moral order, Blake adopted the Devil as his spokesman for the theosophy of desire: 'Those who restrain desire, do so because theirs is weak enough to be restrained.' In his startling 'Proverbs of Hell', he issued paeans to the liberating and visionary power of desire: 'The road of excess leads to the palace of wisdom'; 'He who desires but acts not, breeds pestilence'; 'Sooner murder an infant in its cradle than nurse unacted desires.' All sexual desire is holy, for 'The lust of the goat is the bounty of God'; 'The nakedness of woman is the work of God'; 'the genitals Beauty'.

One possible reader of Blake's *Marriage* was Cosway, who was immersed in Kabbalistic studies and electromagnetic experiments. Through his Polish friends, who had Frankist family connections, he could have learned that the Sabbatians described the 'domain of Edom' as 'the way to Esau' – the way to 'true life', with 'specific connotations of freedom and licentiousness'.[33] In a later self-portrait, Cosway portrayed himself as 'Esau', surrounded with 'occultist emblems of Kabbala, Gnosticism and Freemasonry'.[34] In the verses from Isaiah cited by Blake, the prophet reveals that 'an highway shall be there, and a way, and it shall be called the way of holiness', and 'the ransomed of the Lord shall return and come to Zion'. Did Cosway and Blake decide to embark on the 'way to Esau', where sexual sins become holy?

For both their wives, such an embarkation would be distressing, for its exotic dreams took them far from domestic concerns, while its erotic demands placed great strain on their conjugal relations. After Maria Cosway gave birth to a daughter in 1790, her ill health impelled her to leave husband and child behind, while she returned to Italy. During her absence she begged Richard to educate the child as a Catholic, but he undertook a peculiar project to teach the child Hebrew and to thoroughly Judaise her. When the Loutherbourgs returned from Switzerland, Cosway collaborated in their Cagliostroan rituals and indulged in erotic experiments that further alienated his wife.

Maria confided to a friend that 'the moment he gave himself to Hammersmith, began to lead him from his home'.[35] She reminded her husband, 'Remember my good Mr Cosway, how many years we were happy. My wishes were to follow yours . . . until you began to divide your thoughts, first with occupations in Bedford Square, then a Miss P. Ingrossed them. Afterward with Hammersmith and the L.'[36] Richard Cosway possibly had an affair with Lucy Loutherbourg, who gained a reputation for flirtation and seduction, and Maria's hints at sexual irregularities point to the heightened spiritual-erotic preoccupations among their artistic and Swedenborgian friends. Though we do not know if Blake joined Cosway, Sharp, Bartolozzi and other colleagues who magnetised and ritualised with the Loutherbourgs, several of his works suggest his indulgence in similar experiments, which produced similar spousal distress.

In his unfinished prophecy, *The French Revolution* (1791), Blake hinted at his familiarity with Swedenborgian techniques of 'genital respiration', which had been incorporated into the meditation and breathing rituals of Cagliostro's Egyptian Rite. In what seems an oblique reference to the Cophta's current situation, chained in an Inquisition prison cell perched on a crag in the Apennine mountains, Blake described 'the den nam'd Horror', in which a prisoner is chained to a wall: 'In his soul was the serpent coil'd round his heart, hid from the light, as in a cleft rock.'[37] The coiled serpent, which erupts with phallic energy, was the emblem of the Egyptian Rite, in which techniques of genital breathing and magnetic trance were used to produce visionary euphoria.

Blake praised the Duke of Orleans, initiate of the Egyptian Rite, and portrayed him enacting Cagliostro's ritual in which the Grand Master 'breathes upon the face of the Candidate from the forehead to the chin'.[38] In Blake's version, Orleans 'breath'd on them' and urged them to 'fear not dreams, fear not visions', for the man filled with 'fiery desire' will find that 'Hands, head, bosom, and parts of love' will follow 'their high breathing joy'.

For the artist's simple-natured wife, such *outré* preoccupations must have been frightening, leading her to cautiously back off from willing collaboration. Her husband's irreverent proverbs in *The Marriage of Heaven and Hell* expressed his increasing scorn for her sexual inhibitions and pious timidity: 'Prudence is a rich ugly old maid courted by Incapacity.'[39] For Maria Cosway, who ran away with a castrato singer and dreamed of entering a convent, and for Catherine Blake, who worked slavishly and stayed in her ink-stained parlour, their once-happy marriages moved precariously from heaven to hell.

By 1793, when Blake entered bitter poems in his Notebook, he complained about his wife's 'deceit' and 'secresy', which attempted to replace his love ('Lawless, wing'd & unconfin'd', which 'breaks all chains from every mind') with repressive morality ('Modest, selfish & confin'd / Lawful, cautious and refin'd').[40] He accused her of jealousy when he looked at other pretty roses and of resistance to his fiery sexual and visionary demands: 'I told her all my heart, / Trembling, cold, in ghastly fears – / Ah, she doth depart.'

Inspired by Swedenborgian notions of erectile trance induction and Nordenskjöldian theories of virile potency, Blake hoped to reach the orgasmic state of vision that opened the doors of heaven, only to be thwarted by his wife's religious qualms. In 'The Garden of Love', he lamented this blight upon their chance for conjugial bliss:

I went to the garden of love,
And I saw what I never had seen:
A chapel was built in the midst,
Where I used to play on the green.
And the gates of the chapel were shut,
And 'thou shalt not' writ over the door,
So I turn'd to the garden of love
That so many sweet flowers bore;
And I saw it was filled with graves,
And tomb stones where flowers should be,
And priests in black gowns were walking their rounds
And binding with briars my loves and desires.[41]

Frustrated and angry, Blake defiantly addressed the repressive God of the orthodox, the 'Selfish father of men', and demanded:

Break this heavy chain
That does freeze my bones around.
Selfish! vain!
Eternal bane!
That free Love with bondage bound.[42]

Over the next years Blake's struggle would cause his wife much anguish, as he expected her to kindle his fiery desire until, 'by an improvement of sensual enjoyment', he could achieve the visionary breakthrough, 'when the whole creation will be consumed and appear infinite and holy'. If she could not stimulate perpetual virile potency in her husband, he had Swedenborgian permission to take a concubine.

19

The Frozen Marriage Bed

Can that be Love that drinks another as a sponge drinks
water . . .
. . . Such is self-love that envies all! A creeping skeleton
With lamplike eyes watching around the frozen marriage bed.
William Blake, *Visions of the Daughters of Albion* (1793)

IF CATHERINE BLAKE read her husband's Notebook poems, she must have been deeply hurt by his bitter descriptions of her sexual inadequacies. There may have been good reasons – physical or psychological – for her resistance to her husband's demands. Did he try to mesmerise her – with powerful stare – into compliance? Noting that 'The look of love alarms / Because 'tis fill'd with fire', he implied that she was alarmed enough to cut him off from sexual relations:

Abstinence sows sand all over
The ruddy limbs & flaming hair,
But Desire Gratified
Plants fruits of life & beauty there.
In a wife I would desire
What in whores is always found –
The lineaments of Gratified Desire.[1]

He further complained about clothing that 'hides the Female form / That cannot bear the Mental storm'.[2] Was Catherine frightened by his intense combination of sexual and visionary arousal – of phallic *and* mental storm? Even worse was his rhetorical question, 'Why should I be bound to thee', when 'Love, free love, cannot be bound'.[3] However, Blake may have contributed his own sexual deficiencies, for he hinted at his inability to maintain the prolonged erection necessary to the visionary trance. In an especially bitter poem he wrote:

I saw a chapel all of gold
That none did dare to enter in,
And many weeping stood without
Weeping, mourning, worshipping.

I saw a serpent rise between
The white pillars of the door,
And he forc'd & forc'd & forc'd,
[Till he broke the pearly door – deleted*]*
Down the golden hinges tore,
And along the pavement sweet
Set with pearls & rubies bright,
All his slimy length he drew,
Till upon the altar white

Vomiting his poison out
On the bread and on the wine.
So I turn'd into a sty
And laid me down among the swine.[4]

This painful poem suggests Blake's understanding of Swedenborg's reference in *Conjugial Love* to the 'hinged door' or seminal duct, which must be controlled by the cremaster muscle in order to transform seminal emission into a vehicle of vision. As Swedenborg and his Jewish associates knew, without proper *kawwanah* or reverent concentration, the holy semen becomes contaminated and wasted, and the frustrated mystic becomes a pig – a mere animal of sinful and forbidden flesh.

If Catherine followed her usual practice of assisting her husband in engraving and colouring his illuminated prophecies, then she was surely distressed by his radical manifesto of free love, *Visions of the Daughters of Albion* (1793). The frontispiece immediately places Blake's vision in a Kabbalistic-Illuminist context, for he portrayed 'Bromion' the rapist and 'Oothon' the victim as bound back-to-back, the position of the no-longer copulating Cherubim in the Holy of Holies, when God is separated from his *Shekhinah*.[5] Drawing on that tradition, Swedenborg also revealed that 'two partners who disagree in disposition lie in bed turned back to back'.[6]

Blake decried the imprisoning force of traditional marriage, in which 'she who burns with youth, and knows no fixed lot, is bound / In spells of law to one she loathes . . . and must drag her chains in weary lust'. Instead, he yearned for open and uninhibited sexuality, in which a wife enjoys 'the moment of desire' in broad daylight. Even better, she will no longer jealously deny her husband additional 'girls of mild silver', for she will generously observe them 'in lovely copulation, bliss on bliss'. Then, in a passage that must have wounded Catherine, Blake lamented:

Can that be Love that drinks another as a sponge
drinks water,
That clouds with jealousy his nights, with weepings
all the day,
To spin a web of age around him, grey and hoary, dark,
Till his eyes sicken at the fruit that hangs before his sight?
Such is self-love that envies all, a creeping skeleton
With lamplike eyes watching round the frozen
marriage bed.[7]

As Blake complained that 'a web of age' was spun around him, his wife's condition was even worse. A 'life of hard work and privation' had taken its toll, and she had grown 'common and coarse looking', leading a friend to comment that he 'never saw a woman so much altered'.[8] Faced with her exhaustion and lost beauty, Blake cried out for 'Love happy happy Love! Free as the mountain wind!' And he must have acted or threatened to act on his radical beliefs to provoke the enduring tradition of his wife's jealousy, arguments and floods of tears. Certainly, his continuing scorn for repressive moral laws and his praise for uninhibited sex with multiple partners suggest that Catherine had good grounds for her frightened withdrawal: 'Trembling, cold, in ghastly fears – Ah she doth depart.'[9]

Blake was probably aware that Cosway too was dissatisfied with his wife, who remained in Italy. While Blake was engraving his manifesto of free love, Cosway was carrying on a very public affair with the artist Mary Moser, daughter of the late George Michael Moser, and the two cohabited during an uninhibited sketching tour for six months in 1793. In his sketch-book-cum-journal Cosway reportedly 'gave scope to his lower propensities', making 'lascivious statements about Miss Moser, and invidious comparisons between her and Mrs Cosway'.[10] Though Cosway's journal has disappeared, the similarities between his marital discontent and esoteric-erotic desire and those expressed by Blake suggest a mutual sympathy and situation.

Portraying himself as 'Los', the visionary prophet, and Catherine as 'Enitharmon', his female emanation, Blake described a harrowing sexual relationship: 'He embrac'd her, she wept, she refus'd / In perverse and cruel delight / She fled from his arms.'[11] Her inhibiting will meant that 'No more Los beheld Eternity.' Why would Catherine-Enitharmon be so resistant to his fiery advances? After all, Swedenborg and the

Mrs Blake

Universalists stressed that the reward awaiting 'conjunction by means of ultimate delights' would be 'peace and sweetness, refreshment after temptations, heaven, and the very conjugal happiness'.[12]

Part of the answer may lie in the more revolutionary Swedenborgian and Sabbatian sexual notions practised at Avignon and brought back to London by initiated 'People of the New Israel'. Blake almost certainly knew one of these, William Bryan, who had been instructed in copper-plate printing by his old friend William Sharp.[13] Bryan and John Wright, a journeyman carpenter, heard about Grabianka's society from Samuel, 'a converted Jew' who attended services at Eastcheap.[14] In 1789, the two artisans journeyed by foot to Avignon, where they spent eight months and underwent the gruelling but compelling initiation rituals. Stripped naked, interrogated and hypnotised, they passed through 'all the allegories of the black grade, by all the monstrosities of the earth'.[15] Grabianka then sent them back to London, where they were instructed to be discreet and 'remain hidden', while they secretly looked for candidates for the New Israel. However, Bryan did describe his experiences to friends, including William Sharp, General Rainsford and other Swedenborgians.[16]

From the Kabbalistic oracle, Bryan and Wright received aphorisms and prophecies expressing Grabianka's antinomian theosophy of desire: 'Tread under thy feet the *prudence of men*'; 'Love begets confidence, and confidence heaps prodigies on prodigies'; 'Here is the time in which *God* will break the laws made by the children of earth'; '*Heaven* is already going to permit *Hell* to ransack the earth'; 'Follow the bent, follow the desires of the child of promise, and leave corruption to run into the *sepulchre of the old man*.'[17] The parallels with Blake's 'Proverbs of Hell' in *The Marriage of Heaven and Hell* are striking.

Even more intriguing is the parallel between 'the child of

promise', the 'secret child', prophesied by the oracle and described by Bryan to friends in London, and the secret child portrayed by Blake in his illuminated prophecies, *America*, *The First Book of Urizen*, and *Europe*, engraved in 1793–4.[18] The oracle revealed to Bryan that 'the Turkish Empire would be destroyed by the Instrumentality of a Boy now eleven years of age who resides at Rome conscious of his important destiny and who is under the immediate and daily instruction of Spiritual and Angelic events'.[19] When he reaches puberty and fulfills his revolutionary role, there will be a mass conversion of the Muslims, the downfall of the Papacy and the restoration of the Jews to Palestine, and 'that country will become the beauty and glory of the whole earth'.

The child was being instructed by a charismatic prophet, Ottavio Cappelli, whom Grabianka appointed 'Man-King of the New People'. However, the preparation of the secret child was interrupted in late 1791, when Cappelli was arrested by the papal police and charged with 'depraved and perverse designs, superstitious Kabbalisms, vain and chimerical dreams'.[20] Could Bryan and Sharp have informed Blake about the eleven-year-old child? Three years later Blake would portray a 'secret child' in the fourteen-year-old character of 'Orc', whose name draws on the Greek word for testicles, *orcheis*.[21]

In Blake's prophecies, the rationalist demiurge 'Urizen' enmeshed the human brain in 'The Net of Religion' and 'form'd laws of prudence, and call'd them / The eternal laws of God'.[22] But Urizen could not prevent 'Orc', the pubescent secret child, from exploding with testicular energy to 'rend the links' and seize the 'panting, struggling womb', until 'it joy'd'. If Blake's illuminated neighbours in Lambeth read *America*, they would probably interpret the 'Dark Virgin', who stands 'Invulnerable though naked', as a version of the imprisoned *Shekhinah*, who is freed by the erotic energy of the 'terrible boy' and thus reveals the 'lineaments of gratified desire'. Like Frank and Grabianka, Orc pronounces the reversal of the moral law in the name of sexual and political liberation: 'The fiery joy, that Urizen perverted to ten commands/ . . . That stony law I stamp to dust; and scatter religion abroad.'

Though the Duchés, J. A. Tulk and Barthelemon admired Grabianka, other Swedenborgians disapproved of the count's movement beyond Swedenborg's sexual theosophy to a Frankist-style worship of the Great Mother, which Chastanier attributed to their Catholic proclivities. Even worse, the *Illuminés* at Avignon rejected *Conjugial Love* as their gospel, and rumours circulated about communal sex and orgiastic rituals within their temple. Reports about Avignon's links with London provoked a conservative critic to charge that Illuminist 'clubs' in England sent to the French National Assembly a Memorial, 'in which the Assembly was requested to establish a community of wives'.[23] In the Eastcheap separatists' *New Magazine of Knowledge*, the editor reported that those who reject *Conjugial Love* as divinely inspired are 'now joined in spirit to a certain society' in the south of France, composed of 'mystico-cabbalistico-magnetical practitioners'.[24]

While the *Illuminés* and Blake yearned for the arrival of the secret child, Catherine Blake often seemed baffled and frightened by her husband's sexual demands and visionary adventures. But she also tried to comprehend his increasingly occulted philosophy and to accommodate his sexual and psychological desires. During these turbulent and difficult years there were intermittent periods of domestic harmony and conjugal 'equilibrium'. Moreover, Catherine must have been reassured about the permissibility of his peculiar notions by relatively normal friends, such as his generous patron J. A. Tulk and a new friend, Thomas Butts, who combined respectable public lifestyles with toleration towards Swedenborgian sexual arcana.

As the confidential friend of the Nordenskjölds and

Wadström, Tulk maintained a decades-long effort to get Swedenborg's more explicit manuscripts published. In 1789 he had subsidised Wadström's anonymous translation of *A Sketch of the Delights of Conjugial Love*, consisting of extracts from the manuscript 'Apocalypsis Explicata'. Cosway acquired the translation, and Blake was probably familiar with its daring advocacy of nudity. Affirming that 'Man by means of Conjugial Love becomes the Image and the Likeness of God', Swedenborg stressed that nakedness equals innocence: 'there is nothing lascivious, and thence no subject of shame between married Couples, any more than between little children, when they are naked among themselves'.[25] The plural connotation of 'themselves' provoked objections from the timid, but Tulk continued his campaign for full disclosure.

While working with Chastanier on the manuscripts, Tulk was delighted by supporting passages in 'De Conjugio', and he persuaded a reluctant Hindmarsh to publish them. Noting 'That *Love truly conjugial is Naked*', Swedenborg described the angels of the third heaven, who 'walk with a girdle around their loins when without doors, but without a girdle when at home':

> *in nakedness the married pair behold each other, neither is there anything lascivious therein . . . In bed they lie copulated* as they were created, *and thus they sleep: . . . they say that it cannot be otherwise, because essential conjugial love, which is perpetual, copulates: . . . as it is spoken concerning Adam when he saw Eve his wife, 'behold my bone and flesh' and also that 'they were naked and not ashamed'.*[26]

Then, in a passage that seemed to justify the ritualistic nudity at Avignon, Swedenborg revealed that he was carried to a mountain in the spirit world, where all the husbands and wives were naked. When any newcomers from the natural world arrive, 'they examine them, which is done by stripping off their clothes', to learn whether they embody 'a genuine conjugial principle'.[27] The spirits said that they live in houses with men and maid servants, 'which are all naked'.

From Tulk, who corresponded with James Glen, the Blakes could have learned about the colourful Scot's career as a nudist missionary among the natives of Demerara, to whom he preached Swedenborg's message of angelic nakedness and perpetual potency.[28] Their acceptance of Swedenborgian notions of nudity was perhaps shared by Thomas Butts, who according to family tradition was also a Swedenborgian.[29] Blake felt that he could express himself fully to Butts, who became a steady patron of his revolutionary poetry and designs.

In 1863, Blake's biographer Gilchrist published an anecdote that scandalised his Victorian readers. The source was Butts, who was fond of telling it, and it had since been 'pretty extensively retailed about town'. One day Butts called on the Blakes and found them sitting in the summer-house in their Lambeth garden. The couple was freed from 'those troublesome disguises' that have prevailed 'since the Fall':

> 'Come in!' *cried Blake;* 'it's only Adam and Eve, you know!' *Husband and wife had been reciting passages from* Paradise Lost, *in character, and the garden of Hercules Buildings had to represent the Garden of Eden; a little to the scandal of wondering neighbours, on more than one occasion. However, they knew sufficient of the single-minded artist not wholly to misconstrue such phenomena.*[30]

According to Swedenborgian-Illuminist standards, such Edenic behaviour was not shocking. Moreover, the implication that Blake's 'neighbours' were not distressed by repeated incidents suggests that there were kindred spirits in Lambeth.

Gilchrist further interpreted the nude scene as revealing the acquiescence of Catherine to William's unusual demands:

> *This incident in the garden illustrates forcibly the strength of her husband's influence over her, and the unquestioning manner in which she fell in with all he did or said. When reassured by him that she (for the time) was Eve, she would not dream of contradiction – nay, she in a sense believed it. If therefore the anecdote argues madness in one, it argues it in both.*[31]

Butts's amused tolerance hints at his own acceptance of unconventional sexual behaviour, an attitude evidently seconded by his wife Elizabeth. Two poems by Blake to Mrs Butts suggest that she shared his interest in extramarital sexuality.

In 'The Phoenix / To Mrs Butts', Blake hinted at her flirtation with him in a dialogue between Mrs Butts's Bird and a Fairy gay. Drawing on Shakespearian usage of fairies as 'often ambiguous ministers of sexual joy', Blake made his fairy spokesman 'the traditional symbol of sex'.[32] The poet admits the temptation provoked by the romantic singing and 'names of Love' voiced by Mrs Butts's bird, but he reluctantly sends her back to her husband and children. In another poem, he stressed that she is 'Wife of the Friend of those I most revere' and urges her 'to Go on in Virtuous Seed sowing on Mold / Of Human Vegetation & Behold Your Harvest springing to Eternal life / Parent of Youthful minds & happy wife'.[33]

Bentley suggests that Blake taught at Elizabeth Butts's school for young ladies, in which eighteen unmarried females boarded in their home and provided Thomas Butts with a bevy of 'Daughters of Albion'.[34] At this time, such female boarding schools were suspected of sexual permissiveness; as the *Bon Ton Magazine* reported, they 'were not always the most reputable', for they were 'seminaries of such learning as is often destructive to female virtue'.[35] Despite Blake's radical pronouncements on free love, in this case he urged conjugal fidelity; after all, Thomas Butts was his most important patron. Her attraction to the 'winged fancy' of an adulterous liaison led her from 'her proper attachments to home and children'.[36] Was Elizabeth Butts the proposed second wife who sent Catherine Blake into floods of tears?

While the Blakes maintained their outwardly conventional friendship with the Butts family, William was privately suffering from recurrent bouts of mania, depression and paranoia, which were probably connected with his experiments in Animal Magnetism. Over the next years, he would describe various phenomena associated with the visionary trance: 'they behold / What is within now seen without'; Los has 'sparks issuing from his hair'; emanations produce 'sweet rapturd trance'.[37] Though some Swedenborgians accused Dr de Mainaduc of making 'the art instrumental to horrid enormities', the radicals welcomed the erotic possibilities of female liberation.[38]

One reason that Blake was willing to risk his mental and spiritual health was undoubtedly his hope that he could thaw 'the frozen marriage bed'. He possibly remembered Zinzendorf's exhortation that in order to raise the *Shekhinah* or visualise the 'sapience Archetypal', one must not let middle or old age be an excuse for sexual abstention. Men and women who have 'arrived at the state of continence, must not abstain, but celebrate coition'.[39] Moreover, the elderly 'must cohabit', even 'much the more so'. This Zinzendorfian notion was elaborated by the magnetising Swedenborgians, who pressured their wives to provide enough 'kindling' to elevate their spiritual vision.

General Rainsford, who performed magnetic operations with Loutherbourg, Cosway and Sharp, translated a German 'Account of Magnetic Healing', which affirmed the reality of the 'ecstatic state of the soul' achieved by magnetic manipulation. Blake would certainly have been interested in the conclusion. 'Besides this elevation of the mental faculties during that state of extasy, the organs of the Senses are refined in a most surprising manner.'[40] The ladies know 'nothing of Reserve or Restraint, nothing of that Etiquette, bashfulness or shiness' that commonly inhibits their conversation with the other sex. That Rainsford's magnetic therapy aimed to unrestrain female sexuality was revealed by his friend Lord Percy, who wrote to him: 'I sincerely hope you have operated upon the maid to Effect, and that nine months hence, we shall have proof positive' of the efficacy of Animal Magnetism.[41]

Blake also laboured to gain 'proof positive' that he and his wife could achieve the erotic energy that gives birth to the 'ecstatic state of the soul'. However, as Catherine resisted, withdrew and wept, he pondered 'How to know Love from Deceit'. He noted that 'Love to faults is always blind, / Always is to joy inclin'd, / Lawless, wing'd, & unconfin'd, / And breaks all chains from every mind.'[42] But Deceit is 'Modest, prudish, & confin'd, / Lawful, cautious, & refin'd'. Ultimately, it 'chains in fetters every mind'.

Despite the happy nudist interludes in their Lambeth garden, the Blakes still suffered painful differences concerning conjugial love. But, over the next seven years, William would learn new techniques of sexual thawing, as even more exotic erotica entered his Lambeth milieu from Ethiopia and India. And, as a 'Mental Traveller', he was eventually able to take Catherine along on his voyage to new territories of sexualised spirituality.

20

The Visionary Vulva

As well almost might Paracelsus make a man, without female aid, as can be acquired mystic knowledge without woman, the centre of magnetic attraction.

William Belcher, *Intellectual Electricity* (1798)

WHILE CONSERVATIVE AND liberal Swedenborgians argued about the good or evil propensities of Animal Magnetism, the Illuminists privately studied the visionary connection between female and male sexual energies – between the vulva and the phallus. Swedenborg stressed in 'De Conjugio' that the organs of generation, especially the womb, communicate with heaven.[1] For initiates of the Rite of Heredom, Lambert de Lintot engraved an elaborate Kabbalistic-alchemical design, which featured three nude females with exposed vulvas who dance around a phallic obelisk; the caption reads, 'Nothing without the V-Point.'[2] In another emblem Lintot engraved a circle enclosing three legs emerging from a shared genital area, symbolising the unification of male and female in the V-Point.[3] The motto reads UNA TRINUS AB UNO at the top and DE LOS at the bottom. Did Blake draw upon this emblem for the name of his visionary prophet 'Los'?

Throughout the 1790s, Lintot's friend Dr Ebenezer Sibly (a Swedenborgian Mason) copied Kabbalistic drawings published by Sabbatian Masons, which expressed similar vulvic-phallic symbolism.[4] Like the flamboyant triangular head of Lintot's phallic pillar, Sibly sketched a flamboyant triangle within a

CHAPTER AND GRAND LODGE OF ENGLAND
CHAPITRE ET GRANDE LOGE D'ANGLETERRE

BRUTE STONE
NO R
NO SY
NOTHING WITHOUT THE V POINT

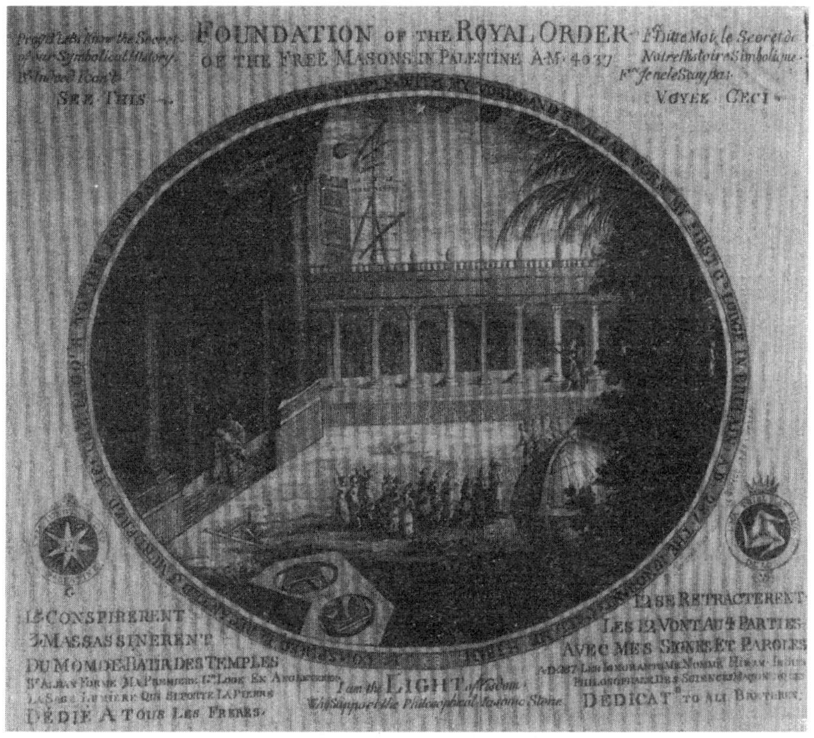
FOUNDATION OF THE ROYAL ORDER
OF THE FREE MASONS IN PALESTINE A.M. 4037
SEE THIS
VOYEZ CECI
LES 12 VONT AU 4 PARTIES
AVEC MES SIGNES ET PAROLES
I am the LIGHT of Wisdom
DÉDIÉ A TOUS LES FRERES

circle that represented 'The invisible incomprehensible Chaos, the Vacuum', next to a vulva (complete with slit and clitoris) inside a circle that represented 'the visible comprehensible Chaos, the Ground'. Together these sexual images formed 'the Philosophic Furnace'. Again, Blake may have drawn on similar traditions for his portrayal of Los labouring at his Hermetic furnace.

As a medical sexologist, Sibly infused these alchemical themes into his therapy for female frigidity, male impotence and infertility. In *The Medical Mirror, or Treatise on the Impregnation of the Human Female* (1794), Sibly's explicit descriptions of the female genitals aimed at improving the sexual responsiveness of women and thus their capacity for conjugial love and spiritual vision. His reproductive diagnoses and techniques were possibly relevant to the alleged reproductive failures of Catherine Blake and the sexual frustration of her husband.

In bitter poems, Blake not only complained about his wife's prudish resistance, but hinted at his own problems with premature ejaculation. Thus his meditative preparation (by intense focus on the *Shekhinah* within his wife) was wasted, along with the divine semen. In 'The Crystal Cabinet', he described his attempt to transform his homely Kate into 'Another Maiden like herself / Translucent lovely shining clear'. Like Lintot's emblem of three legs emerging from the shared V-Point, Blake described a triple-dimensional sexual experience:

Threefold each in the other closd
O what a pleasant trembling fear
O what a smile a threefold Smile
Filld me that like a flame I burnd;
I bent to Kiss the lovely Maid
And found a Threefold Kiss returnd . . .[5]

However, when the narrator attempted to break through to the visionary fourth dimension, he ejaculated prematurely and could not maintain the necessary erectile potency:

I strove to seize the inmost Form
With ardor fierce & hands of flame
But burst the Crystal Cabinet
And like a Weeping Babe became
A weeping Babe upon the wild
And Weeping Woman pale reclind
And in the outward air again
I filld with woes the passing Wind.

Foster Damon suggests that 'The Crystal Cabinet' symbolised the delusions of love, with hints at 'a clandestine love affair' in Lambeth, which ended unhappily because 'the harmony between wife and mistress could not last'.[6] However, Damon's 'threefold' male and two females can also be interpreted as a husband, wife and *Shekhinah*, who almost achieve visionary reintegration until loss of ejaculatory control.

In another painful poem, 'Long John Brown & Little Mary Bell', Blake used his sexualised Fairy to hint at a husband's impotence and wife's vaginal atrophy:

Little Mary Bell had a Fairy in a Nut
Long John Brown had the Devil in his Gut
Long John Brown lovd little Mary Bell
And the Fairy drew the Devil into the Nut-Shell.

Her Fairy Skipd out & her Fairy Skipd in
He laughd at the Devil saying Love is a Sin
The Devil he raged & the Devil he was wroth
And the Devil enterd into the Young Mans broth.[7]

The word 'broth' occurred in esoteric texts to denote sexual fluids.[8] Thus, with his semen spoiled, Long John Brown 'grew thinner & thinner' until he died, while 'the Fairy skipd out of the old Nut shell', leaving Miss Bell 'with her fusty old nut'.

The Blakes' sexual problems were possibly compounded by Catherine's miscarriages, especially one that could have occurred on 26 August 1796. The recent discovery by Tristanne Connolly of the name 'Cath.e Blake' at the British Lying-In Hospital on that date lends a new plausibility to Edwin Ellis's claim that William's proposal to take a second wife so disturbed Catherine that she suffered a miscarriage.[9] Ellis interpreted the poem 'William Bond' as a biographical account of the incident, with 'Mary Green' representing Blake's wife and 'Sister Jane' his sister. When the puritanical 'Angels of Providence' drive away the sexual 'Fairies', William Bond becomes sickened by depression. The alarmed women take pity on his sexual frustration:

> *And on his Right hand was Mary Green*
> *And on his Left hand was his sister Jane*
> *And their tears fell thro the black black Cloud*
> *To drive away the sick mans pain*
>
> *O William if thou dost another Love*
> *Dost another Love better than poor Mary*
> *Go & take that other to be thy Wife*
> *And Mary Green shall her Servant be*
>
> *Yes Mary I do another Love*
> *Another I Love far better than thee*
> *And another I will have for my Wife*
> *Then what Have I do with thee*

Mary trembld & Mary chilld
And Mary fell down on the right hand floor
That William Bond & his Sister Jane
Scarce could recover Mary more . . .[10]

According to Ellis, when Blake 'claimed the right of Abraham to give to Hagar what Sarah refused', his wife 'felt her courage give way, and crying out in her desolation, she fell down in a heap by the bed. Something else as well as her courage gave way' – that is, she aborted a baby. Other critics who believed that Catherine suffered miscarriages detected images of partially formed and premature fetuses in poems ranging from *Thel* to *Jerusalem*.[11] In 1796, Catherine was thirty-eight and an unlikely candidate for a healthy pregnancy. Could the Blakes have utilised the services of Dr Sibly or other Swedenborgian sex doctors to increase her reproductive potential?

If she was indeed pregnant, she would probably be so exhausted and uncomfortable that she rejected her husband's sexual advances. Blake suggests in 'William Bond' that her pity for his sexual frustration triggered his own pity for her misery and that the sexual fairies returned to dance 'round her Shining Head'. However, the return of the fairies may not have been immediate, for 'William Bond' was written several years after the alleged miscarriage. In the intervening years, Blake seemed tormented by sexual desires, obsessions, fantasies and failures, which were intensified by his study of Enochian spiritual erotica.

On paper watermarked 1796, Blake sketched a series of obscene drawings that illustrated the sexual and magical themes of the *Ethiopic Book of Enoch*. The existence of this supposedly lost, apocalyptic book (originally in Hebrew, *c.* second century BC) had long intrigued occultists and students of Kabbalah, for it revealed a sexual-visionary conjunction between angels and men. The Illuminists hoped to discover reinforcement for Swedenborg's linking of the genital organs, especially the womb, with celestial vision.[12] Though critics have assumed that Blake did not make the drawings until 1821, when an English translation of *Enoch* was published, he actually had many opportunities to learn about the rare manuscript soon after its arrival in England. Moreover, his access came through Moravian and Swedenborgian students of the mystical apocalyptic book.

Two manuscripts of *Enoch* were brought to England in 1774 by James Bruce, the Scottish explorer and Ancient Mason, who had recently discussed his Ethiopian discoveries with John Antes, a Moravian missionary in Cairo.[13] Antes hoped to fulfil Zinzendorf's dream of penetrating into the mysterious kingdom – a dream depicted in a 1750 painting of the count studying a map of Ethiopia.[14] Relevant to Blake's later Enochian interests, Antes was the brother-in-law of Benjamin La Trobe, the Moravian minister who almost certainly knew Catherine and Thomas Armitage and John Blake.[15] Through his friendship with Antes, Bruce met the La Trobe family in London and shared his African experiences with them.[16]

Reverend La Trobe, who had been infatuated with Zinzendorf's radical son Christel and who maintained contact with a sect of crypto-Sabbatian Judaeo-Christians in Amsterdam, would not have been shocked by the sexual themes of the Ethiopic text. Neither would his politically radical and sometimes risqué son Benjamin Henry La Trobe, a talented artist and architect, who moved in Blake's artistic circles, and who was privy to Bruce's ongoing translation of the Ethiopic text in the 1780s. The explorer had completed eighteen chapters when he commissioned Benjamin Henry to edit his travel journals.[17]

While working with Bruce, the young architect evidently knew Flaxman, Loutherbourg, Gillray and George Hadfield (brother of Maria Cosway), and he would later praise their works.[18] Though it is presently unknown if he met Blake, Benjamin Henry's biographer suspects that he did, on the basis of 'the unusual Blakean qualities in his watercolour paintings'.[19] Other friends of Blake, such as Cosway, who knew Reverend La Trobe, and William Hayley, who knew James Bruce, could have learned about the 'divine eroticism' of *Enoch*, in which the angelic Watchers copulate with the daughters of men.[20] Most intriguing was the thesis that 'their divinity lies in their organs of generation'.[21] Cosway and Hayley also owned copies of *Le Comte de Gabalis*, in which the angelic copulations of the Book of Enoch were discussed.[22]

Probably informed by Bruce about the Ethiopian version, Hayley published *A Philosophical Essay on Old Maids* (1785), in which Enoch's daughter Kunaza determines to preserve her virginity, even though the Angels 'burned with desire'.[23] Pharmarius, the inventor of magic and dealer in occult machinations, wanted to seduce an unwilling, resistant woman, so he 'infused into the wondering virgin the thrilling flame of desire'. However, the angel Gabriel intervened, so that Kunaza remained 'the original president of Old Maids'. The liberal Hayley, who would subsequently father an illegitimate child, mocked the ideal of celibacy and abstinence; instead, he praised the ancient Jewish traditions of sacramental sexuality. It was perhaps Hayley's comical essay that stimulated Blake's sketch of Enoch around this time.[24]

Blake also had access to a Kabbalistic interpretation of the Book of Enoch, for his Swedenborgian colleague General Rainsford was familiar with an earlier publication of a spurious Ethiopian manuscript, *The History of the Seventy Two Interpreters . . . to which is added, The History of the Angels and Their Gallantry with the Daughters of Men. Written by the Patriarch Enoch* (London, 1715). Rainsford, a Fellow of the

Society of Antiquaries, apparently also read Dr Charles Woide's translation (now lost) made from a third Ethiopian manuscript donated by Bruce to the Royal Library in Paris, which Woide produced for the Antiquaries in London.[25]

As a student of the Kabbalistic techniques of the Avignon oracle, Rainsford drafted his own version, entitled 'The Book of Henoch Which contains the true Cabala of the 72 names of the Angels; which were revealed to Chanoch by the angel Mitratton. Translated into French from an Arabian MS. In the Royal Library at Paris, brought from Abyssinia.'[26] Rainsford shared his Enochian study with his Masonic friends, such as Dr Ebenezer Sibly and Dr William Spence, who interpreted the Ethiopian Enoch from a Swedenborgian perspective and incorporated it into their medical sexology.[27] Blake's Lambeth neighbour J. A. Tulk was so intrigued by the Enochian discovery that he sent to the *New Magazine of Knowledge* the passage in Bruce's *Travels to Discover the Source of the Nile* (1790), which described the 'Gnostic book' and its revelation of the copulation between the sons of God and the daughters of men.[28]

Thus Blake's Enochian illustrations, watermarked 1796, possibly date from that year, when the illuminated Swedenborgians were preoccupied with its themes, and when Blake had a personal stake in the issues raised about phallic potency and spiritual vision.[29] Did he view Catherine as the resistant Kunaza, determined to become a virtual Old Maid? His first Enoch design presents 'an heroic naked man' encircled by four nude females, whose breasts are carefully emphasised, while the angelic Watcher has 'an enormously enlarged penis extending most of the way across his hip'.[30] His giant phallus is 'the reason for his attraction to the surrounding daughters of men'.

While Blake's sketch features a plurality of women and orgiastic implications, a sketch by his friend Flaxman was more discreet, for the figures were 'almost genital-less' and there was only 'one woman per Watcher'.[31] Bentley points to the similarities between Flaxman's more cautious portrayal and his illustration for Swedenborg's *True Christian Religion*, no.134. In that passage, Swedenborg described the descent of light-bringing angels into a spiritual temple.[32] One factor that may have influenced Blake's more orgiastic perspective was the return of Count Grabianka to London in 1796, when he probably called on Tulk and those Swedenborgians still in Lambeth.[33]

In Blake's second drawing, he continued his antinomian interpretation, in which the naked Watcher whispers into the ear of the nude woman as he caresses her belly and she holds his arm gently; then, descending headlong, his outstretched arms reach for her vulva. From this vulvic contact, she will receive the forbidden knowledge of 'sorcery, incantations . . . bracelets and ornaments, the use of paint, the beautifying of the eyebrows, the use of stone, so that the world became altered'.

In the third drawing, the most sexually explicit of the series, a nude woman is poised between 'two enormous, light-giving phalli'. The woman has her left hand on one phallus, while she gazes fixedly at the other; 'her vulva is carefully emphasised', and she seems to have difficulty in choosing which phallus to choose first. As Bentley concludes, the divinity of the Watchers is concentrated on 'their starlike phalli', for their divinity lies in their organs of generation; 'no wonder they were so attractive to the daughters of men – and no wonder their offspring were monsters'.[34]

In the fourth drawing, the vulvas of the two women are again carefully emphasised, while in the fifth the prophet Enoch achieves a vision of the 'Ancient of Days', with the book of the living opened before him. Blake seemed to disagree with the punishment meted out to these antediluvians by an

angry God, for in an additional drawing he portrayed a Watcher who is free to fly from the earth, but on a short tether: 'He is, like all mortals, chained to earth though with immortal aspirations for the stars.'[35] Or, like Grabianka and the Men of Desire, he refuses to accept the limitations placed upon him by the jealous Demiurge, Old Nobodaddy.

In 1796, Blake's commitment to eroticised art was reinforced by his close friend George Cumberland, who employed him to engrave his genitally explicit illustrations of Greek and Roman myths. In *Thoughts on Outline*, Cumberland combined radical political pronouncements with praise for the unashamed nakedness of the Greeks, who freely displayed 'the masculine parts' in their statues. He chastised the increasing prudery of conservative art critics: 'today the index of a narrow mind . . . has a cruel tendency to depress the hand of Art, which is never more elevated than when describing the *human form divine* as it came from the hands of the mysterious great first Cause'.[36] Praising Blake's 'extraordinary genius and abilities', he utilised the engraver's commitment to clear and firm outline to display 'The Conjugal Union of Cupid', with full male genitals and female vulva; 'Anacreon, ode LII', with a nude male grabbing the leg of an embracing nude female, while a satyr thrusts a phallic thyrsis; and 'Ovid: Iron Age', with a Priapic figure in full erection.

Two years later, perhaps influenced by Blake, Cumberland moved beyond Classical explicitness to Ethiopian erotica. In his utopian novella, *The Captive of the Castle of Sennaar: An African Tale* (1798), he located the tale in the Nubian city of Sennaar, where Monsieur Du Roule, an early French ambassador, was murdered by the King of the Nubians, to prevent him from reaching Ethiopia.[37] The affair at Sennaar was well known to the Moravians from the accounts of their missionaries in Egypt, who tried unsuccessfully to visit the secretive Ethiopian kingdom.[38] Like Blake, Cumberland viewed the Enochian copulation between angels and humans positively, and he ignored the punishment imposed by the angry God. His narrator learns from his 'master a Jew' about the island of the Sophis, who live a 'life according to nature'.

Drawing on the Hermetic and Kabbalistic sense of *Sophia* as the female potency within the Godhead, he praised the Sophis' worship of 'the good Energy, whose office is to create', which leads them to affirm, 'O Holy Energy . . . thou art Love!'[39] Among his uninhibited Sophis, early adolescent sexual urges are encouraged, 'for they are fully sensible of the dangers arising from suppression of the natural fires'. Thus, the Energy instructs them in sexual practices, and their colouring becomes 'warm and rosy carnation' from their nude exposure to 'fine air'. In Cumberland's utopian vision of a radical commune, where polygamy and prostitution are accepted, he praised those ancient, exotic statues that still remain and which express the form the Creator gave them. The Sophis would have spurned 'the unnatural depravity that affixed ideas of shame to the most necessary, wonderful and noble organs of the human body'.

Echoing Blake, Cumberland linked this vision of sexual liberation to political liberation, and he called for freedom and virtue, 'although depressed, but not extinct', to triumph over the 'crooked policy of the Machiavellian statesman'. However, Cumberland himself did not triumph, for when he sent the work to a few friends, one persuaded him that 'it would be dangerous under Mr Pitt's maladministration to publish it'.[40] Cumberland subsequently cancelled the edition, and it was never published or sold to anyone. But he had given a few copies to friends.

One of these was Thomas Taylor, the reactionary Platonist, who earlier tried to teach Blake geometry.[41] Taylor urged Cumberland to forgo publication of such 'lasciviousness'.[42] Affirming that he was 'a pronounced Platonist', he insisted that love is '*true* only in proportion as it is *pure*'. Arguing that the love expressed in poetic language is far superior to that 'arising from copulation', he scorned the mere 'union of bodies'. No wonder Blake professed to Crabb Robinson that he was 'very hostile to Plato'.[43] Providing some consolation to Cumberland, Blake wrote enthusiastically about his gift copy, 'Your vision of the Happy Sophis I have devourd. O most delicious book.'[44]

Cumberland was a good friend to the Blakes, and his shared interest in unrestrained sexuality – coupled with that of the Tulks and Buttses – must have assured Catherine that her husband's demands, though sometimes baffling and frightening, were not entirely sinful or illicit. However, Blake's sense of political vulnerablity added an ominous air of paranoia to his erotic and visionary struggles, which would be graphically expressed in the turbulent psychodrama of *Vala, or The Four Zoas*, which he wrote and revised from 1796 to 1807. In the verses and illustrations of this strange and chaotic prophecy he would express his most tormented and eloquent notions of sexuality, with his wife Catherine thrust into a mythic role in the personal and cosmic struggle for spiritual vision.

21

Priapic Prayer and Randy Antiquarians

Alternate Love & Hate his breast: hers Scorn & Jealousy
In embryon passions. they kiss'd not nor embrac'd
for shame & fear
His head beam'd light & in his vigorous voice
was prophecy.
William Blake, *Vala,* or *the Four Zoas* (*c.*1796–1807)

In 1796–7, while Blake produced more than 700 illustrations for Edward Young's pious poem *Night Thoughts*, he began to use the back of proof-sheets to draft his most tormented and provocative prophecy, initially titled *VALA or the Death and Judgement of the Eternal Man: A DREAM of Nine Nights*. Over the next decade, he continually revised and expanded the vast work, which he eventually retitled *The Four Zoas: The Torments of Love & Jealousy in The Death and Judgement of Albion the Ancient Man*. Like the radical Kabbalists and Swedenborgians, Blake believed that human sexuality mirrored that of the divine world, and he determined to courageously and honestly *visualise* it in all its beautiful and perverse forms. Tormented by erotic desires, obsessions, fantasies and failures, he transferred his personal problems to the mythic plane.

In the process, he surrounded his often inchoate verse with shockingly explicit illustrations of a nightmarish world of cosmic sexuality. His capacity for such erotic visualisation was enhanced by the dream techniques of Somnambulism and by the Priapic writings and illustrations of radical antiquarians, who happily discarded the inhibitions of conventional religion to argue for the sexual roots of ancient (and even contemporary) religions. Heated public debates about their theories erupted while Blake worked on *Vala*, and many of his most startling expressions seem to be responses to the revelations by and condemnations of the randy antiquarians.

Since his apprentice days, Blake had been familiar with the work of Baron d'Hancarville, and he copied several of the spectacular engravings in the latter's catalogue, *Collection of Etruscan, Greek and Roman Antiquities from the Cabinet of the Hon'ble William Hamilton* (1766–7).[1] Blake and Cosway, who owned the lavish edition, must have enjoyed the 'exceedingly erotic illustrations', which were presented with a tone of unembarassed, light-hearted gaiety.[2] D'Hancarville described the work as his attempt 'to explore unknown lands'.[3] He followed this with *Monumens du Culte Secret des Dames Romaines* (1770), which featured engravings of ancient stones portraying a profuse variety of sexual positions and animal-human combinations. He argued that these acts were 'very respectable in the Religion of the Ancients'; therefore 'a wife who loves her husband should refuse nothing to him'.[4]

The baron's use of a fake Vatican imprint led to his expulsion from Italy, and he moved to London, where he was welcomed by Townley, Hamilton and Richard Payne Knight. With their support, he next wrote *Veneres et Priapi* (1784), which included better engravings of the obscene images in the *Culte Secret*. Blake may have seen this work, for many of these images reappeared in *Vala*, or *The Four Zoas*.[5] A genuinely erudite art historian, d'Hancarville yearned to move beyond his pornographic work to produce a scholarly treatise on the sexual origins of religion and art in many cultures. His

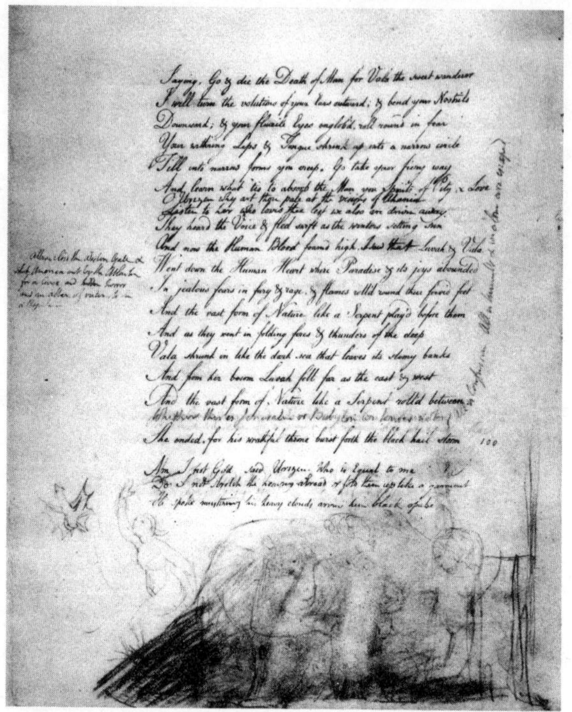

Saying, Go & die the Death of Man for Vala the sweet wanderer
I will turn the volutions of your Ears outward; & bend your Nostrils
Downward; & your fluxile Eyes englob'd, roll round in fear
Your withring Lips & Tongue shrink up into a narrow circle
Till into narrow forms you creep. Go take your fiery way
And learn what 'tis to absorb the Man you Spirits of Pity & Love
O Urizen why art thou pale at the visions of Ahania
Listen to her who loves thee lest we also are driven away
They heard the Voice & fled swift as the winters setting sun
And now the Human Blood foamd high. I saw that Luvah & Vala
Went down the Human Heart where Paradise & its joys abounded
In jealous fears in fury & rage. & flames rolld round their fervid feet
And the vast form of Nature like a Serpent play'd before them
And as they went in folding fires & thunders of the deep
Vala shrunk in like the dark sea that leaves its slimy banks
And from her bosom Luvah fell far as the east & west
And the vast form of Nature like a Serpent rolld between
She ended. for his wrathful throne burst forth the black hail storm

Am I not God said Urizen. Who is Equal to me

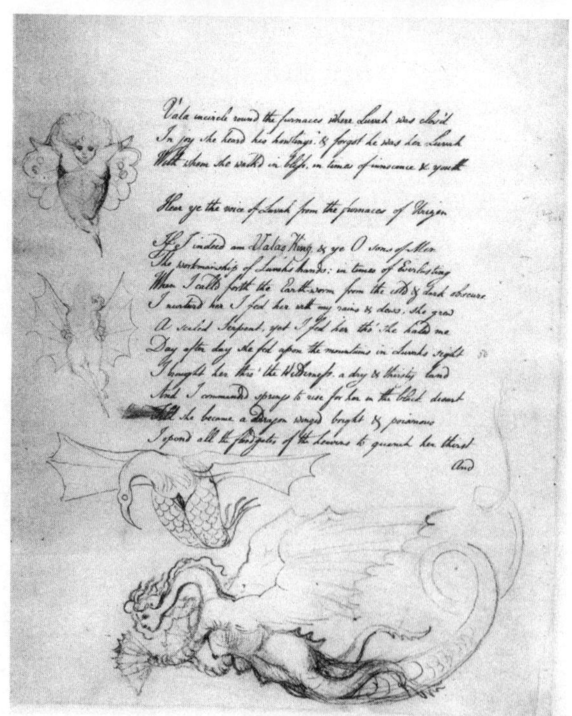

Vala incircle round the furnaces where Luvah was clos'd
In joy she heard his howlings. & forgot he was her Luvah
With whom she walkd in bliss. in times of innocence & youth

Hear ye the voice of Luvah from the furnaces of Urizen

If I indeed am Valas King & ye O sons of Men
The workmanship of Luvahs hands; in times of Everlasting
When I calld forth the Earth-worm from the cold & dark obscure
I nurtured her I fed her with my rains & dews, she grew
A scaled Serpent, yet I fed her tho' she hated me
Day after day she fed upon the mountains in Luvahs sight
I brought her thro' the Wilderness. a dry & thirsty land
And I commanded springs to rise for her in the black desart
Till she became a Dragon winged bright & poisonous
I opend all the floodgates of the heavens to quench her thirst
And

mammoth treatise, *Recherches sur l'origine, l'esprit et les progrés des Arts de la Gréce* (1785), created such a scandal and financial failure that he had to flee England for France. But it also stirred much interest among Blake's artistic and theosophic friends, who flocked to the antiquarians' art collections to see their erotic sculptures, engravings and medals.

According to d'Hancarville, the divine source of creation is 'the Generative Power, or the God of Life'.[6] When the masculine fire unites with the feminine water, life is generated, and worshippers in many ancient religions paid pious devotion to these sexual powers. Though he did not know much about Kabbala, he analysed the Jews' Cherubim and Ark of the Tabernacle according to this thesis and hinted at phallic and uterine meanings behind the Christian cross. Despite occasional lapses into enthusiastic prurience, d'Hancarville stressed that Priapic religion and art were not obscene but genuine expressions of piety, devotion and reverence towards the enormous creative powers of the universe.

While prudes and churchmen expressed horror at d'Hancarville's thesis, many connoisseurs responded positively, which encouraged Richard Payne Knight to go even further. In 1786 he had the Society of Dilettanti print for limited and private distribution *An Account of the Worship of Priapus . . . and its Connexion with the Mystic Theology of the Ancients*. The Dilettanti employed Thomas Spilsbury, member of a Moravian family, to print the controversial book (which is still kept in 'the librarian's poison cupboard').[7] The Moravian connection is suggestive, for Thomas's brother John Spilsbury, an engraver, employed the young Gillray, while another brother Jonathan, a portrait painter, was an acquaintance of Blake.[8] Benjamin Henry La Trobe not only enjoyed the divine eroticism of the Ethiopian Enoch but the Priapic studies of d'Hancarville and

Knight.[9] Apparently, among some Moravians, Zinzendorf's psychoerotic notions of religious art survived the official suppression of 'Sifting Time' themes.

Among the engravers commissioned to illustrate *The Worship of Priapus* was William Sharp, though it is unclear from the unsigned plates whether Sharp produced the explicit portrayals of erect penises, human – animal copulation, the phallic big toe and double oral sex – all copied from religious art objects.[10] In his explanatory text, Knight expressed his belief in 'a broad pantheism', in which the 'emanations' from a 'universal expansion of the creative spirit' permeate all creation – a thesis that would have appealed to Sharp's Swedenborgianism.[11] Boldly describing the phallic and vulvic symbolism at the core of all religions, including Christianity, Knight lamented that hypocritical priests destroyed the joyful and natural religion of its originators: 'one of the greatest curses that ever afflicted the human race is dogmatical theology'. It was a sentiment shared by Blake's Moravian and Illuminist friends.

For General Rainsford, who read the books by Knight and d'Hancarville, their theses reinforced those of Swedenborg about the linkage of phallic and visionary potency. Moreover, d'Hancarville's account in *Recherches* of an ancient phallic religion in Tartary reinforced Swedenborg's claims about the secret, pre-Judaic arcana of conjugial love preserved in that exotic land.[12] The baron also hinted at his own familiarity with Swedenborg's visionary theories, which he compared to those of the Orphean mystics: 'One sees that like Swedenborg, who in our days writes about the marvels of Heaven and Hell "on the evidence of his eyes and ears", Orpheus claimed to see and hear all that passes in Hell.'

From his conversations with Cosway and visiting *Illuminés* in London, d'Hancarville learned more about the sexual theosophy of Swedenborg and the *Hommes de Désir*.[13] Once in

Paris, he published a sequel to *Recherches*, entitled *Antiquités Étrusques, Grecques et Romaines* (1787), in which he compared the encoded phallic symbolism to that of '*artistes initiés*' among the illuminated Freemasons. When asked why ancient artists could express sexual mysteries that speakers and writers were forbidden to mention, he suggested that these portrayals were made by initiated artists, who used an obscure manner that could only be deciphered by fellow adepts: 'Even today the Freemasons present their tableau to people who do not comprehend what the symbols represent and thus cannot give any explication.'[14]

Blake's friend George Cumberland was intrigued by the arguments of the Priapic antiquarians. After returning from Rome, where he visited Cagliostro in his Inquisition cell, Cumberland consulted his friends Townley and Knight about the sexual and mystical interpretations of their mutual collections of engraved medals and intaglios. In May and June 1791, Cumberland called on both men and inspected their *objets d'art*, which resulted in a correspondence about their various explications, with d'Hancarville contributing his thoughts from Paris.[15] In gratitude for their help, Cumberland sent Townley one of his 'pastes', which featured 'an armed head with the P [Priapus] on the inside', and offered to send more 'that will support your Mythology'.[16]

Until 1794, the Priapic studies of the antiquarians reached only limited circles, but in that year an inadvertent footnote by one of Blake's friends, Major Edward Moor, provoked a public scandal and renewed interest in Knight's *Worship of Priapus* and d'Hancarville's publications.[17] While on leave from military service in India, Moor employed Joseph Johnson, who stocked Blake's works, to issue his *Narrative of the Operations of Captain Little's Detachment, and of the Maharatta Army* (1794). In a note, Moor named R. P. Knight as the author of *Priapus* and then dispassionately summarised its theses.

Recounting Knight's argument that the early Christian *agapes* or Love Feasts secretly preserved the phallic religion, Moor outraged a reviewer in the conservative *British Critic*, who condemned him for alerting the public to 'a treatise, of which without his assistance we should happily have been ignorant'.[18] The indignant reviewer continued, 'Much more could we say on this clandestine work, printed without publication, and concealed without suppression; but we consign it, with its impure decorations, to that mystery it courts, and which, we heartily wish may never be revealed.' Of course, with such provocative publicity, curious readers searched for copies of Knight's 'impure' book.

One of these, Thomas Mathias, a reactionary poet, attacked Knight in *The Pursuits of Literature, a Satirical Poem*, which appeared in increasingly virulent editions from 1794 to 1798. Claiming that 'a friend *insisted* that I read *The Worship of Priapus*', Mathias noted that its 'most disgusting plates' have been distributed liberally 'to the *emeriti* in speculative Priapism'.[19] Mathias charged that 'all the ordure and filth, all the antique pictures, and all the representations of the generative organs, in their most odious and degrading protrusion, have been raked together and copulated' with 'a new species of blasphemy'. Dismissing the antiquarians' scholarship as 'records of the stews and bordellos of Greece', he deplored the 'obscene revellings of Greek scholars in their private chambers', where they 'dwell mentally in lust and darkness'.

Mathias further linked Knight's work with Martin Madan's *Thelypthora* as corrupters of youth – a linkage that could place Blake's illuminated poem *Thel* in a scandalous context. In succeeding editions he listed several of Blake's friends – William Hayley, Horne Tooke, Erasmus Darwin and Thomas Paine – as Priapic Jacobins who deserved government surveillance.[20] Despite or because of these intensifying attacks, the 'revelling' antiquarians and their artistic friends became even more committed to the cause of sexually liberated religion.

By 1796, when George Cumberland employed Blake to engrave the genitally explicit illustrations for *Thoughts on Outline*, he viewed Classical art through a thoroughly Priapic prism. He noted that 'Monsieur d'Hancarville, who really was an enthusiast for the Arts of the Ancients', was 'unfortunately not an artist'; nevertheless, he gave us 'a dim, yet not inelegant shadow of those truly great performances'.[21] It was probably no coincidence that in 1796 Blake would attempt to bring similar spiritual-erotic works of art out of the shadows and into the intense visions of *Vala*, his hallucinative psychodrama of fallen and degraded human and divine sexuality.

Blake described 'the bulls of Luvah, breathing fire . . . Round howling Orc', whose beating pulsations 'darted higher & higher to the shrine of Enitharmon'.[22] He thus echoed d'Hancarville's thesis that the bull was the primordial symbol of phallic energy ('*la Puissance Générative*').[23] Affirming that spiritually illuminated artists have expressed this mystery through the ages, d'Hancarville featured engravings of Priapic figures with huge erections, which Blake replicated in *Vala*.[24] As noted earlier, Edward Ellis reported that, among the erased figures in *Vala* was one of an erect phallus, 'an object fitted for sacred art before the degrading spirit of a later civilisation had vulgarised it'.[25] In Blake's design, 'the Priapic attribute is represented as nearly the height of a signpost: three figures are bowing down to it'. According to d'Hancarville, the erotic '*statues Colossales*' were regarded as '*les Simulacres de la Divinité*'.[26]

In *The Worship of Priapus*, Knight also described such 'Images of Divinity', in both their male and female forms. He and Hamilton had brought back from Italy waxen images of the phallus or 'Great Toe' of St Cosmo, who was worshipped at 'the Feast of the Modern Priapus' at Isernia, Italy, until

1781, when the Roman Church banned the practice.[27] The explicit engraving of the phallic toes was possibly produced by William Sharp. Knight lamented that 'the zealous propagators of the Christian faith' had furiously inveighed against the fertility rituals, which he considered both devout and healthy.

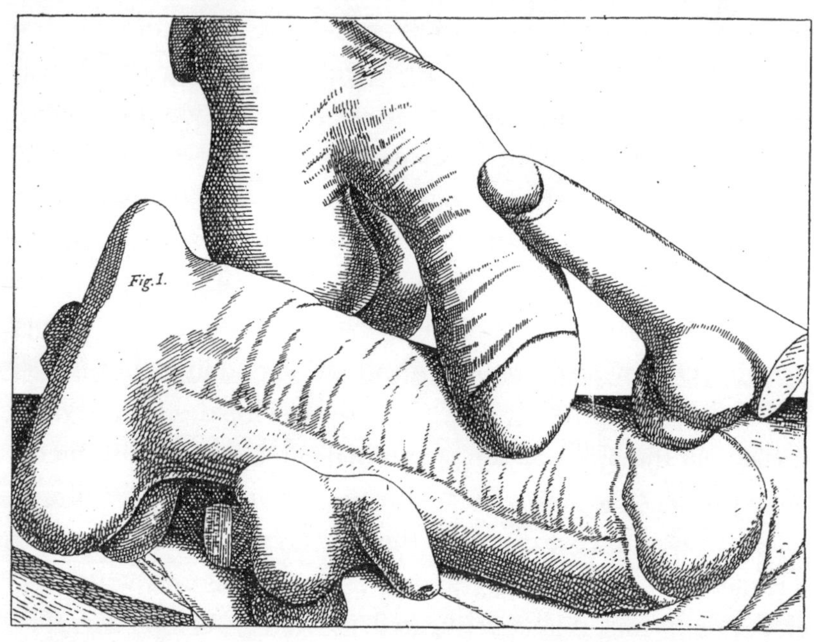

That Blake was aware of this controversy is suggested by his odd drawings of the Great Toe in *Vala*. He possibly remembered Swedenborg's statement that 'the great toe communicates with the genitals', when he drew the female emanation 'Ahania' looking intently at the big toe of Urizen's left foot.[28] In another drawing, Ahania reclines on a regal bed or legless couch that resembles a huge flaccid penis attached to two large testicles; as Peter Otto notes, 'curiously, this flaccid penis/sofa has a toenail, suggesting that it is also a big toe'.[29] According to Kabbalistic and Swedenborgian interpretations of the phallic toe, it can feel the pain created by the

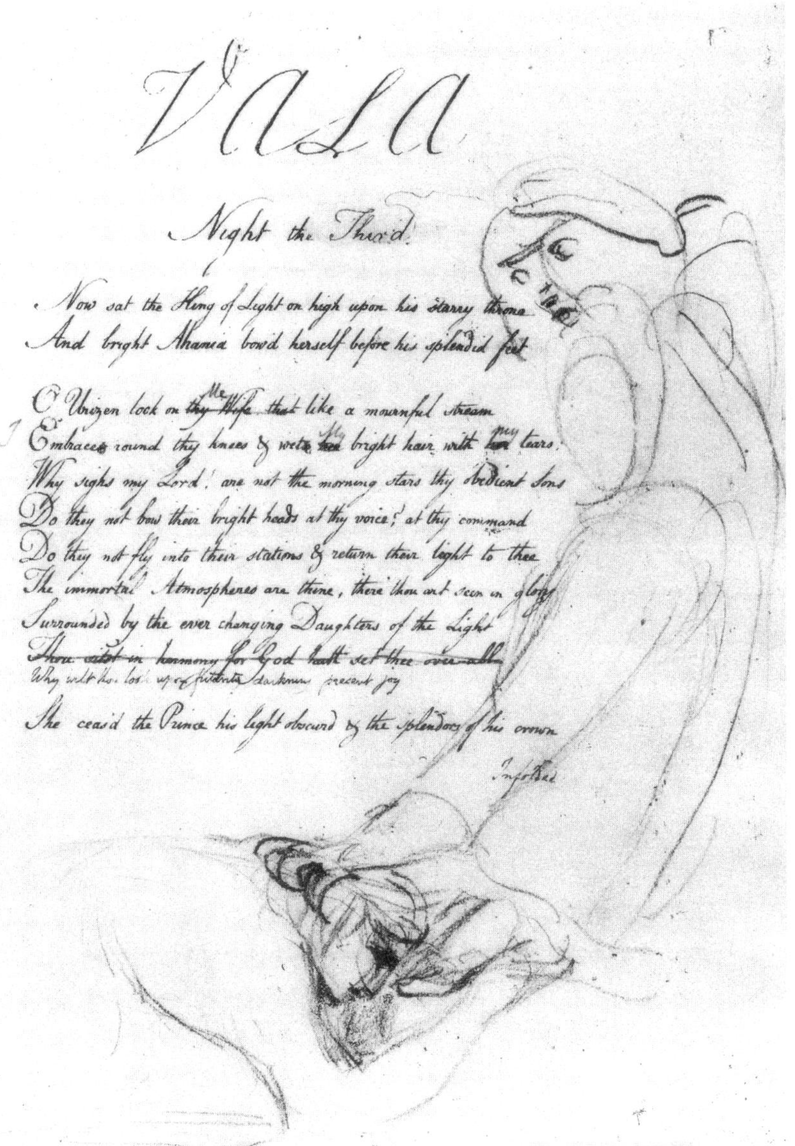

VALA

Night the Third

Now sat the King of Light on high upon his starry throne
And bright Ahania bow'd herself before his splendid feet

O Urizen look on ~~thy Wife that~~ Me like a mournful stream
1 Embrace~~s~~ round thy knees & wet~~s~~ ~~her~~ My bright hair with ~~her~~ my tears:
Why sighs my Lord! are not the morning stars thy obedient Sons
Do they not bow their bright heads at thy voice? at thy command
Do they not fly into their stations & return their light to thee
The immortal Atmospheres are thine, there thou art seen in glory
Surrounded by the ever changing Daughters of the Light
~~Thou sittest in harmony for God hath set thee over all~~
Why wilt thou look upon futurity darkning present joy

She ceas'd the Prince his light obscurd & the splendors of his crown

Infolded

human degradation of divine sexuality. By concentrating intensely upon the 'shards' created by the breaking of the divine vessels, the meditator can release the 'material dross' from the lowly toe and elevate it to its pre-lapsarian, purified place within the Divine Body.[30] Thus, the toe becomes a vehicle of vision, and the male and female 'feet' achieve reunification in the *hieros gamos* (or, in Blake's terminology, in *Beulah*, Hebrew for 'married land').[31]

Thus, when Blake depicted 'Two winged immortal shapes' hovering over the Fallen Man, he illustrated the eloquent lines with an encircled great toe. Like the Cherubim in the Holy of Holies, the winged figures enable the sexually aroused Los to achieve the Divine Vision, despite the barely adequate vulvic 'Gates' of his female emanation Enitharmon:

> *Their wings joind in the Zenith over head*
> *Such is a Vision of All Beulah hovring over the*
> *Sleeper*
> *The limit of Contraction now was fixd & Man began*
> *To wake upon the Couch of Death . . .*
> *. . . Then Los said I behold the Divine Vision thro the*
> *broken Gates*
> *Of thy poor broken heart astonishd melted into*
> *Compassion & Love*
> *And Enitharmon said I see the Lamb of God upon*
> *Mount Zion*
> *Wondring with love & Awe they felt the divine hand*
> *upon them.*[32]

Significantly, the 'poor broken hearted' Enitharmon also achieved a visionary state, which suggests that Catherine Blake occasionally shared in her husband's euphoric trances. Though *Vala* is full of images of perverted or repressed sexuality, which often replicate those in d'Hancarville and Knight, it also includes more sacramental images of female genitalia.[33] D'Hancarville had briefly discussed uterine symbolism, as expressed in one of Townley's marbles and in the Bacchic mitre ('*par leur forme* ovalaire, *l'oeuf de la Création*').[34] Knight went further to describe and present engravings of the female organs and their copulatory function. Noting that the shell or *concha veneris* is a universal emblem of the female genitalia, he stressed that 'The female Organs of Generation were revered as symbols of the generative powers of Nature or matter, as the male were of the Generative powers of God.'[35]

For Blake and his wife, this valorisation of the female genitalia would recall not only Moravian but Swedenborgian teachings. As discussed earlier, the Moravians utilised small coloured cards depicting scenes of domestic marital activities within the female vulva, in which the bed and chair for conjugal intercourse were portrayed within the sanctified sex organ. Edward Moor would also portray the vulva as a religious image, and he argued that the ovoid emblem of the Hindu *Yoni* was transmitted to the West, when it appeared discretely in early church carvings and clerical regalia.[36] In Night One of *Vala*, Blake drew a similar vulvic image, but he left it empty, depicting no scene of marital harmony.[37] Reflecting his own sexual frustration and anger at Catherine, he described the lost opportunity for spiritual vision caused by Enitharmon's frigid refusal of Los's ardent overtures. Though 'Three gates within glorious & bright open into Beulah' from Enitharmon's 'bowels within her loins' and 'inward Parts', she refused to open them: 'she closd and barrd them fast / Lest Los should enter into Beulah through her beautiful gates'.[38] In strange sketches, Blake portrayed the potentially visionary vulva on dragons, serpents and other nightmarish creatures.[39]

The opening of the female gates was considered the most shameful of the engravings in Knight's *Worship of Priapus*, for

Jerusalem his Emanation will soon become a ruin
Her little ones will be slain on the top of every street
And she herself led captive & scatterd into the indefinite
Gird on thy sword O thou most mighty in glory & majesty
Destroy these opressors of Jerusalem & those who ruin Shiloh
So spoke the Messengers of Beulah. Silently removing
The Family Divine drew up the Universal tent
Above Gilead & closd the Messengers in clouds around
Till the time of the End. Then they Elected Seven. called the Seven
Eyes of God & the Seven lamps of the Almighty
The Seven are one within the other the Seventh is named Jesus
The Lamb of God blessed for ever & he followd the Man
Who wanderd in mount Ephraim seeking a Sepulcher
His inward eyes closing from the Divine vision & all
His children wandering outside from his bosom fleeing away
End of The First Night

he revealed that Townley possessed a carving from the Cave of Elephanta in India, which depicted a man and woman performing mutual oral sex, in which her tumescent vulva is raised in a joyful position of uninhibited arousal. According to Knight, the carving was 'a symbol of refreshment and invigoration . . . mutually applied to both their respective Organs of Generation'.[40] However, outraged critics viewed this piece of religious art as the lowest form of perversion and cried out for the suppression of all depictions of female genital arousal. Perhaps reacting to public and domestic resistance to erotic joy, Blake drew tortured images of frustrated sexuality – images of Vala exerting domination over the flaccid penis of Albion; of a female binding a winged phallus with a string; of Urizen's dream of impotence, when two full-breasted females masturbate each other and ignore the male phallic power.[41]

Within the fallen and perverted cosmos of *Vala*, the possibility of sacramental and visionary sexuality remained a distant dream. Blake's drawing of a nude female with a Gothic chapel and phallic altar in her genitals recalls Zinzendorf's positive vision of the female vulva as a place for reverent male worship. It also recalls Swedenborg's affirmation that the womb has communication with heaven. But the frustrated artist placed the image within a world of dolorous groans and shudderings, 'panting in sobs / Thick short incessant bursting sobbing' – a human world in which the 'places of Human Seed' create nothing.[42] Amidst the fragmenting and disintegrating emanations, 'Tharmas' (the sense of touch) cries out, 'O fool to lose my sweetest bliss / Where art thou Enion ah too near to cunning too far off / And yet too near.'

By 1800, Blake's psychological and political vulnerability worried his friends, who determined that he should move from his spy-ridden Lambeth neighbourhood to the seaside village of Felpham, where he would endure the protective but suffocating patronage of William Hayley. For three difficult years, while he laboured at tedious and demeaning commissions for Hayley, he also intensified his experiments in trance-induction, spirit-evocation and automatic writing. His psychic stress was at times intense, for he veered between manic highs when 'voices of Celestial inhabitants are more distinctly heard, & their forms more distinctly seen', and desolate lows when he perceived his worried wife as a confining 'Spectre', who 'Weeps incessantly for my Sin'.[43] He sometimes pitied Catherine, his 'sweet Shadow of Delight', who was 'sick with fatigue', but he also resented her pious and timid responses to his daring psychoerotic adventures:

O'er my Sins Thou sit & moan:
Hast thou no sins of thy own?

Poor pale pitiable form
That I follow in a Storm,
Iron tears & groans of lead
Bind round my aking head.[44]

At Felpham, Blake studied Greek, Latin and Hebrew – the latter especially helpful to his Kabbalistic interpretations of the male and female emanations of the disintegrating Grand Man. When he returned to London in 1803, his 'mental travels' took him further, for he resumed his exploration of Oriental mysticism and Yogic meditation techniques, studies he had begun earlier in Lambeth. In the process he would make the psychosexual breakthrough that enabled not only himself but his wife to enter the blissful land of Beulah, an imaginative space of rejuvenated conjugial love. Reworking and retitling *Vala* as *The Four Zoas*, Blake would portray 'a daughter of Beulah' who 'gave visions toward heaven' and 'made windows into Eden'.[45] The 'incessant bursting sobbing' of Enion-Catherine would give way to her serene acceptance of sacramental sensuality, and Tharmas-William would regain his 'sweetest bliss'.

22

Kabbalistic Cherubim and Yogic Yonis

The Artist having been taken in vision into the ancient republics, monarchies and patriarchates of Asia, has seen those wonderful originals called in the Sacred Scriptures the Cherubim, which were sculptured and painted on the walls of Temples.

William Blake, *A Descriptive Catalogue* (1809)

WHEN GILCHRIST REPORTED that Catherine Blake played a nude Eve to her Adam in their Lambeth garden, he explained that William 'thought the Gymnosophists of India', who 'went naked, were in this wiser than the rest of mankind – pure and wise – and that it would be well if the rest of the world could be as they'.[1] Gilchrist's friend Rossetti also sensed a Yogic influence on Blake: 'Rapt in a passionate yearning, he realised on this earth and in his mortal body, a species of *nirvana*.'[2] Before and after his 'three years' Slumber' in Felpham, Blake was privy to reports and examples of Asiatic sexual mysticism and its symbolic art, brought to England by East India Company employees and Orientalist scholars, artists and collectors.[3] For Blake and his wife, their increasing access to Yogic and Tantric techniques of meditation expanded their capacity to not only visualise but materialise the exotic erotica of the Orient. Moreover, for Catherine the Tantric emphasis on 'worship of the Female partner' as central to the 'yoga of union' elevated her status within her husband's visionary practices.[4] The ageing couple would learn that the Yogis' *nirvana* could be achieved within their humble home.

Baron d'Hancarville argued that the erotic 'colossal statues' of antiquity were 'images of divinity', but he went beyond Western art to hint at their continuing presence in Asiatic temples. He also echoed Swedenborg by claiming that traditions of the 'Generative Potency' were preserved 'in Tartary'.[5] Blake, Tulk and Flaxman would become intrigued by such claims about Tartary, that imagined preserve of the visionary sexuality of Asia.[6] Encouraged by the publications in *Asiatic Researches* and by tales from returning travellers, the Priapic collectors Hamilton, Townley and Knight discreetly displayed their Indian *objets d'art* to friends – including Blake, Cumberland, Flaxman, Hayley and Rainsford.[7] Townley also called on Blake at Lambeth and commissioned him as an engraver.[8]

However, by the mid-1790s the work of Orientalists came under increasing attack, for conservatives argued that their claims about the pre-Mosaic antiquity of Hindu literature undermined Christian chronologies, while their attempts to justify the erotic art and rituals of Asia on religious grounds reeked of obscenity and blasphemy.

The great Sanskrit scholar Sir William Jones was circumspect and euphemistic in his erudite essays on Indian religion, but he was nevertheless accused of inciting heresy and sedition. An indignant reviewer criticised Jones's essay, 'On the Mystical Poetry of the Persians and Indians', for presenting the 'licentious' verse of the great Persian poet, 'the wanton Hafiz', in the garb of religion.[9] Worse still was the Asians' 'gross and frequent personification of the Deity, by the wild rhapsodists, either of India or Europe', which has been the source of 'a thousand errors in theology, and the parent of a thousand sectaries'. Upon the basis of 'their fancied absorption in God, the sect of *Illuminati*, and the *Quietists* of former days, arose a large tribe of modern sectaries, concluding with the *Swedenborgians*, who have built upon it their romantic systems'. If this perverse meditation 'originally comes from the devotees of India', then the government should ban it along with other prohibited products from that fruitful country.

This linking of Yogic, Swedenborgian and Illuminist visionary techniques was the first to appear in public and, despite his hostile intent, the reviewer was actually on the right track – a track that Blake and his wife would soon take. For Catherine, the transformation that eventually occurred in her receptiveness to William's sexual theosophy must have been influenced by the stress on religious permissibility and natural joy that several of their friends not only believed privately but advocated publicly.[10] While sketching an Indian altar at the British Museum, George Cumberland drew 'a female organ' and made notes on the *Lingam* and *Yoni*.[11] Quoting Edward Moor, he compared the Hindu sexual myths to the mystical depictions of phallic erection and divine semen in an Egyptian sarcophagus – all representing the normality of phallic religion.[12]

Moor similarly argued for the healthiness of sex-based theology and called for its revival in the West: 'In countries where religion has not been able to extinguish the flames of love', it would be wise to change the mode of worship, to one in which 'men, animated by the Fire of the Divinity, concur . . . to the continuation of creation, in perpetuating its works'.[13] He urged his readers to imagine beings, who in the 'effervescence of manhood' join their ideas of religion to 'those of the most lively passion' and associate God with their pleasure. They should make God 'palpable and sensible to themselves, by that effusion of souls and senses, where all is mystery, joy and heavenly fervour!' In a passage that Blake would enjoy, Moor described the dancing priestesses in India: 'By the lascivious looks and wanton postures of these priestesses, full of the deity who inspires them, the contagion of enthusiasm and passion, with which they are inflamed, is conveyed to all the senses.' It then goes beyond passion and becomes 'an electric fire'.

Moor hinted at the connection of such joyful eroticism with mystical meditation – the 'divine *absorption* of the pious Yogees', which the more discreet Jones dismissed as 'dissolute contemplation'.[14] Perhaps he discussed Yogic visionary techniques with Blake, who included in *Vala* a *yonic* triangle like an Indian *yantra* and a mystical-sexual *mandala*. From the studies of his Orientalist friend Henry Colebrook, Moor knew that 'Various *yantras*, or mystical figures and marks, are appropriated to the several deities' and that these *yantras*, which possess occult powers, 'are taught in great detail in the *Tantras*'.[15] Though the cautious Colebrook did not reveal any details, he and Moor knew that the meditating Yogi concentrated on the triangular *yantra* in order to visualise the divine *Yoni*, arouse his inner *Lingaṃ*, and achieve 'an internalised union and consequent mystical orgasm'.[16]

In a more troubled version of such symbolism, Blake described the mental division between the sexes ('Why art thou Terrible and yet I love thee?') and illustrated it with a strange scaly serpent. Erdman describes variant versions of the serpent's head, which illustrate the theme 'We hid in secret': 'the head has the shape of an eyed triangle, or cone, similar to an upward-pointing yantra triangle whose central dot stands for the original point of energy of the male seed'.[17] In a second version, the serpent's body extends beside lines of verse in which Tharmas, the sense of touch, defines his counterpart Enion as an expanding and contracting vagina: 'The pointed, searching head recalls the phallic heads which the Gnostics used to display during the rites of the worship of Priapus.' And, of course, the Priapic antiquarians now believed that these images originally came from India.

Among Yogis, the ring-shaped *mandala* served like a *yantra*, a 'magical tool' for visualisation. Erdman notes further that students of alchemy and *mandala* symbolism see in Blake's portrayal of four fantastic erotic figures representations of 'the earthy, airy, watery and fiery species', which all express 'the passion of the female – to capture the male organ? – to transform it into a baby to feed'.[18] In Tantric practice, seminal retention prevents this 'capture' of the divine seed, though the *Yoni* is initially necessary to spiritual arousal of the *Lingam*. Blake's description of a vulva in the shape of a keyhole expressed its role in unlocking the 'doors of perception', which, as he announced earlier, 'will come to pass by an improvement of sensual enjoyment'.[19] Moor's further studies in Tantric Yoga would provide Blake with unusual access to that difficult but inspirational form of visionary eroticism.

Moor was also aware of the similarities between Kabbalistic and Tantric traditions – similarities suggested by Blake, when he described Hebrew Cherubim sculpted on the walls of Asian temples.[20] Moor expressed gratitude to his friend and fellow student of Indian art and religion, the 'learned and ingenious' Thomas Maurice, who brought considerable expertise in Kabbalistic lore to bear on his Oriental studies.[21] David Weir argues that Blake's Asiatic themes were influenced by Maurice, whom he may have met through mutual antiquarian and Swedenborgian friends.[22] While Maurice wrote his multi-volume *Indian Antiquities* (1794–1800), he assimilated the Priapic theories of d'Hancarville and Knight, the Yogic revelations of Moor and Colebrook, and the Kabbalistic notions of the Swedenborgians into an eclectic mix of Christian-Jewish-Indian theosophy – a mix that also emerged in Blake's works.

As an Anglican clergyman, Maurice was initially afraid to write explicitly about Asiatic sexual mysticism, but he was encouraged by Sir Joseph Banks, President of the Royal Society of Sciences, to deal thoroughly and openly with the subject.

Banks assured Maurice that 'the Phallic worship' in its pure state was 'a tribute to an unknown God' celebrated in 'their great secret Mysteries'.[23] He further chided Maurice for his timidity, noting that 'We annex an Idea of immodesty to the Parts of Generation which the Ancients seem not to have felt. They certainly talk'd of them with less reserve than we do and consquently were not impelled to Lust by the mention of the names.' A chastened Maurice replied that he worried about prejudiced modern readers who would react impurely to his descriptions of the 'the symbolical worship of the great *generative and prolific power of nature* represented by its most striking emblem of the rigid Phallus', which was so prominently displayed in the Cave of Elephanta in India.

Banks introduced Maurice to his cousin and neighbour in Soho Square, General Rainsford, who invited the Orientalist to join his private Masonic research lodge, which included Swedenborgians and Illuminists interested in hieroglyphical symbolism and visionary sexuality.[24] Abandoning his earlier denigration of the *Lingam* and *Yoni*, Maurice now confidently praised the work of d'Hancarville, Knight and Moor, who brought this sexual worship out of the shadows. He also compared the Yogis' 'divine raptures of *absorption* in the Deity' to those of 'the modern sect of Swedenborgh', when they speak of 'their imagined Elysium'.[25] J. A. Tulk was especially intrigued by Maurice's work, and he added extracts from *Indian Antiquities* to his discussions of the Ethiopian Enoch in the Swedenborgian journal, *The Aurora, or, the Dawn of Genuine Truth*.[26]

Maurice was also a connoisseur of engraving, which he believed was an ancient holy art, and he may have learned of Blake's exquisite and explicit engravings from their mutual friends.[27] Blake, in turn, would have been interested in Maurice's memories of the deceased Edward Young, his youthful mentor, for Blake combined his illustrations for

Young's *Night Thoughts* with his visionary explorations of sexuality in *Vala*.[28] Thus it is not surprising that Maurice's multi-layered, multi-cultural interpretations of ancient sexual and mystical theories provide an illuminating background for many of the puzzling symbols in *Vala*.

Maurice compared Indian and Jewish esoteric beliefs, citing 'the history of the *Ten Avatars*, or descents of Veeshnu, in a human form' to the '*Ten Sephiroth* of the Hebrews'.[29] He argued that 'in the *Sephiroth*, or *Three Superior Splendours*, of the Ancient Hebrews, may be discovered the three hypostases of the *Christian Trinity*'; similarly, the grand cavern-pagoda of Elephanta is 'a superb Temple of the Tri-une God'. Well read in Kabbalistic literature, he noted that the *Shekhinah* 'had equally the key of the womb and the grave', a point Blake illustrated in his sketch of the vulvic keyhole and in his portrayal of the creative and destructive powers of Vala, the nature goddess. Maurice discussed 'the stupendous symbol of the HEBREW CHERUBIM', who symbolise the 'TWO POWERS in God' (male and female), whose union means that 'God dwelleth between the Cherubim.' As noted earlier, Blake hinted at this Kabbalistic mystery in *Vala*, when he linked the wing-touching Cherubim who hover over the marital bed to the encircled phallic toe.

From Maurice and their mutual Swedenborgian colleagues, Blake could have learned more about Yogic techniques of meditation, which Maurice discussed as 'the most elevated point of holy transport' and which is 'denominated the *absorbed state*'.[30] Robert Essick notes that a drawing by Blake, while he drafted *Vala*, suggests his Yogic interest: 'The figure, backed with what appear to be clouds, sits with eyes closed, or at least lowered with heavy lids, in a posture oddly suggestive of the lotus position in yoga meditation.'[31] From Moor, Blake could have learned about Tantric techniques, for Moor agreed with Henry Colebrook's early judgement that 'the *Tantras* form a branch of literature highly esteemed, though at present much neglected.'[32]

As discussed earlier, the sexual-visionary techniques of Tantra shed light on some of Swedenborg's more fantastic visions. Count Grabianka, who made a third visit to London *c.*1799–1800, could have informed his Swedenborgian friends about the merger of Tantric and Kabbalistic techniques that allegedly occurred in the Illuminist lodges at Avignon and Lyons.[33] Among Rainsford's papers is an account recorded in Paris of a Scottish surgeon, an initiate of Avignon, 'who after some Ceremonies of the Art' evoked the spirit of a dead Englishwoman, who let the astounded observers touch and converse with her.[34] The German theosopher Karl von Eckartshausen similarly recorded his meeting in Paris with a Scot who boasted of making spirits of the dead appear. Claiming that he got the formula from a Jew, the Scot infused the air with a perfume that had 'violent narcotic ingredients', which stimulated Eckartshausen's terrifying visionary experience.[35]

The *Écossais Illuminé* was almost certainly John MacGregor, an exiled veteran of the 1745 Jacobite rebellion, who settled in Avignon, where he joined Grabianka's group.[36] He spent some years in India and became learned in Hindu mysticism, magic and medicine. MacGregor could have learned about the Tantric use of a powerful hallucinogen, *Datura fastuosa*, which was 'employed as a narcotic paste or as wood in a fire ceremony' and was 'easily absorbed through the skin or lungs', thus producing horrific visions and 'the sensation of aerial transport'.[37] Like Swedenborg, who assimilated Yoga and Kabbala into his visionary theosophy, MacGregor evidently infused elements of Tantrism into the erotic rituals at Avignon. Could he have accompanied Grabianka on the count's visits to London in the later 1790s?

That Blake developed a similarly eclectic combination of Tantric, Kabbalistic and Swedenborgian themes is suggested by his startling self-portrait in *Milton*, which he began in 1804 while he was still working on *Vala*. Portraying himself nude with an erect, blackened or charred penis, he flings himself backwards with outstretched arms, as a flaming star descends towards his left foot.[38] In this image and the accompanying verse, Blake seemed to draw upon Swedenborg's description of the Moravian orgiasts, which the artist infused with his own Kabbalistic and Tantric perspective.

After his return to London from Felpham in 1803, Blake's interest in Swedenborg was revived by liberal and heterodox Swedenborgians, who explored not only Enochian but Asiatic sexual theosophy, which they related to Swedenborg's more arcane teachings.[39] Reflecting his own merged interests, Blake praised Swedenborg as a 'Spiritual Preceptor', at the same time as he drew 'an ideal design' of the Brahmins, which portrayed Charles Wilkins translating the *Bhagavad Gita*, which Blake called 'the Hindoo Scriptures'.[40] He was probably familiar with Knight's argument that the Priapic religion was 'very fully explained in the *Bagvat-Geeta*', though buried 'under a mass of poetical mythology'.[41] Blake now described Swedenborg as 'the strongest of men, the Samson shorn by the churches', and he scorned the prudes who had 'perverted' the Preceptor's visions and destroyed 'Jerusalem as a harlot & her sons as reprobates'.[42]

Returning to the visionary sexuality of this more eclectic and esoteric Swedenborg, Blake hoped to redeem the spirit of John Milton, whose relationships with his three wives and three daughters were poisoned by his puritanism and self-love – defects that led England first into civil war and now into European war ('the phallic whip'). Though Blake revered Milton for his republican stand, he was obliged to 'expose the falsehood' of the poet's doctrine, taught in *Paradise Lost*, 'That Sexual intercourse arose out of the Fall – Now that cannot be, for no good can spring out of Evil.'[43] For Milton/Albion

WILLIAM

to be reunited with his fragmented female potencies, he must undergo a reunification of his ancient religious roots – from Asia and Israel.

Thus Blake reported that he was carried in vision to the ancient cities of Asia, where he saw 'those wonderful originals called in the sacred scriptures the Cherubim, which were sculpted and painted on walls of Temples'.[44] Like the Tantric artists of Asiatic temples, he linked his erect and charred penis with the moment of divine influx, when Milton's spirit descends into his foot (and great toe). 'So Milton's shadow fell / Precipitant, loud thundring into the sea of Time & Space':

> *Then first I saw him in the Zenith, as a falling star*
> *Descending perpendicular, swift as the swallow or swift;*
> *And on my left foot falling on the tarsus, enterd there;*
> *But from my left foot a black cloud redounding spread*
> *over Europe.*[45]

Decades earlier, Swedenborg connected the 'toe of the left foot' with 'the genitals; for the genitals correspond to the Word'.[46] He followed Kabbalistic teaching in which the foot functions as 'a euphemism for the phallus, human and divine', while the toes represent the 'ten demonic powers'.[47] Placing hell under the soles of the feet of the Grand Man, he described the 'vastation' that can purge the demonic evil from feet and toes. He also seemed familar with the Yogic significance of the great toe, which plays a crucial role in breath control.[48] The initiate is taught to massage the ankle and great toe, opposite the side through which he wishes the breath to flow. The capacity to breathe on one side was connected with the pre-coital position of the Tantric couple, who mutually visualised the god within the other and achieved a kind of spiritual copulation.

Blake's drawing and lines about the spiritual-erotic influx

into his 'tarsus' suggests his reading of Swedenborg's similar scene, in which Kabbalistic-Tantric meditation and stroking send a stream of fire into the glans penis and 'at the same time into the big toe of the left foot, and through a burning sensation under the midfoot sole, especially into the nail of the big toe of the left foot, which at length co-responds with a fiery burning of such a kind in the glans penis (*bulbo*); it became fiery'.[49] Commenting on the Kabbalistic symbolism of Blake's drawing, Sheila Spector notes that the entry of Milton's spirit into Blake's left foot is an act of sacrificial yet redemptive materialisation that will allow psychic and cosmic sexual reunification.[50]

Just as Swedenborg described the sexual energy progressing from the midfoot sole to the toe of the left foot, so Blake stressed that Milton's spirit entered at the tarsus, which is the space on the sole of the foot just before 'the five long bones which sustain and are articulated with the toes'.[51] After the spirit enters Blake's foot, 'a black cloud redounding' from it 'spread over Europe'. The moment of entry is one of visionary ecstasy in which the toxic poison of repressed sexuality is released. Like the sculpted *Lingams* of India, which were carved out of black stone, Blake's erect penis is blackened or charred.[52] One can only wonder if tarsus and toe stimulated a fiery burning in Blake's *bulbo*! That Blake or his cautious executors added shorts (underpants) to subsequent copies suggests that his erotic self-portrait was deemed too explicit in its original version.

Blake was aware of additional Yogic symbolism about the great toe, for he read Edward Moor's *The Hindu Pantheon* (1810), which included an engraving of 'Narayana with his toe in his mouth, reposing on a lotus leaf'.[53] Moor had first read about this image in M. Sonnerat's *Voyage au Indes Orientales et à la Chine* (1782), one of the first scholarly works on phallic worship in Asia, which included the Frenchman's

WILLIAM

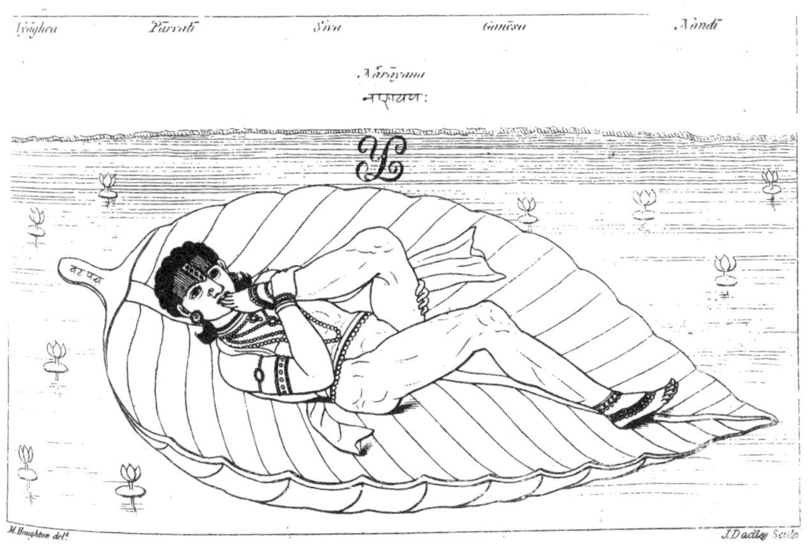

claim that the Indian *Lingam* influenced early Christian art and was even 'carved on the doors of our ancient churches', such as those at Toulouse and Bordeaux.[54] Familiar with the image of phallic toes and double oral sex in Knight's *Rites of Priapus*, Moor recognised similar meanings in the Tantric portrayal of Narayana.

Probably persuaded by his publisher, the increasingly cautious Joseph Johnson, Moor gave a deliberately euphemistic account of 'Linga. Yoni', in which he dismissed the 'puerile conceit' of Narayana's mouth-to-toe copulation as 'symbolical of eternity'. This image was maintained only by 'mystical sectarists' in order to 'furnish enthusiasts with fancies of a corresponding description'. Though Moor did not publish the Tantric purpose of the toe–mouth symbolism, he was undoubtedly aware of it (or he would not have included the engraving of Narayana). In Tantric ritual, 'If one takes his big toe in his mouth and holds it there, he can thereby stop the flow of psychic air within his body.'[55] This technique facilitates control of the seminal flow during the prolonged erection.

Like Maurice and the eclectic Illuminists, Blake merged Yogic with Kabbalistic symbolism. When he again described 'Milton entering my Foot', he placed him within the mysteries of the Grand Man (Adam Kadmon). In this moment of mystical union, 'all this Vegetable World appeard on my left Foot, / As a bright sandal formd immortal of precious stones & gold: I stooped down & bound it on to walk thro' Eternity.'[56] Elliot Wolfson observes that in the *Zohar*, the sandal symbolises the feminine and the foot the masculine, or, more specifically, the phallus: 'the symbols have a twofold connotation; they refer to mundane realities and their correlates in the divine realm, the sandal symbolising the *Shekhinah* and the foot *Yesod*'.[57]

Among Hasidic Kabbalists, the placing of foot into sandal enables 'walking', which serves as a metaphor for sexual activity: 'By means of the movement of one's feet, therefore, sexual unification on high is enhanced', for 'walking is the perfection of the sexual offence brought about through the feet'.[58] Thus, when Blake-Milton encloses his phallic foot in the feminine sandal, the defective mundane marriage is rectified, while the cosmic marriage is consummated. In *Vala*, Blake had sketched two feet, with the words 'B Blake / Catherine Blake / 76'; the number referred to their combined ages in 1797–8.[59] Their joined feet and lifetimes illustrate lines in which the testicular Orc defies the repressive Urizen, who responds: 'Yet thou dost laugh at all these tortures', while 'Walking in joy' and achieving 'visions of sweet bliss'.[60]

Throughout *Milton* there are hints at occasionally achieved sexual harmony between Blake and his wife, and certain lines suggest that he taught her Tantric techniques of visionary sex. Nelson Hilton notes that Blake practised a kind of *coitus interruptus*, which conserved the visionary semen; moreover, the 'sweet River, of milk & liquid pearl' was linked to his putting the bright sandal on his left foot.[61] From Edward Moor, Blake could have learned how Tantric technique reinforced the Kabbalistic symbolism. Moor was familar with Colebrook's description, published in 1797 and again in 1803, of one sect of Tantrists who 'acquired the singular practice of presenting to their own wives the oblations intended for the goddess'.[62] Were these the Moravian-like Kartabhajas, who developed Tantric rituals of conjugal love? Colebrook added that 'there is in most sects a right-handed or decent path, and a left-handed or indecent mode of worship', and the left-handed Tantrists 'require their wives to be naked when attending them at their devotions'.

Moor and Colebrook were aware that the increasing exposure and mockery of traditional Tantric rituals by prudish British officials and scholars had provoked a defensive movement among some Hindu nationalists, who produced a new text (the *Mahanirvana Tantra*), which endorsed 'rituals that would not be threatening to a Western outlook'.[63] These reformed, left-hand Tantrists proclaimed that *maithuna*, ritualised copulation, should be performed only with one's wife. No longer would the initiate seek forbidden women (like Blake's fantasised 'daughters of Albion'), for 'When the weakness of the Kali Age becomes great one's own wife alone should be known as the fifth *tattwa*' (sacred intercourse). Thus, for a British audience, the image of Kali, 'a wild, violent, sexual deity', was domesticated and transformed into an 'approachable maternal goddess'.

Such a domesticated Kali would not have frightened Blake's Kate, and he apparently instructed her in the meditation rituals of *maithuna*: 'Two but one, each in the other sweet reflected; these/ Are our three Heavens beneath the shades of Beulah, land of rest.'[64] Swedenborg hinted at a similar achievement of conjugial union through mutual visualisation: 'partner sees partner in mind', so that 'each partner has the other in himself or herself' and they 'thus cohabit in their inmosts'.[65]

W. B. Yeats, who believed that Blake knew Kabbala and Yoga, described the meditative technique by which an Indian devotee approaches the Self through a transfiguration of sexual desire. However, the adept is not always solitary, for there is another method, that of the Tantric philosophy:

> where a man and woman, when in sexual union, transfigure each other's image into the masculine and feminine characteristics of God, but the man must not finish, vitality must not pass beyond his body, beyond his being. There are married people who, though they do not forbid the passage of the seed, practise, not necessarily at the moment of union, a meditation, wherein the man seeks the divine Self as present in his wife, the wife the divine Self as present in the man. There may be trance . . .[66]

In *Milton*, Blake engraved a nude male with erect penis, gazing upwards towards the eagle of inspiration, while a nude female embraces and gazes lovingly at him. Erdman suggests that the lovers have been interrupted in copulation by the eagle's 'illuminating descent'.[67] But the interruption may have been a deliberate Tantric technique, for they seem to be 'dissolv'd in raptur'd trance'.[68] Two critics suggest that Blake turned against generative sexual relations, for 'the proper response is to withhold the desired seed', but they do not go further to connect this with Tantric meditation.[69]

Blake's hints at seminal retention shed light on a heavily erased drawing in *Vala*, which depicts 'an enormous phallic object' in the left margin, which is 'inner-lined on both sides', suggesting a 'sort of seminal reservoir'.[70] In *Milton*, Blake was more explicit, when he had the phallic Orc instruct the Shadowy Female, 'Behold how I am & tremble lest thou also / Consume in my Consummation; but thou maist take a form / Female & lovely, that cannot consume in Mans consummation.'[71] Among

Tantrists, the withholding of seed from the vaginal suction enabled its energy to ascend to the brain and produce ecstatic visions.

For the Blakes, now in their fifties, such Tantric and Kabbalistic practices seemed to bring periods of sexual equilibrium and serenity to their formerly turbulent conjugal relations. In a late plate of *Milton*, he recalled their earlier sexual problems: 'When I first married you, I gave you all my whole Soul / I thought that you would love my loves & joy in my delights', for then 'thou wast lovely, mild & gentle'. But 'now thou art terrible / In jealousy & and unlovely in my sight, because thou hast cruelly / Cut off my loves in fury till I have no love left for thee'.[72] When Milton/Blake cuts her off, 'intirely abstracting himself from Female loves', she relents and begins 'to give / Her maidens to her husband, delighting in his delight / And then & then alone begins the happy Female joy / As it is done in Beulah.' The illustration to this text is a Hindu *mandala* of four interlocking circles, with an ovoid egg and hint of female *Yoni* in the centre.[73]

Though the post-menopausal Catherine's gift of maidens to her husband was obviously an act of psychological and not physical generosity, it at least ended the battle of wills and stemmed the floods of tears that had bedevilled them for so long. During their stressful Felpham days, Blake sketched a tired-looking wife, who sits on the side of the marital bed and pulls on her stockings, preparing for daily duties, while her (post-coital?) husband remains sleepily on his pillow. In lines accompanying the drawing, he wrote: 'When a Man has Married a Wife / he finds out whether / Her Knees & Elbows are only / glued together.'[74] After their return to more congenial company in London, Catherine seemed no longer frightened by Blake's physical demands, and she entered more easily into his psychosexual fantasies.

In 1807 Blake recorded in his Notebook: 'My Wife was told

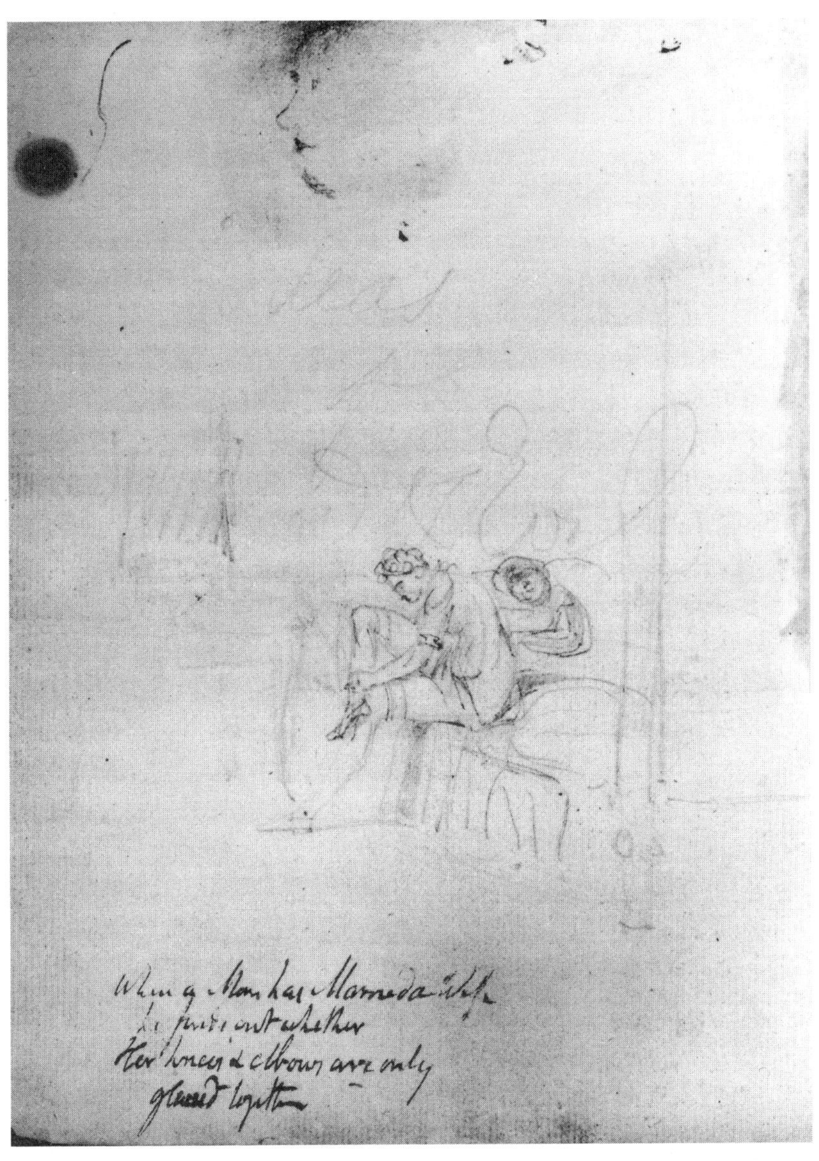
When a Man has Married a Wife
he finds out whether
Her knees & elbows are only
glued together

by a Spirit to look for her fortune by opening by chance a book which she had in her hand', and she opened to 'Enjoyment', an erotic poem by Aphra Behn:

I saw 'em kindle with Desire,
While with soft Sighs they blew the Fire;
Saw the Approaches of their Joy,
He growing more fierce and she less coy;

His panting breast to her's now join'd,
They feast on Raptures unconfin'd:
Vast and luxuriant! Such as prove
The immortality of Love!
For who but a Divinity
Could mingle Souls to that Degree?
And melt them into Ecstasie . . .[75]

Moved by Catherine's delight in Behn's poem, Blake followed these passages with his own verse that paid tribute to her patient devotion: 'I have Mental Joy & Mental Health / And Mental Friends & Mental Wealth / Ive a Wife I love & that loves me / Ive all but riches bodily.'[76] William and Catherine seemed to achieve a kind of suprasexual *nirvana*, a Tantric-Kabbalistic 'state of dream-like consciousness', in which the male-female dynamics reach a blissful equilibrium.[77] Blake could thus serenely affirm, 'There is a place where Contrarieties are equally True / This Place is called Beulah. It is a pleasant lovely Shadow / Where no dispute can come.'[78]

23

Thunder of Thought, & Flames of Fierce Desire

For the Male is a Furnace of Beryl, the Female is a Golden Loom.

William Blake, *Jerusalem* (1804–20)

In the early 1800s, Blake not only resumed his friendships with illuminated Swedenborgians but with liberal Moravians, who would sympathise with the multi-cultural eroticism and visionary millenarianism expressed in *Jerusalem: The Emanation of the Giant Albion*. At the same time, Blake sensed that his explorations of so many theosophical systems – ranging from Moravia to Sweden, Israel, Ethiopia, India and Tartary – could cloud his personal vision, deflect his 'Thunder of Thought'.[1] Thus, he vowed, 'I must Create a system, or be enslav'd by another Mans / I will not Reason & Compare: my business is to Create.' To weave together the disparate strands – to stoke the eclectic 'Flames of Fierce Desire' – he must grant his elderly wife the exalted role of Divine Weaver.

In 1809, Blake gave high praise to Swedenborg, noting that 'the works of this visionary are well worthy the attention of Painters and Poets; they are the foundations of grand things'.[2] His more positive opinion was influenced by his association with open-minded, non-sectarian Swedenborgians, especially John and Nancy Flaxman, John Augustus Tulk and his son Charles Augustus (the latter reportedly rescued the Blakes 'from destitution').[3] Blake was probably aware that the senior Tulks and the Flaxmans were combining their Hebrew and Swedenborgian studies with alchemical experiments, in an attempt to replicate the Hermetic marriage of Nicholas and Pernella Flamel (recalling the Loutherbourgs' earlier attempt).[4]

In 1806, J. A. Tulk anonymously published the *Testament of Nicholas Flamel*, his translation of a French manuscript, sent to him by a Swedenborgian friend in Paris. Drawing on the Kabbalistic decipherment by Antoine Joseph Pernety, an Avignon *Illuminé*, Tulk hoped to decipher Flamel's secret code.[5] The annotations he made in alchemical books reveal his special interest in Hermetic sexual symbolism and themes of conjugial love; they also make clear that he was a practising alchemist. More surprising is the revelation that John and Nancy Flaxman collaborated with him. When Nancy Flaxman gave a talk, 'On the Summary of Alchemy', to their Attic Chest Club, she was not just theorising.[6] In Blake's allusion to those who repeat 'the Smaragdine Table of Hermes' and refuse 'to believe without demonstration', he perhaps referred to their practical experiments.[7]

When J. A. Tulk wrote to the Flaxmans about his discovery of the true identity of Hermes Trismegistus and signed himself 'Philo of the Rosy-Cross', he drew on their quixotic effort to locate the Ethiopian Book of Enoch in Swedenborg's Tartary.[8] In 1807, Tulk published an account of the recent acquisition of the Tartarian Ancient Word, written 'on the rinds of some tree', and of its subsequent sale and disappearance in India.[9] In 1812–13 Tulk and John Flaxman contributed to *The Intellectual Repository of the New Church*, which carried extracts from Latin translations of the Ethiopian manuscript in Paris; these were compared to Swedenborg's tenets.[10] As Tulk wrote excitedly to the Flaxmans:

Edris or Enoch the triple are one and the same with Hermes Trismegistus; whence . . . the Egyptians derived all their arts and sciences. Now if the Book or Books of Enoch are with the Ancient Word preserved by the Mantchou Tartars, it is plain that Hermes Trismegistus is still existing, and may be forthcoming with the Ancient Word, and prove what E. S. [Emanuel Swedenborg] asserts, that this Book is preserved for the use of future churches.[11]

From their current researches, Tulk and Flaxman would understand Blake's strange description in *Jerusalem* of the construction by Urizen and Los of 'a mighty Temple; delivering Form out of confusion', and including all nations of the earth.[12] While Los's 'thunderous hammer' turns the Temple into the body of the Grand Man, 'Ethiopia supports his pillars' and 'his inmost hall is Great Tartary. / China & India & Siberia are his temples for entertainment.' Like Blake, Tulk and Flaxman also studied the *Baghavad Gita*, noting its similarities to Swedenborg's theosophy.[13]

In 1813, the Tulks and Flaxmans were thrilled by the arrival in London of a Swedish *Illuminé*, Fabian Wilhelm Ekenstam, a former Moravian, who now served as an agent for the secret Swedenborgian society *Pro Fide et Caritate*.[14] Bringing with him more extracts from Swedenborg's unpublished journals, Ekenstam re-established the old ties between Tulk's Universalists and the Swedish Masons.[15] He was also determined to consult with British Orientalists and to learn Sanskrit, in preparation for his journey to Tartary to seek the Ancient Word.

Along with Anders Johansen, another former Moravian, the English couples and their Swedish guests plunged deeper into the study of hieroglyphics and alchemy.[16] They also tried to interpret the secrets of a mysterious Danish manuscript, 'Concerning the Spiritual World and the State of Man after

Death', which was revealed 'by the Superior Lights of the 26th and 29th Degrees of Good Purification'. This was apparently produced by members of the Asiatic Brethren in Copenhagen, who had earlier initiated J. C. Lavater (one of Blake's heroes) into their Sabbatian-Rosicrucian system.[17]

Given this heady atmosphere of Hebraic, Hermetic, Enochian and Asiatic studies among his New Jerusalemist friends in London, Blake's renewed respect for Swedenborg's sexual theosophy becomes comprehensible. After the unhappy years in Felpham, he seemed to recognise that his marital problems – his deficiences in conjugial love – were as much his as his wife's fault. Certainly, the Hermetic marriage of the Flamels made clear that the female played an equal role to the male in the quest for physical rejuvenation and divine illumination. Their alchemical system required an equal balancing of male and female energies, which they allegedly embodied in their conjugal relations. Like the Tulks, he added a layer of Kabbalistic and Rosicrucian symbolism to the increasingly eclectic definition of the 'mystical marriage'.

From their residence at 17 South Moulton Street, the Blakes had easy access to fellow students of esoteric erotica. Across the street at no. 51, Richard Cosway 'kept a house for the study of magic', in which one room was 'always consecrated for the purpose of raising spirits' in the magic circle drawn on the floor.[18] According to W. B. Yeats, Blake and Cosway participated in a secret Rosicrucian society, which was possibly the one organised by Dr Sigismund Bacstrom, a Swedenborgian Mason, erudite Hebraist and Kabbalist and a practising alchemist.[19] Bacstrom had been a neighbour of Blake in Lambeth, where on 5 November 1797 he initiated Alexander Tilloch, a friend of Blake, into his Rosicrucian Brotherhood.[20] On that same day, Blake signed a testimonial for Tilloch's 'device to prevent banknote forgeries'.[21] As the great-great-uncle of William Muir, Tilloch was a possible source for Muir's claim that Blakes' parents attended Moravian services at the Fetter Lane Chapel.

Bacstrom and the Rosicrucians assimilated the sexual dynamics of the *Sephiroth* into the male-female principles of alchemy, and he wrote extensively on the 'celestial marriage', in which the male metallic sperm penetrates the female chemical receptacle, thus producing regenerative new life.[22] Yeats further claimed that the London society was directed by 'three brothers named Falk', who instructed Blake in a special, magical use of Hebrew characters and symbols.[23] According to Sheila Spector, in Blake's later years his use of Hebrew became 'purely mystical', and she suggests that *Jerusalem* was infused with themes from the *Kabbala Denudata*.[24]

Like the Illuminist Swedenborgians, Blake viewed the Kabbala as a vehicle for conversion of the Jews to a universalist Christianity. In *Jerusalem*, he made his most direct reference to Adam Kadmon in his address 'To the Jews', which proclaimed that 'You have a tradition that Man anciently containd in his mighty limbs all things in Heaven & Earth.'[25] He challenged them that 'If your tradition that Man containd in his Limbs, all animals, is true', then 'the Return of Israel is a Return to Mental Sacrifice & War. Take up the Cross O Israel and follow Jesus.'

Like the Kabbalists, Blake interpreted 'the Return of Israel' in sexual and visionary terms. In *Jerusalem*, he pointed backwards to his years in Lambeth as the time when he first found Jerusalem, 'by the river', and he illustrated the text with dancing nudes at the top of the page.[26] Hinting at the temporary nature of those intervals of sexual freedom and happiness, he drew at the bottom of the page a nude male with explicit penis, lying on his back, while the fragmenting female emanations weep over him. He now interpreted his wife's earlier withdrawal from him as Albion's fall into division and recalled 'the Judgment that has arisen among / the Zoas of Albion', where 'a Man dare hardly embrace / His own Wife, for the terrors of Chastity that they call / Morality'.[27] Determined to rebuild Jerusalem, 'a city yet a woman', Blake portrayed Los holding his clearly phallic hammer with its erect penis pointing upwards to a downward-pointing winged vulva, into which he boldly gazes.[28]

Drawing on the Kabbalistic notion that circumcision of the penis makes possible the beatific vision, Blake asserted that 'Establishment of Truth depends on destruction of Falsehood continually, / On Circumcision, not on Virginity.'[29] When the 'Satanic Holiness triumphed', a 'Religion of Chastity & Uncircumcised Selfishness' prevailed. With uncircumcision and lack of vision, the sacred vulva became defiled. In a reference to the Kabbalistic tradition concerning the sacking of the Temple by the scornful Antiochus, who publicly displayed the copulating Cherubim, Blake made the degraded Albion chide the inverted Jerusalem: 'dissembler Jerusalem! I look into thy bosom: / I discover thy secret places . . . / Thy Tabernacle taken down, thy secret Cherubim disclosed. / Art thou broken?'

Now the Ark that enclosed the loving couple is carried before war-making armies, for 'they scent the odor of War in the Valley of Vision'. With an illustration of a vulvic ark floating on the waters, Blake recalled the 'Cherubims of Tender-mercy / Stretching their Wings sublime over the Little-ones of Albion'. As Los continues his struggle for *tikkun*, he envisions the re-integrated Grand Man, who encompasses and transcends the sexual polarities:

Humanity knows not of Sex; wherefore are Sexes in Beulah?
In Beulah the Female lets down her beautiful Tabernacle
Which the Male enters magnificent between her Cherubim
And becomes One with her, mingling . . .[30]

His Spectre driv'n by the Starry Wheels of Albions sons, black and
Opake divided from his back; he labours and he mourns!
For as his Emanation divided, his Spectre also divided
In terror of those starry wheels: and the Spectre stood over Los
Howling in pain: a blackning Shadow, blackning dark & opake
Cursing the terrible Los: bitterly cursing him for his friendship
To Albion, suggesting murderous thoughts against Albion.
Los rag'd and stamp'd the earth in his might & terrible wrath!
He stood and stampd the earth! then he threw down his hammer in rage &
In fury: then he sat down and wept, terrified! Then arose
And chaunted his song, labouring with the tongs and hammer:
But still the Spectre divided, and still his pain increas'd!
In pain the Spectre divided: in pain of hunger and thirst:
To devour Los's Human Perfection, but when he saw that Los

While using Kabbalistic meditation to regenerate the sexual and spiritual vision, Blake also hinted at Yogic traditions, citing those 'Ancients' who 'were wholly absorbed in their Gods'.[31]

In Blake's symbolic self-portrait (*c.*1820), he sketched a *menorah* on his forehead. As Raymond Lister explains, 'This symbol, derived from the Jewish seven-branch candlestick modelled on the Tree of Life, expresses spiritual enlightenment, being in effect a third "spiritual" eye.'[32] Geoffrey Keynes recognised that the *menorah* 'gains in significance from being placed in the central point of the forehead; this in Indian Yoga is an important meditation centre (*cakra*) or "third eye"'; moreover, 'Blake would certainly have been familiar with this ancient and fundamental symbolism.'[33]

Blake's assimilation of Asiatic and Yogic symbolism into his Christian Kabbalistic prophecy was perhaps encouraged by his renewed access to Moravian themes, through his friendship with two liberal and artistic Brothers, Jonathan Spilsbury and James Montgomery. Their defence of Moravian history and principles came in a context of renewed attacks on the 'Herrnhutters', which reminded the public of their antinomian and erotic themes – themes that would certainly be attractive to Blake. The hostile campaign had begun in 1799, when the Anglican Divine William Hurd published an enlarged version of his *New and Universal History of the Religious Rites, Ceremonies and Customs of the Whole World*, which included a lengthy, scornful account of the 'secretive' Moravian Brotherhood.

Drawing on the publications of Rimius, Frey and Wesley, Hurd noted that Zinzendorf 'shews a general inclination to all Christian communions' and 'declares that whoever embraces Herrnhuttism need not change his religion'.[34] Like all fanatics, the Moravians 'reject reason, reasoning and philosophy', while Zinzendorf calls 'the theology received by the Christians a dry

one, and good for nothing else than to amuse dogs and swine, unbelievers and atheists, invented by the devil, and that such as teach it are Satan's professors'. In its place, the count presents a sexual religion, in which the Holy Ghost is called 'the eternal wife of God'. The circumcision of the Saviour shows that the male organ is 'the most noble, the most respectable part of a man's body'; even worse, the 'organ of generation of the other sex is no less honourable'.

Having abolished the Mosaic law, the believer is free from all law, 'for Jesus can change the oeconomy of salvation; make criminal what was virtuous, and virtuous what was criminal'. Hurd only hinted at the sexual rituals of the mystical marriage, 'for fear of offending the modesty of our readers' and 'to avoid scandal as much as possible'. He then warned that 'All extremes are connected with insanity; and therefore those who would understand true religion . . . must learn that God is not to be found in the tormenting fire, or the raging whirlwind.' If anything could have revived Blake's interest in Moravianism, these charges certainly would.

In the early 1800s, Blake was in contact with the Moravian engraver and portrait painter Jonathan Spilsbury, whom he probably met in the 1780s, when both exhibited at the Royal Academy.[35] Like the Armitages and John Blake, Spilsbury was raised as an Anglican, but by 1769 he was attracted to Zinzendorf's marriage theology and longed to join the Moravian Congregation.[36] Always close to the La Trobe family, Jonathan shared their liberal sexual and spiritual attitudes. He had earlier engraved the happy nudes on Lord Percy's antique gems, and the Spilsbury family firm printed Knight's *Worship of Priapus* and Chastanier's Swedenborgian appeals to the Masonic *Illuminés*.[37]

Friendly with Cosway, Flaxman and Hayley, Jonathan Spilsbury evidently visited Felpham while Blake was there, and in 1804 Blake reported conversing with him in London.

He applauded Spilsbury's decision to relinquish portrait painting as a profession: 'I conceive that he may be a much better Painter if he practises secretly & for amusement than he could eer be if employd in the drudgery of fashionable dawbing for a poor pittance of money in return for the Sacrifice of Art & Genius.'[38] Blake was pleased by Spilsbury's heartfelt reply, for 'He says he never will leave to practise the Art because he loves it & this Alone will pay its labour by Success if not of money yet of True Art. Which is All –'.

Blake's advice to practise secretly seemed to counter Hurd's criticism of the Moravians' clandestine meetings, which led to charges of 'unnatural practices'. Hurd observed that 'This will always be the case where there are secrets, while the different sexes meet together. Let us only consider the ridiculous stories that have been told concerning the Free-masons, and perhaps all of them are false.'[39] Still, Hurd warned, if the Moravians lock their doors, they 'are guilty of a breach of the toleration act'. Similar suspicions provoked a mob attack on the Fetter Lane Chapel in 1794. Despite the policy of extreme discretion adopted by the post-Zinzendorfian Moravians, the old Jacobite-Jacobin rumours still circulated about their penchant for secrecy.

Like Zinzendorf, Jonathan Spilsbury believed that 'the Spiritual Church is made up of the devoted from every Flock', and he shared the count's interest in foreign cultures and missions – especially those in Asia.[40] His close friend Christian Ignatius La Trobe (brother of the radical architect Benjamin Henry) published the letters he received from the East Indies, which revealed the Moravian missionaries' exposure to the Hindu natives' magical beliefs, use of powerful hallucinogens and good-natured promiscuity.[41] Both Jonathan and Christian Ignatius were readers of *Asiatic Researches*, and they maintained a tolerant attitude towards Indian religion and ritual. In October 1812, a few days before his death, Jonathan preached to 'a congregation of Asiatics who gathered on a Sunday in one of the Moravian chapels, for this was a duty and privilege he greatly enjoyed'.[42] His daughter Maria was so moved by the 'Oriental' scene that she painted a portrait of her father preaching, 'his face lit up with spiritual fervour'.

During this period Spilsbury's Moravian friend James Montgomery, the Sheffield-based poet and publisher, was also in touch with Blake, who was probably aware that Montgomery's non-secret publications led to government surveillance over his activities. Blake may have met the young writer earlier, when Montgomery made periodic visits to London and participated in the radical politics of the London Corresponding Society. As he sardonically remarked, 'one of the first hymns of mine *ever sung* found its way into Billy Pitt's Green Bag', which led to his imprisonment in 1795–6.[43] In *Prison Amusements* (1797), Montgomery revealed his interest in Hindu mysticism and theories of reincarnation.[44] Drawing on earlier Moravian missionary accounts from India and Ceylon, as well as contemporary Oriental scholars, he portrayed in 'The Brahmin' a wise Yogi, whose meditation reveals the unified essence of all living creatures, who survive through cycles of metempsychosis.[45]

When evidence of Montgomery's friendship with Blake first surfaced in 1807, it suggested 'an easy and personal contact between the two men'.[46] Montgomery was an early subscriber to Blake's illustrations for Robert Blair's *The Grave*, and in 1807 he heard from its publisher Robert Cromek that Blake was a 'wild & wonderful genius', who believed that 'What has been called Fancy & Imagination is the Eternal World! & that this World is the only Cheat, Imagination the *only Truth*!'[47] Cromek assured Montgomery that Blake thought highly of his recent publication *The Wanderer of Switzerland* (1806), and believed that it 'will command the applause and admiration of all good men, & of all Lovers of the Higher Kinds of Poetry'. In that volume Montgomery praised the Moravians' missionary and abolitionist efforts, and in May 1807 he began another poem in which he traced the Brethren's history from Hus and Comenius, described the 'Hidden Seed' as 'a Christian Israel', and referred to their belief in the mystical marriage.[48]

Cromek also promised to show his Sheffield friend some prepublication engravings, examples of Blake's 'Noble though extravagant Flights'. Blake, in turn, may have shown Montgomery his manifesto of free love, *Visions of the Daughters of Albion*, for the Moravian called on the 'Daughters of Albion!' to 'Weep!' in his own poem of frustrated love.[49] Montgomery would have been interested in Blake's illustrations to Young's *Night Thoughts*, for he used a quote from Night Nine – 'Of one departed World / I see the mighty shadow' – as the epigraph for his epic poem *The World Before the Flood* (1813). Given their mutual interests, Blake perhaps showed his friend the manuscript of *Vala*, sketched on the back of the proof-sheets of *Night Thoughts*. The linkage is intriguing, for Blake's decision to retitle *Vala* as *The Four Zoas* was possibly influenced by his contact with two open-minded and imaginative Moravians.

While at Felpham and in touch with Spilsbury, Blake had composed and sung a hymn, 'a devotional air', which inspired his listeners.[50] Back in London, he could have learned that Montgomery had started writing hymns again, inspired by the Moravian hymns that had first motivated him to become a poet. Could he have shown the old hymnbooks to Blake, whose mother had once quoted from them? When Montgomery visited London, he stayed with his brother Ignatius, minister to the Moravian Congregation at Fetter Lane; could he have taken Blake to hear the still-powerful choral performances at his mother's former chapel?

In 1754 the Moravians published an enormous hymnbook, which included Hebrew phrases and Asiatic references, revealing their continuing devotion to the Jewish and Oriental missions.[51] In one of Zinzendorf's most beloved hymns, the *Te Matrem*, he referred to 'the Four *Zoa*', defined by the English translator as 'living beings'.[52] In 1807, when Blake used a variant of that phrase to retitle his most disturbingly erotic poem, he 'sought to understand the "Four Mighty Ones" in the psychic alchemy of every man'.[53] In many Moravian hymns the Kabbalistic themes of the mystical marriage were explicitly expressed in Hebrew words and sexualised imagery. Given his earlier frustration with his wife's sexual fears, Blake would find renewed religious sanction for his radical beliefs in these erotic verses, which call on the Brethren to honour the 'parts where Sexes differenc'd are' while they penetrate 'Wedlock's mystery'.[54]

Having weathered their emotional storms, William and an acquiescent Catherine would agree with the hymn-writer that no man should boast of purity while he is still ignorant of marriage's 'mystic Height'.[55] Through 'blessed Theosophy', the meditating Moravian will see the '*Shekhinah as Wisdom*'. In the *Te Matrem*, the Congregation joyfully sang praise to the *Shekhinah* as poetic muse, female sexual potency, wife of God and mother of the God-Man:

Thou didst inspire the Martyrs tongues,
In the last gasp to raise their songs.
Thou dost impel the four Zoa,
Who singing rest not night nor day.

Thou Mother of God's Children all,
Thou Sapience archetypal!

Thou didst fit up the poor Maids Womb
For that awful Conception

That thou the Prophets dost ordain,
And gifts and wonders to them deign.[56]

Like the radical Brethren of the Sifting Time, Blake's Moravian friends would not have been surprised by his merging of Jewish and Asiatic themes. In *Jerusalem*, when Blake affirmed that 'they every one in their bright loins / Have a beautiful golden gate, which opens into the vegetative world', he illustrated it with a young woman enclosed in a Hindu *mandala*, under an arching rainbow and over a dreamily reclining nude male. The filmy, Oriental-looking dress on his 'mild Emanation Jerusalem' suggests a Yogic scene. As Miranda Shaw demonstrates, mutual male-female meditation on the Tantric *mandala* produces orgasmic vision: 'the world of ordinary appearance is replaced by the artistry of enlightened imagination, creating the gossamer, rainbow-like bodies that are the goal of Tantric practice'.[57]

Inspired by his reading of Moor's *Hindu Pantheon*, Blake praised the cosmic principles which, 'governing all by the sweet delights of secret amorous glances', are carved in the great Asiatic temples: 'All things acted on Earth are seen in the bright Sculptures of / Los's Halls, & every Age renews its powers from these Works', while 'Every Affinity of Parents, Marriages and Friendships are here / In all their various combinations wrought by wondrous Art.'[58] Perhaps Moor informed him about a famous but cryptic passage in the *Hejavira Tantra*, which speaks of the four gestures – the smile, gaze, embrace and union – that were considered the most secret language of the *Yoginis*.[59]

The secret gestures were often expressed in the 'wondrous Art' of Hindu shrines. Shaw observes that Tantric couples enjoyed a sexual virtuosity equalling that of the amorous couples *in flagrante delicto* adorning Indian temple towers: 'The mood of exuberant delight, graceful sensuousness and reciprocity that characterises the sculpted couples also suffuses the literary descriptions in the Tantric texts, which exult in an open and unashamed affirmation of sensuality in a religious context.'[60]

One hair nor particle of dust, not one can pass away.
He views the Cherub at the Tree of Life, also the Serpent,
Orc the first born coild in the south: the Dragon Urizen:
Tharmas the Vegetated Tongue even the Devouring Tongue:
A threefold region, a false brain: a false heart:
And false bowels: altogether composing the False Tongue,
Beneath Beulah: as a watry flame revolving every way
And as dark roots and stems: a Forest of affliction, growing
In seas of sorrow. Los also views the Four Females:
Ahania, and Enion, and Vala, and Enitharmon lovely.
And from them all the lovely beaming Daughters of Albion.
Ahania & Enion & Vala, are three evanescent shades:
Enitharmon is a vegetated mortal Wife of Los:
His Emanation, yet his Wife till the sleep of death is past.
Such are the Buildings of Los: & such are the Woofs of Enitharmon:

And Los beheld his Sons, and he beheld his Daughters:
Every one a translucent Wonder: a Universe within,
Increasing inwards, into length and breadth, and heighth:
Starry & glorious: and they every one in their bright loins:
Have a beautiful golden gate which opens into the vegetative world:
And every one a gate of rubies & all sorts of precious stones
In their translucent hearts, which opens into the vegetative world:
And every one a gate of iron dreadful and wonderful,
In their translucent heads, which opens into the vegetative world
And every one has the three regions Childhood: Manhood & Age:
But the gate of the tongue: the western gate in them is clos'd,
Having a wall builded against it: and thereby the gates
Eastward & Southward & Northward, are incircled with flaming fires.
And the North is Breadth, the South is Heighth & Depth:
The East is Inwards: & the West is Outwards every way.

And Los beheld the mild Emanation Jerusalem eastward bending
Her revolutions toward the Starry Wheels in maternal anguish
Like a pale cloud arising from the arms of Beulahs Daughters:
In Entuthon Benythons deep Vales beneath Golgonooza.

Given Moor's increased knowledge about Tantric symbolism, especially that of the *Yoni* in sexual meditation, Blake's radiantly coloured engraving of a male and female sitting upright and facing each other, with legs entwined in copulation, suggests his own practice of this Tantric technique.[61] The design originally included a phallic caterpillar sitting on the lotus lily that provides a bed for the lovers. Again, Blake seemed to draw on Yogic lore, which requires the male to worship the divine *Yoni* of his partner. As his antiquarian colleagues learned, the lotus played a central role in Tantric sexual theosophy.[62]

In Tantra, the female organ is referred to directly as a vulva (*bhaga*, *yoni*) or metaphorically as a lotus (*padma*), for the 'outer opening of the sexual organ resembles the petals of a lotus, while the vulva and cervix are like the heart of the flower'.[63] A Tantric text describes how 'the tip of the phallus distils nectar from the corolla of the woman's lotus', when a 'skillful one worships the yogin's stainless yoni of light'. For some reason, the phallic caterpillar was removed from Blake's lotus. Even worse, like Blake's ecstatically erect penis in *Milton*, which someone covered with undershorts, this emblem of serenely Tantric *nirvana* was erased and the figures awkwardly repositioned to 'a sort of side-saddle sitting'.[64]

In *Jerusalem*, Blake paid loving tribute to Catherine by embedding her name in 'Cathedron', the cathedral in the *Yoni* that makes life and vision possible. Though 'All fell towards the Center, sinking downwards in dire ruin', the visionary artist and his wife continued to rebuild Jerusalem and Albion. In the midst of these fragments 'Is Built eternally the sublime Universe of Los & Enitharmon' and 'Cathedron's golden Hall'.[65] Because the repressive forces of priestcraft condemn the female genitals as shameful, making 'their places of joy & love excrementitious', the sanctification of the *Yoni* is crucial to human and divine reintegration.[66] As another Catherine Blake heard

Jerusalem.
Chap: 2.

Every ornament of perfection. and every labour of love,
In all the Garden of Eden. & in all the golden mountains
Was become an envied horror. and a remembrance of jealousy:
And every Act a Crime. and Albion the punisher & judge.

And Albion spoke from his secret seat and said

All these ornaments are crimes. they are made by the labours
Of loves; of unnatural consanguinities and friendships
Horrid to think of when enquired deeply into; and all
These hills & valleys are accursed witnesses of Sin
I therefore condense them into solid rocks. stedfast;
A foundation and certainty and demonstrative truth:
That Man be separate from Man, & here I plant my seat.

Cold snows drifted around him: ice coverd his loins around
He sat by Tyburns brook, and underneath his heel, shot up!
A deadly Tree, he namd it Moral Virtue, and the Law
Of God who dwells in Chaos hidden from the human sight.

The Tree spread over him its cold shadows. (Albion groand)
They bent down, they felt the earth and again enrooting
Shot into many a Tree! an endless labyrinth of woe!

From willing sacrifice of Self, to sacrifice of (miscall'd) Enemies
For Atonement: Albion began to erect twelve Altars,
Of rough unhewn rocks, before the Potters Furnace
He namd them Justice, and Truth. And Albions Sons
Must have become the first Victims, being the first transgressors
But they fled to the mountains to seek ransom: building A Strong
Fortification against the Divine Humanity and Mercy,
In Shame & Jealousy to annihilate Jerusalem!

in a Moravian hymn of 1749, '*Templum pacis!* Thou mak'st *Templa ex cloacis*' (Temple of Peace! Thou mak'st a Temple out of the place of excrement).[67]

Cathedron's creative and optimistic weaving of the 'Web of Life for Jerusalem' holds humanity and the universe together.[68] In his earlier descriptions of Vala, Blake had drawn on Hindu notions of *maya* as the delusive material veil woven over spiritual reality, which the visionary artist must attempt to penetrate. In *Jerusalem* he seemed to draw on the Tantric view that the universe is a gigantic fabric, in which each being and each object is a fibre.[69] Blake could have learned from Tulk and the Swedish students of Sanskrit that the term *Tantra* derived from the seminal root *tan*, which meant to 'stretch, to spread or to weave, and, metaphorically, to lay out, to explain or to espouse'.[70]

In the Indian cosmogonic hymn, the *Rig-Veda*, *tan* is the key verb to describe the origin of the universe out of 'the sacrificial dismemberment of the primordial man', whose body is spread out into the parts of the universe, just as a thread is spun and woven by a loom.[71] Thus the noun *tantra* was first used in the Vedic hymns to denote 'a kind of weaving machine, a loom, or specifically, the warp and woof'. In a technique strikingly similar to the Yogis' vision of *maya*, meditating Kabbalists visualised the entire sephirotic system as 'the imaginal body'.[72] Through Tantric-Kabbalistic meditation on the divine weaver within one's wife, and through Tantric-Kabbalistic transmutation of the divine semen within one's husband, the loving couple would envision the reweaving of the unravelled God-Man.

As Blake explored the warp and woof of Christian, Jewish and Asian mystical systems, he created his own multi-cultural fabric, his personal 'System'. Unlike Vala's veil of *maya*, Cathedron's was transparent to his fourfold vision, for he could see through, not with the eye.[73] Thus he could visualise his humble bedchamber as 'my first temple & altar' and his 'over joyous' but 'Exhausted' wife as 'a flame of many colours of precious jewels'.[74] In *Jerusalem*, while Los's female emanation joyed in 'the many weaving threads in bright Cathedron's Dome', he joyed in 'Putting on his golden sandals to walk from mountain to mountain', thus 'keeping the Divine Vision in Time of Trouble'.

Through the spiritual-sexual devotion of a man to his wife, worshipping in her vulvic cathedral, the husband *and* wife could be transformed into the bride of Jesus. In one of his more erotic hymns, Zinzendorf had Jesus sing to his male and female brides that his vaginal Side-hole is dear to 'Sinner Hearts', who embrace the Lamb's 'Body Parts from Head to Foot'.[75] Blake similarly portrayed the ecstatic embrace of Albion with Jesus as that of an androgynous bride, whom the heavenly bridegroom presses into his body 'from Head to Foot'.[76]

But Blake also made clear that conjugial love between an earthly husband and wife – which encompasses Moravian, Swedenborgian, Kabbalistic and Tantric elements – is the true key to spiritual vision: 'Embraces are Cominglings from the Head even to the Feet,/ And not a pompous High Priest entering by a Secret Place.'[77]

And I heard the Name of their Emanations they are named Jerusalem
The End of The Song
of Jerusalem

Epilogue

Grant me an old man's frenzy,
Myself I must remake
Till I am Timon and Lear
Or that William Blake
Who beat upon the wall
Till truth obeyed his call;

A mind Michael Angelo knew
That can pierce the clouds
Or inspired by frenzy
Shake the dead in their shrouds;
Forgotten else by mankind
An old man's eagle mind.

W. B. Yeats, 'An Acre of Grass' (1938)[1]

In 1825, when Crabb Robinson met Blake in a London drawing room, the artist was already sixty-eight years old. Rather than mellowing into a comfortable old age, Blake had become even wilder in his erotic spiritual beliefs and more reckless in his anti-moral pronouncements. If Robinson had seen Blake's more radical works, still confined to disorganised manuscripts, he could have traced the trajectory of the artist's developing antinomianism, which intensified into an old man's visionary 'frenzy'. That always Christian trajectory passed through Swedenborgian, Kabbalistic, Tantric, Hermetic and Moravian stages – finally issuing in the full-blown 'heresies' of his old age.

Earlier, in *Vala*, Blake had sketched a proudly resurrected Jesus, with one female breast and an erect penis.[2] Later, in *The Everlasting Gospel* (1818), he portrayed a defiant, rebellious Jesus, who embodies and tolerates human sexuality: 'Was Jesus Chaste or did he / Give any Lessons of Chastity?'[3] Harking back to Zinzendorf's notion of 'humanation', Blake portrayed a Jesus who experienced all the passions with which 'Sinners deal', and he rejected the claim that Jesus 'never fell'.[4] Blake's God tells Jesus, 'Thou art a Man God is no more / Thy own humanity learn to adore.' Though he came close to the Socinianism of the radical Moravians in the *Judenmission*, the idiosyncratic Blake commented in the margin, 'I am sure this Jesus will not do / Either for Englishman or Jew.'

Like the Moravians during the Sifting Time, Blake revered the prostitute Mary Magdalene, who 'was found in Adulterous bed', because her sexual sins gave Jesus the opportunity to display his universal forgiveness. Jesus urges Mary, 'Fear not Let me see / The Seven Devils that torment thee.' Mary then explains her sexual career as 'dark deceit to Earn my bread', which her hypocritical customers condemn:

That they may call a shame & Sin
Loves Temple that God dwelleth in
And hide in secret hidden Shrine
The Naked Human Form Divine
And render that a Lawless thing
On which the Soul Expands its wing.[5]

While W. B. Yeats prepared his ground-breaking edition of Blake's poetry, he was not aware of the Moravian context of Blake's spiritualised sexuality (a context that had been lost to British historians). But he did view him as a student of Swedenborg, whose theosophy of conjugial love drew on Kabbalistic sources. While reading Crabb Robinson's

Reminiscences (1869), Yeats was struck by Blake's statement that Swedenborg was 'a divine teacher', who 'has done much good', but that 'Parts of Swedenborg's scheme are dangerous. His sexual religion is so.'[6] Like the adepts in the *Zohar*, Swedenborg stressed that 'love for the holy' consists in the sacramental 'projection of the semen' and that reverent sexual arousal stimulates spiritual vision.[7]

From Magregor Mathers, his fellow Rosicrucian and translator of the *Kabbala Denudata*, Yeats heard that Blake gained access to the 'unwritten Kabbala', through which 'persons expert in the use of trance' meet each other on 'purely mental territory', especially in 'vision, or waking dream'.[8] Over the next decades, Yeats explored not only Kabbalistic but Tantric notions of divine eroticism, and he became convinced that Swedenborg and Blake were right – that virile potency fuelled the Chariot of Vision. Moreover, it was dangerous fuel for the aged Blake's fiery imagination, in which his 'Thunder of Thought' was linked to 'Flames of Fierce Desire'.

Like Blake with his Kate, Yeats learned that his young bride George possessed the vulvic key to phallic arousal and visionary ecstasy – she was the embodiment of the Kabbalistic *Shekhinah* and Yogic *Yoni*. However, in the latter case, it was the new wife who prodded a reluctant, middle-aged husband into experiments in magnetic trance, automatic writing and sacramental intercourse, on the earthly as well as astral plane. As George trained Yeats in Kabbalistic and Tantric techniques of meditation and copulation, he experienced a surge of visionary energy that infused his greatest poetry. With his wife acting as the medium for automatic writing, the couple produced more than 4,000 pages of script, eventually distilled into *A Vision* (1937), which embodied their sexual and spiritual explorations.

Anne Saddlemyer, George's biographer, explains that the cosmic dance of the *Zohar* revealed the 'direct link between sexual and spiritual union' and the 'uniting of the male and female within one's self'. In a passage that sheds a retrospective light on Blake's erotic technique and visionary cosmos, she stresses that:

> *the greatest visual influence was the Kabbalah, with its tetrads, triads, cones, the four worlds or levels of energy, the three triads of the Tree of Life, down which knowledge descends like 'the Lightning Flash among the sacred leaves'. Zigzagging in the order of Creation . . . the lightning flash is grounded at last in Malkuth . . . or Shekhinah, the female presence, bride or queen, sometimes known as the Holy Spirit, equivalent in Tantra to Shakti, who enters the participant at the moment of orgasm.*[9]

For Mr and Mrs Yeats, sacramental sex stimulated the 'sixth sense', which 'must precede the Beatific Vision'.[10] Remembering Blake's sexagenarian intensity and defiance, the sixty-nine-year-old Yeats even resorted to a Steinach operation (a vasectomy) in the hope of conserving and transmuting the sacred seed into spiritual vision.[11] He described 'the strange second puberty the operation has given me, the ferment that has come upon my imagination'.[12] Through seminal rejuvenation, Yeats transcended the fatigue, disease and 'bodily decrepitude' that threatened to end his creative drive. Though he could not always achieve a full erection and intercourse, he did experience anew the intense sexual arousal and desire that had energised his youthful visions and poetry. Like the white-haired Blake declaiming to Crabb Robinson in a London salon, an exuberant Yeats chanted to the shocked and amused guests at Dublin's soirées:

> *You think it horrible that lust and rage*
> *Should dance attendance upon my old age:*
> *They were not such a plague when I was young;*
> *What else have I to spur me into song?*[13]

And what about their wives during their strange second puberties? For Catherine Blake, the floods of tears were things of the past, and she accepted benignly her husband's most outrageous notions – especially since there was little chance that he would act on them. A visitor reported that 'his excellent old wife was a sincere believer in his visions', and she confided that 'I have very little of Mr Blake's company; he is always in Paradise'.[14] Through their practice of the magnetic trance, especially in its Kabbalistic and Yogic version, Catherine gained access (though limited) to that psychoerotic Paradise. As she echoed the 'violent radicalism' of her husband's religious and political opinions, she drove their good friend Cumberland to remark that Blake 'is a little Cracked, but very honest – as to his wife she is the maddest of the Two'.[15]

The elderly Catherine Blake watched with reverent awe when her husband asked rhetorically, 'Was Jesus Humble or did he / Give any Proofs of Humility?' And she accepted his resounding *No!*, for Jesus and William acted 'with honest triumphant Pride'.[16] For the mature George Yeats, her dying husband's magnificent poetry and *Vision* were more than compensation for his erotic obsessions and indiscreet affairs. Like Blake, who took his wife along on his visionary journey to Jerusalem, Yeats included his magnetic muse when he sailed to golden Byzantium. He knew that:

An aged man is but a paltry thing,
A tattered coat upon a stick, unless
Soul clap its hands and sing, and louder sing
For every tatter in its mortal dress.[17]

That Yeats's old soul required visionary eros – the dangerous sexual religion – in order to clap and sing was accepted by his wife, though she often felt 'like a child of five in charge of a Tiger in a wire cage'.[18] At seventy-one, Yeats continued his 'perilous journey' when he studied Tantric Yoga with an Indian guru, who inspired him to write about the Hindu 'legend of the golden phallus rising'.[19] Justifying his erotic exploits, which fuelled the most productive and creative period of his life, he explained that 'As age increases my chains, my need for freedom grows . . . I repent of nothing but sickness.'[20]

Like Blake's generous 'Oothon', George even helped her husband find young 'daughters of Albion', a gift that Catherine could only give in Blake's poetic fantasy.[21] In the midst of Yeats's final philandering, his wife assured him that when he was gone and she was asked about his love affairs, 'I shall say nothing because I will remember how proud you were.' Like Mrs Blake, Mrs Yeats no longer cried, for both wives believed fundamentally, 'with honest triumphant Pride', that for their dangerously visionary husbands 'the marriage bed is the symbol of the solved antinomy'.[22]

Appendix

1. Moravian Archive: MS. C/36/2. John Blake's letter of petition to join the Congregation of the Lamb (n.d.):

> Dear Brother Beoler I have a Desire to write to you and to our Saviour's Dear Congregation that I may come in a Closer connexont with them, that I may injoy those privilidged with our Dear Saviour as his Congregation have. I made bold to Rite to you to Let you know how it stands with my hart I am a poor missarable unhappy Creature. But for such I know the Saviour Shed his Blood for. May that blood whitch he Shed in ye Garden in the hall before Pilate and on the cross I say may that blood which me Clense and make me one of those that can Rejoyce in hiss wounds, and may his Death and Suffring be the only thing, the one thing neefull for me, to make me happy, I know I a Sinnor and for Sutch the saviour shed his blood. O may I become a happy Sinnor from this moment and to all Eternity. O take me by the hand and hart, and Promise me to our Saviour as one as his purchase, as one he paid so great a price for as one that cost him many Tears Smarts and pain, O Lamb of God grant that I may be a memb'r of thy Congregation and may be quite happy, from your Brother
>
> John Blake
>
> O take me by the hand and
> hart, etc.

2. Moravian Archive: MS. C/36/2/158. Thomas Armitage's letter of petition:

For Brother West
Nov'r the 14th 1750 London

My Dear Brethren

My Dear Saviour has maid me Love you in Such a degree, as I never did Experience before to any Set of People; and I believe it is his will that I should come amongst you; because he has done it himself, for I could not bear the Doctrine of his Bloody Corps, till; very lately, till non but my Dr Saviour could show me; perfectly, & he over came me so sweetly that I shall never forget, when I only went out of curiosity to hear Bro'r Cennick, which was to be the last Time I thought I wod care in hearing any of the Brethren; & my Jesus Show'd me that I had been seeking something else besides him, nor could I then bear the thought of hearing anything Else; but of him being Crucified & of his Bleeding wounds, which I Experienced very Sweet & the only food for my Soul then; I am but very poor in my Self & weak and find my Love very cool sometime toward him, for all hes done for me so much, but when my Loveing Saviour comes again and kindles that Spark, then I feel I can love him dearly; so he makes me love him or Else I should not love him at all –; & I can feel my Saviour, forgive me all my base actions from time to time; for all that my Dr Lords Love is such, as bad as I am I know he Loves me with that ever lasting Love, that nothing shall separate us, as St Paul sais, from Your Unworthy Brother in the Suffering Jesus

Thos Armitage

3. Moravian Archive: MS. C/36/2/159. Catherine Armitage's letter of petition (n.d.):

My Dear Bretheren & Sistors

I have very littell to say of my self for I am a pore crature and full of wants but my Dear Saviour will satisfy them all I should be glad if I could allways lay at the Cross full as I do know thanks be to him last Friday at the love feast our Saviour was pleased to make me Suck his wounds and hug the Cross more than Ever and I trust will more and more till my fraile nature can hould no more at your request I have rit but I am not worthy of the blessing it is desird for I do not Love our Dear Savor halfe enough but if it is his will to bring me among his happy flock in closer conection I shall be very thankful I would tell you more of my self but itt is nothing thats good so now I will rite of my Savour that is all Love

Here let me drink for ever drink
nor never once depart
for what I tast makes me to cry
fix at this Spring My heart
Dear Savour thou has seen how oft
Ive turnd away from thee
O let thy work renewd to day
Remain eternally
Catherine Armitage

Notes

Acknowledgements

1. Marsha Keith Schuchard, 'Why Mrs Blake Cried: Swedenborg, Blake and the Sexual Basis of Spiritual Vision', *Esoterica: The Journal of Esoteric Studies*, 2 (2000), 45–93. http.www.esoteric.msu. This was written before my discovery of the Moravian documents in June 2001.

Introduction

1. Arthur Symons, *William Blake* (London: Archibald Constable, 1907), 253. Symons reprints the passages about Blake recorded in Crabb Robinson's diary and reminiscences.
2. Ibid., 269. In German, *Frauen* means both women and wives.
3. Ibid., 74–5.
4. John Thomas Smith, *Nollekens and His Times* (London, 1828); reprinted in Gerald E. Bentley, *Blake Records* (Oxford: Clarendon, 1969), 459, 474.
5. Alexander Gilchrist, *Life of William Blake, 'Pictor Ignotus'* (London: Macmillan, 1863), 316.
6. Ibid., 331.
7. Algernon Charles Swinburne, *William Blake: A Critical Essay* (1868; rpt. New York: AMS, 1973), 14.
8. Edwin John Ellis and William Butler Yeats, *The Works of William Blake* (1893; rpt. New York: Benjamin Blom, 1967), I, 42.
9. Edwin John Ellis, *The Real Blake* (London: Chatto & Windus, 1907), 90.

10. Ibid., 168.
11. William Michael Rossetti, *The Poetical Works of William Blake* (London: G. Bell, 1874), lvii.
12. David Erdman, *The Illuminated Blake* (London: Oxford UP, 1975), 248.
13. Ellis, *Real Blake*, 411–12.
14. Symons, *Blake*, 260.
15. Rossetti, *Poetical Works*, lxxx.
16. Ellis and Yeats, *Works*, I, 24–5.
17. William Butler Yeats, *Essays and Introductions* (1961; New York: Macmillan, 1986), 112–13.
18. Thomas Wright, *The Life of William Blake* (1929; rpt. New York: Burt Franklin, 1969), I, 2.
19. Margaret Lowery, *Windows of the Morning: A Critical Study of William Blake's Poetical Sketches* (New Haven: Yale UP, 1940), 14–15, 210 n.57.
20. For the Moravian claim, see Nancy Bogen, 'The Problem of William Blake's Early Religion', *The Personalist*, 49 (1968), 509, 517; and Jack Lindsay, *William Blake: His Life and Works* (London: Constable, 1978), 3–4, 275–6. For the Muggletonian argument, see E. P. Thompson, *Witness Against the Beast: William Blake and the Moral Law* (Cambridge: Cambridge UP, 1993). For the Dissenter-Baptist claim, see Gerald E. Bentley, *The Stranger from Paradise: A Biography of William Blake* (New Haven: Yale UP, 2001), 7–11.
21. For the anti-Swedenborgian argument, see David Erdman, 'Blake's Early Swedenborgianism: A Twentieth-Century Legend', *Comparative Literature*, 5 (1953), 247–57.

Chapter 1: Religion of the Heart

1. Alexander Gilchrist, *Life of William Blake*, rev. edn; ed. Ruthven Todd (1880; London: J. M. Dent, 1942), 82.
2. E. P. Thompson, *Witness Against the Beast*, 120–1; Keri Davies, 'William Blake's Mother: A New Identification'. *Blake: An Illustrated Quarterly*, 33 (1999), 36–50.
3. The letters of application to join the Moravian Congregation

of the Lamb written by John Blake, Thomas Armitage and Catherine Armitage are reproduced in the Appendix. See also Keri Davies and Marsha Keith Schuchard, 'Recovering the Lost Moravian History of William Blake's Family', *Blake: An Illustrated Quarterly*, 38 (2004), 36–43.

4. Moravian historians differ on the dates of the Sifting Time, but for the Fetter Lane Congregation the years 1743–53 were the most significant. For the most accurate histories of the Sifting Time, see Colin Podmore, *The Moravian Church in England, 1728–1760* (Oxford: Clarendon, 1998); Paul Peucker, "Blut auf unsre grüne Bänchen: Die Sichtungzeit in der Herrnhuter Brüdergemeine", *Unitas Fratrum: Zeitschrift für Geschichte und Gegenwartsfragen der Brüdergemeine*, 49/50 (2002), 41–94; and Craig Atwood, *Community of the Cross: Moravian Piety in Colonial Bethlehem* (University Park: Pennsylvania UP, 2004).
5. Peter Ackroyd, *London: The Biography* (London: Chatto & Windus, 2000), 230.
6. Ibid., 231–7.
7. London, Moravian Church Library and Archive: MS. C/36/2/158. Henceforth cited as Moravian Archive.
8. Ibid., MS. C/36/2/159.
9. Ibid., MS. C/36/2/168.
10. For introductory biographies, see John Weinlick, *Count Zinzendorf* (New York: Abingdon, 1956); and Arthur Freeman, *An Ecumenical Theology of the Heart: The Theology of Count Nicholas Ludwig von Zinzendorf* (Bethlehem, PA: Moravian Church in America, 1998).
11. Atwood, *Community*, 45; Pierre Deghaye, *La Doctrine Ésotérique de Zinzendorf* (Paris: Klincksieck, 1969), 161–2.
12. J. Taylor Hamilton and Kenneth G. Hamilton, *History of the Moravian Church* (Bethlehem, PA: Moravian Board of Christian Education, 1967), 18–19.
13. Gerald E. Bentley, *Blake Records* (Oxford: Clarendon, 1969), 543.
14. Arthur James Lewis, *Zinzendorf, the Ecumenical Pioneeer: A Study in the Moravian Contribution to Christian Mission and Unity* (Philadelphia: Westminster, 1962), 25.

15. Christiane Dithmar, *Zinzendorfs Nonkonformistische Haltung zum Judentum* (Heidelberg: C. Winter, 2000), 56.
16. Lewis, *Zinzendorf*, 26.
17. Dithmar, *Zinzendorfs*, 76, 80.
18. Atwood, *Community*, 97.
19. John Sadler, *J. A. Comenius and the Concept of Universal Education* (London: Allen & Unwin, 1966), 42.
20. Andrew Weeks, *Boehme: An Intellectual Biography of the Seventeenth-Century Philosopher and Mystic* (Albany: State University of New York, 1991), 43.
21. Gershom Scholem, *Major Trends in Jewish Mysticism* (1941; rev. edn New York: Schocken, 1954).
22. B. J. Gibbons, *Gender in Mystical and Occult Thought: Behmenism and its Development in England* (Cambridge: Cambridge UP, 1996), 205.
23. Dithmar, *Zinzendorfs*, 104–7.
24. For his movement, see Gershom Scholem, *Sabbatai Zevi: The Mystical Messiah, 1626–1676*, trans. R. J. Zwi Werblowsky (Princeton: Princeton UP, 1973).
25. Atwood, *Community*, 44.
26. Freeman, *Ecumenical*, 7.
27. Craig Atwood, 'Blood, Sex, and Death: Life and Liturgy in Zinzendorf's Bethlehem' (Ph.D. dissertation: Princeton University, 1995), 73–4.
28. Deghaye, *Doctrine Ésotérique*, 167.
29. Bentley, *Blake Records*, 542.

Chapter 2: The Mystical Marriage

1. Erich Beyreuther, 'Zinzendorf und das Judentum', *Judaica*, 19 (1963), 193–246.
2. Dithmar, *Zinzendorfs*, 104–7.
3. See Raphael Patai, *The Hebrew Goddess* (New York: Ktav, 1967), 101–3, 120–2; David Biale, *Eros and the Jews* (New York: Doubleday, 1988), 101–2.
4. For development of 'Marriage Theology' by the late 1730s, see Craig Atwood, 'Sleeping in the Arms of Jesus: Sanctifying

Sexuality in the Eighteenth-Century Moravian Church', *Journal of the History of Sexuality*, 8 (1997), 189–214.

5. J. P. Lockwood, *Memorials of the Life of Peter Böhler, Bishop of the Church of the Moravian Brethren*, introd. Thomas Jackson (London: Wesleyan Conference Office, 1868), 35; W. R. Ward, 'Peter Boehler', in Donald Lewis, ed., *The Blackwell Dictionary of Evangelical Biography: 1730–1860* (Oxford: Blackwell, 1955), 115.
6. John Wesley, *The Journal of John Wesley*, ed. Nehemiah Curnock (1916; rpt. London: Epworth, 1938), I, 436.
7. Gibbons, *Gender*, 95.
8. The Non-Jurors believed that William III illegally deposed the Stuart king, James VII and II, and they refused to swear allegiance to the new regime or its Hanoverian successors. Wesley's parents (and initially he himself) were sympathetic to the Non-Juring and Jacobite causes.
9. Daniel Benham, *Memoirs of James Hutton* (London: Hamilton, Adams, 1856), 31. For the controversy about Wesley's shorter draft, see J. Wesley, *Journal*, I, 459.
10. Moravian Archive: MS. C/36/2/159.
11. Podmore, *Moravian Church*, 31.
12. Colin Podmore, 'The Fetter Lane Society, 1738', *Proceedings of the Wesley Historical Society*, 47 (1989), 140.
13. Ibid., 151.
14. Podmore, *Moravian Church*, 61–2.
15. Podmore, 'Fetter Lane Society', 165.
16. Dithmar, *Zinzendorfs*, 122, 145, 215.
17. Complaint made in 1741 and published in George Tennent, *Some Account of the Principles of the Moravians* (London: S. Mason, 1743), 13.
18. Symons, *Blake*, 255.
19. Julius Sachse, *The German Sectarians of Pennsylvania, 1742–1800* (1899–1900; rpt. New York: AMS, (1971), 164.
20. Henry Rimius, *A Candid Narrative of the Rise and Progress of the Herrnhutters* (London: A. Linde, 1753), Appendix, xx; Henry Rimius, *A Solemn Call on Count Zinzendorf* (London: A. Linde, 1754), 18. Deghaye, *Doctrine Ésotérique*, 93–4.
21. Atwood, 'Sleeping', 44; Biale, *Eros*, 54, 101–8.

22. Sachse, *German Sectarians*, II, 69–80.
23. Podmore, *Moravian Church*, 130.
24. Ibid., 131.
25. Aaron Fogleman, 'Jesus is Female: The Moravian Challenge in the German Communities of British North America', *The William and Mary Quarterly*, 60 (2003), 326.
26. Ibid., 325.
27. Podmore, *Moravian Church*, 31.
28. Many of the Fetter Lane records were censored or destroyed in the wake of public attacks on the Moravians from 1753 onwards.
29. Peter Vogt, 'Zinzendorf's Theology of the Sabbath', in Craig Atwood and Peter Vogt, eds, *The Distinctiveness of Moravian Culture: Essays and Documents in Moravian History in Honor of Vernon H. Nelson* (Nazareth, PA: Moravian Publication Society, 2001), 218.
30. Abraham Reincke, *A Register of Members of the Moravian Church . . . Between 1727 and 1754* (Bethlehem, PA: H. T. Clauder, 1873), 14.
31. For the probable fraternal relation between John and James Blake, see Bentley, *Stranger*, 3.

Chapter 3: Sex, Wounds and Blood

1. Moravian Archive: C/36/2/168.
2. Atwood, *Community*, 11–19.
3. For the tradition, see Leo Steinberg, *The Sexuality of Christ in Renaissance Art and Its Modern Oblivion*, 2nd rev. edn (1983; Chicago: Chicago UP, 1996).
4. Ibid., 57.
5. Atwood, 'Sleeping', 191–205.
6. Elliot Wolfson, 'The Cut that Binds: Time, Memory and the Ascetic Impulse', in Shaul Magid, ed., *God's Voice from the Void: Old and New Studies in Bratslav Hasidism* (Albany: State University of New York, 2002), 113.
7. Nicholas Ludwig von Zinzendorf, *Maxims, Theological Ideas and Sentences*, ed. J. Gambold (London: J. Beecroft, 1751), 137–8.
8. Atwood, 'Sleeping', 191.
9. Rimius, *Candid Narrative*, 66.

10. Moravian Archive: C/36/1/2.
11. William Blake, *Complete Poetry and Prose of William Blake*, rev. ed, eds. David Erdman and Harold Bloom (New York: Doubleday, 1988), 50. Henceforth cited as Blake, *CPP*, 50.
12. Atwood, 'Sleeping', 172, 204–5.
13. Moravian Archive: C/36/7/3.
14. Zinzendorf, *Maxims*, 228.
15. Craig Atwood, 'Zinzendorf's "Litany of the Wounds of the Husband"' , *Lutheran Quarterly*, 11 (1997), 202.
16. Ibid., 142.
17. For Andrea del Sarto's *Tallard Madonna* (*c*.1515), see Steinberg, *Sexuality*, 286, plate 2.
18. Rimius, *Candid Narrative*, 46–7. A version of this hymn appeared in the hymnbook apparently owned by Catherine Armitage; see [James Hutton], *A Collection of Hymns: Consisting Chiefly of Translations from the German Hymnbook of the Moravian Brethren* (London: James Hutton, Bookseller in Fetter Lane, 1749), 54.
19. Steinberg, *Sexuality*, 374–5.
20. Piero Campresi, *Juice of Life: The Symbolic and Magic Significance of Blood*, trans. Robert Barr; introd. Umberto Eco (New York: Continuum, 1995), 70.
21. Zinzendorf, *Maxims*, 229.
22. Rimius, *Candid Narrative*, 56–7.
23. Ibid., 63.
24. Peter Ackroyd, *Blake: A Biography* (New York: Alfred Knopf, 1996), 281; William Blake, *The Four Zoas*, ed. Cettina Magno and David Erdman (Lewisburg: Bucknell UP, 1987), 158.
25. From the German word *Delikatesse* (delicacy, dainty); see Atwood, *Community*, 110.
26. [Hutton], *Collection of Hymns*, 138.
27. Atwood, *Community*, 219.
28. Atwood, 'Blood', 178, 232.
29. Atwood, *Community*, 214.
30. Atwood, 'Blood', 242. For similar experiences of spiritual-erotic catharsis in the 'hymns to blood' of various Catholic saints, see Campresi, *Juice of Life*, 68–70.
31. Moravian Archive: C/36/2/158.

32. The image of Elisha lying on top of the widow's son was also assimilated into Scottish and Jacobite Masonic rituals, with King Charles II representing the widow's son and the 'five points of fellowship' (a frontal, full-body embrace) representing the revivification of the Stuart cause. See David Stevenson, *The Origins of Freemasonry: Scotland's Century, 1590–1710* (1988; Cambridge: Cambridge UP, 1993), 143–4.
33. Benham, *Memoirs*, 596.
34. Moravian Archive: C/36/2/168.

Chapter 4: The Mirth of the Justified-Sinner Community

1. Rimius, *Candid Narrative*, 52–3.
2. Atwood, 'Zinzendorf's Litany', 197–8.
3. Moravian Archive: C/36/7/3 (28 August 1749).
4. Nicolaus Ludwig von Zinzendorf, *Nine Public Lectures on Important Subjects in Religion Preached in the Fetter Lane Chapel in the Year 1746*, trans. and ed. George Forell (Iowa City: Iowa UP, 1973), 4.
5. Ibid., 15.
6. Moravian Archive: C/36/10/3 (17 February 1749).
7. Symons, *Blake*, 74–5.
8. Hans-Walter Erbe, 'Herrnhaag: eine religiöse Kommunität im 18. Jahrhundert', *Unitas Fratrum*, 23–4 (1988), 196–9.
9. Rimius, *Solemn Call*, 19–20.
10. Paul Peucker, '"Inspired by Flames of Love": Homosexuality and 18th Century Moravian Brothers', *Journal of the History of Sexuality* (forthcoming).
11. Ibid.; also Erbe, 'Herrnhaag', 148, 161–4.
12. Elijah Schochet, *The Hasidic Movement and the Gaon of Vilna* (Northvale/London: Jason Aronson, 1994), 45–7.
13. Peucker, 'Inspired by Flames'.
14. Ibid.
15. Atwood, 'Blood', 179–80.
16. Podmore, *Moravian Church*, 135.
17. Peucker, 'Inspired by Flames'.
18. Zinzendorf, *Maxims*, 224.

19. John Cennick, *Sacred Hymns* (Bristol: Felix Farley, 1743), part I, hymn XXIII.
20. Fogleman, 'Jesus is Female', 326.
21. Peucker, 'Inspired by Flames'.
22. Andrew Frey, *A True and Authentic Account: Containing the Occasion of his Coming among the Herrnhutters or Moravians*, trans. from German (London: J. Robinson, 1753), 16–17.
23. Ibid., 20.
24. Atwood, *Community*, 17 n.57, 90.
25. Fogleman, 'Jesus is Female', 327.
26. Craig Atwood, 'Zinzendorf's 1749 Reprimand to the *Brüdergemeine*', *Transactions of the Moravian Historical Society*, 29 (1996), 59–84. The shocking letter was later destroyed, along with other evidence of Christel's 'irregular' activities.
27. Ibid., 74.
28. Peucker, 'Inspired by Flames'.
29. Podmore, *Moravian Church*, 228–65.
30. Moravian Archive: C/36/14/2.
31. Ibid., C/36/1/2, p.10.
32. Ibid., C/36/7/5, p.61.
33. Ibid., C/36/7/5, p.80.
34. Ibid., C/36/11/14.
35. Ibid., C/36/7/3 (13 September 1749).
36. Ibid., C/36/7/5 (13 September 1751).
37. Ibid., C/36/7/5 (27 May 1750).
38. Ibid., C/36/11/6. For the terms of the will, see Gerald Bentley, *Blake Records,* 2nd rev. edn (New Haven: Yale UP, 2004), 5–6.
39. Swedenborgian translators use 'conjugial' instead of 'conjugal' to connote the special spiritual sense of the word. I will follow this usage when referring to Swedenborg's meaning.

Chapter 5: Swedenborg and Kabbalistic Science

1. For Brockmer's full account, see Emanuel Swedenborg, *Swedenborg's Dream Diary*, ed. Lars Bergquist; trans. Anders Hallengren (West Chester: Swedenborg Foundation, 2001), 54–7.

2. Anecdote recounted in Benedict Chastanier, *Tableau Analytique et Raisonée de la Doctrine Celéste* (London, 1786), 21–4.
3. For his family background, see Signe Toksvig, *Emanuel Swedenborg: Scientist and Mystic* (1948; New York: Swedenborg Foundation, 1983), 7–42. For the most accurate biography of Swedenborg, see Lars Bergquist, *Swedenborgs Hemlighet* (Stockholm: Natur och Kultur, 1999), 26–61. For his role in diplomatic espionage, see my article, 'Emanuel Swedenborg: Deciphering the Codes of a Celestial and Terrestrial Intelligence', in Elliot Wolfson, ed., *Rending the Veil: Concealment and Secrecy in the History of Religions* (New York: Seven Bridges, 1999), 177–207.
4. Emanuel's surname was also Swedberg until 1721, when he was ennobled by the queen and given the new name Swedenborg. I use the latter name throughout to avoid confusion.
5. Rudolph Tafel, *Documents Concerning the Life and Character of Emanuel Swedenborg* (London: Swedenborg Society, 1875), I, 103, 194–5.
6. Dithmar, *Zinzendorfs*, 54–5; Elisheva Carlebach, *Divided Souls: Converts from Judaism in Germany, 1500–1700* (New Haven: Yale UP, 2001), 81–3.
7. Hugo Valentin, *Judarnas Historia I Sverige* (Stockholm: Albert Bonniers, 1924), 26–7, 84.
8. William White, *Emanuel Swedenborg: His Life and Writings*, 2nd rev. edn (London: Simpkin, Marshall, 1868), 11–12. An exception was Jesper, his youngest son, who was born on his birthday.
9. Ibid., 5, 13.
10. Swedenborg's first autograph appears on the title-page of a dissertation on Hebrew, *Exercitium academicum . . . seu lucos Hebraeorum* (Stockholm, 1699); see Cyriel Sigstedt, *The Swedenborg Epic* (New York: Bookman, 1952), 461 n.343.
11. Toksvig, *Swedenborg*, 23.
12. Ibid., 20–1, 28.
13. Ibid., 5.
14. The following draws on the detailed discussion of Benzelius's career and influence on Swedenborg in my article, 'Leibniz, Benzelius and Swedenborg: The Kabbalistic Roots of Swedish

Illuminism', in Allison Coudert, Richard Popkin and Gordon Weiner, eds, *Leibniz, Mysticism and Religion* (Dordrecht: Kluwer Academic, 1998), 84–106.

15. Van Helmont was the anonymous author of the concluding treatise, the 'Adumbratio Kabbalae Christianae', which pressed the analogy between the Kabbalistic concept of Adam Kadmon as microcosmic man and the Christian concept of Jesus as primordial man. Leibniz probably informed Benzelius that he believed Van Helmont was a Rosicrucian. See Allison Coudert, *The Impact of the Kabbalah in the Seventeenth Century: The Life and Thought of Francis Mercury van Helmont (1614–1698)* (Leiden: Brill, 1999), 308–29.
16. The current Sabbatian movement was discussed in [Francis Lee], *A Letter to Some Divines, concerning the Question, Whether God since Christ's Ascension, doth anymore reveal himself to Mankind by means of Divine Apparitions* (London, 1695).
17. Valentin, *Judarnas*, 84–5; Hans Joachim Schoeps, *Barocke Juden, Christen, Judenchristen* (Berne and Munich: Francke, 1965), 60–7.
18. Elliot Wolfson, 'Messianism in the Christian Kabbalah of Johann Kemper', in Matt Goldish and Richard Popkin, eds, *Jewish Messianism in the Early Modern Period* (Dordrecht: Kluwer Academic, 2001), 138–87.
19. George Dole, 'Philosemitism in the Seventeenth Century', *Studia Swedenborgiana*, 7 (1990), 5–17.
20. Wolfson, 'Messianism', 141–2.
21. *History of the Works of the Learned* (1710–11), IX, 708. Swedenborg wrote to Benzelius that he would give him an account of 'all I have read' in this journal; see Alfred Acton, *The Letters and Memorials of Emanual Swedenborg* (Bryn Athyn: Swedenborg Scientific Association, 1955), I, 23.
22. Acton, *Letters*, I, 30.
23. John Wilkins, *The Mathematical and Philosophical Works* (London, 1708), 42. For Wilkins's Rosicrucian interests and Masonic contacts, see my book, *Restoring the Temple of Vision: Cabalistic Freemasonry and Stuart Culture* (London: Brill, 2002), 569, 597–605, 625.
24. John Smith, *Select Discourses* (London, 1660), 203, 252–7, 304.

25. Acton, *Letters*, I, 120.
26. John Norris, *The Theory and Regulation of Love* (London, 1688), 160, 167–8.
27. Ibid., 171.
28. Ibid., 100.

Chapter 6: Erotic Dreams and Ecstatic Visions

1. For an important revisionist study of the so-called 'Age of Liberty' under Chancellor Arvid Horn, see Anthony Upton, *Charles XI and Swedish Absolutism* (Cambridge: Cambridge UP, 1998), especially p.261. For Swedenborg's political activities and frustrations, see my article, 'Jacobite and Visionary: the Masonic Journey of Emanuel Swedenborg', *Ars Quatuor Coronatorum*, 115 (2002), 33–72. I plan to publish a book-length study, 'Emanuel Swedenborg, Secret Agent on Earth and in Heaven: A Political and Masonic Biography'.
2. Bergquist, *Swedenborgs Hemlighet*, 129–30, 205–6, 236–44; Swedenborg, *Dream Diary* (Bergquist edn), 12, 30–8.
3. Emanuel Swedenborg, *Psychologia Empirica*, trans. Alfred Acton (Philadelphia: Swedenborg Scientific Society, 1923), 90.
4. His visit to Prague is described in Alfred Acton, 'The Life of Emanuel Swedenborg . . . 1688–1744', p.382. Typescript in library of the Academy of New Church, Bryn Athyn, PA. I am grateful to Reverend Chris Baun for use of his copy, which provides important unpublished information on Swedenborg.
5. 'Hussites' and 'Jonathan Eibeschuetz', *Encyclopaedia Judaica* (Jerusalem, 1972). Gustaf Dalman, 'Documente eines Christlichen Geheimbundes unter den Juden in achtzehnen Jahrhundert', *Saat und Hoffnung. Zeitschrift für die Mission der Kirche an Israel*, 12 (1890), 18–37; Yehudah Liebes, 'A Crypto Judaeo-Christian Sect of Sabbatian Origin', *Tarbiz*, 57 (1988), 110, 349–84 [in Hebrew].
6. Swedenborg, *Psychologia*, 22, 158–60.
7. Eberhard Zwink, '"Schrauben-förmige Bewegung is in allem": Oetinger lenkt den Blick auf Swedenborgs Irrdische Philosophie'; *Contubernium*, 63 (2005), 197–229.

8. Sigstedt, *Swedenborg Epic*, 115.
9. Swedenborg, *Psychologia*, 76, 92.
10. On Schurig's work, see Peter Wagner, *Eros Revived* (London: Secker & Warburg, 1988), 12–13.
11. For details on these travels, see Schuchard, 'Jacobite and Visionary', 41–5.
12. Inge Jonsson, 'Köpenhamn-Amsterdam-Paris: Swedenborgs Resa 1737–1738', *Lychnos* (1967–8), 74; Nils Jacobsson, *Den Svenska Herrnhutismens Uppkomst* (Uppsala, 1908), 106–20.
13. Acton, 'Life', 450–4.
14. Emanuel Swedenborg, *An Introduction to the Word Explained*, ed. Alfred Acton (Bryn Athyn: Academy of New Church, 1927), 27.
15. Emanuel Swedenborg, *The Word of the Old Testament Explained*, trans. Alfred Acton (Bryn Athyn: Academy of New Church, 1928–48), no. 6905
16. Swedenborg, *The Economy of the Animal Kingdom*, trans. A Clissold (New York: Swedenborg Scientific Association, 1955), I, 241.
17. Ibid., I, 9.
18. Swedenborg probably referred to 'Rabbi' Lieberkuhn and those Moravians who joined Jews in discussions of the *Geheimlehre* (secret or esoteric teachings). Unfortunately, after Swedenborg's death, his heirs destroyed the pages of his 1739 journal in which he recorded his erotic dreams and visions. Moravian officials would similarly censor the names of those Jews involved in the Dutch *Geheimbund*. Dithmar, *Zinzendorfs*, 22, 105, 129–30. Emanuel Swedenborg, *The Spiritual Diary*, trans. Alfred Acton (1962; rpt. London: Swedenborg Society, 1977), no. 2097. On Lieberkuhn's career, see Gustaf Dalman and Diakonus Schulze, *Zinzendorf und Lieberkuhn: Studien der Geschichte der Judenmission* (Leipzig: J. E. Hinrich, 1903).
19. Jakob Meyer, *The Story of Moses Haim Luzzatto at Amsterdam, 1736–1743* (Amsterdam: Joachimstael's Boekhandel, 1947).
20. Simon Ginzburg, *The Life and Times of Moses Hayim Luzzatto* (Philadelphia: Dropsie College, 1931), 112–17. On Jewish Masons in Holland, see Margaret Jacob, *Living the Enlightenment: Freemasonry and Politics in Eighteenth-Century Europe* (New York: Oxford UP, 1991), 173.

21. Moses Chaim Luzzatto, *Derech ha Shem: The Way of God*, trans. A. Kaplan (New York: Feldheim, 1977), 185–95.
22. On his secret journey, see Schuchard, 'Jacobite and Visionary', 44–5.
23. Swedenborg, *Economy*, II, 209, 239, 313.
24. Acton, 'Life', 554–5.
25. [Abbé N. De Montfaucon de Villars], *Le Comte de Gabalis* (Paris: Claude Barbin, 1670), 158–9. I quote from the English translation, *Comte de Gabalis* (London: William Rider, 1922), 101–5.
26. Emanuel Swedenborg, *A Philosopher's Notebook*, ed. Alfred Acton (Philadelphia: Swedenborg Scientific Association, 1923), 89.
27. For the intensely mystical-political atmosphere at this time in Sweden, see Claude Nordmann, *Grandeur et Liberté de la Suède (1660–1792)* (Paris: Beatrice-Nauwelaerts, 1971), 418 n.37.
28. Swedenborg, *Economy*, III, 340.
29. Ibid, III, 351.
30. Acton, *Letters*, II, 630.
31. Tennent, *Some Account*, 13, 27, 46.
32. John Stinstra, *A Pastoral Letter Against Fanaticism*, trans. Henry Rimius (1750; London: A. Linde, 1753), 59–60, 92.
33. Zinzendorf, *Maxims*, 152.
34. Frey, *True and Authentic Account*, 52–3.
35. Luzzatto, *Derech ha-Shem*, 183–5, 129–31, 167–8.
36. Elliot Wolfson, '*Tikkun ha-Shekhinah:* Redemption and the Overcoming of Gender Dimorphism in the Messianic Kabbalah of Moses Hayyim Luzzatto', *History of Religions*, 36 (1997), 332.
37. Villars, *Gabalis*, 27.
38. Giacomo Casanova, *History of My Life*, trans. Willard Trask (New York: Harcourt Brace, and World, 1966), II, 198.
39. Emanuel Swedenborg, *Emanuel Swedenborg's Journal of Dreams*, trans. J. J. G. Wilkinson, ed. W. R. Woofenden (New York: Swedenborg Foundation, 1986), no. 14. Unless otherwise indicated, all quotations are from this edition, cited as Swedenborg, *Journal of Dreams*.
40. C. T. Odhner, 'Swedenborg's Dreams or Diary of 1744', *New Church Life*, 34 (1914), 391.

41. Toksvig, *Swedenborg*, 78. Bergquist suggests that he visited brothels in 1744; see his edition, *Dream Diary*, 232.
42. Emanuel Swedenborg, *The Generative Organs*, trans. J. J. G. Wilkinson (London: William Newberry, 1852), 32–3. Though planned as part of *The Animal Kingdom*, this treatise was published posthumously.
43. Swedenborg, *Journal of Dreams*, no. 14.
44. Ibid., nos 12, 14.
45. Ginzburg, *Luzzatto*, 82–3.
46. Swedenborg, *Journal of Dreams*, nos 12–15, 46.
47. Ibid., no. 65.
48. Ibid., nos 47–8.
49. Ibid., nos 87–8.
50. Fogleman, 'Jesus is Female', 54.
51. Moshe Idel, 'Sexual Metaphors and Praxis in the Kabbalah', in David Kraemer, ed., *The Jewish Family: Metaphor and Memory* (Oxford: Oxford UP, 1989), 200–1.
52. Swedenborg, *Journal of Dreams*, no. 171.
53. Ibid., no. 172. In his edition Bergquist supplies the elided word 'ejaculation', found in the original Swedish manuscript, but omitted in Wilkinson's and Odhner's translations.
54. Louis Jacobs, *Jewish Mystical Testimonies* (New York: Schocken, 1977), 141.
55. Ibid., 141.
56. Swedenborg, *Generative Organs*, 71.
57. Emanual Swedenborg, *Journal of Dreams*, trans. C. T. Odhner (Bryn Athyn: Academy of New Church, 1918), no. 179.
58. Schochet, *Hasidic Movement*, 45.

Chapter 7: Sacramental Sexuality

1. Schuchard, 'Jacobite and Visionary', 47–50.
2. Moravian Archive: C/36/11/4; Swedenborg, *Journal of Dreams*, nos 191, 197.
3. Ibid., no. 120, Fredrik Ruoth, 'Johan Wilhelm von Archenholtz', *Studien Historische*, H. 131 (1915), 150–7.
4. Swedenborg, *Journal of Dreams*, no. 197.

5. Swedenborg, *Dream Diary* (Bergquist edn), 53.
6. Swedenborg, *Journal of Dreams*, nos 51–4.
7. Ibid. (Odhner trans.), no. 132.
8. Luzzatto, *Derech ha-Shem*, 109.
9. Ginzburg, *Luzzatto*, 34–5.
10. Scholem, *Major Trends*, 272.
11. Swedenborg, *Journal of Dreams*, no. 173.
12. Sachse, *German Sectarians*, I, 462.
13. Christoph Gottlieb von Murr, *Über den wahren Rosenkreutzer und des Freymaurerordens* (Sulzbach: J. E. Semler, 1803), 81.
14. Rimius, *Supplement*, xlix; Sachse, *German Sectarians*, I, 465.
15. Swedenborg, *Dream Journal* (Bergquist edn), p. 336.
16. Zinzendorf, *Maxims*, 173, 175.
17. Emanuel Swedenborg, *The Animal Kingdom*, trans. J. J. G. Wilkinson (1744; London: W. Newberry, 1843), I, 235.
18. Swedenborg, *Dream Journal* (Bergquist edn), nos 114–16.
19. Carl Gustaf Tessin, *Tessin och Tessiniana*, ed. Fredrik von Ehrenheim (Stockholm, 1819), 301–2; Casanova, *History*, V, 107–57.
20. Swedenborg, *Journal of Dreams*, no. 200. Klemming, the first editor of the manuscript, dated this entry May 1744.
21. Ibid., no, 283–5.
22. The year 1744 marked the infusion of Rosicrucian themes into Swedish Freemasonry, according to Karl Frick, *Die Erleuchteten* (Graz, 1973), 300.
23. On Falk and Swedenborg, see my articles, 'Yeats and the Unknown Superiors: Swedenborg, Falk and Cagliostro', in Marie Roberts and Hugh Ormsby-Lennon, eds, *Secret Texts: The Literature of Secret Societies* (New York: AMS, 1993), 114–68, and 'Dr Samuel Jacob Falk: A Sabbatian Adventurer in the Masonic Underground', in Matt Goldish and Richard Popkin, eds, *Millenarianism and Messianism in Early Modern European Culture: Jewish Messianism in the Early Modern World* (Dordrecht: Kluwer Academic, 2001), 203–26.
24. Swedenborg, *Journal of Dreams* (Bergquist edn), 55–7.
25. For Smith's founding of the Northern Harodim, see Norman Hackney, 'Some Notes on the Royal Order of Scotland' (1954),

typescript in the Grand Lodge Library, London, pp.15–16. For his authorship of Masonic works, see Cecil Adams, 'The Freemasons' Pocket Companions of the Eighteenth Century', *Ars Quatuor Coronatorum*, 45 (1932), 183–4.

26. For Smith and Falk, see Cecil Roth, 'The King and the Cabalist', *Essays and Portraits in Anglo-Jewish History* (Philadelphia: Jewish Publication Society of America, 1962), 148.
27. William Smith, MD, *A Dissertation on the Nerves* (London: printed for the author, 1768), 8–9, 67.
28. Ibid., 290.
29. [Rudolph Tafel], 'New Documents Concerning Swedenborg', *New Church Magazine*, 4 (1885), 382.
30. The Swedish Church was in the adjoining Prince's Square (now named Swedenborg Square), and the Swedish ministers maintained a residence in Wellclose Square. Zinzendorf urged the Moravians also to attend their native churches.
31. William Smith, MD, *A Sure Guide to Sickness and Health* (London, 1776), 1–17.
32. I am grateful to Mrs Cecil Roth, who allowed me to read her unpublished translation of the diary of Kalisch, Falk's factotum. The diaries of Kalisch and Falk are published in Hebrew in Michal Oron, *Mib'al Shed Leba'al Shem: Schmuel Falk, Haba'al Sehm Mi-London* (Jerusalem: Mosad Bialik, 2003). An English translation is forthcoming.
33. Michal Oron, 'Dr Samuel Jacob Falk and the Eibeschuetz-Emden Controversy', in Joseph Dan and Karl Grözinger, eds, *Mysticism, Magic and Kabbalah in the Ashkenazic Judaism* (New York: Walter de Gruyter, 1995), 254 n.50.
34. Ibid., 252.
35. Edgar Samuel, 'Dr Meyer Schomberg's Attacks on the Jews of London, 1746', *Transactions of Jewish Historical Society of England*, 20 (1959–60), 103–4.
36. Swedenborg, *Journal of Dreams*, no. 212.
37. Ibid., no. 213.
38. Swedenborg, *Generative Organs*, 155–60.
39. Atwood, 'Blood', 103 n.160, 104, and *Community*, 110–11.
40. Rimius, *Candid Narrative*, 63 n.3.

41. Fogleman, 'Jesus is Female', 309.
42. Rimius, *Candid Narrative*, 46–7.
43. Schochet, *Hasidic*, 47.
44. Swedenborg, *Journal of Dreams* (Odhner trans.), no. 157. Wilkinson translates it, 'I rose up now a whole God up.'
45. Swedenborg, *Generative Organs*, 20–8. One wonders if the popular rock band 'The Cremasters' was familiar with Swedenborg's psychosexual theories.
46. Ibid., 155–60.
47. Emanuel Swedenborg, *On the Worship and Love of God* (Boston: John Allen, 1832), 116, 119, 212–13.

Chapter 8: Judaised Yoga

1. Stockholm, Riksarkiv: Hollandica, no. 896; Valentin, *Judarnas*, 115–36; R. D. Barnett, 'The Correspondence of the Mahamad', *Transactions of Jewish Historical Society of England*, 20 (1959–60), 22.
2. Emanuel Swedenborg, *The Word of the Old Testament Explained*, trans. Alfred Acton (Bryn Athyn: Academy of the New Church, 1928–48), no. 5292. This enormous manuscript was published posthumously.
3. Ibid., no. 187.
4. Ibid., nos 1510–11, 1645, 3142, 5141, 5314, 5588, 5618.
5. Ibid., no. 541.
6. Ibid., no. 4663; see also nos 4694–5.
7. Ibid., no. 3345.
8. Schuchard, 'Jacobite and Visionary', 50–1.
9. Ingerich, 'Swedenborg', 34.
10. Dithmar, *Zinzendorfs*, 185–6.
11. Swedenborg, *Spiritual Diary*, no. 151, p. 41; no. 357.
12. Ibid., no. 308.
13. Scholem, *Major Trends*, 63–4; also, his *Kabbalah* (1974; New York: Dorset, 1987), 14–21.
14. Ginsburg, *Luzzatto*, 82–3.
15. Swedenborg, *Spiritual Diary*, no. 488.
16. Ibid., no. 3208.

17. Patai, *Hebrew Goddess*, 268.
18. Lewis, *Zinzendorf*, 24–5.
19. William Addison, *The Renewed Church of the United Brethren, 1722–1930* (London: Society for Promoting Christian Knowledge, 1932), 58, 99, 311.
20. For Marco Polo's account, see David Gordon White, *The Alchemical Body: Siddha Traditions in Medieval India* (Chicago: Chicago UP, 1996), 9, 72, 276.
21. François Bernier, *Travels in the Mogul Empire*, trans. Irving Brock; rev. edn Archibald Constable (1891; Delhi: S. Chand, 1969), 320–1, 345. The French version appeared in many editions from 1670 on.
22. Ibid., 346.
23. Quoted in Jeff Bach, *Voices in the Wilderness: The Sacred World of Ephrata* (University Park: Pennsylvania State UP, 2003), 188.
24. Christopher McIntosh, *The Rosicrucians: The History, Mythology and Rituals of an Occult Order*, 2nd rev. edn (Wellingborough: Crucible, 1987), 80–1.
25. For Moravian missions in India, see David Cranz, *The Ancient and Modern History of the Brethren*, trans. Benjamin La Trobe (London: W. and H. Strahan, 1780); E. Arno Lehmann, *It Began at Tranquebar*, trans. M. J. Lutz (London: Christian Literature Society, 1956).
26. Zinzendorf, *Maxims*, 206.
27. Cranz, *Ancient*, 225, 324; August Spangenberg, *The Life of Nicholas Ludwig Count Zinzendorf*, trans. Samuel Jackson (London: Samuel Holdsworth, 1838), 356.
28. Johannes Lucas Niekamp, *Missions-Geschichte* (Halle, 1740), I, 79, 105.
29. Paintings by Johan Valentin Haidt in 1747–8; see Paul Peucker and Stephen Augustin, eds, *Graf ohne Grenze: Leben und Werk von Nikolaus Ludwig Graf von Zinzendorf* (Herrnhut: Unitätsarchiv/Comeniusbuchhandlung, 2000), plates 326, 327.
30. Scholem, *Major Trends*, 139.
31. Swedenborg read accounts of Jewish-Indian influences and sexual customs in *History of the Works of the Learned*, 1 (1699),

149–50; 11 (1708), 259–69; 13 (1711), 323–8; and *Memoirs of Literature*, 39 (1710), 155–6.

32. Swedenborg, *Dream Diary* (Bergquist edn), 160; Arvid Gradin, *A Short History of the Bohemian-Moravian Church* (London: J. Hutton, 1743).
33. Emanuel Swedenborg, *Catalogus Bibliothecae Emanuelis Swedenborgii*, ed. Alfred Stroh (Holmiae: Aftonbladet, 1907).
34. De La Créquiniére, *The Agreement of the Customs of the East-Indians with Those of the Jews*, trans. John Toland (1705; rpt. New York: AMS, 1999), 16–17, 67–9.
35. Swedenborg, *Spiritual Diary*, no. 6061.
36. Ibid., nos 2411–12.
37. Emanuel Swedenborg, *The Delights of Wisdom Concerning Conjugial Love*, trans. Alfred Acton (1768; London: Swedenborg Society, 1970), nos 56, 76.
38. For the visits to Herrnhaag of Lieberkuhn and missionaries and converts from Malabar, Tartary, Ceylon and other Asian locations, see Hans-Walter Erbe, 'Die Grundseinlegung zum Brüderhaus in Herrnhaag', *Unitas Fratrum*, 6 (1979), 38–41.
39. Hugh Urban, *The Economics of Ecstasy: Tantra, Secrecy and Power in Colonial Bengal* (Oxford: Oxford UP, 2001), 143. Urban suggests a Christian influence on the Kartabhajas; it could well have come from the Moravian missionaries.
40. Peucker, 'Inspired by Flames'.
41. Frey, *True and Authentic Account*, 42.
42. Urban, *Economics*, 143.
43. Ibid., 37.
44. David Gordon White, *Kiss of the Yogini* (Chicago: Chicago UP, 2003), 320 n.44.
45. Urban, *Economics*, 47, 88, 148.
46. Ibid., 113.
47. Swedenborg, *Spiritual Diary*, nos 4989–92.
48. Ibid., no. 402.
49. In *The Generative Organs*, 126–7, he quoted Schurig's and Leeuwenhoek's descriptions of the sperm as 'little worms' and 'tailed worms'.
50. Swedenborg, *Spiritual Diary*, nos 3066–9.

51. Ibid., nos 2411–12.
52. Ibid., no. 6067.
53. For example, see Stephen Larsen, 'The Visionary Tradition', in Robin Larsen, ed., *Emanuel Swedenborg: A Continuing Vision* (New York: Swedenborg Foundation, 1988), 192–4.
54. Swedenborg, *Journal of Dreams*, nos 134, 209, p.127.
55. Toksvig, *Swedenborg*, 218–19.
56. Ibid., 315. For further similarities between Swedenborgian and Yogic theory and practice, see D. Gopaul Chetty, *New Light Upon Indian Philosophy: or Swedenborg and Saiva Siddhanta* (London: J. M. Dent, 1923), especially the chapter 'Was Swedenborg a Yogi?'
57. Jacob Sessler, *Community Pietism Among Early American Moravians* (New York: Henry Holt, 1933), 176.

Chapter 9: Phallic Feet and Tantric Toes

1. F. G. Lindh, 'Swedenborgs Ekonomi', *Nya Kyrkans Tidning* (Sept.–Oct. 1929), 89–91; Bergquist, *Swedenborgs Hemlighet*, 400–14.
2. Swedenborg, *Spiritual Diary*, nos 3492, 4814.
3. Ibid., nos 5886–95.
4. Peucker, 'Inspired by Flames'.
5. Swedenborg, *Spiritual Diary*, no. 5989.
6. Frey, *True and Authentic Account*, 34.
7. Rimius, *Supplement*, xli–xliii.
8. Swedenborg, *Spiritual Diary*, nos 5886, 5988–95.
9. Dithmar, *Zinzendorfs*, 183, 187. For Lieberkuhn's conversion strategies, see *Periodical Accounts Relating to the Missions of the Church of the United Brethren, Established among the Heathen*, 12 (1831), 345–9; 14 (1838), 309–14; 15 (1840), 153–8.
10. Hans-Christoph Hahn and Helmut Reichel, *Zinzendorf und die Herrnhuter Brüder* (Hamburg: F. Wittig, 1977), 435.
11. Peucker, 'Inspired by Flames'.
12. Some of the scenes in the diary (late 1748) may have taken place in Moravian gatherings in Holland, where Christel's innovations also influenced the more radical Brethren.

13. Swedenborg, *Spiritual Diary*, nos 3453, 3439, 3447.
14. Ibid., nos 3450–2.
15. Peucker, 'Inspired by Flames'.
16. Swedenborg, *Spiritual Diary*, no. 3451, n.1.
17. Frey, *True and Authentic Account*, 42. Comparisons were frequently made between the 'Eva Society' and Zinzendorf's 'United Brethren'; see Willi Temme, *Krise der Leiblichkeit: Die Sozietät der Mutter Eva (Buttlarsche Rotte) und der Radikale Pietismus um 1700* (Göttingen: Vandenhoeck und Ruprecht, 1998), 373, 396, 416.
18. Rimius, *Animadversion*, 43–4.
19. Scholem, *On the Kabbalah*, 348 n.23.
20. *History of the Works of the Learned*, 10 (1708), 268–9.
21. Swedenborg, *Spiritual Diary*, no. 3453.
22. For Blake's self-portrayal with 'a black penis erect against his body', see Erdman, *Illuminated Blake*, 248.
23. Swedenborg, *Spiritual Diary*, nos 3455, 5989.
24. Scholem, *Kabbalah*, 337.
25. Elliot Wolfson, 'Images of God's Feet: Some Observations on the Divine Body in Jerusalem', in Howard Eilberg-Schwarz, ed., *People of the Body: Jews and Judaism from an Embodied Perspective* (Albany: State University of New York, 1992), 154, 163.
26. Ibid., 171.
27. Swedenborg, *Spiritual Diary*, no. 3909.
28. Ibid., nos 5106–7.
29. Jeffrey Kripal, *Kali's Child: The Mystical and Erotic Life and Teaching of Ramakrishna*, 2nd edn (1995; Chicago: Chicago UP, 1998), 202–4.
30. For the following Tantric interpretation, I draw on Mircea Eliade, *Yoga: Immortality and Freedom*, trans. Willard Trask (Princeton: Princeton UP, 1969), 232–3, 246–9; Michael Volin and Nancy Phelan, *Yoga and Sex* (London: Pelham, 1970), 62–5; Omar Garrison, *Tantra: the Yoga of Sex* (London: Academy Editions, 1972), 23; George Feurstein, *Tantra: The Path of Ecstasy* (Boston: Shambala, 1998), 134–8, 232–49.
31. Fan Fu Ruan, *Sex in China* (New York: Plenum, 1991), 62–3.
32. Richard Davis, 'Becoming a Siva and Acting as One, in Saiva

Worship', in Teun Goudriaan, ed., *Ritual and Speculation in Early Tantrism: Studies in Honour of André Prevoux* (Delhi: Sri Satguru, 1993), 113.
33. Volin and Phelan, *Yoga*, 64.
34. André Van Lisebeth, *Tantra: The Cult of the Feminine* (1988; New York: Samuel Weiser, 1995), 307–22.
35. Ibid., 305, 312.
36. Swedenborg, *Spiritual Diary*, no. 3325.
37. Ibid., no. 3453.
38. Shyam Ghosh, *The Original Yoga* (Munshiram Manoharlal, 1980), 70.
39. Ruan, *Sex in China*, 62.
40. Eliade, *Yoga*, 232.
41. Lisebeth, *Tantra*, 315.
42. Swedenborg, *Journal of Dreams*, no. 184.
43. Lisebeth, *Tantra*, 310, 327.

Chapter 10: Moravian Deaths and Blake Beginnings

1. Swedenborg, *Spiritual Diary*, nos 5989–90. It is unclear how many Moravians (if any?) enacted the weird scenes in Swedenborg's diary, but the radicals clearly constituted a small minority. He absolved his friend Brockmer and publisher Lewis from involvement, and he maintained friendships with several members. Though some Single Brethren pressed the Fetter Lane Elders to tell them what really went on at Herrnhaag, the Congregation as a whole was kept in the dark; see Moravian Archive: C/36/7/4/f.123.
2. Moravian Archive: C/36/7/4 / f.123.
3. Ibid., C/36/7/3–6 (1749–52), *passim*.
4. Ibid., C/36/11/6. For the terms of the will, see Bentley, *Blake Records* (2nd edn), 5–6.
5. Ibid., C/36/5/1, p.44.
6. Ibid., C/36/11/6.
7. Dr Keri Davies is investigating the identifications and genealogies of all these Blakes.
8. Bentley, *Stranger*, 5.

9. Ibid., 7–12, for the Dissenter claims.
10. Podmore, *Moravian Church*, 176–7.
11. Moravian Archive: C/36/7/3 (3 May 1749).
12. Bentley, *Blake Records*, 543.
13. Gilchrist, *Life* (1880), 6.
14. Henry Meyer, *Child Nature and Nurture According to Nicolaus Ludwig von Zinzendorf* (New York: Abingdon, 1928), 94–105.
15. Atwood, 'Blood', 192–3, and *Community*, 178–83.
16. Meyer, *Child Nature*, 138, 142. He acknowledged that some parents were unable to give their children the necessary home training and must therefore 'use the advantages offered by the congregation'. For children of missionaries and travelling ministers, who had to be away from home, Moravian boarding schools were established. But home-schooling was the ideal.
17. Ibid., 103.
18. Bentley, *Blake Records*, 477.
19. Rimius, *Candid Narrative*, 48.
20. Freeman, *Ecumenical Theology*, 83; Blake, *CPP*, 84, 852.
21. Atwood, *Community*, 78.
22. Sessler, *Communal*, 174.
23. For the erotic mother-child portrayals, see Steinberg, *Sexuality of Christ*, 3, 10, 78.
24. Blake, *CPP*, 468, 852.
25. Ibid., 49.
26. Atwood, *Community*, 178–9.
27. Moravian Archive: C/36/7/3.
28. Blake, *CPP*, 285.
29. Zinzendorf, *Nine Public Lectures*, 81.
30. Ibid., 82–3.
31. Symons, *Blake*, 264.
32. Zinzendorf, *Nine Public Lectures*, 84–5.
33. I discuss other Moravian artists in my article 'Young William Blake and the Moravian Tradition of Visionary Art,' *Blake: An Illustrated Quarterly* (forthcoming).
34. Vernon Nelson, 'Johan Valentin Haidt's Theory of Painting', *Transactions of the Moravian Historical Society*, 13 (1984), 71–8.
35. Bentley, *Stranger*, 49–51.

36. Vernon Nelson, *Johan Valentine Haidt* (Williamsburg: Abby Aldrich Rockefeller Folk Collection, 1966), 9–13.
37. Bentley, *Blake Records*, 421.
38. Sessler, *Communal*, 166–7.
39. Atwood, 'Blood', 74.
40. Moravian Archive: C/36/7/3. Elaborate 'emblematical' and 'hieroglyphical' paintings and transparencies were described at the celebration of Zinzendorf's birthday.
41. Sachse, *German Sectarians*, I, 354–64, 401–2.
42. Bach, *Voices*, 144–5.
43. Henry Borneman, *Pennsylvania German Illuminated Manuscripts* (Norristown: Pennsylvania German Society, 1937), 47.
44. Podmore, *Moravian Church*, 150–1; Atwood, 'Blood', 171.
45. Bentley, *Stranger*, 5.
46. John Joseph Stoudt, *Pennsylvania Folk-Art* (Allentown: Schlecter, 1948), 138. Like Blake, the Ephratans included Boehmenist symbolism in their illuminated art, and the frontispiece to the *ABC Book* includes a small flying angel who is 'Virgin Sophia, Boehme's ideagraph of Heavenly Wisdom'.
47. For Blake's interest, see Frank Parisi, 'William Blake and the Emblem Tradition' (University of Edinburgh: Ph.D. thesis, 1975).
48. Sadler, *Comenius*, 28, 42–3, 201, 282.
49. John Cennick, *The Life of Mr John Cennick*, 2nd edn (Bristol: printed for the Author and sold by J. Lewis and Mr Hutton, London, 1745), 24. For the influence of Hugo on Comenius and Blake, see Rosemary Freeman, *English Emblem Books* (New York: Octagon, 1966), 27–30, 88–9, 229.
50. Moravian Archive: C/36/7/3 (30 December 1749; 19, 24 May 1751).
51. Mario Praz, *Studies in Seventeenth-Century Imagery* (London: Warburg Institute, 1939), 11.
52. Ibid., 12.
53. Ibid., 133–4.
54. Zinzendorf, *Nine Public Lectures*, 81.
55. Geoffrey and Margaret Stead, *The Exotic Plant: A History of the Moravian Church in Britain, 1742–2000* (Peterborough: Epworth, 2003), 300.

56. Herman Hugo, *Pia Desideria* (1624; Antwerp: Henry Aertssens, 1632), 334.
57. Erdman, *Illuminated Blake*, 31.
58. See *L'Âme Amante de son Dieu, représentée dans les Emblémes de Hermannus Hugo*, ed. J. M. B. de la Mothe-Guyon (1717; Paris, 1790), preface.
59. Ibid., 273, 31.
60. Praz, *Studies*, 136.
61. Benham, *Memoirs*, 417.

11. School of Art and Eros

1. Bentley, *Blake Records*, 477.
2. Nelson, 'Haidt's Theory', 76–7.
3. Bentley, *Blake Records*, 477.
4. Bentley, *Stranger*, 22.
5. D. G. C. Allan, *William Shipley: Founder of the Royal Society of Arts*, rev. edn (1968; London: Scolar, 1979), 77, 144; also, Joseph Moser's account of Shipley in *European Magazine* (September 1803).
6. Allan, *Shipley*, 8, 27–9, 50–3. Though many non-initiates today think of Masonic lodges as dining clubs for businessmen, some high-degree lodges maintain the esoteric and Rosicrucian interests of their seventeenth- and eighteenth-century precursors.
7. For Messiter's Masonic and Swedenborgian associations, see Achatius Kahl, 'La Nouvelle Église dans ses Rélations avec la Franc-maçonnerie', in Johan Tybeck, ed., *La Nouveau Salem* (Basle, 1871), 128–48. The name James Blake appears in the Atholl Register, Lodge no.38, from 1757 to 1761 (in the Library of the Grand Lodge of London). The name William Armitage (brother or cousin of Thomas?) appears in Lodge no.72 in 1781 and no.305 in 1802.
8. Laurence Dermott, *Ahiman Rezon* (1756; facs. rpt. Bloomington: Masonic Book Club, 1972), xiv, 37. For his background, see Cecil Adams, '*Ahiman Rezon*, the Book of Constitutions', *Ars Quatuor Coronatorum*, 46 (1933), 239–57.

9. London, Royal Society of Arts: 'The Minutes of the Society for the Encouragement of Arts, Manufactures and Commerce', I, 11–12.
10. Allan, *Shipley*, 77–8.
11. Richard Cosway, *A Catalogue of the Very Curious, Extensive and Valuable Library of Richard Cosway, R.A.* (London: Stanley, 1821). I am grateful to Dr Stephen Lloyd for sending me a copy of this important catalogue. On Cosway and the Moravians, see John Nichols, *Literary Anecdotes of the Eighteenth Century* (1812–15; rpt. New York: AMS, 1961), III, 435–7; Horace Walpole, *The Correspondence of Horace Walpole*, ed. W. S. Lewis (New Haven: Yale UP, 1937–83), XXXIII, ii, 511. On Messiter and the Moravians, see D. G. Goyder, *A Concise History of the New Jerusalem Church* (London: Thomas Goyder, 1829), xxiii.
12. A record of Cosway's extensive collection of Swedenborg's works is given in the MS. 'Catalogue, Schedule or Inventory of Household Goods and Furniture, Books, . . . made between Richard Cosway and Maria, his Wife' (15 April 1820). The late Diana Wilson's copy of this MS. is in the Huntington Library.
13. H. N. Morris, *Flaxman, Blake, Coleridge and Other Men of Genius Influenced by Swedenborg* (London: New Church, 1915).
14. Bogen, 'Problem', 509.
15. For the students and teachers at Pars, see Lloyd, *Cosway*, 20–3; David Bindman, *Blake as an Artist* (Oxford: Phaidon, 1977), 12.
16. Bentley, *Stranger*, 24; Nelson, 'Haidt's Theory', 76–7.
17. Alfred Rubens, 'Early Anglo-Jewish Artists', *Transactions of Jewish Historical Society of England*, 14 (1935–9), 101. He identifies Cosway, not Jeremiah Meyer, as the painter of Casanova's ring.
18. For Cosway's precocious and pronounced sexuality, see Stephen Lloyd, *Richard and Maria Cosway: Regency Artists of Taste and Fashion* (Edinburgh: Scottish National Portrait Gallery, 1995), 23.
19. Hyde, *Bibliography*, no. 2400. She had been selling Swedenborg's works since 1763.
20. Swedenborg, *Catalogus*; Cosway, *Catalogue*.

21. Nicholas Venette, *Conjugal Love*, 20th edn (1750; rpt. New York: Garland, 1984), 8, 116, 142.
22. Roy Porter, *The Facts of Life: The Creation of Sexual Knowledge in Britain* (New Haven: Yale UP, 1995), 72.
23. Ibid., 73.
24. Swedenborg, *Catalogus*; Cosway, *Catalogue*.
25. Anon., *Onania*, 15th edn (London: J. Isted, 1730), I, 65, 141, 157.
26. It is curious that this tradition of the 'English wanker' versus the 'virile Gael' persists in today's popular culture, especially in the cinema.
27. Emanuel Swedenborg, *The Apocalypse Explained*, trans. J. C. Agar (New York: American Swedenborg Society, 1894), no. 992 n.2.
28. Swedenborg drew on his volumes of Thomas Herbert's *Relation du Voyage de Perse et des Indes Orients* (1663) and Gemelli Careri's *Voyage du Tour du Monde* (1719). See his *Catalogus* and *Philosopher's Notebook*, 487–9.
29. John Wesley, *The Arminian Magazine*, 4 (1781), 46–9; 5 (1782), 676–80; 6 (1783), 438–40, 606–12.
30. Rimius, *Candid Narrative*, 5.
31. Rimius, *Solemn Call*, 12.
32. Rimius, *Supplement*, xxiv.
33. Beverly Smaby, '"Other Measures to Keep the Candles Lit": The 1752 Transatlantic Travel Diary of Anna Johanna Piesch', in Atwood and Vogt, *Distinctiveness*, 113 n.36.
34. Schuchard, 'Falk', 210–15.
35. Emanuel Swedenborg, *The Delights of Wisdom Concerning Conjugial Love*, trans. Alfred Acton (1768; London: Swedenborg Society, 1970), nos 42–3. Henceforth cited as *Conjugial Love*.
36. Ibid., nos 6–9, 54.
37. Ibid., nos 37, 54.
38. Ibid., no. 144.
39. Ibid., no. 210.
40. Dithmar, *Zinzendorfs*, 192–203.
41. Gershom Scholem, *The Messianic Idea in Judaism* (New York: Schocken, 1971), 117, 349 n.36.

42. Swedenborg, *Conjugial Love*, no. 310.
43. Ibid., nos 55, 112.
44. According to Rabbi Israel Baal Shem Tov, late leader of the Polish Hasidim; see Biale, *Eros*, 131–2.
45. Louis Jacobs, *Their Heads in Heaven: Unfamiliar Aspects of Hasidim* (London: Valentine Mitchell, 2005), 3.
46. Idel, 'Sexual Metaphors', 200, 205–6.
47. Swedenborg, *Conjugial Love*, no. 55.
48. Ibid., no. 107 n.1.
49. Ibid., no. 374.
50. Lisebeth, *Tantra*, 312.
51. Swedenborg, *Conjugial Love*, no. 146.
52. Lisebeth, *Tantra*, 100.
53. D. G. White, *Alchemical Body*, 276.
54. Wolfson, '*Tiqqun ha-Shekhinah*', 300 n.35, 318 n.127.
55. For this Masonic background, see my articles, 'Yeats', 142–6, and 'Secret Masonic History', 40–6.

Chapter 12: Apprentice in Art and Romance

1. Uxorius, *Hymen – An Accurate Description of the Ceremonies in Marriage by Every Nation in the Known World* (London: I. Pottinger, 1760), 1–18, 42, 131, 162.
2. Swedenborg, *Conjugial Love*, no. 296.
3. Ibid., nos 450–9.
4. Blake, *CPP*, 34.
5. Swedenborg, *Conjugial Love*, no. 453.
6. Gerard Vaughan, 'The Collecting of Classical Antiquities in England in the Eighteenth Century: A Study of Charles Townley (1737–1805)' (Ph.D. dissertation: Oxford University, 1988), 6–16.
7. David Stevenson, *The Beggar's Benison: Sex Clubs of Enlightenment Scotland and their Rituals* (Edinburgh: Tuckwell, 2001), 96–8.
8. Vaughan, 'Collecting', 13; British Museum: Townley Papers, TY 7/20/28 (Cosway to Townley, 24 February 1772); partially quoted in Lloyd, *Cosway*, 29.

9. Anon., *The Joys of Hymen, or, the Conjugal Directory* (London: D. Davis, 1768), preface, x.
10. Ibid., 5, 12.
11. Lloyd, *Cosway*, 32.
12. Bentley, *Blake Records* (2nd edn), 81–2.
13. Zinzendorf, *Nine Public Lectures*, 81.
14. [Hutton], *Collection of Hymns*, 18–19.
15. James Harris, *Hermes, or a Philosophical Inquiry Concerning Universal Grammar*, 3rd rev. edn (London: printed for John Nourse and Paul Vaillant, 1771), 44, 324–6, 383. According to the Smaragdine Tablet of Hermes Trismegistus, 'that which is above is like that which is below'. The Renaissance development of the science of micro-macro correspondences and hieroglyphics drew on this notion.
16. Cosway, *Catalogue*.
17. Bentley, *Stranger*, 36.
18. Bentley, *Blake*, 13. For the Masonic 'art of memory' or visualisation, see David Stevenson, *The Origins of Freemasonry: Scotland's Century, 1590–1710* (Cambridge: Cambridge UP, 1988), 87–124; also, Schuchard, *Restoring the Temple of Vision*, 192, 199–207, 355, 383.
19. Moravian Archive: Church Book of the Brethren, Congregation in London, p.28; Congregation Diary, VI (1752), p.111.
20. Bentley, *Stranger*, 45.
21. The following quotes are from Blake's *Poetical Sketches* (1783); *CPP*, 408–10, 413, 416.
22. Nelson Hilton, 'Some Sexual Connotations', *Blake: An Illustrated Quarterly* (Winter 1982–3), 166–71.
23. David Erdman, 'William Blake's Debt to James Gillray', *Art Quarterly*, 12 (1949), 165–70.
24. Moravian Archive: Church Book of the Brethren, Congregation in London, p.28; Congregation Diary, VI (1952), p.111.
25. Richard Godfrey and Mark Hallet, *James Gillray: The Art of Caricature* (London: Tate Gallery, 2001), 12.
26. British Library: Add. MSS. 27,337 ff.2–15. 'James Gillray Correspondence, Hints for Caricatures, 1796–1830'.
27. Thomas Wright and R. H. Evans, *The Works of James Gillray*

(1851; rpt. New York: B. Blom, 1968), includes the forty-five 'suppressed plates'.

28. Godfrey and Hallett, *Gillray*, 62.
29. Ibid., 14–15, 20–1, 52.
30. Draper Hill, *Fashionable Contrasts: Caricatures by James Gillray* (London: Phaidon, 1966), 6.
31. Speech reprinted in *The Principles and Practices of the Most Ancient and Honourable Society of Free and Accepted Masons* (London, 1786), 150–65.
32. Benedict Chastanier, *A Word of Advice to a Benighted World* (London, 1795), 23–4.
33. Blake, *CPP*, 707–8.

Chapter 13: The Celestial Bed

1. Flaxman and his father worked continuously with operative stonemasons, and Flaxman owned an engraving of 'The Free-Masons' School', produced for Masonic brethren; see John Flaxman, *Catalogue of a Valuable Assemblage of Engravings . . . of the late John Flaxman, Esq., R.A.* (London: Christie's, 1 July 1828). In 1787–8, Sharp's name, along with those of George Gordon and his radical secretary Robert Watson, appears in the Grand Lodge, London: Grand Master's Lodge Record, 13, 17, 23–4. For Stothard's Masonic affiliation, see Andrew Tuer, *Bartolozzi and His Works* (London: Field and Tuer, 1881), I, 5.
2. For his career, see Rüdiger Joppien, *Philippe Jacques de Loutherbourg, R.A.* (London: Greater London Council, 1973).
3. Hyde, *Bibliography*, no. 3404.
4. Though Cecil and Irene Roth believed the portrait of Falk was by John Singleton Copley, Stephen Lloyd (who examined it with Mrs Roth's permission) concluded that it was almost certainly by Loutherbourg.
5. Anon., 'The Reverend Jacob Duché', *The Monthly Observer*, 1 (1857), 81.
6. Clarke Garrett, 'The Spiritual Odyssey of Jacob Duché', *Proceedings of the American Philosophical Society*, 119 (1975), 144–6; Sachse, *German Sectarians*, II, 403–10.

7. For the walks, see Bentley, *Stranger*, 28.
8. Blake, *CPP*, 417. For the poem's allusion to the American Revolution and George III's oppression of his own people, see David Erdman, *Blake: Prophet Against Empire*, 2nd rev. edn (1954; Princeton: Princeton UP, 1969), 20–9.
9. Blake, *CPP*, 448.
10. Ibid., 811.
11. For Graham's Masonic affiliation, see Kenneth Mackenzie, *The Royal Masonic Cyclopaedia*, ed. Robert Gilbert and John Hamill (1877: Wellingborough: Aquarian, 1987), 100.
12. Barbara Schnorrenberg, 'A True Relation of the Life and Career of James Graham, 1745–1794', *Eighteenth-Century Life*, 15 (1991), 69.
13. Roy Porter, 'The Sexual Politics of James Graham', *British Journal for Eighteenth-Century Studies*, 5 (1982), 202.
14. Roy Porter, 'Sex and the Singular Man: The Seminal Ideas of James Graham', *Voltaire and the Eighteenth-Century*, 228 (1984), 14, 20.
15. Ibid., 19.
16. Graham's lecture quoted in Richard Altick, *The Shows of London* (Cambridge: Cambridge UP), 83.
17. Porter, 'Sex and the Singular Man', 9–10.
18. 'An Eccentric Lecture', *Rambler's Magazine* (April 1783), 121.
19. Anon., *The Celestial Beds, or a Review of the Votaries of the Temple of Health, Adelphi and the Temple of Hymen, Pall Mall* (London: G. Kearsley, 1781), 34.
20. Porter, 'Sexual Politics', 199.
21. William Whitwell, 'James Graham: Master Quack', *Eighteenth-Century Life*, 4 (1977), 47.
22. For a revisionist account of Gordon's history and motives, see my article, 'Lord George Gordon and Cabalistic Freemasonry: Beating Jacobite Spears into Jacobin Ploughshares', in Martin Mulsow and Richard Popkin, eds, *Secret Conversions to Judaism in Early Modern Europe* (Leiden: Brill, 2004), 183–231.
23. T. Wright, *Life of Blake*, I, 8.
24. Erdman, *Prophet*, 10.
25. Bentley, *Blake Records*, 518.

26. Iain McCalman, *The Last Alchemist: Count Cagliostro, Master of Magic in the Age of Reason* (New York: HarperCollins, 2003), 158.
27. *Town and Country Magazine* (June 1786), 289–90.
28. Reginald Blunt, *Mrs Montague: Queen of the Blues* (London: Constable, 1923), II, 93.
29. Porter, 'Sex and the Singular Man', 14.
30. Blake, *CPP*, 37.
31. Gerald Bentley, *A Bibliography of George Cumberland, 1754–1848* (New York: Garland, 1975), 49–51.
32. For the imposed undershorts on Blake's design, see Erdman, *Illuminated Blake*, 248.
33. Blake, *CPP*, 642.
34. Atwood, *Community*, 89 n.65.
35. Bentley, *Stranger*, 22–4.

Chapter 14: The Temple of Hymen

1. Joppien, *Loutherbourg*, 4.
2. Stephen Daniels, 'Loutherbourg's Chemical Theatre: Coalbrook at Night', in John Barrell, ed., *Paintings and the Politics of Culture: New Essays on British Art, 1700–1850* (Oxford: Oxford UP, 1992), 199–224.
3. J. W. Oliver, *The Life of William Beckford* (London: Oxford UP, 1932), 90–1.
4. *The Valuable Library of Books in Fonthill Abbey* (London: Phillips, 9 September–23 October 1823). He also acquired the *Kabbala Denudata* and many books on alchemy and magic.
5. Lloyd, *Cosway*, 41–5.
6. Vaughan, 'Collecting', 257.
7. Stephen Lloyd, 'The Life and Art of Richard Cosway, R.A. (1742–1821) and Maria Cosway (1760–1838)' (Ph.D. dissertation: Oxford University, 1995), 162.
8. For the rumours, see Basil Long, *British Miniaturists* (London, 1929), 95.
9. Gilchrist, *Life* (1880), 32–3.
10. Bentley, *Blake Records*, 517–18.
11. Jacques Ferrand, *A Treatise on Love-Sickness*, eds. Donald Beecher

and Massimo Ciavolella (1640; Syracuse: Syracuse UP, 1900), 121, 197.

12. Bentley, *Blake Records*, 518.
13. James Graham, *A Clear, Full and Faithful Portraiture . . . of a Certain Most Beautiful and Spotless Virgin Princess* (Bath: R. Cruttwell, 1792), 5, 13.
14. Porter, 'Sexual Politics', 203.
15. Roy Porter, 'A Touch of Danger: The Man-Midwife as Sexual Predator', in Roy Porter and George Rousseau, eds, *Sexual Underworlds of the Enlightenment* (Manchester: Manchester UP, 1987), 208.
16. Lady Hamilton, *Memoirs of Emma Lady Hamilton*, ed. W. H. Long (1815; Philadelphia: Lippincott, 1891), 17–23; Altick, *Shows*, 82.
17. *Rambler's Magazine*, 1 (June 1783), 187–9.
18. B. L. K. Henderson, *Romney* (New York: Frederick Stokes, 1922), 22, 58.
19. A. Stuart Brown, 'Gustavus Katterfelto: Mason and Magician', *Ars Quatuor Coronatorum*, 69 (1956), 136–8.
20. *Rambler's Magazine*, 1 (May 1783), 198.
21. David Erdman, *Prophet*, 96, 104.
22. Altick, *Shows*, 83.
23. *Arminian Magazine*, 4 (1781), 46–9; 5 (1782), 676–80; 6 (1783), 483–540, 607–12.
24. Bryn Athyn, Academy of the New Church: Academy Collection of Swedenborg Documents, no. 1664.31. Henceforth cited as ACSD.
25. James Graham, MD, of the Temple of Health, *A Discourse . . . on the Nature, and Manner of the Resurrection of the Human Body*, 5th rev. edn (1783; Hull: T. Briggs, 1787), 2, 16, 18, 26.
26. Long, *British Miniaturists*, 95.
27. Bryn Athyn, Academy of the New Church: ACSD, no. 1664.3101. 'List of Those Devoted to Swedenborg's Doctrines in 1784.'
28. [Benedict Chastanier], *Plan Général d'une Société Universelle* (London: Robert Hawes, 1782). My translation from the French.

29. Detailed documention for the following account is given in my article, 'Secret Masonic History', 40–51.
30. For the brothers' background, see Jan Häll, *I Swedenborgs Labyrint: Studier I de Gustavianska Swedenborgarnes Liv och Tänade* (Stockholm: Atlantis, 1995).
31. For background, see Schuchard, 'Secret Masonic History', 41–3.
32. Bryn Athyn, Academy of the New Church: ACSD, no. 1664.31.
33. James Hyde, 'James Glen: The New Church Pioneer and Hermit', *New Church Review*, 19 (1912), 532–72.
34. For the 'Mystic International', see Clarke Garrett, *Respectable Folly: Millenarians and the French Revolution* (Baltimore: Johns Hopkins UP, 1975), 97–120.
35. Blake, *CPP*, 460.

Chapter 15: Merry Making and Edifying Discourses

1. In *Stranger in Paradise*, 73 n., Bentley states than an advertisement for one of Reverend Mathew's sermons was 'printed in the copy of Emanuel Swedenborg's *Wisdom of Angels Concerning Divine Love and Wisdom* (1788), which Blake annotated'. The Mathews' daughter Harriet married the Swedish diplomat and *Illuminé* Baron Göran Ulrik Silverhjelm, a kinsman of Swedenborg and member of the Royal Order of Heredom. The Mathews supported the Swedenborgian colonisation projects of the Nordenskjöld brothers. They were also friendly with James Hutton, the Moravian minister.
2. For Thomas Spence's alchemical studies, see British Library, Rainsford Papers: Add. MSS. 26,669 ff.129–30.
3. Blake, *CPP*, 441–3, 413, 438, 425.
4. See Erdman's comments in Blake, *CPP*, 884.
5. These drawings were attributed or discovered in the 1980s. See Christopher Heppner, 'Blake's "New Jerusalem Descending": A Drawing Identified', *Blake: An Illustrated Quarterly*, 20 (1986), 4–11; Martin Butlin, 'Six New Early Drawings by William Blake and a Reattribution', *Blake: An Illustrated Quarterly*, 23 (1989), 107–12.
6. Blake, *CPP*, 450, 458.

7. William Blake, *An Island in the Moon*, ed. Michael Phillips (Cambridge: Cambridge UP, 1987), 8. An English translation was not published until 1787, but the Swedenborgians often translated Latin extracts at their discussion meetings.
8. Blake, *CPP*, 460.
9. Ibid., 449.
10. Charles Higham, 'Francis Barthelemon', *New Church Magazine*, 15 (1896), 1–13.
11. David Erskine Baker and Isaac Reed, *Biographica Dramatica* (1812; rpt. New York: AMS, 1966), II, 260–1. The play opened in 1780 and was frequently revived over the next five years.
12. George Williamson, *Richard Cosway, R.A.* (London: George Bell, 1927), 23.
13. Peter Pindar [John Wolcot], *More Lyric Odes to the Royal Academicians for 1783* (London, 1783), VI.
14. Anthony Pasquin [John Williams], *The Royal Academicians: A Farce* (London, 1786), 22.
15. Ibid., 23.
16. Stevenson, *Beggar's Benison*, 39, 238. The prince was elected on 2 August 1783; his friend and the Cosways', the balloonist Vincent Lunardi, was elected on 10 October 1785.
17. Blake, *CPP*, 457.
18. Erdman, *Prophet*, 31–2 n.6.
19. In a 1784 wash drawing Romney included William Hayley, a reader of Swedenborg and admirer of Blake's work, in company with Emma and Greville.
20. Eliza Meteyard, *The Life of Josiah Wedgwood* (1866; facs. rpt. London: Cornmarket, 1970), II, 577, 582.
21. Blake, *CPP*, 449.
22. Ibid., 450.
23. Sybil Rosenfeld, 'The *Eidophusikon* Illustrated', *Theatre Notebook*, 18 (1963–4), 52–4.
24. Altick, *Shows*, 125–7.
25. Genevieve Levallet-Haig, 'Philippe Jacques de Loutherbourg, 1740–1813', *Archives Alsaciennes de'Histoire de l'Art*, n.s. 27 (1948), 88.
26. Blake, *CPP*, 450–1.

27. Ibid., 462.
28. George Speight, *The History of the English Puppet Theatre* (London: George Harrap, 1955), 128.
29. Blake, *CPP*, 462.
30. Anthony Pasquin [John Williams], *Memoirs of the Royal Academicians* (London: H. D. Symonds, 1796), 80.
31. Pasquin [Williams], *The Royal Academicians: A Farce*, [8]. His annotated copy is in the Bodleian Library.
32. *Rambler's Magazine* (December 1785).
33. For a more detailed study of D'Eon's role in Blake's milieu, see my article, 'Blake's "Mr Femality": Freemasonry, Espionage and the Double Sex'd', *Studies in Eighteenth-Century Culture*, 22 (1992), 20–31.
34. For his diplomatic and espionage career, see Michel Decker, *Madame Le Chevalier d'Eon* (Paris: Librairie Académique, 1987).
35. For his struggles with Modern Masonry, see Chetwode Crawley, 'The Chevalier d'Eon', *Ars Quatuor Coronatorum*, 16 (1908), 231–51.
36. Blake, *CPP*, 452; Erdman, *Prophet*, 98, 124.
37. Blake, *CPP*, 465.
38. For D'Eon's friends and parties, see Henry Angelo, *The Reminiscences of Henry Angelo*, ed. Lord Howard de Walden and H. Lavers Smith (London: Kegan Paul, 1904), II, 85; also, *Angelo's Pic-Nic* (London: Thomas Kelly, 1834), XIII, 172–3.
39. *Catalogue of the Scarce Books and Valuable Manuscripts of the Chevalier d'Eon* (London: Christie's, 1791).
40. Blake, *CPP*, 845.
41. Ibid., 113.
42. Autopsy report in the *London Times* (25 May 1810).

Chapter 16: Animal Magnetism and the *Furor Uterinus*

1. Bentley, *Stranger*, 89–94.
2. Gilchrist, *Life of Blake*, 50–1.
3. Blake, *CPP*, 306.
4. Butlin, *Paintings*, I, nos 113–20.
5. Bindman, *Blake*, 37–9.
6. Gilchrist, *Life of Blake*, 59.

7. Symons, *Blake*, 261.
8. Bentley, *Blake Records*, 460.
9. Ellis, *Real Blake*, 55.
10. For background, see Robert Darnton, *Mesmerism and the End of the Enlightenment in France* (Cambridge, MA: Harvard UP, 1968).
11. Ibid., 24.
12. Ibid., 4.
13. Barbara Stafford, *Body Criticism: Imaging the Unseen in Enlightenment Art and Medicine* (Cambridge, MA: Massachusetts Institute of Technology, 1991), 457–8.
14. Darnton, *Mesmerism*, 4.
15. J. C. Colquhoun, trans., *Report of the Experiments on Animal Magnetism* (Edinburgh: Robert Cadell, 1833), 101–3.
16. Lisebeth, *Tantra*, 37.
17. Blake, *CPP*, 474.
18. Anon., 'Animal Magnetism', *British and Foreign Medical Review*, 14 (1839), 9.
19. Blake, *CPP*, 474.
20. For his arrival in London, see Joseph Banks, *The Banks Letters*, ed. W. R. Dawson (London: British Museum, 1958), 66.
21. For details of Mainaduc's role in Blake's milieu, see my article, 'Blake's Healing Trio: Magnetism, Medicine and Mania', *Blake: An Illustrated Quarterly*, 23 (1989), 20–32.
22. *Journal Encylopédique*, 6 (1785), 320.
23. Chastanier, *Word of Advice*, 30–1.
24. J. B. de Mainaduc, MD, *The Lectures of J. B. de Mainaduc* (London: printed for the Executrix, 1798). The copy in the Royal College of Surgeons, London, includes a list of the paying customers. These included General Rainsford, Lord Percy and William Bousie, all associates of the Universal Society.
25. Ibid., xi, 28–9, 81–3, 97.
26. Stafford, *Body Criticism*, 449, 459.
27. Mainaduc, *Lectures*, 106.
28. Joseph Farington, *The Diary of Joseph Farington*, ed. K. Garlick and A. Macintyre (New Haven: Yale UP, 1978), III, 710.
29. Blake, *CPP*, 314.
30. Mainaduc, *Lectures*, 207.

31. Thomas Jefferson, *The Papers of Thomas Jefferson*, ed. Julian Boyd (Princeton: Princeton UP, 1950), IV, 3–4.
32. Anon., 'Animal Magnetism', 9; Anon., *A Letter to a Physician in the Country* (London: J. Debrett, 1786), 32.
33. *The Gazetteer and New Daily Advertiser* (30 June 1787).
34. Anon., 'Animal Magnetism', 19.
35. Cosway, *Catalogue.*
36. D. T. De Bienville, *Nymphomania, or, a Dissertation concerning the Furor Uterinus*, trans. E. S. Wilmot, MD (London: J. Pew, 1775), 30, 65–8, 157.
37. Ibid., 75–8.
38. Ibid., 107.

Chapter 17: The Men of Desire

1. The term *Les Hommes de Désir* was used by the crypto-Jewish Kabbalist Martines de Pasqually for his initiates into the Masonic rite of *Élus Coens*. It was borrowed by his disciple Louis Claude de Saint-Martin as the title for a famous book (Strasbourg, 1790), which Saint-Martin began writing during a visit to the Illuminists and Swedenborgians in London in 1787. The conference of *Philaléthes* in Paris, which included Swedenborgian delegates from London, described themselves as 'a body of Masons or *men of desire* highly capable of searching for truth'.
2. For Grabianka's career, see M. L. Danilewicz, '"The King of the New Israel": Thaddeus Grabianka (1740–1807)', *Oxford Slavonic Papers*, n.s., 1 (1968), 49–74.
3. Chastanier, *Word of Advice*, 26–7.
4. Alice Joly, 'La "Sainte Parole" des Illuminés d'Avignon', *La Tour Saint-Jacques*, II–IV (1960), 98–116.
5. Garrett, *Respectable Folly*, 97–120.
6. James Hyde, 'Benedict Chastanier and the Illuminati of Avignon', *New Church Review*, 14 (1907), 181–205.
7. Danilewicz, 'King', 58.
8. Chastanier, *Word of Advice*, 34.
9. Erdman, *Prophet*, 137–8.
10. For the rituals and teachings, see Micheline Meillassoux-Le

Cerf, *Dom Pernety et les Illuminés d'Avignon* (Milan: Arché, 1992).

11. Micheline Meillassoux-Le Cerf, 'Dom Pernety (1715–1796) et son Milieu' (Ph.D. thesis: University of Sorbonne, 1988), II, 231.
12. Danilewicz, 'King', 59, 66–7.
13. Frederick Daniell, *A Catalogue Raisonné of the Engraved Works of Richard Cosway* (London: Daniell, 1890), 4, 21–4; Arthur Mandel, *The Militant Messiah* (Atlantic Highlands: Humanities Press, 1979), 110–11.
14. For his colourful career, see Constantin Photiades, *Count Cagliostro*, trans. K. S. Shelvankar (London: Rider, 1932).
15. For background on the relationship between Falk and Cagliostro, see my articles, 'Yeats and the Unknown Superiors', 114–68; and 'Dr Samuel Jacob Falk', 203–26.
16. [Monsignor Barberi], *The Life of Joseph Balsamo, Commonly Called the Count Cagliostro* (Dublin, 1792), 152–3. Cosway owned this volume.
17. McCalman, *Last Alchemist*, 69.
18. Jacques Grot, ed., *Lettres de Grimm à l'Impératrice Catherine II*, 2nd rev. edn (St Petersburg, 1884), vol. 44, 212–13. (Empress Catherine to Baron Grimm, 1781.) My translation.
19. William Spence, MD, *Essays in Divinity and Physic . . . With an Exposition of Animal Magnetism and Magic* (London: Robert Hindmarsh, 1792), xiii. Cosway owned multiple copies of this book.
20. London, Wellcome Institute of the History of Medicine: Lalande Collection, MS. 1048. My translation.
21. Quoted in Francis Mossiker, *The Queen's Necklace* (New York: Simon & Schuster, 1961), 554.
22. Patricia Fara, 'An Attractive Therapy: Animal Magnetism in Eighteenth-Century England', *History of Science*, 23 (1995), 139.
23. Cyrus Redding, *Fifty Years Recollections* (London, 1858), III, 114–15.
24. Photiades, *Cagliostro*, 19.
25. Joppien, *Loutherbourg*, 4, no. 62; McCalman, *Last Alchemist*, 164–8.
26. Gerald Bentley, 'Mainaduc, Magic and Madness: George

Cumberland and the Blake Connection', *Notes and Queries*, 236 (September 1991), 294–6.

27. Percy Colson, *The Strange History of Lord George Gordon* (London: Robert Hale, 1937), 169–72. For more on Gordon's 'Judaisation', see my article, 'Lord George Gordon', 183–231.
28. *Rambler's Magazine* (September 1785), 342–3.
29. See the articles on 'Lord George Gordon' and 'William Blake' in the *Encyclopaedia Judaica* (Jerusalem, 1972).
30. [Barberi], *Life*, 153–4, 165.
31. Butlin, 'Six New Early Drawings', 108–9. Butlin suggests a Swedenborgian context for these drawings, which he dates *c.*1785. I believe 1786 is the more likely date.
32. Butlin, *Paintings*, I, 113, 127–8, 251.
33. Photiades, *Cagliostro*, 222.
34. [Barberi], *Life*, 166–7.
35. Ibid., 152–3.
36. Swedenborg, *Conjugial Love*, no. 505.
37. For the techniques, see Terry Castle, 'Phantasmagoria: Spectral Technology and the Metaphorics of Modern Reverie', *Critical Inquiry*, 15 (1998), 27, 33, 38.
38. For more background, see my article, 'William Blake and the Promiscuous Baboons: A Cagliostroan Séance Gone Awry', *British Journal for Eighteenth-Century Studies*, 18 (1993), 185–200.
39. Blake, *CPP*, 42.
40. Ibid., 44.
41. Thompson, *Witness*, 145 n.47.
42. W. Harry Rylands, *Records of the Lodge Original, Number 1, now the Lodge of Antiquity, Number* 2, 2nd rev. edn (London: privately printed, 1928), II, 31–2; *General Advertiser* (2 December 1786).
43. T. Wright, *Works of Gillray*, II, plate 37.
44. McCalman, *Last Alchemist*, 180–1.
45. Blake, *CPP*, 1.
46. Auguste Viatte, *Les Sources Occultes du Romantisme* (1927; Paris: Honoré Champion, 1968), I, 165, 170. Lavater corresponded with Swedenborg, collected manuscripts on the Moravians, called on Cagliostro and received Kabbalistic revelations from

Gablidone. Blake's friend Henry Fuseli was privy to Lavater's esoteric explorations.

47. Blake, *CPP*, 591.
48. Ibid., 590, 600.

Chapter 18: Perpetual Virile Potency

1. For the following annotations, see Blake, *CPP* 602–9.
2. Ibid., 593. In his annotations to Lavater's *Aphorisms* (1788).
3. Ibid., 605.
4. For more on this conference, see Marsha Keith Schuchard, 'The Secret Masonic History of Blake's Swedenborg Society', *Blake: An Illustrated Quarterly*, 26 (1992), 44–6; also, Morton Paley, 'A New Heaven is Begun: William Blake and Swedenborgianism', *Blake: An Illustrated Quarterly*, 12 (1979), 64–90.
5. London, Swedenborg Society, Conference Library: 'Minutes of the Great Eastcheap Conference' (7 May 1787–7 November 1791).
6. Philip K. Nelson, *Carl-Bernhard Wadström: Mannes Bakomyten* (Norrköping: Föreningen Gaml Norrköpping, 1998), 20, 28, 126.
7. Swedenborg, *Conjugial Love*, nos 462–77.
8. Swinburne, *Blake*, 14.
9. [Augustus Nordenskjöld], *Plan for a Free Community Upon the Coast of Africa* (London: Robert Hindmarsh, 1790), 135.
10. Ibid., iii–v, x.
11. Ibid., 34–5.
12. His alchemical broadside is reprinted in my article, 'Secret Masonic History', 48–51. Original in Helsinki University Library.
13. For the detailed context, see my article, 'Blake's *Tiriel* and the Regency Crisis: Lifting the Veil on a Royal Masonic Scandal', in Jackie de Salvo, G. A. Rosso and Christopher Hobson, eds, *Blake, Politics and History* (New York: Garland, 1988), 115–35.
14. Spence, *Essays*, 52, 57–8.
15. Blake, *CPP*, 6.
16. Gustav Davidson, *A Dictionary of Angels* (New York: Free Press, 1967), 288.

17. Martin Madan, *Thelypthora* (London: J. Dodsley, 1780–1), II, 336; III, 273–9.
18. Blake, *CPP*, 609–11.
19. Anon., 'Epistolary Correspondence of the Earlier Members of the Church', *Monthly Observer*, 2 (1858), 281; James Hyde, 'Some Notes Respecting Robert Hindmarsh', *New Church Magazine* (March 1905), 118–19.
20. Garrett, 'Spiritual Odyssey', 153. Though Jacob Duché resigned the Asylum chaplaincy in 1789, he continued to participate in Swedenborgian affairs in Lambeth until his return to America in 1793.
21. Barthelemon lived at 8 Kennington Place, Vauxhall, and Tulk on Kennington Lane, Vauxhall.
22. Emanuel Swedenborg, *Marriage (De Conjugio)*, in *Posthumous Theological Works*, trans. John Whitehead (1914; New York: Swedenborg Foundation, 1978), II, 523–4, 551.
23. Ibid., II, 440–2.
24. *New Jerusalem Magazine*, 2 (February 1790), 89, 92.
25. The Swedenborgian Masons Lambert de Lintot, General Charles Rainsford and Dr Ebenezer Sibly collected publications about the Frankists and their Masonic affiliate, the Order of Asiatic Brethen. For the Brethren's activities, see Gershom Scholem, *Du Frankisme au Jacobinisme* (Paris: le Seul Gallimard, 1981), 28–39.
26. Blake, *CPP*, 34. For colour reproductions of the plates, see William Blake, *The Early Illuminated Books*, eds. Morris Eaves, Robert Essick and Joseph Viscomi (London: Tate Gallery, 1993), 141–93.
27. Garrett, *Respectable Folly*, 116; Scholem, *Kabbalah*, 303.
28. Scholem, *Messianic Idea*, 138; Mandel, *Militant Messiah*, 52.
29. Scholem, *Kabbalah*, 293–4.
30. Mandel, *Militant Messiah*, 113.
31. Blake, *CPP*, 39; Erdman, *Illuminated Blake*, 111.
32. Ibid., 111, 120. For the sexual-visionary function of *yod*, see Fischel Lachower and Isaiah Tishby, *The Wisdom of the Zohar: An Anthology of Texts*, trans. David Goldstein (Oxford: Oxford UP, 1989), I, 343.

33. Scholem, *Kabbalah*, 293–4.
34. Lloyd, *Cosway*, 127, no. 161.
35. Fawn Brodie, *Thomas Jefferson: An Intimate History* (New York: W. W. Norton, 1974), 20, 519.
36. Francis Beretti, *Pascal Paoli à Maria Cosway: Lettres et Documents, 1782–1803* (Oxford: Voltaire Foundation, 2003), 14.
37. Blake, *CPP*, 287, 294.
38. Review of Barberi's *Life of Cagliostro*, in the *European Magazine* (December 1791), 438–9.
39. Blake, *CPP*, 35.
40. I quote the Notebook poems from Geoffrey Keynes's edition, *Blake: Complete Writings* (Oxford: Oxford UP, 1985), 161–87, which presents a clearer chronological version than Erdman's edition.
41. Ibid., 162–3.
42. Blake, *CPP*, 18.

Chapter 19: The Frozen Marriage Bed

1. Keynes, *Blake*, 178, 182.
2. Blake, *CPP*, 481.
3. Ibid., 469.
4. Ibid., 163.
5. Erdman, *Illuminated Blake*, 127–36.
6. Swedenborg, *Conjugial Love*, no. 171.
7. Blake, *CPP*, 50.
8. Gilchrist, *Life* (1880), 99, 316. The friend was probably Flaxman, who returned from Italy in 1794; see Bentley, *Blake Records*, 24.
9. Keynes, *Blake*, 161.
10. Barnett, *Cosway*, 125–6.
11. Blake, *CPP*, 79.
12. *New Jerusalem Magazine*, 5 (May 1790), 207. This journal was funded by J. A. Tulk to present the liberals' views.
13. John Timbs, *English Eccentrics and Eccentricities* (1875; Detroit: Singing Tree, 1969), 190.

14. John Wright, *A Revealed Knowledge of Some Things that Will Speedily Be Fulfilled in the World, Communicated to a Number of Christians, Brought Together at Avignon, by the Power of the Spirit of the Lord, From All Nations* (London, 1794), 4–5. For more on Samuel, see my article, 'William Blake and the Jewish Swedenborgians', in Sheila Spector, ed., *The Jews and British Romanticism* (New York: Palgrave Macmillan, 2005), 61–86.
15. For the rituals, see Viatte, *Sources Occultes*, I, 100.
16. Alnwick Castle: MS. 599 ff.107–21. Bryan explained the working of the Kabbalistic oracle to Rainsford.
17. Wright, *Revealed Knowledge*, 30, 32, 52–7.
18. Bryan described the child to Quaker friends in 1791 and to General Rainsford in the early 1790s. For Bryan's Grabiankan-style criticism of Swedenborg, see David Worrall, 'William Bryan, Another Anti-Swedenborgian Visionary of 1789', *Blake: An Illustrated Quarterly*, 34 (2000), 14–22.
19. London, Friends' House Library: John Thompson MS. JT35.
20. Garrett, *Respectable Folly*, 105–6, 115–16; Meillassoux-Le Cerf, *Dom Pernety*, 189. Cappelli was executed in 1798; records of the case are still kept secret by the Vatican.
21. Erdman, *Prophet*, 26 n.7.
22. Blake, *CPP*, 51–4, 66, 82–3.
23. John Robinson, *Proofs of a Conspiracy Against All the Religions and Governments of Europe, Carried on in the Secret Meetings of the Freemasons, Illuminati and Reading Societies*, 4th rev. edn (London: Caldwell and Davis, 1798), 470.
24. *New Magazine of Knowledge Concerning Heaven and Hell*, 9 (November 1790), 406. Hindmarsh started this rival magazine as the mouthpiece of the conservatives, who planned to gain a Dissenters' licence for a separate, sectarian church.
25. Emanuel Swedenborg, *A Sketch of the Chaste Delights of Conjugial Love* [trans. C. B. Wadström] (London: J. Denew, 1789), 9, 41.
26. *New Magazine of Knowledge* (May 1791), 193–5.
27. Ibid., 195.
28. Higham, 'James Glen', 541–3.
29. Gerald Bentley, 'Thomas Butts, White Collar Maecenas', *PMLA*

(*Publications of the Modern Language Association*), 71 (1956), 1052–66. The assertion that Butts was a Swedenborgian was published by his great-granddaughter, Mary Butts, who had carefully studied the family history; see her autobiographical novel, *The Crystal Cabinet*, ed. Camilla Bragg (Manchester: Carcanet, 1988), 12–13, 155.

30. Gilchrist, *Life* (1863), 54. Though the pious John Linnell, who met Blake in 1818, regarded the nudity story 'with incredulity', Gilchrist stressed that 'Mr Butts' authority in all that relates to the early and middle period of Blake's life, must be regarded as unimpeachable.' W. M. Rossetti backed up Gilchrist, noting that 'the fact might have occurred, without Mr Linnell's knowing, by any possibility anything about it.' Though Bentley acknowledges that the story was circulating at the Royal Academy by 1815, he rejects it as a 'red herring'; see *Blake Records* (2nd edn), xxvii.
31. Gilchrist, *Life* (1880), 96–7.
32. John Adlard, 'A Blake Poem', *Times Literary Supplement* (21 September 1984), 1055. For a romantic biographical interpretation, see Geoffrey Keynes, 'An Unpublished Poem by William Blake', *Times Literary Supplement* (14 September 1984), 1021.
33. Blake, *CPP*, 714.
34. Bentley, *Stranger*, 187; also his article, 'The Daughters of Albion and the Butts Household', *Blake: An Illustrated Quarterly*, 18 (1984), 116.
35. *The Bon Ton Magazine; or Microscope of Fashion and Folly*, 1 (September 1791), 264.
36. Robert Essick, 'William Blake's "The Phoenix": A Problem in Attribution', *Philological Quarterly*, 67 (1988), 378.
37. Blake, *CPP*, 314, 332, 371.
38. Anon., 'Epistolary Correspondence', 420.
39. Rimius, *Supplement*, 420.
40. British Library, Rainsford Papers: Add. MSS. 23,675 ff.34–6.
41. Ibid., Add. MSS. 23,668 f.9.
42. Keynes, *Blake*, 175.

Chapter 20: The Visionary Vulva

1. Swedenborg, *Marriage (De Conjugio)*, II, 523–4.
2. John Lane, 'A Symbolic Chart of 1789', *Ars Quatuor Coronatorum*, 3 (1890), 37. Lintot reprinted his engravings over the years, and his papers were inherited by General Rainsford.
3. Erich Lindner, *The Royal Art Illustrated*, trans. Arthur Lindsay (Graz: Akademische Druck, 1976), 136.
4. London, Wellcome Institute: Ebenezer Sibly, MS. 4594. For his career, see Eric Ward, 'Ebenezer Sibly – A Man of Parts', *Ars Quatuor Coronatorum*, 71 (1959), 48–52.
5. Blake, *CPP*, 488.
6. S. Foster Damon, *A Blake Dictionary: The Ideas and Symbols of William Blake* (1965; London: Thames and Hudson, 1973), 95, 233.
7. Blake, *CPP*, 496.
8. For example, Tantrists used 'broth' to describe the proper relationship between the female's vaginal fluids and the male's semen; see Ruan, *Sex in China*, 64; Feurstein, *Tantra*, 232–4, 248.
9. Tristanne Connolly, *William Blake and the Body* (New York: Palgrave Macmillan, 2002), 105–9.
10. Blake, *CPP*, 496–8.
11. Kerrison Preston, *Blake and Rossetti* (London: Alexander Moring, 1944), 29; S. Foster Damon, *A Blake Dictionary*, rev. edn (1965; 1988), 401.
12. In Sweden, the Kabbalistic stories of the ascension of Enoch into heaven, where he became the angel Metatron, were woven into an Illuminist Masonic rite. Documents of the Metatron Rite in the Grand Lodge archives in Stockholm include eighteenth-century transcriptions of Swedenborg's writings.
13. John Antes, 'Extract of the Narrative of the Life of Our late dear and venerable Brother, John Antes, Written by himself', *Periodical Accounts Relating to the Missions of the Church of the United Brethren Established Among the Heathen*, 20 (1851), 164–5.
14. Peucker and Augustin, eds, *Graf ohne Grenzen*, 94.
15. Benjamin Henry Latrobe, *The Correspondence and Miscellaneous*

Papers of Benjamin Henry Latrobe, ed. John C. Van Horne and Lee W. Formwalt (New Haven: Yale UP, 1984), III, 931. After emigrating to America in 1795, he elided the spelling of his surname.

16. J. M. Reid, *Traveller Extraordinary: The Life and Times of James Bruce of Kinnaird* (London: Eyre & Spottiswoode, 1968), 303. Reid confuses Reverend La Trobe with his son Benjamin Henry.
17. John Antes, *Observations and Customs of the Egyptians* (1799; Dublin: John Jones, 1801), 9–15; Jeffrey Cohen and Charles Brownell, *The Architectural Drawings of Benjamin Henry Latrobe* (New Haven: Yale UP, 1987), 40.
18. Talbot Hamlin, *Benjamin Henry Latrobe* (New York: Oxford UP, 1955), 98, 198.
19. Ibid., 246, 540–1.
20. For Cosway's friendships with James Hutton and Benjamin La Trobe, see Walpole, *Correspondence*, XXXIII, ii, 510. The editor tentatively identifies 'the chief of the Moravians' as Hutton, whose portrait Cosway painted, but he was more likely the sociable La Trobe, who participated in liberal and artistic circles.
21. Gerald E. Bentley, 'A Jewel in an Ethiop's Ear: The Book of Enoch as Inspiration for William Blake, John Flaxman, Thomas Moore and Richard Westall', in Robert Essick and David Pierce, eds, *Blake in His Time* (Bloomington: Indiana UP, 1978), 213.
22. Cosway, *Catalogue*; William Hayley, *A Catalogue of the . . . Library of the Late William Hayley* (London: Evans, 1821); rpt. in A.N.L. Munby, ed., *Sale Catalogues of Libraries of Prominent Persons* (London: Sotheby Parke-Bernet, 1971–5), II, 120.
23. William Hayley, *A Philosophical, Historical and Moral Essay on Old Maids* (London: T. Cadell, 1785), II, 6–37.
24. Butlin dates 'Enoch walked with God' towards the end of 'ca. 1780–85'; see his *Paintings*, I, 55.
25. Richard Laurence, *The Book of Enoch the Prophet . . . now first translated from an Ethiopic MS. In the Bodleian Library*, 2nd rev. edn (1821; Oxford: John Henry Parker, 1838), vi–vii.
26. Rainsford gave the MS. to his Swedenborgian-Masonic friend Lord Percy (from 1786, Sixth Duke of Northumberland), where he preserved it in the archives of Alnwick Castle (MS. 619).

27. Ebenezer Sibly, *Magazine of Natural History* (London: Chapante and Widrow, 1794), 137; Spence, *Essays*, 19–20.
28. *New Magazine of Knowledge* (October 1791), 421–4.
29. John Beer also suggests a 1796 date; see his article, 'Blake's Changing View of History: The Impact of the Book of Enoch', in Steve Clark and David Worrall, eds, *Historicizing Blake* (New York: St Martin's, 1994), 159–78.
30. Bentley, 'Jewel', 231, plate 139. I follow Bentley's interpretations of the original drawings, which are difficult to decipher in reproductions.
31. Ibid., 231.
32. Emanuel Swedenborg, *True Christian Religion*, trans. W. C. Dick (London: Swedenborg Society, 1950), no. 134. Blake owned this work, which expressed Swedenborg's most explicitly Masonic themes.
33. Tulk had moved to 21 Sloane Street, Knightsbridge, by this time, but he stayed in touch with the Swedenborgians in Lambeth. I was informed about Grabianka's friendship with Tulk and his return to England in 1796 by Denis Duckworth, then serving as archivist of the Swedenborg Society in London, but he was unable to retrieve the relevant documents (which he had read), which are now missing.
34. Bentley, 'Jewel', plate 141.
35. Ibid., 234, plate 144.
36. George Cumberland, *Thoughts on Outline* (London: W. Wilson, 1796), 17, 29, 44–5, plates 15, 18.
37. Bentley, 'Jewel', 215, 236 n. 10. Cumberland was interested in Bruce's experiences and writing; see Bentley, *Bibliography of George Cumberland*, 96.
38. See the account by Benjamin La Trobe's brother-in-law, John Antes, in his *Observations*, 22. Antes's manuscript was dated 20 April 1788.
39. George Cumberland, *The Captive of the Castle of Sennaar* (London: printed for the author, 1798), 28, 52, 61, 83, 95, 191, 208.
40. Bentley, *Blake Records* (2nd edn), 96.
41. Ibid., 500.

42. Geoffrey Keynes, *Blake Studies*, 2nd edn (Oxford: Clarendon, 1971), 240–1.
43. Symons, *Blake*, 256.
44. Robert Essick and Morton Paley, '"Dear Generous Cumberland": A Newly Discovered Letter and Poem by William Blake', *Blake: An Illustrated Quarterly*, 32 (1998), 4–5.

Chapter 21: Priapic Prayer and Randy Antiquarians

1. Bindman, *Blake*, 17.
2. Francis Haskell, 'Baron d'Hancarville: An Adventurer and Art Historian in Eighteenth-Century Europe', *Past and Present in Art and Taste: Selected Essays* (New Haven: Yale UP, 1987), 40.
3. [Baron d'Hancarville], *Collection of Etruscan, Greek and Roman Antiquities from the Cabinet of the Hon'ble William Hamilton* (Naples, 1766–7), III, 3.
4. [Baron d'Hancarville], *Monumens du Culte Secret des Dames Romaines* (Rome: de l'imprimerie du Vatican, 1777; rpt. 1787), vii.
5. [Baron d'Hancarville], *Veneres et Priapi* ([London], 1784), nos 52, 59, 62, etc.
6. Baron d'Hancarville, *Recherches sur l'origine, l'esprit et les progrés des Arts de la Gréce* (London: B. Appleyard, 1785), I, xii, 48, 224–5, 241, 310.
7. Nikolaus Pevsner, 'Richard Payne Knight', *Art Bulletin*, 32 (1949), 298.
8. Hill, *Mr Gillray*, 14; Bentley, *Blake Records*, 114.
9. Benjamin Henry Latrobe, *The Virginia Journals of Benjamin Henry Latrobe*, ed. Edward Carter (New Haven: Yale UP, 1977), 222–5.
10. London, Society of Antiquaries: 'Minutes of the Society of Dilettanti (1778–1798)', February 1785, 4 May 1788; MS. Correspondence D. Vol. I, ff.315–16, 325 (June and July 1785).
11. Pevsner, 'Knight', 297.
12. D'Hancarville, *Recherches*, I, 89, 147, 447; Charles Rainsford, *A Catalogue of the Valuable Library of Books of General Rainsford, Deceased* (London: Christie, 1809), 9.
13. D'Hancarville was a devoted friend of Maria Cosway and acted

as her liaison with Thomas Jefferson in Paris. While in London, he met Louis Claude de Saint-Martin, a student of Swedenborg and Boehme, who began writing *Les Hommes de Désir* in 1787.

14. Baron d'Hancarville, *Antiquités Étrusques, Grecques et Romaines* (Paris: F. A. David, 1787), III, 134–6.
15. British Library, Cumberland Papers: Correspondence, vol. VI. Add. MSS. 36496 ff.344; vol. XXVI, Add. MSS. 36516 f.259.
16. British Museum, Townley Papers: MS. TY 7/15/1511; 7/1512.
17. When Moor returned to London in 1791–6, he sought out engravers to copy his Indian collections, including Moses Haughton, who was friendly with Blake. Moor and Blake both attended dinners at Joseph Johnson's bookstore, and the Orientalist-soldier would later be considered 'a fresh channel of information' on Blake. See Beth Lau, 'William Godwin and the Joseph Johnson Circle: the Evidence of the Diaries', *Wordsworth Circle*, 33 (2002), 106; she lists him as 'Major Moore'. Also, Joe Riehl, 'Bernard Barton's Contribution to Cunningham's "Life of Blake": a New Letter', *Blake: An Illustrated Quarterly*, 17–18.
18. *The British Critic*, 4 (September 1794), 223–4, 388–91.
19. Thomas Mathias, *The Pursuits of Literature, a Satirical Poem*, 16th edn (1794–8; London: Becket and Porter, 1812), I, 1, 79–80.
20. Ibid., I, lxi.
21. Cumberland, *Thoughts*, 17, 29.
22. Blake, *Four Zoas*, 191,
23. D'Hancarville, *Recherches*, I, 74.
24. D'Hancarville, *Antiquités*, II, 5; III, 134–6, plates 64, 66, 71, 72.
25. Ellis, *Real Blake*, 411–12.
26. D'Hancarville, *Recherches*, I, vi.
27. Richard Payne Knight, *An Account of the Remains of the Worship of Priapus* (London: J. Spilsbury, 1786), 5–7, 23, plate 1.
28. Magno and Erdman, *Four Zoas*, 151.
29. Peter Otto, 'A Pompous High Priest: Urizen's Ancient Phallic Religion', *Blake: An Illustrated Quarterly*, 34 (2001), 20–1.
30. For the complex theory of the 'breaking of the vessels', see Scholem, *Major Trends*, 265–8, and *Kabbalah*, 137–40.

31. For the Jewish use of Beulah to mean 'married', see Isaiah, lxii: 4: 'thy land [shall be called] Beulah; for the Lord delighteth in thee, and thy land shall be married'. See Damon, *Blake Dictionary*, 42.
32. Blake, *CPP*, 372.
33. For Knight's influence on Blake's erotic designs, see Otto, 'Pompous', 6–7.
34. D'Hancarville, *Recherches*, I, 84, 132, 310, 389.
35. Knight, *Account*, 5, 47, 81, plates IX and X.
36. Edward Moor, *Oriental Fragments* (London: Smith and Elder, 1834), 79, 147, 283–5, 293, plate IV.
37. Blake, *Four Zoas*, 135.
38. Blake, *CPP*, 313.
39. Blake, *Four Zoas*, 140.
40. Knight, *Account*, 5, 47, 81, plate XI.
41. Blake, *Four Zoas*, 47–9, 83–4.
42. Ibid., 158; Blake, *CPP*, 329–30.
43. Ibid., 710, 475.
44. Ibid., 137, 477.
45. Ibid., 304, 824.

Chapter 22: Kabbalistic Cherubim and Yogic Yonis

1. Gilchrist, *Life* (1863), 115.
2. Rossetti, *Poetical Works*, xi.
3. Besides Edward Moor, Blake was friendly with the artists Ozias Humphrey and Thomas and William Daniell, who spent years in India and brought back pictures of Indian temple art, including the sculptured *Lingam* and *Yoni*.
4. Shaw, *Passionate Enlightenment*, 152.
5. D'Hancarville, *Recherches*, I, vi; II, 82.
6. Blake, *CPP*, 208. For their Tartarian interests, see Carl-Michael Edenborg, *Fabian Wilhelm Ekenstam och Mötet Mellan Romantiken och Alekemin* (Stockholms Universitet, HT, 1994), 19, 26; also, his *Alkemiens Skam* (Stockholm: Caudex, 2002), 175–7.
7. British Museum, Townley Papers: MSS. TY 7/1802, 1803, 1985;

TY 8/59. For Blake's access to Townley's collections, see Morton Paley, *The Traveller in the Evening: The Last Works of William Blake* (Oxford: Oxford UP, 2003), 119.

8. Bentley, *Stranger*, 180–1.
9. *The British Critic*, 3 (January 1794), 153–6.
10. Cumberland, Cosway, Flaxman, Fuseli and Hayley all began to collect and sketch Indian *objets d'art*, and they followed the publications of Moor and his Orientalist colleagues.
11. Bentley, *Bibliography of George Cumberland*, 113.
12. British Library, Cumberland Papers: Add. MSS. 36,522 ff.1–2.
13. Moor, *Narrative*, 401–2, 358.
14. Ibid., 54, 58.
15. Henry T. Colebrook, 'On the Religious Ceremonies of the Hindus', *Asiatick Researches*, 8 (1808), 86. Colebrook and Moor discussed this subject in the 1790s.
16. Heinrich Zimmer, *Artistic Form and Yoga in the Sacred Images of India*, trans. Gerald Chapple and James Lawson (Princeton: Princeton UP, 1984), 30–1; David Gordon White, *The Practice of Tantra* (Princeton: Princeton UP, 2000), 15.
17. Blake, *Four Zoas*, 28.
18. Ibid., 38–9.
19. Blake, *CPP*, 39.
20. Ibid., 531.
21. Edward Moor, *The Hindu Pantheon* (London: Joseph Johnson, 1810), 177, 188, 363.
22. David Weir, *Brahma in the West: William Blake and the Oriental Renaissance* (Albany: State University of New York, 2003), 21.
23. London, Museum of Natural History, Dawson Turner Collection: 'Correspondence of Sir Joseph Banks', vol. VIII, ff.117–21; IV, ff.143–5.
24. Gordon Hills, 'Notes on Some Masonic Personalities at the End of the Eighteenth Century', *Ars Quatuor Coronatorum*, 25 (1912), 141–2. Some possible members of this private lodge were Cosway, Chastanier, J. A. Tulk, Ebenezer Sibly, Alexander Tilloch and Dr Sigismund Bacstrom. Lord Percy (now Duke of Northumberland) and George Adams, mutual friends of Maurice and Rainsford, may also have attended.

25. Thomas Maurice, *Indian Antiquities* (London: Elmsley and Richardson, 1792–1800), V, 1001. The first volume actually appeared in 1794.
26. 'Spiritus Novitius' [Tulk], *Aurora*, I (May 1799), 28. Tulk financed this journal as a mouthpiece for the liberal Swedenborgians.
27. Maurice, *Indian Antiquities*, VII, 785.
28. Thomas Maurice, *Memoirs* (London: Rimington, 1819–20), I, 19; II, 139.
29. Maurice, *Indian Antiquities*, I, xxxvi; III, vii; IV, 502, 594.
30. Ibid., II, 307.
31. Robert Essick, 'Blake in the Marketplace, 2003', *Blake: An Illustrated Quarterly*, 37 (2004), 118, plate 1.
32. Henry Colebrook, 'Enumeration of Indian Classes', *Asiatic Researches*, 5 (Calcutta, 1798), 54.
33. For Grabianka's third visit to London, see Danilewicz, 'King', 64. For Tantra at Lyons, see Hugh Urban, 'Elitism and Esotericism: Strategies of Secrecy and Power in South Indian Tantra and French Freemasonry', *History of Religions*, 37 (1998), 1–37.
34. British Library, Rainsford Papers: Add. MSS. 23,675 ff.33–4.
35. Antoine Faivre, *Eckhartshausen et la Théosophie Chrétienne* (Paris: Klingsieck, 1969), 107.
36. Meillassoux-Le Cerf, 'Dom Pernety', 134. Rainsford knew another Scottish physician, Dr Caerni, who also visited Avignon.
37. Ronald M. Davidson, *Indian Esoteric Buddhism: A Social History of the Tantric Movement* (New York: Columbia UP, 2002), 200.
38. William Blake, *Milton a Poem*, ed. Robert Essick and Joseph Viscomi (London: Tate Gallery, 1993), 112.
39. For the esoteric Swedenborgian researches of the Flaxmans and Tulks, see Chapter 23 of this book.
40. Blake, *CPP*, 548.
41. Knight, *Account*, 81–2.
42. Blake, *CPP*, 117, 546.
43. Bentley, *Blake Records*, 544.
44. Blake, *CPP*, 531.
45. Blake, *Milton*, 100, plate 29A; Blake, *CPP*, 110.

46. Swedenborg, *Spiritual Diary*, nos 5106–7.
47. Wolfson, 'Images of God's Feet', 163, 168.
48. Garrison, *Tantra*, 123; Ghosh, *Original Yoga*, 101.
49. Swedenborg, *Spiritual Diary*, no. 3453.
50. Sheila Spector, 'Blake's *Milton* as Kabbalistic Vision', *Religion and Literature*, 25 (1993), 19–33.
51. According to eighteenth-century anatomical descriptions; see 'tarsus' in the *Oxford English Dictionary*.
52. On the black stone *Lingam*, see Lisebeth, *Tantra*, 206.
53. Edward Moor, *The Hindu Pantheon* (London: Joseph Johnson, 1810), 103, 124, 194, plate 20.
54. M. Sonnerat, *Voyage aux Indes Orientales et à la Chine* (Paris, 1782), I, 175, 181, 294.
55. Ghosh, *Original Yoga*, 101.
56. Blake, *CPP*, 115.
57. Wolfson, 'Images of God's Feet', 166–7.
58. Elliot Wolfson, 'Walking as a Sacred Duty: Theological Transformation of Social Reality in Early Hasidism', in Gershon Hundert, ed., *Essential Papers on Hasidism: Origins to Present* (New York: New York UP, 1991), 199, 206.
59. Blake, *Four Zoas*, 69, 192.
60. Blake, *CPP*, 354.
61. Hilton, 'Some Sexual Connotations', 167.
62. Colebrook, 'Religious Ceremonies', 280.
63. For this sanitised Tantra, see Hugh Urban, *Tantra: Sex, Secrecy and Politics in the Study of Religion* (Berkeley: California UP, 2003), 63–6.
64. Blake, *CPP*, 113.
65. Swedenborg, *Spiritual Diary*, no. 4408.
66. W. B. Yeats, 'The Mandukya Upanishad', in *Essays and Introductions* (New York: Collier, 1968), 484.
67. Erdman, *Illuminated Blake*, 258.
68. Blake, *CPP*, 323.
69. Leopold Damrosch, *Symbol and Truth in Blake's Myth* (Princeton: Princeton UP, 1980), 203. See also Otto, 'Pompous High Priest', 19, for a depiction of 'chaste' ejaculation, without contact between the sexes.

70. Description by John Grant, 'Visions in *Vala*: a Consideration of Some Pictures in the Manuscript', in Stuart Curran and Joseph Wittreich, eds, *Blake's Sublime Allegory* (Madison: Wisconsin UP, 1973), 188–9.
71. Blake, *CPP*, 184.
72. Ibid., 132.
73. Edward Moor, who was intrigued by the *Yoni* symbolism he deciphered in Christian art and high-degree Masonic rituals, would later publish explicit explanations of the mystical significance of the vulvic ovoid; see his *Oriental Fragments*, 79, 147, 283–5, 293, plate IV.
74. Keynes, *Blake*, 418, 906. Keynes dates the poem 1800–3, during the Felpham period, which I find more convincing than Erdman's date of 1788. I also agree with critics who see the emerging figure as the wife. For the drawing and differing interpretations of who (wife or husband?) is getting out of bed, see David Erdman and Donald Moore, *The Notebook of William Blake* (Oxford: Clarendon, 1973), 8 n.4, [N14 (4)].
75. Bentley, *Stranger*, 71. Blake quoted the poem from Edward Bysshe's *The Art of Poetry* (London, 1705), 116–17.
76. Blake, *CPP*, 481; Erdman and Moore, *Notebook*, N8.
77. Blake, *Milton*, 112.
78. Blake, *CPP*, 129.

Chapter 23: Thunder of Thought, & Flames of Fierce Desire

1. Blake, *CPP*, 145, 153.
2. Ibid., 546.
3. Bentley, *Stranger*, 348. For the friendship of the Tulks and Blakes, see Raymond Deck, 'New Light on C. A. Tulk, Blake's 19th-Century Patron', *Studies in Romanticism*, 16 (1977), 217–36; also Richard Lines, 'Charles Augustus Tulk – Swedenborgian Extraordinary', *Arcana*, 3 (1997), 10–16. Both J. A. and C. A. Tulk bought and promoted Blake's works; it was the son who introduced Coleridge to Blake and who published early praise of his mystical and artistic genius.
4. Edenborg, *Ekenstam*, 28–9. I am grateful to Dr Edenborg for

informing me about J. A. Tulk's alchemical studies and experiments.

5. [J. A. Tulk], *Testament of Nicholas Flamel* (London: J. and E. Hodson, 1806), III, 20. Hodson was a Swedenborgian publisher. Tulk's inscribed author's copy is in his collection of alchemical books, preserved in Eric Benzelius's old library in Linköping, Sweden.
6. British Library: Flaxman Papers. Add. MSS. 39,788 f.1.
7. Blake, *CPP*, 251.
8. British Library: Flaxman Papers. Add. MSS. 39,788. f.447.
9. *The First Report of the London Society* (1807), page E. Blake's friends Flaxman and Joseph Proud participated in this new Swedenborg society, which maintained links with Illuminist Masons in Sweden, France, Germany and Russia.
10. *Intellectual Repository for the New Church* (1812), 1, 42–8, 463–5; II, 81; (1813), VIII, 463.
11. British Library: Flaxman Papers. Add. MSS. 39,781 f.101. Tulk's source was 'Ahamed ben Wahshish', quoted in Joseph Hammer's *Ancient Alphabets and Hieroglyphic Characters Explained* (London, 1806).
12. Blake, *CPP*, 207–8.
13. *Intellectual Repository* (1814–15), II, 154.
14. British Library: Flaxman Papers. Add. MSS. 39,781 ff.113, 121; Edenborg, *Ekenstam*, 10–28.
15. Hyde, *Bibliography*, 694, no. 3500. J. A. Tulk's notes on this MS. (written in 1814) reveal his earlier friendship and collaboration with Chastanier, Wadström, the Nordenskjölds, and Manoah Sibly (brother of Ebenezer). He was currently negotiating the purchase of the late J. P. Moët's French translation of Swedenborg's works, and he stayed in touch with the Swedenborgian *Illuminés* in France. See further in Hyde, nos 3494–9.
16. For Moravian influence on the Johansen family, see Häll, *Swedenborgs Labyrint*, 233–5.
17. For Lavater, the Asiatic Brethren and Danish Rosicrucians, see Antoine Faivre, 'J. C. Lavater, Charles de Hesse et l'École du Nord', in his *Mystiques, Théosophes et Illuminés au Siécle des*

Lumiéres (Hildesheim: Georg Olms, 1976), 175–90. Henry Fuseli, a lifelong friend of Lavater and confidant of Blake, acquired the physiognomist's *Reise nach Kopenhagen* (1793) and planned to describe his visionary experiences in a biography (which was never completed).

18. Ellis and Yeats, *Works of Blake*, 1, 24–5; Barnett, *Cosway*, 171.
19. Biographical information on Bacstrom is preserved at Kew, Royal Botanic Gardens: Joseph Banks Collection, II, ff.152–3 (Bacstrom to Banks, 18 November 1796); Los Angeles, Getty Library: Bacstrom MSS., III, nos 5–6; Ron Charles Hogart, *Alchemy: A Comprehensive Bibliography of the Manly P. Hall Collection of Books and Manuscripts* (Los Angeles: Philosophical Research Society, 1986).
20. Glasgow University: Ferguson MS. 22. Quoted in Edenborg, *Alkemins Skam*, 298 n.43. See also Adam McLean, 'Bacstrom's Rosicrucian Society', *Hermetic Journal*, 6 (1979), 25–9.
21. Bentley, *Blake Records*, 59. Keri Davies argues that Tilloch was the model for 'Tilly Lally', the eccentric scientist in Blake's *Island in the Moon*; see his 'William Blake in Contexts' (Ph.D. dissertation: University of Surrey, 2003), 147, 256.
22. Los Angeles, Getty Library: Bacstrom MSS., II, no. 8; Hogart, *Alchemy*, 224–5.
23. Yeats, *Poems of William Blake*, xxiv–xxv. For possible identifications of the Falk brothers, see Schuchard, 'Yeats', 115–16.
24. Sheila Spector, 'Blake's Graphic Use of Hebrew', *Blake: An Illustrated Quarterly*, 37 (2003), 78; also her *'Wonders Divine': The Development of Blake's Kabbalistic Myth* (Lewisburg: Bucknell UP, 2001), 32–5.
25. Blake, *CPP*, 171, 174.
26. Ibid., 164. For the illustrations, see William Blake, *Jerusalem, The Emanation of the Giant Albion*, ed. Morton Paley (Princeton: Princeton UP, 1991), plate 19.
27. Blake, *CPP*, 179.
28. Blake, *Jerusalem*, plate 6.
29. Ibid., plate 24; Blake, *CPP*, 205, 210, 166–7, 169.
30. Ibid., 193.
31. Ibid., 145, 158.

32. Raymond Lister, *George Richmond: A Critical Biography* (London: Robin-Gorton, 1981), 132.
33. Geoffrey Keynes, *The Complete Portraiture of William and Catherine Blake* (Clairvaux: Trianon, 1977), 131–3. Yeats also pointed to Blake's familiarity with Yogic symbols, noting that his usage of 'the egg of Brahma' in *Milton* would be recognised by 'Students of the occult philosophy of the Tatwas' as a 'certain symbol associated with Akasa'. See Ellis and Yeats, *Works of William Blake*, I, 317.
34. William Hurd, *A New Universal History of the Religious Rites, Ceremonies and Customs of the Whole World*, rev. edn (1788; London: Blackburn, Hemingway, 1799), 783–813.
35. Bentley, *Blake Records*, 100, 114. Keri Davies will publish a study of Blake's friendship with Spilsbury and its Moravian significance.
36. Ruth Young, *Father and Daughter: Jonathan and Maria Spilsbury, 1737–1812: 1777–1820* (London: Epworth, 1952), 10–11, 20–6, 32, 41.
37. *A Collection of Fifty Prints from Antique Gems. In the Collections of the Rt. Hon. Earl Percy, the Hon. C. F. Greveller and T. M. Slade, Esq.*, engraved by John Spilsbury (London: John Boydell, n.d.). For Spilsbury as publisher of Chastanier's publications, see Hyde, *Bibliography*, nos 1170, 1915.
38. Blake, *CPP*, 755.
39. Hurd, *New Universal History*, 813.
40. Young, *Father*, 26.
41. John Gottfried Haensal, *Letters on the Nicobar Islands . . . to the Reverend C. I. Latrobe* (London: Fetter Lane, 1812), 47–57.
42. Young, *Father*, 30.
43. Samuel Ellis, *Life, Times and Character of James Montgomery* (London: Jackson, Walford, and Hodder, 1864), 12–16, 22, 36.
44. 'Paul Positive' [James Montgomery], *Prison Amusements* (London: Joseph Johnson, 1797), 155–60.
45. He retained his interest in Hinduism and yogic meditation over the next decades; see John Holland and James Everett, eds, *Memoirs of the Life and Writings of James Montgomery* (London: Longman's, 1854), IV, 19, 303.

46. Gerald Bentley, *Blake Records Supplement* (Oxford: Clarendon, 1988), 45–50.
47. Bentley, *Blake Records* (2nd edn), 235.
48. James Montgomery, *The Wanderer in Switzerland and Other Poems* (London: Verner and Hood; Sheffield: printed by J. Montgomery at the Iris Office, 1806), 167; James Montgomery, 'The West Indies: a Poem', in *Poems on the Abolition of the Slave Trade* (London: Bowyer and Bensley, 1809), 35, 39. In the Preface, Montgomery says he started the poem in May 1807.
49. Montgomery, the poem 'Hannah' in *Wanderer*, 11, 135, 147.
50. Bentley, *Blake Records Supplement*, 18–19.
51. *A Collection of Hymns for the Children of God in All Ages . . . Designed Chiefly for the Use of the Congregations in Union with the Brethren's Church* (London, 1754), II, 103, 215, 220, 284–5, 314.
52. Ibid., II, 297, 386.
53. Erdman, *Prophet*, 293. *Zoa* in Greek is the plural form of *Zoon*, meaning animals or living beings. Blake used an English plural form, *Zoas*.
54. *Collection of Hymns*, II, 206–8.
55. Ibid., II, 299–300.
56. Ibid., II, 297–8.
57. Miranda Shaw, *Passionate Enlightenment: Women in Tantric Buddhism* (Princeton: Princeton UP, 1994), 166.
58. Blake, *CPP*, 161.
59. Urban, *Tantra*, 30.
60. Shaw, *Passionate Enlightenment*, 156–7.
61. Blake, *Jerusalem*, plate 28.
62. With the botanical assistance of Sir Joseph Banks, Townley, Knight and Maurice examined the structure of the Indian lotus, which helped them understand the sexual and spiritual symbolism of the flower.
63. Shaw, *Passionate Enlightenment*, 155–7.
64. Erdman, *Illuminated Blake*, 307.
65. Blake, *CPP*, 209.
66. Ibid., 247.
67. [Hutton], *Collection of Hymns*, 32.

68. Blake, *CPP*, 242, 247.
69. Lisebeth, *Tantra*, 286.
70. Urban, *Tantra*, 25.
71. Ibid., 26.
72. Elliot Wolfson, 'Mantra and Divine Name in Hindu and Jewish Meditation Techniques', paper given at the Annual Meeting of the American Academy of Religion, Atlanta, Georgia (23 November 2003).
73. Blake, *CPP*, 492, 860. 'We are led to Believe a Lie / When we see [With – *deleted*] not Thro the Eye.'
74. Ibid., 709.
75. [Hutton], *Collection of Hymns*, 56.
76. Blake, *Jerusalem*, 296, plate 99.
77. Ibid., plate 99 E; Blake, *CPP*, 223.

Epilogue

1. William Butler Yeats, *Yeats's Poems*, ed. A. Norman Jeffares and Warwick Gould (London: Macmillan, 1989), 419.
2. Blake, *Four Zoas*, 222; Peter Otto, *Blake's Critique of Transcendence: Love, Jealousy and the Sublime in the The Four Zoas* (Oxford: Oxford UP, 2000), 270.
3. Blake, *CPP*, 520–4.
4. Ibid., 876–8.
5. Ibid., 522.
6. Ellis and Yeats, *Works*, I, 143–4.
7. Swedenborg, *Journal of Dreams*, nos 171–2.
8. Ellis and Yeats, *Works*, I, 24–5.
9. Anne Saddlemyer, *Becoming George: The Life of Mrs W. B. Yeats* (Oxford: Oxford UP, 2002), 122–4.
10. Ibid., 119.
11. On Yeats's Steinach operation, see Brenda Maddox, *George's Ghosts: A New Life of W. B. Yeats* (London: Picador, 1999), 265–7. On the operation and his Tantric studies, see Roy Foster, *W. B. Yeats: A Life, II: The Arch-Poet* (Oxford: Oxford UP, 2003), 496–500, 537–8.
12. Richard Ellmann, *W. B. Yeats's Second Puberty* (Washington:

Library of Congress, 1985).

13. Yeats, *Yeats's Poems*, 430.
14. Gilchrist, *Life* (1880), 327.
15. Bentley, *Blake Records*, 221.
16. Blake, *CPP*, 518–19.
17. Yeats, *Yeats's Poems*, 301.
18. Saddlemyer, *Becoming George*, 502.
19. Yeats, *Essays*, 485.
20. William Butler Yeats, *The Letters of W. B. Yeats*, ed. Allan Wade (London: Macmillan, 1955), 852. Influenced by his Tantric studies, Yeats increasingly feared that his sickness was caused by the excessive masturbation of his youth, which wasted the visionary semen; see Maddox, *George's Ghosts*, 267–8.
21. Ibid., 280, 303, 312.
22. Saddlemyer, *Becoming George*, 119.

Works Cited

Manuscripts

Academy of New Church, Bryn Athyn, Pennsylvania: Academy Collection of Swedenborg Documents, no. 1664.31; Alfred Acton, 'The Life of Emanuel Swedenborg . . . 1688–1744' (typescript).

Alnwick Castle, Alnwick: Rainsford Papers; Catalogue of Manuscripts, MS. 619.

British Library, London: Cumberland Papers, Add. MSS. 36,494; 36,522.

—— Flaxman Papers, Add. MSS. 39,781, f.101; 39, 788, f.1.

—— Rainsford Papers, Add MSS. 26,668–9.

British Museum, London: Townley Papers, MSS. TY 7/1511–12, 1802–3, 2028–9; TY 8/59.

Friends' Reference Library, London: John Thompson Collection, MS. JT35.

Grand Lodge Library, London: Atholl Register, Lodge no. 138.

—— Grand Masters' Lodge Record.

—— Norman Hackney, 'The Royal Order of Heredom of Kilwinning' (typescript, 1954).

Huntington Library, Pasadena, California: Diana Wilson's transcript of 'Catalogue, Schedule, or Inventory of Household Goods, Furniture, Books, . . . made between Richard Cosway and Maria, his Wife (15 April 1820).

John Rylands Library, University of Manchester: Eng. MS. 420, Catalogue of George Cumberland's Library.

Moravian Church Library, London: Congregation Diaries, Obituaries, Records of Births and Burials, Petitions for Membership.

Museum of Natural History, London: Dawson Turner Collection, Correspondence of Sir Joseph Banks, IV, ff.143–5; VIII, ff.117–21.

Philosophical Research Society, Los Angeles, California: Bacstrom MSS., III, nos 5–6. Since moved to Getty Center.

Riksarkiv, Stockholm: Hollandica, no. 896.

Royal Botanical Gardens, Kew: Sir Joseph Banks Collection, MS. I, ff.122, 240; II, ff.152–3.

Royal Order of Scotland, Edinburgh: Record Book, 1750–1937.

Royal Society of Arts, London: 'Minutes of the Society for Encouragement of Arts, Manufactures, and Commerce'.

Royal Society of Sciences, London: Journal Book, XVIII; Register Book, XVI.

Society of Antiquaries: 'Minutes of the Society of Dilettanti (1778–1798)'.

Stiftsbibliothek, Linköping: Eric Benzelius d.y., MS. B53, Diarium; Bref til Benzelius, V, 40; Catalogus Librorum.

Swedenborg Society, London: Conference Library, 'Minutes of the Great East Cheap Conference (7 May 1787 to 7 November 1791)'.

Wellcome Institute for the History of Medicine, London: Lalande Collection, MS. 1045; Ebenezer Sibly, MS. 4594.

Books, Articles and Dissertations
University presses are abbreviated as UP.

Ackroyd, Peter, *Blake: A Biography* (New York: Alfred Knopf, 1995).

—— *London: The Biography* (London: Chatto & Windus, 2000).

Acton, Alfred, *An Introduction to the Word Explained* (Bryn Athyn: Academy of the New Church, 1927).

—— *The Letters and Memorials of Emanuel Swedenborg* (Bryn Athyn: Swedenborg Scientific Association, 1955).

Adams, Cecil, '*Ahiman Rezon*, the Book of Constitutions', *Ars Quatuor Coronatorum*, 46 (1933), 239–57.

—— 'The Freemasons' Pocket Companions of the Eighteenth Century', *Ars Quatuor Coronatorum*, 45 (1932), 165–231.

Addison, William, *The Renewed Church of the United Brethren, 1722–1930* (London: Society for Promoting Christian Knowledge, 1932).

Adlard, John, 'A Blake Poem', *Times Literary Supplement* (21 September 1984), 1055.

Allan, D. G. C., *William Shipley: Founder of the Royal Society of Arts*, rev. edn (1968; London: Scolar, 1979).

Altick, Richard, *The Shows of London* (Cambridge, MA Harvard / Belknap, 1978).

Angelo, Henry, *Angelo's Pic-Nic* (London: Thomas Kelly, 1834).

—— *The Reminiscences of Henry Angelo*, eds. Lord Howard de Walden and H. Lavers Smith (London: Kegan Paul, 1904).

Antes, John, 'Extract of the Narrative of the Life of our late dear Brother, John Antes, Written by Himself', *Periodical Accounts Relating to the Missions of the Church of the United Brethren Established Among the Heathen*, 20 (1851), 155ff.

—— *Observations on the Manners and Customs of the Egyptians* (1799; Dublin: John Jones, 1801).

Atwood, Craig, 'Blood, Sex, and Death: Life and Liturgy in Zinzendorf's Bethlehem' (Ph.D. dissertation: Princeton University, 1995).

—— *Community of the Cross: Moravian Piety in Colonial Bethlehem* (University Park: Pennsylvania State UP, 2004).

—— Sleeping in the Arms of Jesus: Sanctifying Sexuality in the Eighteenth-Century Moravian Church', *Journal of the History of Sexuality*, 8 (1997), 25–51.

—— 'Zinzendorf's Litany of the Wounds of the Husband', *Lutheran Quarterly*, 11 (1997), 189–214.

—— 'Zinzendorf's 1749 Reprimand to the *Brüdergemeine*', *Transactions of the Moravian Historical Society*, 29 (1996), 59–84.

—— and Vogt, Peter, *The Distinctiveness of Moravian Culture: Essays and Documents in Moravian History in Honor of Vernon H. Nelson on his Seventieth Birthday* (Nazareth, PA: Moravian Historical Society, 2003).

Bach, Jeff, *Voices in the Wilderness: The Sacred World of Ephrata* (University Park: Pennsylvania State UP, 2003).

Baker, David Erskine, and Reed, Isaac, *Biographica Dramatica* (1812; rpt. New York: AMS, 1966).

Banks, Joseph, *The Banks Letters*, ed. W. R. Dawson (London: British Museum, 1958).

Barberi, Monsignor, *The Life of Joseph Balsamo, Commonly Called the Count Cagliostro* (Dublin, 1792).

Barnett, Gerald, *Richard and Maria Cosway* (Tiverton: West Country Books, 1995).

Barnett, R. D., 'The Correspondence of the Mahamad', *Transactions of the Jewish Historical Society of England*, 20 (1959–60), 22–3.

Beckford, William, *The Valuable Library of Books in Fonthill Abbey* (London: Phillips, 9 September–23 October 1823).

Beer, John, 'Blake's Changing View of History: The Impact of the Book of Enoch', in Steve Clark and David Worrall, eds, *Historicizing Blake* (New York: St Martin's, 1994), 159–78.

Belcher, William, *Intellectual Electricity, Novum Organum of Vision, and Grand Mystic System . . . by a Rational Mystic* (London, 1798).

Benham, Daniel, *Memoirs of James Hutton* (London: Hamilton, Adams, 1856).

Bennett, Shelley, *Thomas Stothard: The Mechanisms of Art Patronage in England circa 1800* (Columbia: Missouri UP, 1985).

Bentley, Gerald E., *A Bibliography of George Cumberland (1754–1848)* (New York: Garland, 1975).

—— *Blake Records* (Oxford: Clarendon, 1969).
—— *Blake Records*, 2nd edn (New Haven: Yale UP, 2004).
—— *Blake Records Supplement* (Oxford: Clarendon, 1988).
—— 'The Daughters of Albion and the Butts Household', *Blake: An Illustrated Quarterly*, 18 (1984), 116.
—— 'A Jewel in an Ethiop's Ear: The Book of Enoch as Inspiration for William Blake, John Flaxman, Thomas Moore, and Richard Westall', in Robert Essick and Donald Pierce, eds, *Blake in His Time* (Bloomington: Indiana UP, 1978), 213–40.
—— 'Mainaduc, Magic, and Madness: George Cumberland and the Blake Connection', *Notes and Queries*, 236 (September 1991), 294–6.
—— *Stranger from Paradise: A Biography of William Blake* (New Haven: Yale UP, 2001).
—— 'Thomas Butts, White Collar Maecenas', *PMLA: Publications of the Modern Language Association*, 71 (1956), 1052–66.
Bereti, Francis, *Pascal Paoli à Maria Cosway: Lettres et Documents, 1782–1803* (Oxford: Voltaire Foundation, 2003).
Bergquist, Lars, *Swedenborgs Hemlighet* (Stockholm: Natur och Kultur, 1999).
Bernier, François, *Travels in the Mogul Empire (1670)*, trans. Irving Brock; rev. edn Archibald Constable (1891; Delhi: S. Chand, 1969).
Beyreuther, Eric, 'Zinzendorf und das Judentum', *Judaica*, 19 (1963), 193–246.
Biale, David, *Eros and the Jews* (New York: Basic Books, 1992).
Bienville, D. T. de, *Nymphomania, or, A Dissertation Concerning the Furor Uterinus*, trans. E. S. Wilmot (London: J. Pew, 1775).
Bindman, David, *Blake as an Artist* (Oxford: Phaidon, 1977).
—— *John Flaxman* (London: Thames and Hudson, 1979).
Blake, William, *Blake: Complete Writings*, 2nd rev. edn, ed. Geoffrey Keynes (1966; Oxford: Oxford UP, 1985).

—— *The Complete Poetry and Prose of William Blake*, rev. edn, eds. David Erdman and Harold Bloom (1965; New York: Doubleday, 1988).

—— *The Early Illuminated Books*, eds. Morris Eaves, Robert Essick and Joseph Viscomi (London: Tate Gallery, 1993).

—— *The Four Zoas by William Blake*, eds. Cettina Tramontano Magno and David Erdman (Lewisburg: Bucknell UP, 1987).

—— *An Island in the Moon*, ed. Michael Phillips (Cambridge: Cambridge UP, 1987).

—— *Jerusalem, The Emanation of the Giant Albion*, ed. Morton Paley (Princeton: Princeton UP, 1991).

—— *Milton a Poem*, eds. Robert Essick and Joseph Viscomi (London: Tate Gallery, 1993).

Blunt, Reginald, *Mrs Montague: Queen of the Blues* (London: Constable, 1923).

Bogen, Nancy, 'The Problem of William Blake's Early Religion', *The Personalist*, 49 (1968), 509–20.

Borneman, Henry, *Pennsylvania German Illuminated Manuscripts* (Norristown: Pennsylvania German Society, 1937).

Brodie, Fawn, *Thomas Jefferson: An Intimate Portrait* (New York: W. W. Norton, 1974).

Brown, A. Stuart, 'Gustavus Katterfelto: Mason and Magician', *Ars Quatuor Coronatorum*, 69 (1956), 136–8.

Bruce, James, *Travels to Discover the Source of the Nile* (Edinburgh / London: Ruthven, J. Robinson, 1790).

Butlin, Martin, *The Paintings and Drawings of William Blake* (New Haven: Yale UP, 1981).

—— 'Six New Early Drawings by William Blake and a Reattribution', *Blake: An Illustrated Quarterly*, 23 (1989), 107–12.

Campresi, Piero, *Juice of Life: The Symbolic and Magic Significance of Blood*, trans. Robert Barr; introd. Umberto Eco (New York: Continuum, 1995).

Carlebach, Elisheva, *Divided Souls: Converts from Judaism in Germany, 1500–1700* (New Haven: Yale UP, 2001).

—— *The Pursuit of Heresy: Rabbi Moses Hagiz and the Sabbatian Controversies* (New York: Columbia UP, 1990).

Casanova, Giacomo, *History of My Life*, trans. Willard Trask (New York: Harcourt, Brace, and World, 1966).

Castle, Terry, 'Phantasmagoria: Spectral Technology and the Metaphorics of Modern Reverie', *Critical Inquiry*, 15 (1998), 26–61.

Cennick, John, *An Account of a Late Riot at Exeter* (London: printed by J. Hart and sold by J. Lewis, 1745).

—— *The Life of Mr John Cennick*, 2nd edn (Bristol: printed for the author, 1745).

—— *Sacred Hymns for the Children of God in the Days of their Pilgrimage* (London: B. Miller, 1741).

Chastanier, Benedict, *Journal Novi-Jerusalemite* (London, 1788–9).

—— *Plan Général d'une Société Universelle* (London: Robert Hawes, 1782).

—— *Tableau Analytique et Raisonée de la Doctrine Celéste* (London, 1786).

—— *A Word of Advice to a Benighted World* (London, 1795).

Chetty, D. Gopaul, *New Light Upon Indian Philosophy: or Swedenborg and Saiva Siddhanta* (London: J. M. Dent, 1923).

Clarke, Michael, and Penny, Stephen, eds, *The Arrogant Connoisseur: Richard Payne Knight, 1751–1824* (Manchester: Manchester UP, 1982).

Cohen, Jeffrey, and Brownell, Charles, *The Architectural Drawings of Benjamin Henry Latrobe* (New Haven: Yale UP, 1994).

Colebrook, Henry T., 'Enumeration of Indian Classes', *Asiatic Researches*, 5 (Calcutta, 1798).

—— *Essays on the Religion and Philosophy of the Hindus*, ed. Michael Franklin (1837; rpt. London: Ganeesha, 2001).

A Collection of Hymns of the Children of God in All Ages . . .

Designed Chiefly for the Use of the Congregations in Union with the Brethren's Church (London, 1754).

Colquhoun, J. C., trans., *Report of the Experiments on Animal Magnetism* (Edinburgh: Robert Cadell, 1833).

Colson, Percy, *The Strange History of Lord George Gordon* (London: Robert Hale, 1937).

Connolly, Tristanne, *William Blake and the Body* (New York: Palgrave Macmillan, 2002).

Cosway, Richard, *Catalogue of the Very Curious, Extensive and Valuable Library of Richard Cosway, R.A.* (London: Stanley, 1821).

Coudert, Allison, *The Impact of the Kabbalah in the Seventeenth Century: The Life and Thought of Francis Mercury Van Helmont, 1614–1698* (Leiden: Brill, 1999).

Cranz, David, *The Ancient and Modern History of the Brethren*, trans. Benjamin La Trobe (London: W. and A. Strahan, 1780).

Crawley, Chetwode, 'The Chevalier d'Eon', *Ars Quatuor Coronatorum*, 16 (1908), 231–51.

Créquinière, M. de la., *The Agreement of the Customs of the East-Indians with Those of the Jews*, trans. John Toland, introd. Joel Reid (1705; facs. rpt. New York: AMS, 1999).

Cumberland, George, *The Captive of the Castle of Senaar* (London: Egerton, 1798).

—— *A Catalogue of the Collection of Books on Art . . . of George Cumberland* (London: Christie and Mason, 6 May 1835).

—— *Thoughts on Outline* (London: W. Wilson, 1796).

Dalman, Gustaf, 'Documente eines Christlichen Geheimbundes unter den Juden im achtzehnen Jarhhundert', *Saat und Hoffnung. Zeitschrift für die Mission der Kirche an Israel*, 12, (1890), 18–37.

—— and Schulze, Diakonus, *Zinzendorf und Lieberkuhn: Studien der Geschichte der Judenmission* (Leipzig: J. E. Hinrich, 1903).

Damon, S. Foster, *A Blake Dictionary* (1965; London: Thames and Hudson, 1973).

Damrosch, Leopold, *Symbol and Truth in Blake's Myth* (Princeton: Princeton UP, 1980).

Danilewicz, M. L. 'The King of the New Israel: Thaddeus Grabianka (1740–1897)', *Oxford Slavonic Papers*, n.s. 1 (1968), 49–74.

Daniell, Frederick, *A Catalogue Raisonné of the Engraved Works of Richard Cosway* (London: Daniell, 1890).

Daniels, Stephen, 'Loutherbourg's Chemical Theatre: Coalbrook at Night', in John Barrell, ed., *Painting and the Politics of Culture: New Essays on British Art, 1700–1850* (Oxford: Oxford UP, 1992), 199–224.

Darnton, Robert, *Mesmerism and the End of the Enlightenment in France* (Cambridge, MA: Harvard UP, 1968).

Davidson, Gustav, *A Dictionary of Angels* (New York: Free Press, 1967).

Davidson, Ronald M., *Indian Esoteric Buddhism: A Social History of the Tantric Movement* (New York: Columbia UP, 2002).

Davies, Keri, 'William Blake in Contexts: Family, Friendships and Some Intellectual Microcultures of Eighteenth- and Nineteenth-Century England' (Ph.D. dissertation: University of Surrey, 2003).

—— 'William Blake's Mother: A New Identification', *Blake: An Illustrated Quarterly*, 33 (1999), 36–50.

—— 'William Muir and the Blake Press at Edmonton with Muir's Letters to Kerriston Preston', *Blake: An Illustrated Quarterly*, 27 (1993), 14–25.

—— and Schuchard, Marsha Keith, 'Recovering the Lost Moravian History of William Blake's Family', *Blake: An Illustrated Quarterly*, 38 (2004), 36–43.

Davis, Richard, 'Becoming a Siva and Acting as One, in Saiva Worship', in Teun Goudrian, ed., *Ritual and Speculation in*

Early Tantrism: Studies in Honour of André Prevoux (Delhi: Sri Satguru, 1993).

Deck, Raymond, 'New Light on C. A. Tulk, Blake's 19th Century Patron', *Studies in Romanticism*, 16 (1977), 217–36.

Deghaye, Pierre, *La Doctrine Ésotérique de Zinzendorf* (Paris: Klincksieck, 1969).

Dermott, Laurence, *Ahiman Rezon* (1756; facs. rpt. Bloomington: Masonic Book Club, 1972).

Dithmar, Christiane, *Zinzendorfs Nonkonformistische Haltung zum Judentum* (Heidelberg: C. Winter, 2000).

Dole, George, 'Philosemitism in the Seventeenth Century', *Studia Swedenborgiana*, 7 (1990), 5–17.

Edenborg, Carl-Michael, *Alkemins Skam* (Stockholm: Caudex, 2002).

—— *Fabian Wilhelm af Ekenstam och Mötet Mellan Romantiken och Alekemin* (Stockholm: Stockholms Universitet, 1994).

Eliade, Mircea, *Yoga: Immortality and Freedom*, trans. Willard Trask (Princeton: Princeton UP, 1969).

Ellis, Edwin, *The Real Blake* (London: Chatto & Windus, 1907).

—— and Yeats, William Butler, *The Works of William Blake* (1893; rpt. New York: AMS, 1973).

Ellis, Samuel, *Life, Times and Character of James Montgomery* (London: Jackson, Walford and Hodder, 1864).

Ellmann, Richard, *W. B. Yeats's Second Puberty* (Washington: Library of Congress, 1985).

Eon, Chevalier d', *Catalogue of the Scarce Books and Valuable Manuscripts of the Chevalier d'Eon* (London: Christie's, 1791).

Erbe, Hans-Walter, 'Herrnhaag: Eine religiöse Kommunität im 18 Jahrhundert', *Unitas Fratrum*, 23/24 (1988), 13–224.

—— 'Herrnhaag – Tiefpunkt oder Höhepunkt der Brüdergeschichte', *Unitas Fratrum*, 26 (1989), 37–51.

Erdman, David, *Blake: Prophet Against Empire*, rev. edn (1954; Princeton: Princeton UP, 1969).

—— 'Blake's Early Swedenborgianism: A Twentieth-Century Legend', *Comparative Literature*, 5 (1953), 247–57.

—— *The Illuminated Blake* (London: Oxford UP, 1975).

—— 'William Blake's Debt to James Gillray', *Art Quarterly*, 12 (1949), 165–70.

—— and Moore, Donald, *The Notebook of William Blake* (Oxford: Clarendon, 1973).

Essick, Robert, 'Blake in the Market Place', *Blake: An Illustrated Quarterly*, 37 (2004), 120.

—— 'William Blake's "The Phoenix": a Problem in Attribution', *Philological Quarterly*, 67 (1988), 378.

—— and Paley, Morton, '"Dear Generous Cumberland": A Newly Discovered Letter and Poem by William Blake', *Blake: An Illustrated Quarterly*, 32 (1998), 4–12.

Faivre, Antoine, *Eckartshausen et la Théosophie Chrétienne* (Paris: Klincksieck, 1969).

Fara, Patricia, 'An Attractive Therapy: Animal Magnetism in Eighteenth-Century England', *History of Science*, 23 (1995), 127–77.

Farington, Joseph, *The Diary of Joseph Farington*, eds. K. Garlick and A. Macintyre (New Haven: Yale UP, 1978).

Ferrand, Jacques, *A Treatise on Lovesickness*, trans. and ed. Donald Beecher and Massimo Ciavollella (1640; Syracuse: Syracuse UP, 1900).

Feurstein, George, *Tantra: The Path of Ecstasy* (Boston: Shambala, 1998).

Flaxman, John, *A Catalogue of a Valuable Assemblage of Engravings . . . of the late John Flaxman, R.A.* (London: Christie's, 1 July 1828).

Fogleman, Aaron, 'Jesus is Female: The Moravian Challenge in the German Communities of British North America', *The*

William and Mary Quarterly, 60 (2003), 295–332.

Foster, Roy, *W. B. Yeats: A Life, II: The Arch-Poet* (Oxford: Oxford UP, 2003).

Freeman, Arthur J., *An Ecumenical Theology of the Heart: The Theology of Count Nicholas Ludwig von Zinzendorf* (Bethlehem, PA: Moravian Church in America, 1998).

Freeman, Rosemary, *English Emblem Books* (New York: Octagon, 1966).

Frey, Andrew, *A True and Authentic Account: Containing the Occasion of his Coming among the Herrnhutters or Moravians*, trans. from German (London: J. Robinson, 1753).

Frick, Karl, *Die Erleuchteten* (Graz: Akademische Druck-u. Verlagsandstadt, 1973).

Garrett, Clarke, *Respectable Folly: Millenarians and the French Revolution* (Baltimore: Johns Hopkins UP, 1975).

—— 'The Spiritual Odyssey of Jacob Duché', *Proceedings of the American Philosophical Society*, 119 (1975), 143–55.

Garrison, Omar, *Tantra: The Yoga of Sex* (London: Academy Editions, 1972).

Ghosh, Shyam, *The Original Yoga* (Delhi: Munshiram Nahoharlal Publishers, 1980).

Gibbons, B. J., *Gender in Mystical and Occult Thought: Boehmenism and its Development in England* (Cambridge: Cambridge UP, 1996).

Gilchrist, Alexander, *Life of William Blake, 'Pictor Ignotus'* (London: Macmillan, 1863; rev. edn 1880; ed. Ruthven Todd, 1942).

Ginzburg, Simon, *The Life and Times of Moses Hayim Luzzatto* (Philadelphia: Dropsie College, 1931).

Godfrey, Richard, and Hallet, Mark, *James Gillray: The Art of Caricature* (London: Tate Gallery, 2001).

Goyder, D. G., *A Concise History of the New Jerusalem Church* (London: Thomas Goyder, 1829).

Gradin, Arvid, *A Short History of the Bohemian-Moravian Church*

(London: J. Hutton, 1743).

Graham, James, *A Clear, Full, and Faithful Portraiture . . . of a Certain Most Beautiful and Spotless Virgin Princess* (Bath: R. Cruttwell, 1792).

—— *A Discourse . . . [on] the Nature, and Manner of the Resurrection of the Human Body*, 5th rev. edn (1783; Hull: T. Briggs, 1787).

—— *The General State of Medical and Chirurgical Practices Exhibited*, 6th edn (Bath, 1778).

Grant, John, 'Visions in *Vala*: a Consideration of some Pictures in the Manuscript', in Stuart Curran and Joseph Wittreich, eds, *Blake's Sublime Allegory* (Madison: Wisconsin UP, 1973), 141–202.

Grimm, Baron, *Lettres de Grimm à l'Impératrice Catherine II*, 2nd rev. edn, ed. Jacques Grot (St Petersburg, 1884).

Haensal, John Gottfried, *Letters on the Nicobar Islands . . . to the Reverend C. I. Latrobe* (London: Fetter Lane, 1812).

Hahn, Hans-Christoph, and Reichel, Helmut, *Zinzendorf und die Herrnhuter Brüder* (Hamburg: Friedrich Wittig, 1977).

Häll, Jan, *I Swedenborgs Labyrint: Studier i de Gustavianska Swedenborgarnes Liv och Tänande* (Stockholm: Atlantis, 1995).

Hallengren, Anders, 'The Secret of Great Tartary', *Arcana*, 1 (1995), 35–54.

Hamilton, Emma, Lady, *Memoirs of Emma Lady Hamilton*, ed. W. H. Long (1815; Philadelphia: Lippincott, 1891).

Hamilton, J. Taylor, and Hamilton, Kenneth G., *History of the Moravian Church* (Bethlehem, PA: Moravian Board of Christian Education, 1967).

Hamilton-Jones, J. W., *Bacstrom's Alchemical Anthology* (London: J. M. Watkins, 1960).

Hamlin, Talbot, *Benjamin Henry Latrobe* (New York: Oxford UP, 1955).

Hancarville, Baron dé [Hugues, Pierre François], *Antiquité Étrusque, Gréques, et Romaines* (Paris: F. A. David, 1787).

—— *Collection of Etruscan, Greek and Roman Antiquities from the Cabinet of the Hon'ble William Hamilton* (Naples, 1766–7).

—— *Monumens du Culte Secret des Dames Romaines* (1777; rpt. Rome: de la Imprimerie du Vatican, 1787).

—— *Recherches sur l'Origine, l'Esprit, et les Progrés des Arts de la Gréce* (London: B. Appleyard, 1785).

—— *Veneres et Priapi* ([London], 1784).

Harris, James, *Hermes, or a Philosophical Inquiry Concerning Universal Grammar*, 3rd rev. edn (London: John Nourse and Paul Vaillant, 1771).

Haskell, Francis, 'Baron d'Hancarville: an Adventurer and Art Historian in Eighteenth-Century Europe', in his *Past and Present in Art and Taste: Selected Essays* (New Haven: Yale UP, 1987).

Hayley, William, *A Catalogue of the . . . Library of the Late William Hayley* (London: Evans, 1821; facs. rpt. in A. N. L. Munby, ed., *Sale Catalogues of the Libraries of Prominent Persons* (London: Sotheby Parke-Bernet, 1971–5), II.

—— *A Philosophical, Historical and Moral Essay on Old Maids* (London: T. Cadell, 1785).

Henderson, B. L. K., *Romney* (New York: Frederick Stokes, 1922).

Heppner, Christopher, 'Blake's "New Jerusalem Descending": a Drawing Identified', *Blake: An Illustrated Quarterly*, 20 (1986), 4–11.

Herbert, Thomas, *Some Years Travels into Diverse Parts of Africa and Asia* (London, 1665).

Higham, Charles, 'Blake and the Swedenborgians', *Notes and Queries*, 11 (1915), 276–7.

—— 'Francis Barthelemon', *New Church Magazine*, 15 (1896), 1–13.

—— 'James Glen: the New Church Pioneer and Hermit', *New Church Review*, 19 (1912), 532–72.

Hill, Draper, *Fashionable Contrasts: Caricatures by James Gillray* (London: Phaidon, 1966).

Hills, Gordon P., 'Notes on the Rainsford Papers in the British Museum', *Ars Quatuor Coronatorum*, 26 (1913), 93–129.

—— 'Notes on Some Contemporary References to Dr Falk, the Baal Shem of London, in the Rainsford MSS. in the British Museum', *Transactions of Jewish Historical Society of England*, 8 (1915–17), 122–8.

—— 'Notes on Some Masonic Personalities at the End of the Eighteenth Century', *Ars Quatuor Coronatorum*, 141–64.

Hilton, Nelson, 'Some Sexual Connotations', *Blake: An Illustrated Quarterly* (Winter 1982–3), 166–71.

Hindmarsh, Robert, *Rise and Progress of the New Jerusalem Church* (London: Hodgson, 1861).

Holland, John, and Everett, James, eds, *Memoirs of the Life and Writings of James Montgomery* (London: Longmans, 1854).

Hugo, Hermann, *Pia Desideria* (1624; Antwerp: Henry Aertssens, 1632).

Hurd, William, *A New and Universal History of Religious Rites, Ceremonies and Customs of the Whole World*, rev. edn (1788; London: Blackburn, Hemingway, 1799).

[Hutton, James], ed., *A Collection of Hymns: Consisting Chiefly of Translations from the German Hymnbook of the Moravian Brethren*, Part III, 2nd edn (London: James Hutton, Bookseller in Fetter Lane, 1749).

Hyde, James, 'Benedict Chastanier and the Illuminati of Avigon', *New Church Review*, 14 (1907), 181–205.

—— *A Bibliography of the Works of Emanuel Swedenborg* (1906; facs. rpt. London: Swedenborg Society, 2002).

—— 'Some Notes Respecting Robert Hindmarsh', *New Church Magazine* (March 1905), 118–19.

Idel, Moshe, 'Sexual Metaphors and Praxis in the Kabbalah', in David Kraemer, ed., *The Jewish Family: Metaphor and Memory* (Oxford: Oxford UP, 1989), 199–204.

Jacob, Margaret, *Living the Enlightenment: Freemasonry and Politics in Eighteenth-Century Europe* (New York: Oxford UP, 1991).

Jacobs, Louis, *Jewish Mystical Testimonies* (New York: Schocken, 1977).

—— *Their Heads in Heaven: Unfamiliar Aspects of Hasidism* (London: Valentine Mitchell, 2005).

Jefferson, Thomas, *The Papers of Thomas Jefferson*, ed. Julian Boyd (Princeton: Princeton UP, 1950).

Joly, Alice, 'La "Sainte Parole" des Illuminés d'Avignon', *La Tour Saint-Jacques*, 2–4 (1960), 98–116.

Jonsson, Inge, 'Köpenhamn–Amsterdam–Paris: Swedenborgs Resa 1737–1738', *Lychnos* (1967–8), 30–76.

Joppien, Rüdiger, *Philippe Jacques de Loutherbourg, R.A.* (London: Greater London Council, 1973).

Joys of Hymen, or the Conjugal Directory (London: D. Davis, 1768).

Kahl, Achatius, 'La Nouvelle Église dans ses Rélations avec la Franc-maçonnerie', in Johan Tybeck, ed., *Le Nouveau Salem* (Basle, 1871), 128–48.

Keynes, Geoffrey, *Blake Studies*, 2nd ed (Oxford: Clarendon, 1971).

—— *The Complete Portraiture of William and Catherine Blake* ([Clairvaux]: Trianon, 1977).

—— 'An Unpublished Poem by William Blake', *Times Literary Supplement* (14 September 1984), 1021.

Knight, Richard Payne, *An Account of the Remains of the Worship of Priapus* (London: T. Spilsbury, 1786).

Kripal, Jeffrey, *Kali's Child: The Mystical and the Erotic in the*

Life and Teaching of Ramakrishna, 2nd edn (1995; Chicago: Chicago UP, 1998).

Kroyer, Peter, *The Story of Lindsey House, Chelsea* (London: Country Life, 1956).

Lachower, Fischel, and Tishby, Isaiah, *The Wisdom of the Zohar*, trans. David Goldstein (Oxford: Oxford UP, 1989).

Lane, John, 'The Symbolic Chart of 1789', *Ars Quatuor Coronatorum*, 3 (1890), 109.

Larsen, Robin, ed., *Emanuel Swedenborg: A Continuing Vision* (New York: Swedenborg Foundation, 1988).

Latrobe, Benjamin Henry, *The Correspondence and Miscellaneous Papers of Benjamin Henry Latrobe*, ed. John C. Van Horne and Lee W. Formwalt (New Haven: Yale UP, 1984).

—— *The Virginia Journals of Benjamin Henry Latrobe*, ed. Edward Carter (New Haven: Yale UP, 1977).

Lau, Beth, 'William Godwin and the Joseph Johnson Circle: the Evidence of the Diaries', *Wordsworth Circle*, 33 (2002), 106.

Laurence, Richard, *The Book of Enoch the Prophet . . . now first Translated from an Ethiopic MS. in the Bodleian Library*, 2nd rev. edn (1821; Oxford: J. H. Parker, 1838).

Lee, Francis, *A Letter to Some Divines, concerning the Question, whether God since Christ's Ascension, doth anymore reveal Himself to Mankind by the Means of Divine Apparitions* (London, 1695).

Lehmann, E. Arno, *It Began At Tranquebar*, trans. M. J. Lutz (London: Christian Literature Society, 1956).

Levellet-Haig, Genevieve, 'Philippe Jacques de Loutherbourg, 1740–1813', *Archives Alsaciennes d'Histoire de l'Art*, n.s. 27 (1948), 77–134.

Lewis, A. J., *Zinzendorf: The Ecumenical Pioneer* (Philadelphia: Westminster, 1962).

Liebes, Yehudah, 'A Crypto Judaeo-Christian Sect of Sabbatian Origin', *Tarbiz*, 57 (1988), 110, 349–84. [Hebrew.]

Lindh, F. G., 'Swedenborgs Ekonomi', *Nya Kyrkans Tidning* (May 1927 – October 1929).

Lindner, Erich, *The Royal Art Illustrated*, trans. Arthur Lindsay (Graz: Akademische Drück, 1976).

Lindsay, Jack, *William Blake: His Life and Work* (London: Constable, 1978).

Lines, Richard, 'Charles Augustus Tulk – Swedenborgian Extraordinary', *Arcana*, 3 (1997), 5–32.

Lisebeth, André Van, *Tantra: The Cult of the Feminine* (1992; York Beach: Samuel Weiser, 1995).

Lloyd, Stephen, 'The Accomplished Maria Cosway: Anglo-Italian Artist, Musician, Salon Hostess and Educationalist,' *Journal of Anglo-Italian Studies*, 2 (1992), 108–39.

—— 'The Life and Art of Richard Cosway, R.A. (1742–1821) and Maria Cosway (1760–1838)' (Ph.D. dissertation: Oxford University, 1995).

—— 'Richard Cosway: the Artist as Collector, Connoisseur and *Virtuoso*', *Apollo* (June 1991), 398–405.

—— *Richard and Maria Cosway: Regency Artists of Taste and Fashion* (Edinburgh: Scottish National Portrait Gallery, 1995).

Lockwood, J. P., *Memorials of the Life of Peter Boehler, Bishop of the Church of the Brethren*, introd. Thomas Jackson (London: Wesleyan Conference Office, 1868).

Long, Basil, *British Miniaturists* (London, Geoffrey Bles, 1929).

Lowery, Margaret, *Windows of the Morning: A Critical Study of William Blake's Poetical Sketches* (New Haven: Yale UP, 1940).

Lucia, *The Life of Count Cagliostro* (London: T. Hookham, 1787).

Luzzatto, Moses Chaim, *Derech ha Shem: The Way of God*, trans. A. Kaplan (Jerusalem / New York: Feldman, 1977).

McCalman, Iain, *The Last Alchemist: Count Cagliostro, Master of Magic in the Age of Reason* (New York: HarperCollins, 2003).

McIntosh, Christopher, *The Rose Cross and the Age of Reason* (Leiden: Brill, 1992).

—— *The Rosicrucians: The History, Mythology and Rituals of an Occult Order*, 2nd rev. edn (1980; Wellingborough: Crucible, 1987).

Mackenzie, Kenneth, *The Royal Masonic Cyclopaedia*, introd. Robert Gilbert and John Hamill (1877; Wellingborough: Aquarian, 1987).

McLean, Adam, 'Bacstrom's Rosicrucian Society', *Hermetic Journal*, 6 (1979), 25–9.

McLynn, Frank, *Charles Edward Stuart: A Tragedy in Many Acts* (1988; Oxford: Oxford UP, 1991).

Madan, Martin, *Thelyphthora* (London: J. Dodsley, 1780–1).

Maddox, Brenda, *George's Ghosts: A New Life of W. B. Yeats* (London: Picador, 1999).

Mainaduc, John Bonniot de, *The Lectures of J. B. de Mainaduc* (London, 1798).

Mandel, Arthur, *The Militant Messiah* (Atlantic Highlands: Humanities, 1979).

Mathias, Thomas, *The Pursuits of Literature, a Satirical Poem*, 16th edn (1794–8; London: Becket and Porter, 1812).

Maurice, Thomas, *Indian Antiquities* (London: Elmsley and Richardson, 1792–1800).

—— *Memoirs* (London: Rimington, 1819–20).

Maxted, Ian, *The London Book Trades, 1775–1800* (Folkestone: Dawson, 1977).

Meillassoux-Le Cerf, Micheline, *Dom Pernety et les Illuminés d'Avignon* (Milan: Arché, 1992).

—— 'Dom Pernety (1716–1796) et son Milieu' (Ph.D. dissertation: University of Sorbonne, 1988).

Meteyard, Eliza, *The Life of Josiah Wedgwood* (1866; facs. rpt. London: Cornmarket, 1970).

Meyer, Henry, *Child Nature and Nurture According to Nicolaus Ludwig von Zinzendorf* (New York: Abingdon, 1928).

Meyer, Jacob, *The Story of Moses Haim Luzzatto at Amsterdam, 1736–1743* (Amsterdam: Joachimstael's Boekhandel, 1947).

Montgomery, James, *Poems on the Abolition of the Slave Trade* (London: Bowyer and Bensley, 1809).

—— [Positive, Paul], *Prison Amusements* (London: Joseph Johnson, 1797).

—— *The Wanderer of Switzerland and Other Poems* (London: Verner and Hood, 1806).

Moor, Edward, *The Hindu Pantheon* (London: Joseph Johnson, 1810).

—— *A Narrative of the Operations of Captain Little's Detachment, and of the Mahratta Army* (London: Joseph Johnson, 1794).

—— *Oriental Fragments* (London: Smith and Elder, 1834).

Morris, H. N., *Flaxman, Blake, Coleridge and Other Men of Genius Influenced by Swedenborg* (London: New Church, 1915).

Mossiker, Frances, *The Queen's Necklace* (New York: Simon & Schuster, 1961).

Murr, Christoph Gottlieb von, *Über den wahren Ursprung der Rosenkreutzer und des Freymaurerordens* (Sulzbach: J. E. Semler, 1803).

Murray, E. B., 'Thel, *Thelyphthora*, and the Daughters of Albion', *Studies in Romanticism*, 20 (1981), 275–97.

Nelson, Philip K., *Carl-Bernhard Wadström: Mannes Bakomyten* (Norrköping: Föreningen Gamla Norrköping, 1998).

Nelson, Vernon, *Johan Valentin Haidt* (Williamsburg: Abby Aldrich Rockefeller Folk Collection, 1966).

—— 'John Valentin Haidt's Theory of Painting', *Transactions of the Moravian Historical Society*, 13 (1984), 71–8.

Niekamp, Johann Lucas, *Missions-Geschichte* (Halle, 1740).

Nixon, Edna, *Royal Spy: The Strange Case of the Chevalier d'Eon* (New York: Reynal, 1965).

[Nordenskjöld, Augustus], *Plan for a Free Community Upon the Coast of Africa* (London: Robert Hindmarsh, 1790).

Nordmann, Claude, *Grandeur et Liberté de la Suède (1660–1792)* (Paris: Beatrice-Nauwelaerts, 1971).

Norris, John, *The Theory and Regulation of Love* (London, 1688).

Odhner, Carl Theophilus, 'Swedenborg's Dreams or Diary of 1744', *New Church Life*, 34 (1914).

Oliver, J. W., *The Life of William Beckford* (London: Oxford UP, 1932).

Onania, 15th edn (London: J. Isted, 1750).

Oron, Michal, 'Dr Samuel Jacob Falk and the Eibeschuetz-Emden Controversy', in Joseph Dan and Karl Grözinger, eds, *Mysticism, Magic, and Kabbalah in Ashkenazic Judaism* (New York: Walter de Gruyter, 1995), 243–56.

—— *Miba'al Shed Leba' al Shem: Schmuel Falk, Haba'al Shem Mi-London* (Jerusalem: Mosad Bialik, 2003). [Hebrew.]

Otto, Peter, *Blake's Critique of Transcendence: Love, Jealousy, and the Sublime in The Four Zoas* (Oxford: Oxford UP, 2000).

—— 'A Pompous High Priest: Urizen's Ancient Phallic Religion', *Blake: An Illustrated Quarterly*, 34 (2001), 4–22.

Paley, Morton, 'A New Heaven is Begun: William Blake and Swedenborgianism', *Blake: An Illustrated Quarterly*, 12 (1979), 64–90.

—— *Traveller in the Evening: The Last Works of William Blake* (Oxford: Oxford UP, 2003).

—— 'William Blake, the Prince of the Hebrews, and the Woman Clothed with the Sun', in Morton Paley and Michael Phillips, eds, *William Blake: Essays in Honour of Sir Geoffrey Keynes* (Oxford: Clarendon, 1973), 260–93.

Pasquin, Anthony [John Williams], *Memoirs of the Royal Academicians* (London: H. D. Symonds, 1796).

—— *The Royal Academicians: A Farce* (London, 1786).

Patai, Raphael, *The Hebrew Goddess* (New York: Ktav, 1967).

—— *The Jewish Alchemists* (Princeton: Princeton UP, 1994).

Peucker, Paul, '"Blut auf unsre grüne Bänchen": Die Sichtungzeit in der Herrnhuter Brüdergemeine', *Unitas Fratrum*, 49/50 (2002), 41–94.

—— '"Inspired by Flames of Love": Homosexuality and 18th Century Moravian Brothers,' *The Journal of the History of Sexuality* (forthcoming).

—— 'Kreuzbilder und Wundenmalerei: Form und Funktion in der Herrnhuter Brüdergemeine um 1750', *Unitas Fratrum*, 55/56 (2005), 125–74.

—— and Stephen Augustin, eds, *Grah ohne Grenze: Leben und Werke von Nikolaus Ludwig von Zinzendorf* (Herrnhut: Unitätsarchiv / Comenius Buchhandlung, 2000).

Pevsner, Nickolaus, 'Richard Payne Knight', *Art Bulletin*, 31 (1949), 293–309.

Photiades, Constantin, *Count Cagliostro*, trans. K. S. Shelvankar (London: Rider, 1932).

Pindar, Peter [John Wolcot], *More Lyric Odes to the Royal Academicians for 1783* (London, 1783).

Podmore, Colin, 'The Fetter Lane Society, 1738–1740', *Proceedings of the Wesley Historical Society*, 46 (1988), 125–53; 47 (1989), 156–81.

—— *The Moravian Church in England, 1728–1760* (Oxford: Clarendon, 1998).

Podmore, Frank, *From Mesmer to Christian Science* (New York: University Books, 1963).

Porter, Roy, *The Facts of Life: The Creation of Sexual Knowledge in Britain, 1650–1950* (New Haven: Yale UP, 1995).

—— 'Sex and the Singular Man: The Seminal Ideas of James Graham', *Studies on Voltaire and the Eighteenth Century*, 228 (1948), 3–24.

—— 'The Sexual Politics of James Graham', *British Journal for Eighteenth-Century Studies*, 5 (1982), 199–206.

—— 'A Touch of Danger: the Man-Midwife as a Sexual Predator', in Roy Porter and George Rousseau, eds, *Sexual Underworlds of the Enlightenment* (Manchester: Manchester UP, 1987), 206–27.

Praz, Mario, *Studies in Seventeenth-Century Imagery* (London: Warburg Institute, 1939).

Preston, Kerriston, *Blake and Rossetti* (London: Alexander Moring, 1944).

Rainsford, Charles, *A Catalogue of the Valuable Library of Books of Gen. Rainsford. Deceased* (London: Christie, 1809).

The Rambler's Magazine (1783–5).

Redding, Cyrus, *Fifty Years' Recollections* (London, 1858).

Reid, J. M., *Traveller Extraordinary: The Life and Times of James Bruce of Kinnaird* (London: Eyre & Spottiswoode, 1968).

Reincke, Abraham, *A Register of Members of the Moravian Church . . . Between 1727 and 1754* (Bethlehem PA: H. T. Clauder, 1873).

Riehl, Joe, 'Bernard Barton's Contribution to Cunningham's "Life of Blake": a New Letter', *Blake: An Illustrated Quarterly*, 33 (1999), 17–18.

Rimius, Henry, *A Candid Narrative of the Rise and Progress of the Herrnhutters* (London: A. Linde, 1753).

—— *A Solemn Call on Count Zinzendorf* (London: A. Linde, 1754).

—— *A Supplement to the Candid Narrative of the Rise and Progress of the Herrnhutters* (London: A. Linde, 1755).

Robison, John, *Proofs of a Conspiracy Against All the Religions and Governments of Europe, Carried on in the Secret Meetings of the Freemasons, Illuminati and Reading Societies*, 4th rev. edn (London: Caldwell and Davis, 1798).

Rosenfeld, Sybil, 'The *Eidophusikon* Illustrated', *Theatre Notebook*, 18 (1963–4), 52–4.

Rossetti, William Michael, ed., *The Poetical Works of William Blake* (London: G. Bell, 1874).

Roth, Cecil, *Essays and Portraits in Anglo-Jewish History* (Philadelphia: Jewish Publication Society of America, 1962).

Ruan, Fan Fu, *Sex in China* (New York: Plenum, 1991).

Rubens, Alfred, 'Early Anglo-Jewish Artists', *Transactions of Jewish Historical Society of England*, 91–129.

Ruoth, 'Johan Wilhelm von Archenholtz', *Studien Historische*, 131 (1915), 150–7.

Rylands, W. Harry, *Records of the Lodge Original, Number 1, now the Lodge of Antiquity, Number 2*, 2nd rev. edn (London: privately printed, 1928).

Sachse, Julius Frederich, *The German Sectarians of Pennsylvania, 1742–1800* (1899–1900; rpt. New York: AMS, 1971).

Saddlemyer, Anne, *Becoming George: The Life of Mrs W. B. Yeats* (Oxford: Oxford UP, 2002).

Sadler, John, *J. H. Comenius and the Concept of Universal Education* (London: Allen & Unwin, 1963).

Samuel, Edgar, 'Dr Meyer Schomberg's Attacks on the Jews of London, 1746', *Transactions of Jewish Historical Society of England*, 20 (1959–60), 83–111.

Schnorrenberg, 'A True Relation of the Life and Career of James Graham, 1745–1794', *Eighteenth-Century Life*, 15 (1991), 58–75.

Schochet, Elijah, *The Hasidic Movement and the Gaon of Vilna* (Northvale / London: Jason Aronson, 1994).

Schoeps, Hans Joachim, *Barocke Juden, Christen, Judenchristen* (Berne and Munich: Francke, 1965).

Scholem, Gershom, *Du Frankisme au Jacobinisme* (Paris: Le Seul, Gallimard, 1981).

—— *Kabbalah* (New York: Quadrangle / New York Times, 1974).

—— *Major Trends in Jewish Mysticism* (1941; rev. edn New York: Schocken, 1954).

—— *The Messianic Idea in Judaism* (New York: Schocken, 1971).

—— *On the Kabbalah and its Symbolism* (New York: Schocken, 1965).

—— *Sabbatai Zevi: The Mystical Messiah*, trans. R. J. Zwi Werblowsky (Princeton: Princeton UP, 1973).

—— 'Ein verschollener jüdischer Mystiker der Aufklärungzeit in Deutschland: E. J. Hirschfeld', *Yearbook of the Leo Baeck Institute*, 7 (1962), 254–5.

Schuchard, Marsha Keith, 'Blake's Healing Trio: Magnetism, Medicine, and Mania', *Blake: An Illustrated Quarterly*, 23 (1989), 20–31.

—— 'Blake's Mr Femality: Freemasonry, Espionage, and the Double-Sex'd', *Studies in Eighteenth-Century Culture*, 22 (1992), 51–71.

—— 'Blake's *Tiriel* and the Regency Crisis: Lifting the Veil on a Royal Masonic Scandal', in Jackie DeSalvo, G. A. Rosso and Christopher Hobson, eds, *Blake, Politics, and History* (New York: Garland, 1998), 115–35.

—— 'Dr Samuel Jacob Falk: A Sabbatian Adventurer in the Masonic Underground', in Matt Goldish and Richard Popkin, eds, *Millenarianism and Messianism in Early Modern European Culture: Jewish Messianism in the Early Modern World* (Dordrecht: Kluwer Academic, 2001), 203–26.

—— 'Emanuel Swedenborg: Deciphering the Codes of a Terrestrial and Celestial Intelligencer', in Elliot Wolfson, ed., *Rending the Veil: Concealment and Secrecy in the History of Religions* (New York: Seven Bridges, 1999), 177–207.

—— 'Jacobite and Visionary: The Masonic Journey of Emanuel Swedenborg', *Ars Quatuor Coronatorum*, 115 (2003), 33–72.

—— 'Leibniz, Benzelius, and Swedenborg: the Kabbalistic Roots of Swedish Illuminism', in Allison Coudert, Richard

Popkin and Gordon Weiner, eds, *Leibniz, Mysticism, and Religion* (Dordrecht: Kluwer Academic, 1998), 84–106.

—— 'Lord George Gordon and Cabalistic Freemasonry: Beating Jacobite Swords into Jacobin Ploughshares', in Martin Mulsow and Richard Popkin, eds, *Secret Conversions to Judaism in Early Modern Europe* (Leiden: Brill, 2004), 183–231.

—— *Restoring the Temple of Vision: Cabalistic Freemasonry and Stuart Culture* (Leiden: Brill, 2002).

—— 'The Secret Masonic History of Blake's Swedenborg Society', *Blake: An Illustrated Quarterly*, 26 (1992), 40–51.

—— 'Why Mrs Blake Cried: Swedenborg, Blake, and the Sexual Basis of Spiritual Vision', *Esoterica: The Journal of Esoteric Studies*, 2 (2000), 45–93. http.www.esoteric.msu.

—— 'William Blake and the Jewish Swedenborgians', in Sheila Spector, ed., *The Jews and British Romanticism: Politics, Religion, Literature* (London: Palgrave, 2005), 61–86.

—— 'William Blake and the Promiscuous Baboons: A Cagliostroan Séance Gone Awry', *British Journal for Eighteenth-Century Studies*, 18 (1993), 185–200.

—— 'Yeats and the Unknown Superiors: Swedenborg, Falk, and Cagliostro', in Hugh Ormsby-Lennon and Marie Roberts, eds, *Secret Texts: The Literature of Secret Societies* (New York: AMS, 1993), 114–68.

Sessler, Jacob John, *Communal Pietism among Early American Moravians* (New York: Henry Holt, 1933).

Shaw, Miranda, *Passionate Enlightenment: Women in Tantric Buddhism* (Princeton: Princeton UP, 1994).

Sibly, Ebenezer, *The Medical Mirror, or . . . Treatise on the Impregnation of the Human Female*, 2nd edn (London, 1794).

Sigstedt, Cyriel, *The Swedenborg Epic* (New York: Bookman, 1952).

Smaby, Beverly, 'Other Measures to Keep the Candles Lit': The 1752 Transatlantic Travel Journal of Anna Johanna Piesch', in Atwood and Vogt, *Distinctiveness*, 97–120.

Smith, John, *Select Discourses* (1660; facs. rpt. Delmar: Scholars Facsimiles, 1979).

Smith, William, *A Dissertation on the Nerves* (London: W. Owen, 1768).

—— *A Sure Guide to Sickness and Health* (London: J. Bew; J. Walter, 1776).

Sonnerat, M., *Voyage au Indes Orientales et à la Chine* (Paris, 1782).

Spangenberg, August, *The Life of Nicholas Ludwig Count Zinzendorf*, trans. Samuel Jackson (London: Samuel Holdsworth, 1838).

Spector, Sheila, 'Blake's Graphic Use of Hebrew', *Blake: An Illustrated Quarterly*, 37 (2003), 63–79.

—— 'Blake's *Milton* as Kabbalistic Vision', *Religion and Literature*, 25 (1993), 19–33.

—— '*Tiriel* as Spenserian Allegory Manqué', *Philological Quarterly*, 71 (1992), 313–35.

—— *'Wonders Divine': The Development of Blake's Kabbalistic Myth* (Lewisburg: Bucknell UP, 2001).

Speight, George, *The History of the English Puppet Theatre* (London: George Harrap, 1955).

Spence, William, *Essays in Divinity and Physic . . . with an Exposition of Animal Magnetism and Magic* (London: Robert Hindmarsh, 1792).

Stafford, Barbara, *Body Criticism: Imaging the Unseen in Enlightenment Art and Medicine* (Cambridge, MA: Massachusetts Institute of Technology, 1991).

Stead, Geoffrey, 'The Moravian Settlement at Fulneck, 1742–1790', *Publications of the Thoresby Society*, 2nd series, 9 (1998).

—— and Stead, Margaret, *The Exotic Plant: A History of the Moravian Church in Britain, 1742–2000* (Peterborough: Epworth, 2003).

Steinberg, Leo, *The Sexuality of Christ in Renaissance Art and its Modern Oblivion*, 2nd rev. edn (1983; Chicago: Chicago UP, 1996).

Stevenson, David, *The Beggars' Benison: Sex Clubs of Enlightenment Scotland and Their Rituals* (Edinburgh: Tuckwell, 2001).

—— *The Origins of Freemasonry: Scotland's Century, 1590–1710* (Cambridge: Cambridge UP, 1988).

Stinstra, John, *A Pastoral Letter Against Fanaticism*, trans. Henry Rimius (1750; London: A. Linde, 1753).

Stoudt, John Joseph, *Pennsylvania Folk Art* (Allentown: Schlecter, 1948).

Swedenborg, Emanuel, *The Animal Kingdom*, trans. J. J. Garth Wilkinson (London, 1843–4).

—— *The Animal Kingdom, Parts 4 and 5 on Generation*, trans. Alfred Acton (1912; rpt. Philadelphia: Boericke and Tafel, 1955).

—— *The Apocalypse Explained* (New York: American Swedenborg Printing and Publishing Society, 1894).

—— *Catalogus Bibliothecae Emanuelis Swedenborgii*, ed. Alfred Stroh (Holmiae: Aftonbladet, 1907).

—— *The Delights of Wisdom Concerning Conjugial Love*, trans. Alfred Acton (London: Swedenborg Society, 1970).

—— *The Economy of the Animal Kingdom*, trans. A. Clissold (New York: Swedenborg Scientific Association, 1955).

—— *Emanuel Swedenborg's Diary, Recounting Spiritual Experiences During the Years 1745 to 1765*, trans. Durban Odhner (Bryn Athyn: General Church of the New Jerusalem, 1998–2002).

—— *Emanuel Swedenborg's Journal of Dreams*, trans. J. J. Garth Wilkinson, ed. W. R. Woofenden (New York: Swedenborg Foundation, 1986).

—— *The Generative Organs*, trans. J. J. Garth Wilkinson (London: William Newberry, 1852).

—— *Journal of Dreams*, trans. C. T. Odhner (Bryn Athyn: Academy of New Church, 1918).

—— *On the Worship and Love of God* (Boston: John Allen, 1832).

—— *A Philosopher's Notebook*, ed. Alfred Acton (Philadelphia: Swedenborg Scientific Association, 1931).

—— *Posthumous Theological Works*, trans. John Whitehead (1914; New York: Swedenborg Foundation, 1978).

—— *Psychologia, being Notes and Observations on Christian Wolf's Psychological Empirica*, trans. Alfred Acton (Philadelphia: Swedenborg Scientific Association, 1923).

—— *A Sketch of the Chaste Delights of Conjugal Love* [trans. C. B. Wadström] (London: J. Denew, 1789).

—— *The Spiritual Diary*, trans. Alfred Acton (1962; rpt. London: Swedenborg Society, 1977).

—— *Swedenborg's Dream Diary*, ed. Lars Bergquist, trans. Anders Hallengren (Westchester: Swedenborg Foundation, 2001).

—— *True Christian Religion*, trans. W. C. Dick (London: Swedenborg Society, 1950).

—— *The Word of the Old Testament Explained*, trans. Alfred Acton (Bryn Athyn: Academy of the New Church, 1928–48).

Swinburne, Algernon Charles, *William Blake: A Critical Essay* (1868; rpt. New York: Benjamin Blom, 1967).

Symons, Arthur, *William Blake* (London: Archibald Constable, 1904).

Tafel, Rudolph, *Documents Concerning the Life and Character of Emanuel Swedenborg* (London: Swedenborg Society, 1875).

—— 'New Documents Concerning Swedenborg', *New Church Life*, 4 (885), 371–92.

Temme, Will, *Krise der Leiblichkeit: Die Sozietät der Mutter Eva (Buttlarsche Rotte) und der Radikale Pietismus um 1700* (Göttingen: Vandenhoeck und Ruprecht, 1998).

Tennent, George, *Some Account of the Principles of the Moravians* (London: S. Mason, 1743).

Tessin, Carl Gustaf, *Tessin och Tessiniana*, ed. Fredrik von Ehrenheim (Stockholm, 1819).

Thompson, Edward Palmer, *Witness Against the Beast: William Blake and the Moral Law* (Cambridge: Cambridge UP, 1993).

Timbs, John, *English Eccentrics and Eccentricities* (1875; Detroit: Singing Tree, 1969).

Toksvig, Signe, *Emanuel Swedenborg: Scientist and Mystic* (1948; New York: Swedenborg Foundation, 1983).

Tuer, Andrew, *Bartolozzi and His Works* (London: Field and Tuer, 1881).

[Tulk, John Augustus, ed], *The Aurora, or, the Dawn of Genuine Truth* (London: Aurora Press, 1799).

—— *Testament of Nicholas Flamel* [trans. J. A. Tulk] (London: J. and E. Hodson, 1807).

Upton, Anthony, *Charles XI and Swedish Absolutism* (Cambridge: Cambridge UP, 1988).

Urban, Hugh, *The Economics of Ecstasy: Tantra, Secrecy and Power in Colonial Bengal* (Oxford: Oxford UP, 2001).

—— 'Elitism and Esotericism: Strategies of Secrecy and Power in South Indian Tantra and French Freemasonry', *History of Religions*, 37 (1998), 1–37.

—— *Tantra: Sex, Secrecy, and Politics in the Study of Religion* (Berkeley: California UP, 2003).

Uxorius, *Hymen: An Accurate Description of the Ceremonies in Marriage by Every Nation in the Known World* (London: I. Pottinger, 1760).

Valentin, Hugo, *Judarnas Historia I Sverige* (Stockholm: Albert Bonniers, 1924).

Vaughan, Gerard, 'The Collecting of Classical Antiquities in England in the Eighteenth Century: A Study of Charles Townley (1737–1805)' (Ph.D. dissertation: Oxford University, 1988).

Venette, Nicholas, *Conjugal Love*, 20th edn (1750; rpt. New York: Garland, 1984).

Viatte, Auguste, *Les Sources Occultes du Romantisme* (1927; Paris: Honoré Champion, 1928).

Villars, Abbé N. de Montfaucon de, *Le Comte de Gabalis* (Paris: Claude Barbin, 1670).

—— *Comte de Gabalis* (London: William Rider, 1922).

Vogt, Peter, 'Zinzendorf's Theology of the Sabbath', in Atwood and Vogt, *Distinctiveness*, 205–31.

Volin, Michael, and Phelan, Nancy, *Sex and Yoga* (London: Pelham, 1967).

Wagner, Peter, *Eros Revived* (London: Secker & Warburg, 1988).

Walpole, Horace, *The Correspondence of Horace Walpole*, ed. W. S. Lewis (New Haven: Yale UP, 1937–83).

Walsh, Donald, ed., *Blackwell Dictionary of Evangelical Biography* (Oxford: Blackwell, 1995).

Ward, Eric, 'Ebenezer Sibly – A Man of Parts', *Ars Quatuor Coronatorum*, 71 (1959), 48–52.

Weeks, Andrew, *Boehme: An Intellectual Biography of the Seventeenth-Century Philosopher and Mystic* (Albany: State University of New York, 1991).

Weir, David, *Brahma in the West: William Blake and the Oriental Renaissance* (Albany: State University of New York, 2003).

Wesley, Charles, *The Journal of Charles Wesley* (London: Robert Colley, 1909).

Wesley, John, *The Arminian Magazine* (1781–3).

—— *The Journal of John Wesley*, ed. Nehemiah Curnock (1916; rpt. London: Epworth, 1938).

White, David Gordon, *The Alchemical Body: Siddha Traditions in Medieval India* (Chicago: Chicago UP, 1996).

—— *The Kiss of the Yogini* (Chicago: Chicago UP, 2003).

—— *The Practice of Tantra* (Princeton: Princeton UP, 2000).

White, William, *Emanuel Swedenborg: His Life and Writings*, 2nd rev. edn (London: Simpkin Marshall, 1868).

Whitwell, William, 'James Graham: Master Quack', *Eighteenth-Century Life*, 4 (1977), 37–49.

Wilkins, John, *The Mathematical and Philosophical Works* (London, 1708).

Williamson, George, *Richard Cosway, R.A.* (London: George Bell, 1927).

Wolfson, Elliott, 'The Cut that Binds: Time, Memory, and the Ascetic Impulse', in Shaul Magid, ed., *God's Voice from the Void: Old and New Studies in Bratslav Hasidism* (Albany: State University of New York, 2002), 103–54.

—— 'Images of God's Feet: Some Observations on the Divine Body in Jerusalem', in Howard Eilberg-Schwartz, ed., *People of the Body: Jews and Judaism from an Embodied Perspective* (Albany: State University of New York, 1992).

—— 'Mantra and Divine Name in Hindu and Jewish Meditation Traditions', paper given at Annual Meeting of American Academy of Religion (Atlanta, Georgia, 23 November 2003).

—— 'Messianism in the Christian Kabbalah of Johann Kemper', in Matt Goldish and Richard Popkin, eds, *Jewish Messianism in the Early Modern Period* (Dordrecht: Kluwer Academic, 2001), 138–87.

—— '*Tikkun ha-Shekhinah:* Redemption and the Overcoming of Gender Dimorphism in the Messianic Kabbalah of Moses Hayyim Luzzatto', *History of Religions*, 36 (1977), 289–332.

—— 'Walking as a Sacred Duty: Theological Transformation of Social Reality in Early Hasidism', in Gershon David Hundert, *Essential Papers on Hasidism: Origins to Present* (New York: New York UP, 1991), 179–207.

Wonnacott, William, 'The Rite of Seven Degrees in London', *Ars Quatuor Coronatorum*, 39 (1926), 63–98.

Worrall, David, 'William Bryan, Another Anti-Swedenborgian Visionary of 1789', *Blake: An Illustrated Quarterly*, 34 (2000), 14–22.

Wright, John, *A Revealed Knowledge of Some Things that Will*

Steadily Be Fulfilled in the World, Communicated to a Number of Christians, Brought Together at Avignon, by the Power of the Spirit of the Lord, from All Nations (London, 1794).

Wright, Thomas, *The Life of William Blake* (1929; rpt. New York: Burt Franklin, 1969).

Wright, Thomas and Evans, R. H., *The Works of James Gillray* (1851; rpt. New York: B. Blom, 1968).

Yeats, William Butler, *Essays and Introductions* (1961; New York: Macmillan, 1986).

—— *The Letters of W. B. Yeats*, ed. Allan Wade (London: Macmillan, 1955).

—— *The Poems of William Blake* (London: Muses' Library, 1893).

—— *Yeats's Poems*, eds. A. Norman Jeffares and Warwick Gould (London: Macmillan, 1989).

Young, Ruth, *Father and Daughter: Jonathan and Maria Spilsbury, 1737–1812; 1777–1820* (London: Epworth, 1952).

Zimmer, Heinrich, *Artistic Form and Yoga in the Sacred Images of India*, trans. Gerald Chapple and James Lawson (Princeton: Princeton UP, 2000).

Zinzendorf, Nicholas Ludwig von, *Maxims, Theological Ideas and Sentences, Out of the Present Ordinary of the Brethren's Churches . . . 1737 till 1747*, ed. J. Gambold (London: J. Beecroft, 1751).

—— *Nine Public Lectures on Important Subjects in Religion Preached in Fetter Lane in the Year 1746*, ed. George Forell (Iowa City: Iowa UP, 1973).

Zwink, Eberhard, '"Schrauben-förmige Bewegung ist in allem": Oetinger lenkt den Blick auf Swedenborgs "Irrdische Philosophie"' 'Philosophie', *Contubernium*, 63 (2005), 197–299

Index